WORKING TIME IN

BRITAIN

THE EFFECTS OF

CHANGES IN PATTERN

AND DURATION IN

SELECTED INDUSTRIES

Trade Union Research Unit
Ruskin College
Oxford

The research for this publication was financed by the
ANGLO-GERMAN FOUNDATION FOR THE STUDY OF INDUSTRIAL SOCIETY
as part of its programme of study of social and economic
policy issues

St. Stephen's House, Victoria Embankment, London SW1A 2LA

The Anglo-German Foundation for the Study of Industrial Society was established by an inter-governmental agreement between the Federal Republic of Germany and the United Kingdom following a generous initiative of the German Federal Government which was given expression during a state visit to Britain of the then Federal President, the late Dr. Gustav Heinemann. It was incorporated by a Royal Charter granted on the 5th December 1973. The Patrons of the Foundation are HRH The Prince Philip, Duke of Edinburgh, and Prof. Dr. Karl Carstens, President of the Federal Republic of Germany.

Financial support for the Foundation is now provided by both Governments, which each appoint six Members to the Board of Trustees.

The Foundation initiates and supports the study of the social, economic and political problems of Western industrial society, drawing particularly on the resources of the two countries in tackling common problems. A major part of the programme is concerned with the dissemination by publication, conferences or seminars of the results of such studies.

The opinions expressed in this report are entirely those of the authors.

Printed by David Green Printers Limited
Kettering, Northamptonshire

ISBN 0 905492 32 3   Price: £15.00

CONTENTS

WORKING TIME IN BRITAIN
THE EFFECTS OF CHANGES IN PATTERN AND DURATION IN SELECTED INDUSTRIES

PART 1

WORKING TIME: TRENDS AND ISSUES OF THE 1970s

PART 2
GENERAL ECONOMIC AND WORKING TIME TRENDS AT INDUSTRY AND CASE STUDY LEVEL

PART 3   WORKING TIME: ALTERNATIVES IN THE 1980s

INTRODUCTION TO THE PROJECTS

This book is one of a number of reports on research into aspects of the question of the duration and pattern of working time which are published simultaneously by the Anglo-German Foundation on the completion of research work which it has sponsored. This summary is published in each of the reports.

THE ORIGIN OF THE PROJECTS

One of the objects for which the Foundation was established was "to promote the study and to deepen the understanding of modern industrial society with a view to advancing the knowledge of the citizens . . . in regard to that industrial society and in the problems which arise therefrom or in relation thereto, and in ways and means of resolving, circumventing, counteracting, alleviating or reducing such problems". There are many ways in which such objects could be achieved. The Foundation has sought to use such methods as will bring together the experience and abilities of people in the two countries in the examination of common problems.

Whilst bringing together people to look at common problems has resulted in many "conventional" research projects, it has also been the practice of the Foundation to take initiatives in less conventional ways. Bearing in mind the great difficulties which are foreseen with regard to employment in most of the Western European countries over the next ten or fifteen years, the Foundation decided to explore the extent to which some of the key issues in this matter could be studied and worked upon profitably and jointly by people in Britain and Germany. Of course there was consciousness of the fact that many people and institutions were already studying these problems in the two countries and that there was little point in duplicating their work. It was therefore considered that the Foundation should concentrate on specific issues rather than the whole field, and should try to initiate research which stayed close to the practical situations. A further decision was taken at the outset (and later, after some discussion by the Board of Trustees, confirmed) that no attempt would be made to involve all of the "social partners" in any one project. The reasons for this and the consequences will appear later.

There are existing connections between German and British trade unions and German and British employers' associations, in addition to connections at government, official and political levels and many individual business and social contacts. However, it is something new for such institutions to conduct or be involved in joint trans-national research. The decision was therefore taken to try to find out whether there were issues of common concern which would be suitable for research, which would be carried out by qualified researchers but would also have the advice of specific representative institutions.

The initial discussions were opened with representatives of British and German trade unions and the trade union confederation in each country. After a number of meetings it became clear that the issue which these representatives wished to have researched was the possibility of a reduction in working time and what the consequences for increased employment opportunities might be. It was agreed eventually that the whole question of the duration and pattern of working time was an important and currently topical segment of the future employment question and that it would be appropriate to investigate it, since little or no work was being done other than at a rather high level of macro-economic abstraction. As the proposed project was being formulated, it was decided that there should be much more concentration on specific consequences at the level of an industry or a company.

The two trade union groups were invited to suggest who might conduct the research. The German trade unions proposed Professor Michael Bolle of the Free University in Berlin, and the British trade unions proposed Mr John Hughes of the Trade Union Research Unit at Ruskin College, Oxford. Some time was required to formulate the precise research proposal which was to be put to the Board of Trustees of the Foundation. During these discussions, Professor Burkhard Strümpel (also of the Free University Berlin) became a member of the German team, and some initial steps were taken by which the Institute of Manpower Studies would have been associated with some of the quantitative aspects of the British study. It was intended that the research should be comparable with regard to industries and the structure of the research programme, and if possible that the reports which would emerge at the end of the project would also have similar structures so that they could be compared. In the event, and after the projects had got under way, there were some slight deviations from this plan. It did not prove possible to associate the Institute of Manpower Studies with the work at Ruskin College in the way which had been intended, and the structure of the Ruskin College research and report turned out to be somewhat different from that of the Free University Berlin, whilst retaining a common approach of sectoral and company studies within the same industries.

The research programme was arranged with the idea that the two research teams would maintain contact as they progressed, and that there would be regular review meetings at which both sides would be present. The two trade union groups were reconstituted into an advisory panel (with some slight changes in membership but a no less representative result) and this panel took part also in the review meetings. During these meetings a good deal

(ii)

was learned about differences in style and method and many of the exchanges at these meetings were in themselves a valuable development of the Foundation's work.

As mentioned earlier, there had been a discussion about whether it would be more appropriate to have a project with which both trade unions and employers (and possible other groups and even government representatives) would be involved. This idea was turned down for a number of reasons:

— The research teams chosen valued their reputation for academic objectivity and although the advisory panel on the project first launched was drawn entirely from the trade unions, they considered that the consequences of their work would stand up to objective criticism from other directions.

— The view was expressed that a steering committee on which all the representative institutions were involved might feel some need to take up early positions about some of the more contentious issues which might emerge, with the result that the research reports might have a "lowest common denominator" quality.

— A more practical reason was that the employers' associations were not sure whether or not they wished to be involved in such a research project at that time, largely because the length of the working week was a current bargaining issue.

Subsequently (and following two successful exchanges organised by the Foundation between the senior officials of the two organisations) the Foundation was approached by the Engineering Employers' Federation in Britain and the Gesamtverband der Deutschen Metallindustriellen Arbeitgeberverbände (the Association of Metalworking Industry Employers' Associations—the nearest equivalent to the EEF), to discuss whether a parallel project could be set up. Of course, it was clear that the trade union sponsoring group had originally been mainly interested in the extent to which shorter working time would provide new employment places, whereas the employers were more concerned about the economic consequences of shorter working time. However it was not considered necessary that the project with the employers' advisory group should be exactly the same in structure or objectives as that with the trade union advisory group.

After some discussion it was decided that the basis of the project should be an examination of the economic and similar consequences of an immediate significant reduction in working time. In the event, this was interpreted slightly differently in the two countries.

The Engineering Employers' Federation in conjunction with the Foundation invited five research bodies to submit proposals for research, generally along the lines mentioned above, and the choice was made of PA International

Consultants Limited for a project designed to study the effects of immediate changes in working time on competitiveness in specific companies. Gesamtmetall selected Professor Ott of the Institut für Angewandte Wirtschaftsforschung in Tübingen, and agreed upon a project which set out to study the global effect of accelerated reductions in working time. For these projects, an advisory panel was constituted from the two employers' associations, together with representation from the Confederation of British Industry and the Engineering Industries Association, and this advisory panel has kept in touch with the development of the research. Although in this case the approach of the two research teams was quite different from the outset, they met together with the advisory panel and exchanged reports on their work.

When all these arrangements had been properly drafted and approved for financial support by the Board of Trustees of the Foundation (the total sum being £108,900 and DM384,935) three projects (Berlin, Ruskin and PA) involved a micro-economic study of specific industries and firms, and one project (Tübingen) involved a macro-economic study. In the case of Berlin and Ruskin the study was of specific industries and services which had been agreed beforehand; in the case of PA, the research was concerned with selected firms which were representative and therefore displayed a number of factors which might have a bearing on the question under review, but which were chosen from manufacturing industry only. Each research team was to apply itself to the problem in its own way with the advice of the panels and the assistance of the Foundation secretariat, and whilst it was hoped that the three micro-economic studies would be able to present comparable information (particularly in the Berlin and Ruskin cases) no attempt was to be made at any early stage to distil out common results or impressions.

This attitude was subsequently confirmed by discussion at the Board of Trustees and with a meeting representing all research teams and all members of the advisory panel. For this reason the reports of the different research teams are being published quite separately, although simultaneously. The Foundation's belief is that it is necessary for all this (for the most part new) information to find its way into the public debate; once this has happened, the question of a consolidated publication covering all the projects will be discussed. The arrangements for publication are as follows:

— The Foundation will publish the Ruskin report, an English translation of a major summary of the Berlin report, and the PA report.

— Berlin will publish the full version of the Berlin report in German.

— Tübingen will publish the full version of the Tübingen report in German; this project started later than the others and in consequence the final report will be completed later. At the date of writing this common introduction to the three books to be published by the Foundation no decision has been taken about an English version of the Tübingen report. This introduction also will not seek to distil out common or conflicting ideas from the three reports in which it will appear. The concentration will be on trying to bring out some of the highlights from each of the three research programmes, drawing upon the conclusions of the research teams themselves.

1. TRADE UNION RESEARCH UNIT, RUSKIN COLLEGE OXFORD

The TURU project was defined as "The investigation of the duration and pattern of working time and the possible employment, output, and other consequences of changing the present duration and pattern in selected industries and services". Six sectors of the economy were selected:

— Motor vehicles
— Chemicals
— Electrical engineering
— Distributive trades
— Passenger transport
— The National Health Service.

For each sector, a detailed industry study was prepared, utilising published data to build up a picture of working time patterns and manpower utilisation. At the same time, the researchers undertook case studies at the level of the individual enterprise. In the case studies, the objective was to analyse the economic and social factors which had historically and were currently determining working time patterns for specific workforces.

The report is divided into three main sectors:

— Part I
Working time: Trends and issues of the 1970s

— Part II
General Economic and Working Time Trends at Industry and Enterprise level

— Part III
Why Change?
How to change?

Apart from the case for a shortening of working time as a method of increasing employment places and as a way of improving the quality of

(v)

working life in general, as advocated by trade unions in both countries, the British trade unions argue specifically for a reduction of the normal working week from 40 to 35 hours as a way of removing discrimination between manual and non-manual workers, the case being that many non-manual workers and some manual workers already work a 35-hour week. Despite these attempts to secure a reduction of the working week, the statistics presented in the TURU report show that almost two-thirds of male manual workers worked overtime of the order of ten hours per week. Only one-fifth of male non-manual workers worked and were paid for working overtime and for them the average overtime hours were 7.2. These figures contrast with the manual man's average basic hours of 39.8 and the non-manual man's basic hours of 37.1 but the statistics must be looked at with care, since many non-manual workers do not get paid for overtime. Shiftworking also plays a more important part in the working time of manual workers than of non-manual workers (23.6% as compared with 5.6%).

The report also examines the question of worker preferences for overtime and for methods of shortening working time; most women workers prefer normal hours without systematic overtime and the people who are most prepared to work overtime are male employees between 25 and 50, i.e. when their domestic commitments are at their greatest. Elsewhere the report draws attention to the fact that if there were a question of reducing the working week, men would prefer it to be reduced in a block of useable time, whereas women would prefer to have it reduced as a proportion of each working day or possibly by the elimination of Friday afternoon work.

The persistence of overtime working as a regular feature of industrial life was supported by the fact that the costs of additional recruitment to employers were rising during the 1970s whilst the real cost of high levels of overtime fell; combined with the impression that there was a shortage of many specific skills and the desire of some of the workers to earn more money, the maintenance of high overtime levels went unopposed. This is in spite of the fact that the Department of Employment calculated in 1978 that if half of the hours then worked by manual men in excess of 48 per week were worked instead by additional full-time workers, the unemployment register could be reduced by over 100,000. This was at a time when normal basic hours were of the order of 40 hours per week.

The TURU report shows to the satisfaction of the authors that the cost of increases which might result from a shortening of working time from 40 to 35 hours per week over a period of a few years (estimated at 6 to 8%) would be small in comparison with the other factors at work on the economy such as other increases in earnings as a result of negotiations which took inflation into account and changes in the exchange rates. If the possibility of achieving better working arrangements inside plants were taken at the same time as the reduction in working hours took place, it was possible (they argue) that the reduction of working time might lead to better use of capital, and more flexible working hours for employees and for factories, with a resulting improvement in efficiency.

In summary, Part I of the report sets out the existing situation in some detail, largely on the basis of published statistics. Although most of the analysis was in relation to the working week, consideration was also given to changes in holiday entitlement.

The 12 case studies were chosen so as to reflect a broad cross-section of the labour/capital mix in the UK economy with various employment forms and to provide reasonable comparisons as between high and low technology industries, male-dominated and female-dominated workforces, public and private sector ownership and the secondary and tertiary sectors of the economy. In addition all of the industries chosen display a variety of shiftwork systems and embrace an equally diverse range of collective bargaining structures. The industry studies are based mainly on published data, supplemented in some cases by data from major organisations and authoritative studies and reports on aspects of industrial organisation. The industry studies were supported by a number of case studies at plant level. These case studies set out to discover:

— Why the present working time and duration patterns existed in a particular situation.

— How payment for different time and duration patterns varied.

— What problems or disadvantages were associated with existing patterns and to quantify these, if possible.

— What preferences management and employees would have with respect to forms of reduction in working time, particularly with respect to a shorter worker week or a shorter working year.

— What organisational consequences might flow from proposed forms of shorter working time and the output and employment effects of these.

— What effects on costs, particularly labour costs the changes might involve.

— What benefits (or elimination of disadvantages) might result from the changes.

— What potential ''least cost'' solutions there might be.

The data was gathered by means of semi-structured interviews with representatives of management and trade unions at site level (all the companies and organisations concerned were trade union organised). However, the researchers make the point that although a common core of questions was utilized for both sets of interviews, differences in terms of access to basic information and experience of the particular site varied considerably between individuals so that comparisons of either management or trade union responses across case studies are rendered problematic. There was also a problem in that the researchers found difficulty of access to key individuals in management and management data. In only one case was there difficulty in gaining the confidence of the local trade union representative.

In the concluding remarks of the second section of the report, some attention is given to a number of specific issues.

Labour Market Constraints

Here it is suggested that an improvement in working conditions through a reduction in working time—if it were a relative improvement compared with other employers in the area—would improve the attractiveness of that company to the external labour market and improve (by reducing absenteeism) the internal labour market. However, as the authors point out, such beneficial effects do depend upon the advantages being relative and on there being a high degree of mobility and availability of the right kind of labour. In the case of engineering workers, the situation appeared to be that there was a shortage of skilled workers more or less irrespective of geographic location and there were difficulties in moving people within the establishment because of the lack of differential between skilled and semi-skilled workers and the demarcation defences of the former. Therefore both external and internal mobility of labour were poor and the solution which was adopted was overtime working for skilled workers. The authors say "it may be that in bargaining for reduced hours a trade union may also find itself arguing for a parallel boost in training provision in order to combat the labour market constraints operating on their claim". It suggests that this may have long awaited benefits. These internal and external labour market constraints apply almost entirely to skilled workers.

Social and Economic Determinants of Working Time

The authors point out that while overtime may for a time obscure the need for changes and provide a temporary escape valve for pressure that has built up within a working time system, in the long run changes are made because of social and economic pressures, the latter including technological developments. The fact that the real cost of overtime has been reduced and that other factors have affected the earning possibilities of employees during normal time have led to a maintenance of overtime.

(viii)

Costs and Competition

The authors draw attention to how bargainers in some of the case studies have tackled the adverse cost argument. In two of the case studies, reductions of the working week were achieved without adding significantly to costs—in one case, by the creation of a fifth shift, and in the other case as a result of a change-over from predominantly day-working to two-shift working. In both cases, overtime was reduced substantially.

The authors attribute part of the fall in effective overtime costs to successive "incomes policies" which granted pay increases as supplements that were not consolidated into the basic rate used in calculating overtime premia.

Bargaining Structures

The report draws attention to the fact that the most significant reductions in the working week took place where the bargaining was mainly local and not constrained by national or sectoral considerations.

Worker Preferences

Apart from the differences in worker preferences on account of sex, as indicated earlier the authors point out that despite the disadvantages in terms of employment creation of a low relative cost of overtime, a change to a high relative cost of overtime might accelerate the substitution either of capital for labour or of female labour for male labour.

The report concludes by arguing the case for change in the working week and by giving advice, especially to bargainers, on how the process of change might be accelerated.

2. ### FORSCHUNGSSTELLE SOZIALÖKONOMIE DER ARBEIT—FREIE UNIVERSITÄT BERLIN

The Berlin study concentrated on four industrial sectors:

— The chemical industry

— The motor industry

— Electrical engineering

— The retail trade

In addition to the sectoral analysis, considerable attention was given to the implementation of working time agreements at plant level. The report is divided into four principal parts:

— PART A
Working-time and working-time policy in the 1960s and 1970s
— PART B
Company working-time policy
— PART C
Adjustment problems with changes in working-time systems
— PART D
The possibilities of changes in working-time systems.

By comparing the sectoral analysis and the plant level investigations it was possible to test whether a large part of the possible employment effects (i.e. increased employment to balance the reduction in hours worked by each employee) of a reduction in working time is lost through "adjustment processes inside the plant". Approximately 20 case studies were carried out in substantial plants in the industries concerned and these case studies were related to the mathematical calculations at the macro-economic sectoral level.

A number of matters of principal concern emerged from the research.

The "Steering Function" of Negotiated Working Time

A central question which arises from negotiations of reduced working time is whether or not actual working time follows the trend of the negotiated working time. For example it would be quite possible for a reduction in negotiated working time to result merely in an increase in overtime, so that the only consequence would be increased payment for the same work by the same people. It is quite obvious that this question is a central issue in the discussion of the possibility of a reduction in working time, since only if actual working time follows negotiated working time with a more or less constant relationship, is it possible to proceed to any further investigation of the other consequences which might flow from a reduction.

In order to examine this relationship with the required degree of rigour, Berlin had to create its own data base, a contribution which was of great value in itself. The researchers followed in general the Institut für Arbeitsmarkt und Berufsforschung (IAB) breakdown of the components of working time but they disaggregated it to sector level. The information on the labour market and on working time which resulted from this has not so far been available in such detail.

The interesting and clear conclusion of this part of the study was that for the economy as a whole and for the individual sectors considered over the entire period from 1960 to 1978 a reduction in negotiated annual working time brought about a roughly parallel reduction in actual working time. In the 1970s however, negotiated working time lost some of its predominance, since cyclical factors (changes in overtime and the use of short time) came to have a greater influence on actual working time. But these were only short-term reactions of actual working time to fluctuations in production and/or demand. Over the longer term they did not greatly affect the largely stable relationship between developments of negotiated and actual working time. In Germany therefore it can be said that negotiated working time "steered" actual working time. This implies that when reduced working time is negotiated in Germany some adjustment process will always be necessary. It was also possible to draw conclusions about the relationship between growth and employment for particular industries: In the 1960s in electrical engineering a 2 per cent growth in output was necessary to produce a 1 per cent growth in employment: by the 1970s a 2.8 per cent growth was required to produce 1 per cent growth in employment; in the motor industry 3.5 per cent growth was required.

The study examines the extent to which companies can operate their own working time policies independently of the negotiated working time and the resulting underlying trend in actual working time. This varies from industry to industry but it is quite clear that overtime and short term policies at the company level operate in the German industries studied mainly as a short term response to cyclical variations and demand.

Faced with the reduction in the negotiated working time companies need to devise their own "adjustment policies". Because of specific technology there will be a range of specific qualifications of labour which are needed and shortages may arise. The aim of the company will be to achieve functional flexibility in its work force and in doing so to improve the quality of its internal labour market. This has the incidental but not unimportant consequence that the work force becomes better qualified and the qualified work force is greater in number so that it is possible to cope with increased demand in the upswing without having to go to the external labour market and incur hiring and training costs, even if such labour is available at that time.

The study goes on to examine the employment effects which might be expected from different speeds of reduction in working time and which component of working time has been responsible for the decline in actual working time. In a number of tables the influence of the different forms of reduction in working time on employment in the industrial sectors is shown and a forecast is made of the number of workers who will be required in the industries concerned in 1990 with different variants of reduction in working time and with different growth rates in production. It is assumed (because of

(xi)

existing agreements) that a reduction of the agreed working week will not take place in Germany before 1985. In this section of the report the interesting concept of critical growth rate in output emerges; if the growth rate in output drops below this critical rate, employers will be more inclined to make workers redundant than to reduce hours.

In assessing the employment effects of reductions in working time the Berlin study deals also with rationalisation. It recognises that one of the strategies which might be employed by a company faced with a reduction in working time would be investment to save labour. The immediate impact would be to reduce the expected employment effect of a reduction in working time. However the increase in efficiency would stabilize the economic growth trend and this will be a decisive factor in improving the situation on the labour market. Over the longer term rationalisation investment which increases productivity secures future growth and this is a prerequisite for any further reduction in working time. It is also possible for such rationalisation investment to improve the conditions in unpopular jobs, either by removing the more objectionable features of the job or by reducing the working hours of those who have to do them by increasing productivity.

Company Adjustment Problems

In this section of the report the study examines the extent to which productivity improvements resulting from a reduction in working time would balance the employment effects which might be expected. The study of the 1960s and 1970s showed that the working time reductions were largely carried out in periods of low economic growth and the productivity increases which they entailed prevented a greater decline in employment. A series of graphs is displayed relating the development of actual employment in an industry with that which might have been expected if working time had remained constant, if productivity and working time had remained constant, or if productivity only had remained constant. In all industries and in the economy as a whole the authors conclude that the reduction in working time in the 1960s and 1970s prevented a possible decline in employment which would have otherwise have taken place because of productivity improvement.

The study looks at different factors which affect company adjustment processes.

—   Technology, organisation, and working time

—   Job structures and work intensification possibilities

— Internal labour markets
— External labour markets
— Working time and costs.

The main conclusion from these studies is that there are a number of alternative possible adjustment strategies even within one set of technological or organisational structures and that the possibilities of work intensification vary very greatly from one industry, company or even part of a company to another. In analysing these adjustment policies, the research team developed the concept of "elasticity of job requirements"; the lower the elasticity the easier it is to maintain production without increasing employment, i.e. the lower the degree of utilisation of labour was before the "adjustment" began. The scope for more intensive working depends on the elasticity of job requirements. In the electrical engineering industry, elasticity is high, in chemicals low, in the motor industry high and in retailing low. Moves by companies to make themselves less dependent on the external labour market by expanding their internal labour markets have already been commented upon. The same forms of reduction in working time can have different effects in different sectors because of the varying cost structures and working time induced costs in those sectors. Generalised statements about the cost consequences of a reduction in working time are viewed with some scepticism.

Flexible Working Time Systems

The study also looks at the options open to workers with regard to a reduction in working time to see whether increased flexibility would reduce the conflict between individual preferences and existing patterns of working time. The development of greater flexibility is not looked upon as having entirely positive effects; in certain cases greater flexibility can have negative effects with regard to employment consequences (for example by increasing the number of part-time workers in certain sectors) and the opening up of working time to very large variations in individual preferences can weaken the collective bargaining position.

The possibilities of shorter working time are often stated to depend upon the availability of skilled labour. It is argued that skilled labour is always in short supply and that this presents insuperable obstacles to a reduction in working time. The research team distinguishes between "job-induced" and "standard-induced" qualification requirements. The old "skilled" categories were in the "job-induced" qualification category. But observation in Germany suggests that as people change jobs, they often move into jobs in which their specific craft skills are not required: it is their flexibility, adaptability and work habits which fit the "standard-induced" qualification requirements. This leads to the interesting conclusion that if the

(xiii)

demand is for "standard-induced" qualifications, the lack of qualification is a result of unemployment (since such habits cannot be obtained if one is not in work). This conflicts with the traditional view, based upon a demand for "job-induced" qualifications, that lack of qualifications causes unemployment.

Of course it must be emphasised that these findings derive from research in German industry: the findings in Britain might be quite different, if (for example) different attitudes to demarcation imposed precise and narrow restrictions on which jobs were available to which employees.

3. PA INTERNATIONAL CONSULTANTS LIMITED

As has been previously explained, the precise focus of the project carried out by PA International Management Consultants was somewhat different from the research carried out by Ruskin and Berlin.

In particular, concentration was upon the economic consequences of an immediate reduction in working time. Drawing on the special strength of management consultants, the method was to go into detail in 30 manufacturing establishments in an attempt to assess the precise consequences of such changes. Set alongside the other two reports, the PA report gives a certain view of the reactions of specific companies, the characteristics of whose businesses were chosen so as to give a reasonably characteristic spread in relation to British industry in general in respect of size, location, resource structure, exposure to international competition and proportion of women employed. All of these factors are clearly defined in the case studies and readers can therefore form their own judgement about the reactions of the companies to the proposed working time reduction. The published report is in two main sections:

— Part I—Summary of Findings and Conclusions

— Part II—Main Report, which includes an analysis of the findings of the 30 case studies, of which 5 are described in some detail as representative of the whole.

The remaining 25 case studies are contained in Part III of the report, which is not being generally published, although if there is sufficient demand, it will probably be made available in the Foundation's "Research Papers" series. The PA study was of information provided by the managements of the companies only.

Although the greatest interest from the trade union side was with regard to the shortening of the working week, it was decided to look at all the options which were open to negotiators in reducing working time, that is:

— To shorten the working week

— To extend holidays

— To reduce or eliminate overtime

— To extend early retirement

— To delay the start of working life for young people, possibly by giving them community services tasks or longer education.

It was decided that the reduction in working time under each of these headings should be the same and an arbitrary figure of 10 per cent reduction was chosen. The figure and the choice of an equal reduction was partly to simplify calculation, although trade unions were in fact claiming reductions of the order of 10 per cent in the working week whilst under another heading, a reduction of working life from approximately 50 years to approximately 45 years would be implied for many people by a general reduction in the retirement age for men to 60. The reduction investigated was not therefore unreasonable, although it could be argued that it would be most unlikely for such a large change to be achieved in one step, if historical trends are followed.

There was a wide range of estimates between companies of the effects of the postulated changes; the researchers could not generally correlate the causes of this variation with the characteristics by which they classified the organisation interviewed, with the exception of the much higher than average impact on labour costs of continuous operations in process industry which would result from the need to move from four shift to five shift cover, if the working week were reduced by 10 per cent to 36 hours. Factors specific to each company, such as the extent to which their resources were currently utilized, were much more important.

Although none of the participating companies would alter the working patterns voluntarily, some said that if forced to do so they felt a need to choose an approach suited to their own circumstances. The researchers had some reservations about whether these companies would welcome in practice a situation in which their working pattern differed markedly from neighbouring companies or others in their industry.

Underlying assumptions affecting the results included the following:

— Most companies assumed that employees would expect their real earnings to be maintained in the event of a reduction in working time; in the case of a possible reduction in overtime, some companies thought that a reduction in real earnings would be accepted, and some other companies thought that a reduced pension for early retirement might be acceptable.

— On average, employers assessed that they would be able to achieve a 7 per cent increase in productivity during the process of reducing working time by 10 per cent. However, this average conceals a wide range in the forecast changes in productivity from improvements of 16 per cent to reductions of 21 per cent. This variation results from the wide range of action on shift patterns, working practices, investment and trading policies, which are likely to be appropriate to meet the needs of individual companies.

— As an initial assumption in planning their reactions to reduction in working time, companies postulated that they would try to maintain output at current levels and would recruit extra people to do so.

— In nearly every case companies said that there would be potential recruits available for semi and unskilled jobs, but skilled trades, i.e. instrument mechanics and electronic tradesmen were in short supply. Generally, extensive retraining and re-grading would be required, if dislocation of operations was to be avoided during the period of change. Removal of demarcations and alterations to working practices would be required.

In order to evaluate the effects of early retirement and late starting on company costs, it was necessary to decide by whom the costs would be borne. For the purposes of this study it has been assumed that the total cost be borne either nationally or by the companies. Taking this into account, the five options for changing the patterns of working life became seven.

The following comments include figures which are averages, and they should be interpreted with caution, as there are wide variations in the results between companies, as can be seen from the individual case studies.

The findings of the study indicate that reductions in working time achieved by a shorter working week or longer holidays applied uniformly over British manufacturing industry could result in increases in numbers employed by some companies, but would put at risk the jobs of other people in other companies. The latter would have to reduce costs and eliminate unprofitable activities, in order to preserve their businesses. Whether the balance between these two pressures would result in increases in overall employment, is difficult to assess. The researchers estimated that at the time of preparing the drafts of the report, in May 1980, the overall increase in employment over all 30 companies from a 10 per cent reduction in working time would be some 3 per cent.

The costs of the 10 per cent reduction in working time would have been covered by a 7 to 8 per cent increase in productivity, and a rise of about 3 per cent in prices.

However, the researchers felt that even this interpretation gave an over-optimistic view of employment opportunities, and given the deepening recession, the safety-valve of higher prices would be available to even fewer companies than at the time of this study, and consequently the increase in employment would only be about 1 per cent.

Negative factors affecting employment would include the possible closure of some companies, if employers failed to force through reductions in costs in order to stem losses, whilst action to reduce costs might well include measures to reduce numbers employed. Furthermore it would be expected that employers would attempt to increase productivity, and the opportunities for doing so certainly appeared to exist in some of the companies studied. This would reduce the need for extra labour. Some of the companies which were already making efficient use of labour and operating in competitive markets would tend to cut out marginally profitable activities and reduce numbers employed. It was therefore the opinion of the researchers that the overall increase in employment would probably be less than 1 per cent under present trading conditions.

The researchers point out that decreases in working time or increases in leisure time must be paid for, and that there are only four real choices:

— Lower real earnings for the existing work force

— Reduced company profits

— Higher prices to the consumer, or

— Higher productivity.

Since it was assumed that employees would not accept lower real earnings in exchange for increases in leisure time, decreases in working time became equivalent to increases in wages, although they were less preferred by employers since they are less easy to operate and control. This does not take into account the consequences of overtime, which would merely be an accentuation of these trends.

The researchers came to the conclusion that there were significant possibilities for particular companies to achieve higher productivity and reduce working time without injuring the company's financial position. However, this would not result in any significant increase in employment. They point out that from their research it appears that the only way in which decreases in working time would improve employment prospects of the UK economy would be if such a measure as a 10 per cent immediate reduction forced management and unions alike to face up to the need to improve productivity. A number of companies reported that the prospect of a one-step immediate 10 per cent reduction, as opposed to a gradual phasing-in, would be far more likely to result in both management and unions facing up to the issues involved.

CONCLUSION

The Foundation now offers for discussion a substantial contribution in empirical research-based facts. As has already been indicated, at this stage no attempt will be made to draw out the common threads of the three reports, nor where their conclusions are in conflict. But it is possible to frame some questions, which are fundamental to consideration of the problem, which arise in one way or another in all three reports:

— Would an immediate reduction in working time create more employment places, and does the nature of the reduction affect how many places will be created?

— Could these extra places be filled by labour market operations without increasing overtime?

— If not, are there artificial or traditional obstacles to labour market operations the removal of which would have the effect of enabling such vacancies to be filled?

— What would be the economic consequences of reductions in working time under various degrees of competition? Is it in fact possible to introduce a shortening of working time which does not worsen the competitive position, but still results in more employment places being created?

In their different ways, the three reports give the answers of the research teams to these questions and can now be studied in detail by those who have to deal with this question at the practical level of policy and negotiation.

The Foundation would like to thank not only the research teams who have carried out the work, but also the members of the advisory panels from employers and trade unions, who have so willingly contributed to this rather unusual enterprise.

Finally, it would like to thank all those companies and individuals within companies, which have helped to provide the data base on which the research has been founded.

February 1981   Peter McGregor

(Peter McGregor was Secretary General of the Foundation from 1974 to 1981. He is now Industrial Director of the National Economic Development Office)

PREFACE

The final version of this report has been built up from extensive discussions and reconsideration of drafts, and considerable teamwork, on the part of the staff of the Trade Union Research Unit. Part One of the report is mainly the work of John Hughes, with Robin Beddoe contributing the analysis of trends in annual holidays with pay, and the study of shift premia. Part Two is the work of many hands. Bernard Casey was responsible for the original case study fieldwork in retailing, motors, chemicals, and electronics, and Denis Gregory for that in the health service. Denis Gregory was also responsible for editing the case study material for the final report and contributed the chapter on key points for bargainers. A number of people contributed to the industry studies at various stages. Susan Hastings produced the study on road passenger transport, Richard Bird that on the National Health Service, John Hughes those on chemicals and electrical and electronic engineering (incorporating some earlier material from Bernard Casey), and Richard Bird developed the final form of the motor vehicle manufacturing study, while Denis Gregory again assisted with the final version of the retail trade study. Finally, Part Three of the report was written by John Hughes. All of this work rested on co-operation and support from many people which we have acknowledged elsewhere. And, of course, the report would never have appeared without the untiring assistance of our secretaries, Diana Crayk and Mary Williams.

Our results, conclusions and thoughts are presented in the body of the report, however, it is timely here to note that we do not regard this as anything more than a crucial first step in helping to advance and clarify this important debate.

Trade Union Research Unit
May 1980

xix

PART 1: WORKING TIME: TRENDS AND ISSUES OF THE 1970s

Chapter 1: The Changing Structure of Employment and Working Time

The 1970s in Britain witnessed some quite startling changes in employment in the economy. It is very much in the context of, and in the light of, such employment changes that much of the contemporary re-examination of working time has developed.

In this section, official data are used to identify some of the most striking changes in the balance of employment in the economy. Unavoidably it is also necessary to chronicle in outline the substantial rise in unemployment, especially in the last half of the 1970s, and to project that forward into the early 1980s.

Working time patterns intrude directly on the study of what has been happening to employment because of the very marked increase in part-time employment in Britain. This can be measured in some detail from 1971 to 1977 (and in part more recently). Unless the swing to part-time employment is taken into account a misleading impression of employment trends would be gained. Thus, between 1971 and 1977 female employment rose by over 800,000; but this was entirely due to a rise of over 30% in part-time employment. Full-time employment of female workers actually fell slightly.

To start with we set out series indicating the main developments in the decade 1968 to 1978. The information is derived both from Department of Employment estimates and from the National Income accounts. Major changes were taking place within the largely unchanged total of employees in employment in the UK (close to 22.7 million in both 1968 and 1978), and in the relationship between labour supply and employment.

In outline the Tables show the following:

i) The total of employees in employment fell by around half a million in the recession of the early 1970s and then restored that fall in the single year of 1973. A minor cyclical swing (plus or minus less than 1% at most) around a level trend of 22.7 million is in evidence since then.

ii) But a very significant shift occurred as between employment in the public sector and the private sector of the economy. Within the rhythm of some cyclicality private sector employment fell by close to one million over the decade. This is the more ominous since 1978 has to be interpreted as representing a relatively favourable level of cyclical activity in the private sector of the economy.

1

Table 1.1   Employees in Employment, UK 1968-1978   (in millions)

	All Employees in Employment	Private Sector	Public Sector*
1968	22.65	16.65	6.00
1969	22.62	16.59	6.03
1970	22.47	16.35	6.12
1971	22.12	15.89	6.23
1972	22.12	15.81	6.31
1973	22.66	16.25	6.42
1974	22.79	16.22	6.57
1975	22.71	15.78	6.93
1976	22.54	15.56	6.98
1977	22.61	15.55	7.06
1978	22.67	15.60	7.07

* Excluding the armed forces.

Source: Department of Employment Gazette, and National Income Accounts, 1979.

iii) By contrast the public sector of employment (leaving aside the size of the armed forces) was responsible for a compensatory increase in employment of one million over the same ten year period. Most of that growth (some 800,000) was actually concentrated into the five year period 1970/75. This served both to counteract the recessions of 1971-72 and of 1975, as well as lending reinforcement to the cyclical upswing in private sector employment in 1973. The expansion of public sector employment was mainly a phenomenon of central government services (which include the health service) and local government (which includes much of education). It owed little overall to public corporation employment; such corporations tend to shed labour in the process of rationalisation, and this was apparent in the early 1970s. There was some increase in employment in public corporations in the latter half of the 1970s as the public corporation sector was extended (with an offsetting reduction of private sector employment).

But the style of public policy towards the public sector and its employment has changed since the mid 1970s. The near plateau of such employment since 1975 signals one change of tempo towards the restraint of public sector activity and expenditure. At the very end of the decade and in the early 1980s this is being replaced by a more evident scaling down of services and employment in the public sector.

Manufacturing Employment

If it has been particularly the expansion of public service employment that lay behind the rise in public sector employment in the 1970s, it has been the decline of manufacturing employment that has particularly dominated the level of private sector employment.

What is unusual about the employment decline of recent years is that it is no longer the product of cyclical growth and fairly marked increases in labour productivity. It is now associated with the disappearance of cyclical growth (overall) and a much slower improvement in labour productivity. One of the reasons for increased attention to the possible reduction of working time is the contemporary context in which further major falls in manufacturing employment must be expected, in the early 1980s, without this being offset by any major process of job creation elsewhere in the economy (and least of all in public employment).

The table that follows highlights the pattern of the 1970s.

Table 1.2   **British Manufacturing: Employment, Output, Labour Productivity**   (1975 = 100)

	Employment* (millions)	Employment Index	Output Index	Labour Productivity Index
1970	8.16	111.0	98.0	88.3
1971	7.89	107.4	97.4	90.8
1972	7.61	103.9	100.0	96.3
1973	7.66	104.5	108.3	103.7
1974	7.70	104.7	106.5	101.8
1975	7.33	100.0	100.0	100.0
1976	7.10	97.0	101.4	104.6
1977	7.15	97.7	102.8	105.2
1978	(7.11)	(97.1)	103.7	(106.8)
1979	(7.03)	(96.0)	(104.5)	(108.8)

* The employment numbers relate to Great Britain (June count of each year): the indices are for the United Kingdom.

Source: Department of Employment Gazette and Economic Trends. Bracketed data are still provisional.

It is not possible to interpret the information on manufacturing without taking into account the timing of trade cycles. But it is also necessary to

3

supplement the data presented for the 1970s with some earlier information. The following are key points:

i) The 1970s saw a serious loss of forward momentum in the output of UK manufacturing. Earlier periods had shown in round terms a growth of manufacturing output of around 16% in each trade cycle of four or five years. Output in the trade cycle measured from the trough of 1975 to 1978/9 shows *no overall growth* as compared with the broadly equivalent years in the previous cycle, 1971-74. Output has notably failed to reach—let alone surpass—the peak levels of 1973/4.

Understandably, this, and associated weaknesses in the trading performance of UK manufacturing,* has led to widespread discussion of "de-industrialisation". Moreover, the forecasts for the first half of the 1980s are not merely pointing to a further recession but to a slow and limited recovery. Manufacturing output rose over 30% between equivalent years in the early 1960s and the early 1970s; but from the recession of the early 1970s to that of the early 1980s the expectation is that "growth" may be only around 3% in a decade.

ii) In such a context what appears surprising is that the fall in employment in UK manufacturing has not been even more substantial. Even so we are looking at a fall of over 1,100,000 over the decade. Within that total male employment fell by over 700,000 (or 13%) to just under five million. Female employment fell by nearly 400,000 (or 16%) to just over two million. A further major fall is to be anticipated in the opening years of the 1980s (this is discussed further below).

iii) Labour productivity was rising rapidly in the trade cycle of the early 1970s. Indeed, from the earlier peak in 1968 to the peak in 1973 productivity (per person employed) rose by over 20%. By contrast, from the 1973 peak to 1978 labour productivity increased by a mere 3%, and if we measure from 1973 to 1979 the rise is only some 5%. This poor recent performance is to some extent a reflection of the fact that output was affected in both 1978 and 1979 by high levels of industrial disputes. Thus both the failure to restore previous peak levels of output, and the very limited growth in output per person employed, can be linked to industrial disputes. In the two years taken together 30 million working days were lost in disputes in manufacturing industries; which are high levels compared with most

* Thus (on an Overseas Trade Statistics basis) in 1970 manufactured exports were 48% higher than the manufactured imports of that year. In 1979 manufactured exports only exceeded manufactured imports by around 5%.

4

earlier years. But in addition manufacturing output was affected by disputes outside the sector, notably in the transport industry.

iv) The argument of the previous paragraph implies that in the late 1970s manufacturing industry was maintaining employment, or in some cases actually increasing it, to meet expected market demand, but that actual performance fell short of such plans. But in the early 1980s there is the prospect of another recession, and in a context of worsening comparative costs.

The fall in employment in the two recessions of the 1970s can be identified from Table 1.2: a drop of 550,000 from 1970 to 1972, and one of 600,000 from 1974 to 1976. Thus it is difficult to avoid the expectation of a further decline in employment of equivalent dimensions a 7% employment fall implying the loss of another half a million jobs. That is, unless initiatives in work sharing and reduction of working time help ameliorate such arithmetic.

v) It is important to recognise that the large scale displacement of labour from jobs in manufacturing that we have noticed in the UK in the 1970s, and that is anticipated for the early 1980s, is not yet associated with any *acceleration* of labour productivity improvements. On the contrary it has emerged in the context of a *slowing* of productivity gains. The possible effects of new technology, both in displacement and possible job creation, still lie substantially in the future (though one of the "case study" sectors, electronics, is already materially affected).

There is a further set of official estimates which throw more light on the connection between labour displacement in manufacturing and movements in working time. This consists of estimates for "operatives" alone (that is for male and female manual workers). Occupational shifts in the UK economy are discussed in detail in the next part of this report, but it should be noted that the proportion of manual workers in manufacturing has been declining, and consequently their displacement from employment is more marked than that of non-manuals.

The official data include estimates of both a series of total weekly hours worked by all operatives, that is what might be termed total weekly labour input, and a series of average weekly hours "per operative". The latter series would be, for instance, affected by an increase in the proportion of part-time workers. The series uses a different information base from that of the New Earnings Survey, which concentrates mainly on the working time of adult workers working a full week. Instead, a six monthly survey of manual workers is used; this measures *actual* hours of all workers who worked *any* hours during the survey week (and therefore picks up the *net*

5

effect of the basic week, overtime, and absence or late starting. Moreover, it also has the advantage of continuity over many years.

Table 1.3   Working Time: Operatives in Manufacturing   (1970 = 100)

	Total Weekly Hours of All operatives	Average Weekly Hours Worked Per Operative
1960	115	105.6
1970	100	100
1971	94	98
1972	90	98
1973	92	99
1974	90	97
1975	84	96
1976	82	96
1977	83	97
1978	82	97
1979	80	96

Source: Department of Employment Gazette, Table 121; 1.12 in recent issues.

The table demonstrates an overall fall of 20% during the decade in the "input" of manual working hours in manufacturing, which in turn followed a 13% fall in the previous decade of the 1960s. The column of average hours worked by contrast shows a fall of over 5% in the 1960s and of some 4% in the 1970s.

Another way to analyse the data is to measure the pattern of change over each trade cycle (comparing equivalent, e.g. peak, years). The last two trade cycles each show a 10% fall in total manual labour input, but only a 2½% fall in average weekly hours worked.

There is very little indication from such data that any near stabilisation of manufacturing (or more widely, production instustries') employment can realistically be expected to emerge in the 1980s in Britain, at least within the existing patterns of working time. But before turning to look more closely at what relationship between employment trends and unemployment may be developing at the opening of the 1980s, it is important to examine a further aspect of changes in working time in the 1970s.

The Growth of Part Time Work in the 1970s

The analysis so far has been largely conducted in terms of employment aggregates and their change. But *within* these totals a profoundly import-

6

ant development has affected much of the economy. In directly affecting employment it has also represented an important dimension of change in working time. We have to measure and explain the dramatic and disproportionate increase in part-time work, particularly in the first half of the 1970s.

It is, of course, difficult to measure part-time work reliably and in a consistent way. For instance a change in the basis of compilation of the New Earnings Survey sample made a material difference to its measurement of part-time work, and prevented the development of consistent series. What we do have, from 1971 to 1977, is the Census of Employment, which over those years has measured part-time and full-time workers on a regular basis. *

Even for that limited group of years the information is sufficiently important to modify quite sharply the picture of employment and working time emerging from the overall figures examined so far. Over the period 1971 to 1977 the employment series for Great Britain show an increase in the total number of employees in employment of 478,000. How do the figures for part-time workers modify this? In the first place what is revealed is that *full-time jobs* actually *fell* by almost the same figure (a fall of 479,000) to just over 17.8 million. The remarkable increase in part-time employment was heavily concentrated on female employment; the number of part-time female employees rose in the six years by 860,000 to 3,617,000 (a 31% increase). Female full-time employment by contrast actually fell by 35,000. Part-time male employment is on a smaller scale and rose more modestly from 584,000 to 681,000 (a 17% rise). But we need to look again at the employment total. This can be adjusted to "full-time equivalents". From data on the local authorities, which represent a major concentration of part-time employment, and from evidence in the distributive trades, we would treat 1 part-time as equivalent to 0.4 of a full-time worker. On that basis total employment in Great Britain, measured in full-time equivalents, fell by 100,000 to just over 19½ million between 1971 and 1976. It is an important corrective to the appearance presented by the unadjusted figures.

Production Industries

The fall in overall employment in manufacturing industries has already been commented on. Over the six years covered by part-time statistics employment in production industries fell by 800,000—most of this (736,000) concentrated in manufacturing. Part-time work is limited in

* The 1977 data has only been published in early 1980 due to computer difficulties.

7

production industries other than manufacturing, where part-time employment actually increased slightly from 542,000 in 1971 to 566,000 in 1976. (There the fall in full-time employment by contrast was 760,000). Most part-time employment in manufacturing (489,000 in 1976) is of females and the small overall increase in part-time employment to 1967 thus masks an important change within the period. Part-time female employment rose rapidly to 1974 (by 117,000 a 25% increase) and then fell sharply in 1975. In other words, part-time employment is more unstable in face of cyclical fluctuations in manufacturing than is full time employment.

The Service Sectors

The most striking developments in part-time employment are found in the service sectors of the economy, which in 1977 accounted for nearly 13 million of the 22 million employees in employment in Great Britain. In these sectors both male and female employment has been increasing, and there is less cyclicality. In terms of aggregates, male employment in 1971 in the service sectors was slightly higher than that for females; but by 1977 the rapid increase of female employment had put their total employment (just under 6.7 millions) two-thirds of a million ahead of that of males. Yet as the following table shows, a very large part of this expansion of employment has involved part-timers:

Table 1.4   Service Sectors: Employees in Employment, 1971 and 1977

	1971 (000s)	1977 (000s)	Change, 1971-77 (000s)	As %
Male, full-time	5,261	5,445	+ 184	+ 3.5%
Female, full-time	3,418	3,636	+ 218	+ 6.4%
Male, part-time	473	561	+ 88	+ 18.6%
Female, part-time	2,207	3,037	+ 831	+ 37.6%
Totals	11,358	12,679	+ 1,321	+ 11.6%

Source: Census of Employment, Department of Employment Gazette (Data are for Great Britain; all sectors other than production industries and agriculture).

Thus over the six years part-time employment of females rose nearly six times as fast, in percentage terms, and almost four times as fast numerically, as that of full-timers. Although part-time male employment is a much smaller element, its proportional rate of increase was more than five times that of full-time males. Clearly, the increase of part-time female employment by 831,000 (over 37%) is the most significant development recorded in the table.

In consequence, on an unweighted basis the growth in part-time workers accounted for around 920,000 of the 1,320,000 increase in service sector employment in these six years. On a weighted basis (using one part-timer as equivalent to 0.4 of a full-timer) part-timers accounted for nearly half the increase (of 770,000 in full-time equivalents).

The rise in the proportion of women workers in the service trades who are part-timers is obviously significant. By 1977 part-timers constituted 46% of the total of female employment there; however on a "full-time equiv-alent" basis they probably still accounted for only one quarter of the total female labour input.

Within these totals some important differences in the patterns of change are revealed for service trades that are major employers of part-time labour. It is important to identify these since otherwise the analysis of what has been happening will be defective.

Official comment on the Census of Employment figures draws attention to the fact that much of the increase in part-time employment was concen-trated in the years 1973-75, and seems to invite the conclusion that a much more limited rate of increase in part-time employment is likely to be the subsequent trend. There was certainly one special factor at work in 1973-74; the raising of the school-leaving age to 16 removed a "cohort" of young people (who would have been entering the labour market) and, in a period of high activity, this must have encouraged the recruitment of part-timers.

But in the service sectors we need to distinguish between public and private services. In the case of *public* services the expansion of employment in the years to 1976, and notably in health and education services, rested heavily on part-timers. Thus educational services (mainly public) increased part-time employment of females by a third to 691,000 and medical and dental services showed an increase of 43% to 390,000 in their part-time female employment. Since then growth of employment has been sharply checked as a result of constraints on public expenditure; in 1977 part-time employment in medical and dental services still increased, though by only eight thousand, while in educational services it fell slightly (by over five thousand). So far as female employment in medical and dental services was concerned, the changes in the six years to 1977 meant that part-time workers had increased in numbers twice as much as full-time workers (by + 125,000, and + 60,000 respectively).

Thus, the effect of public spending constraints in the later 1970s appears to have been largely to freeze the numbers in the main public services close to their 1976 levels. (Some further growth resumed briefly between 1978 and

9

1979 so far as local authority employment was concerned, but this was already being reversed in the second half of 1979). This is substantially checking one major source of increased employment—full- and part-time—that was influential until 1976.

However, in the *private* service sectors there was also a dramatic advance in part-time work after 1971 and this has largely continued over the whole period to 1977. It must therefore be assumed that this growth in part-time employment—one that is disproportionately larger than the increase in full-time employment—is continuing.

It is helpful to distinguish two patterns. In one, exemplified by retail trade, full-time female employment falls while part-time employment increases. In the other, exemplified by financial services and miscellaneous services, both full- and part-time employment rise, but part-time female employment increases disproportionately. In these latter two sectors part-time employment continued to grow markedly through to 1977 for female employees, as did full-time employment (though at a slower pace). Table 1.6 illustrates these trends.

Table 1.5   Education and Health Services

Female Employment (thousands)

Full-Time	1971	1977
Educational Services	466.6	562.5
Medical and Dental Services	506.4	567.1
Part-Time		
Educational Services	519.2	685.6
Medical and Dental Services	272.8	397.6

Source: Census of Employment.

Table 1.6   Retail Distribution, Financial and Miscellaneous Services

Female Employment (thousands)

			Change 1971-77	
	1971	1977	(000s)	As %
Full-Time				
Retail Distribution	633.3	560.7	− 72.6	− 11%
Insurance, Financial Serv.	365.9	406.6	+ 40.7	+ 11%
Miscellaneous Services	548.6	562.9	+ 14.3	+ 3%
Part-Time				
Retail Distribution	534.6	673.6	+ 139.0	+ 26%
Insurance, Financial Serv.	123.8	176.7	+ 52.9	+ 43%
Miscellaneous Services	482.7	755.6	+ 272.9	+ 57%

Source: Census of Employment.

The six years, therefore, saw a marked change in the ratio of part-time to full-time female employees. For instance in retailing the number of part-timers increased from 84% of that of full-time employees to 120%. Indeed the fall in full-time female employment in retailing means that on a "full-time equivalent" basis there was an overall drop in retail employment during the six years. In 1976-77 the movement in both full and part-time numbers was negligible (this was a period of depressed trading volume). So it may be that by then many retail establishments had adjusted their ratios of full- and part-time staff to something of a new equilibrium (there is some indication of this from employee information in major retail company reports). Consequently, the future pace of advance in part-time employment in retailing may well be slower than in the mid 1970s.

Miscellaneous Services,* and on a smaller scale Financial Services, show the most vigorous advance in part-time employment. In Miscellaneous Services the ratio of part-time to full-time female workers increased from 88% to 134% and there was no sign of any check to this. As in retailing, at the end of the period a clear majority of female employees were part-time workers.

Changes on this scale in the structure of employment, and with it changes in patterns of working time (new combinations of full- and part-time workers over extended hours and shift systems), have important implications for the sectors affected. These include the lack of security, including legal rights, of many part-time workers, and disadvantages in pay and fringe benefits. But on the expectation (which is common to all official projections of the future labour force) of further rises in the "activity rates" of married women, we are looking here at one of the main and most flexible labour reserves in the modern economy. It has to be assumed that in the 1980s more women workers in particular will be seeking jobs; many will be seeking part-time work, others may find offers of part-time work more readily available than that of full-time work. The great acceleration in the use of part-time labour in the 1970s needs, therefore, to be understood in detail in specific contexts. The studies in retail distribution and in the hospital service particularly help in this.

Employment and Unemployment

But perhaps one of the most significant points to note about the phenomenon of rapidly rising part-time employment after 1971 is that it largely coincided with a massive rise in unemployment. By June 1977* unemployment in the UK economy stood at 1,450,000 or *twice* its 1971

---

*These include e.g. hotels and restaurants, public houses and clubs, hairdressers and laundries.

level. And certainly the check set on additional recruitment into the public services from 1976 onwards—which was noted in the previous section as eventually slowing the overall rise in part-time employment —was one major factor generating and then helping to maintain high unemployment levels.

Earlier the relative stability of overall numbers of employees in employment in the UK economy was emphasised. But that has to be set alongside the rather wave-like changes in the total working population, influenced both by demography and activity rates. The working population increased in the first half of the 1960s to reach a peak in 1966 as the high birth rate peak of the immediate post-war years moved into the labour force. There was then a slow decline in the working population until 1971 followed by a renewed expansion. This was fed initially from an increase in female activity rates, and after 1974 from a rising number of young workers entering the labour force. This increase in the size of the cohorts entering the labour force for the first time will continue until 1981-83. It is the combination of the trade cycle, the weak performance of the manufacturing sector, the curbing of public expenditure after 1976, and these demographic factors that have produced the movements in unemployment.

Table 1.7   Unemployment in the UK (June count)

In thousands	1970	555
	1971	724
	1972	804
	1973	575
	1974	542
	1975	866
	1976	1,332
	1977	1,450
	1978	1,446
	1979	1,344

Source: Economic Trends.

Within these high total figures for the later years of the 1970s the unemployment of young workers is particularly severe. Typically around half a million young workers under 25 have been unemployed, with the figure going above that as school leavers enter the labour market in the summer of each year.

* The time of the Employment Census.

12

The official estimates of unemployment by age groups are revealing:

Table 1.8   Unemployed Rates by Age, Great Britain, January 1979

Age Group	Percentages	
	Males	Females
Under 18	11.4	12.3
18–19	10.6	10.1
20–24	9.4	8.3
25–34	6.6	4.2
35–44	5.4	1.9
45–54	4.7	2.1
55–59	6.2	3.0
60 +	10.0	0.2
Average	7.0	4.3

Source: Department of Employment Gazette, March 1979.

It is apparent that the trends that have led to a build up of persistently high unemployment in the UK economy have particular impact on younger workers. Moreover, recent official research has established that the unemployment of younger workers follows the overall changes in unemployment but with greater amplitude. We have, therefore, to assume a yet more serious increase in young workers' unemployment in the early 1980s. To some extent, then, immediate interest in the possibilities of reducing working time is directed at the grave levels of unemployment of young workers to be expected if present trends of employment and patterns of working time persist.

Although the later 1970s appear as years of peak post-war unemployment rates, a number of our case studies suggested that companies were constrained in their working time policies by what were perceived as difficulties in recruitment in the labour market, at least in particular regions. It is important to recognise that marked imbalances and segmentation have developed in labour markets, both occupationally and regionally. The time of our case study work (1979) did represent a somewhat frustrated peak in a wide range of manufacturing industries, and a period of high consumer spending that affected a wide range of service industries. A clear sign of this is to be found in the marked shift in the ratio of unemployed manual craftsmen to job vacancies between 1977 and 1979.* Such ratios have to be treated warily, since not all job vacancies are among

* See also the article "Skill Shortage Indicators" Dept. of Employment Gazette, October 1979. Nearly half the manufacturing establishments reporting defined "hard-to-fill" skilled vacancies were in the South East.

those officially recorded, but they do identify trends. The marked regional imbalances are also evident:

Table 1.9   Manual Craftsmen: Ratios of Unemployed to Job Vacancies (JV).

Region	Sept. 1977 Unemployed: JV.	Sept. 1979 Unemployed: JV.
South East	2.3 : 1	0.9 : 1
East Anglia	2.0 : 1	0.9 : 1
South West	4.4 : 1	1.4 : 1
West Midlands	3.8 : 1	2.3 : 1
East Midlands	1.9 : 1	1.0 : 1
Yorkshire & Humberside	2.7 : 1	1.5 : 1
North West	6.7 : 1	2.9 : 1
Northern	4.6 : 1	4.2 : 1
Wales	5.0 : 1	1.9 : 1
Scotland	4.6 : 1	2.7 : 1

Source: Department of Employment Gazette.
(Data relate to "craft and similar occupations, including foremen, in processing, production, repairing, etc.")

These statistics must serve to emphasise that in so mismatched a labour market the role of a positive manpower policy needs to be a persistent one, even in a context of high unemployment. It happened that industrial disputes and problems stemming from comparative cost and competitiveness constrained the potential industrial expansion of the late 1970s. But the need that has to be understood and met in the context of the 1980s is both to innovate in the handling of working time so as to reduce the social burden of structural unemployment, and to plan to minimise or avoid the constraints of skill shortages. There is no reason in Britain, at least, to think that the context of the 1980s is in these respects qualitatively different from that of the late 1970s.

That said, it is necessary to project—albeit cautiously—the likely employment and unemployment trends of the early 1980s. In the two recessions of the 1970s the fall in manufacturing employment was respectively 7% and 10%; it was proportionately a heavier fall in female than in male employment. In round terms—and assuming a recession of a severity of similar dimensions—manufacturing employment may be expected to fall to around 6½ million by the second half of 1981 (between half a million and 600,000 less than in 1979). Private sector employment outside of manufacturing was largely unchanged in the last two recessions; again, it seems reasonable to repeat this assumption. Public sector civil employment rose in each of the recessions of the 1970s (by around 200 and 400

14

thousand respectively); this assumption cannot be repeated. In policy terms a fall is clearly intended; in practice, in face of trade union resistance and public concern, the employment fall may be limited.

These elements, taken together, suggest an employment fall of around 600,000 to 1981. The labour force projections suggest a rise of a quarter of a million in the number of young workers (under 25); projections of a further rise in activity rates may be frustrated by the lack of job opportunities in the recession. All of this suggests a rise in the unemployment rate for Great Britain from 5½% in mid 1979 to around 9% (2.2 million) by the latter half of 1981. No serious forecaster has been able to project more than a very slow "recovery" beyond that date; in some parts of the industrial economy the dangers of cumulative weakening or collapse cannot be disregarded.

This is the context for a critical review of traditional patterns of working time.

Chapter 2: Working Time and the Occupational Structure

In the British economy very significant differences in patterns of working time have developed as between manual and non-manual work. There are further important differences between the working time of men and women manual workers, and some further differentiation between that of non-manual men and women. This section therefore examines some of the main changes in the occupational balance of the labour force coming through in the 1970s, and relates these to differences in the patterns of working time of the four main categories (manual men, manual women, non-manual men, non-manual women).

In sequence, the following ground is covered:

a) The very large scale changes in the occupational balance of the employees in employment in the 1970s. These include a fall of some one and a half million full-time adult manual workers and a rise of nearly one million full-time non-manual workers.

b) The main characteristics of the patterns of working time of the four main categories of worker, on the latest official data.

c) A closer look at the tendency for the basic week of many non-manual workers to fall, particularly in the first half of the 1970s; this led to a majority of non-manual men, and over three fifths of non-manual women, having a basic working week of 37 hours or less.

d) Some consideration of changes in relative pay, and in the occupational balance of pay costs, that have resulted from the 1970s. We note also that non-manual workers still on longer basic weeks (e.g. 40 hours) have relatively low earnings; this affects the possible costs of reducing such basic weekly hours.

The Occupational Balance Changes:
The Numbers Involved

In this section an attempt is made to identify the numbers involved, as employees in employment, in the main categories of manual and non-manual work. There are, however, no official estimates on precisely the lines that we required. To start with we sought to establish the salient figures for full-time adult employees.

There are problems of estimation in seeking to do so, since it is only by grossing up from the New Earnings Survey (nominally a one in a hundred sample but in practice one in 120/130) that the numbers in each category can be assessed. Besides, there are also some problems regarding the employment totals.* But with some margin of error it is possible to present the data for *full-time adult employees* for 1970 and 1978:

Table 1.10   Estimated Numbers of Full-Time Adult Employees, in 1970 and 1978 (millions)

	Manual Men	Manual Women	All Manual
1970	8.03	2.00	10.03
1978	6.86	1.57	8.43
Change	− 1.17	− 0.43	− 1.6
	Non-Manual Men	Non-Manual Women	All Non-Manual
1970	3.93	3.13	7.06
1978	4.40	3.57	7.97
Change	+ 0.47	+ 0.44	+ 0.91
	All Men	All Women	All Employees
1970	11.96	5.13	17.09
1978	11.26	5.14	16.40
Change	− 0.7	− 0.01	− 0.69

Notes: Estimates based on grossing up from NES; 1970 using grossing up factors of 123 for men and 130 for women (lower than those suggested in the 1970 NES to allow for the revised basis of collection of employment data in use since 1971); 1978 using grossing up factors of 120 for men and 128 for women.

Estimates are for employees. There are also some 1.9 million self-employed in the economy (though not all of these will necessarily be adults). Definition of adult age; 21 and over for men; 18 and over for women.

What is immediately apparent is the major decline in the numbers of manual workers—of both sexes—and the more moderate increase in the numbers of non-manual workers. By 1978 the process had already gone so far that there were in total only half a million fewer non-manual full-time

* A new employment series was developed from 1971, so that an attempt has to be made to adjust earlier data to be consistent with the later series. Employment data after 1976 are still "provisional".

workers (nearly 8 million) than manual workers (just under 8½ million). Nevertheless, manual men remain the largest of the four categories (accounting for about 42% of total full-time adult employees), although their numbers appear to have fallen by over one million between 1970 and 1978. The rise in the number of non-manual men (just under half a million) did not match this and the number of men employed full-time fell by some 700,000. By contrast the decline in the number of full-time manual women and the increase in non-manual women are virtually identical.

These changes have quite important implications for the make up of the total pay bill for full-time workers in the British economy. They have more than offset the fact that proportionately hourly earnings over these years—for both men and women—were rising faster for manual workers than for non-manual workers. With the scale of full-time employment set out in the previous table the total hourly pay bill in 1970 split evenly between manual earnings and non-manual earnings (manual men 44% of the total, manual women 6½%; non-manual men 34½% of the total, non-manual women 15%). By 1978 the balance had tilted towards the higher proportion of non-manual workers. By then manual workers only accounted for 45% of the total hourly pay bill of all full-time workers, non-manual workers for 55% of the total (men manual workers 39%; women manual workers 6%; non-manual men 37%; non-manual women 18%).

So far we have looked only at the main categories of full-time adult workers. In order to get a more complete picture of the composition of the labour force, and the ways in which it has been changing, we need to extend the comparison of manual and non-manual occupational employment trends to juveniles and to part-time workers.

The range of error in identifying the other members of the employed labour force—young workers and in particular part-time workers—is rather greater. We have assumed the same grossing up factors for young workers (the NES only indicates a single set of factors for grossing up). In the case of part-time workers we have made an estimate of total numbers which seems compatable with the national employment data (this is itself uncertain for both 1970 and 1978), and allocated to the four categories in the same ratio as NES sample numbers of part-time workers. With these qualifications the complete picture of paid employment in the British economy in 1970 and 1978 appears as follows:

Table 1.11 Estimates of Numbers of Employees in Great Britain, 1970, 1978   (millions)

	Manual		Non-Manual	
	1970	1978	1970	1978
Full-Time Men	8.03	6.86	3.93	4.40
Full-Time Women	2.00	1.57	3.13	3.57
Youths (F.T.)	0.88	0.80	0.33	0.26
Girls (F.T.)	0.17	0.11	0.33	0.19
Part-Time Male	(0.36)	(0.35)	(0.18)	(0.33)
Part-Time Female	(1.67)	(2.00)	(1.03)	(1.73)
All Full-Time	11.08	9.33	7.72	8.41
All Part-Time	(2.03)	(2.35)	(1.21)	(2.06)
Totals	(13.11)	(11.69)	(8.93)	(10.48)

Estimates: Based on NES and on employment data; bracketed figures involve higher risk of error.

The numbers of young workers have been influenced by demographic change (increasing the numbers in the relevant age groups), the raising of the school leaving age and increased proportions staying in full-time education after the minimum school leaving age, and sharply increased juvenile unemployment. Part-time employment has been increasing rapidly; exactly comparable figures are available from 1971 to 1977 (and are discussed elsewhere). The estimate here is for an increase broadly from 3.2 million in 1970 to 4.4 million in 1978. On the estimates given above the part-time employment of manual women has been increasing while full-time employment has fallen (within an almost unchanged total employment of manual women), and the number of part-time manual female workers exceeds that of full-timers.

Differentiation in Patterns of Working Time: Manual and Non-Manual

The importance of the changing occupational balance for patterns of working time is that there are important differences as between the four main categories (manual men, manual women, non-manual men, non-manual women) in such important parameters of working time as the length of the basic week, the proportion working overtime and the overtime hours worked, and the proportion working on shifts (as revealed through the New Earnings Survey by shift premia payments). The following table summarises these salient features of working time and the differences between the four categories for the latest (1979) New Earnings

19

Survey data. (There have only been very minor and irregular changes in the pattern revealed since the information was compiled in this form*).

Table 1.12   Occupational Working Time Patterns: Full Time Adult Employees in April 1979

Weekly	Manual		Non-Manual	
All employees	Men	Women	Men	Women
Average Basic Hours	39.8	38.5	37.1	36.3
Average Overtime Hours	6.3	1.1	1.6	0.4
Total Average Hours	46.2	39.6	38.8	36.7
Overtime Pay as % of Average Earnings	15.0%	3.5%	3.5%	1.2%
Shift Premia as % of Average Earnings	3.2%	1.9%	0.6%	0.8%
Those receiving overtime pay				
% of all Employees	58.5%	17.5%	20.3%	10.3%
Average Overtime Hours	10.6	6.1	7.2	4.0
Overtime Pay as % of Earnings	23.4%	16.4%	17.1%	11.1%
Those receiving shift premia				
% of all Employees				
Shift Premia as % of	23.6%	11.4%	5.6%	9.5%
Average Earnings less Overtime Pay	14.1%	14.7%	11.6%	8.9%
Normal Basic Hours	39.4	38.7	38.5	38.9
Overtime Hours	7.4	2.0	5.0	0.6

Source: New Earnings Survey.

There are a number of points to observe, several of which will be examined at more length subsequently:

— The basic week of non-manual workers is closer to 35 hours than to 40 hours on average. It is only the category of manual men for whom the basic week is close to 40 hours.

— Overtime working is far more important for manual men than for any other category. Overall overtime only adds 3½% to the earnings of manual women and non-manual men, and it accounts for even less of the earnings of non-manual women. But it accounts for 15% of total manual men's earnings.

* Since 1974, but there were deficiencies in that year's returns.

20

— When overtime working is looked at more closely, it becomes apparent that (in the survey week, which may be regarded as typical) it affected nearly three out of every five manual men, but only one in five non-manual men, and lower proportions of women workers. For the manual men who did work overtime, the average overtime hours worked were over 10 and the pay resulting accounted for nearly a quarter of total pay. For other categories of workers in the table the figures are lower.

— Shift work played a more important part in the working time of manual workers; 23.6% (of manual men) received shift premia. The main contrast is with the non-manual men where only 5.6% received shift premia. Shift premia, where received, only accounted for around 14% of basic earnings for manual workers—and even less for non-manuals. It is noteworthy that the basic week of non-manuals working shifts is on average longer than for non-manuals as a whole. This is (particularly for non-manual women shift workers*) connected with the importance of shift working for the hospital service, where many of the workers concerned have remained on a 40 hour basic week (there are currently agreements to reduce this for nursing staff). Generally, non-manual workers on shift work appear as having not only longer basic weeks, but they are also lower paid (despite the shift premia) than the average non-manual man or woman not working shifts. In basic hours and pay they are closer to their manual shift-working equivalents.

The Basic Week of Non-Manuals: Falling Trend

The fact that in the main the basic weekly hours for non-manual workers in Britain are below 40 hours and have tended to fall further, at least in the first half of the 1970s, is an important element in discussions on the reduction of working time. Important for at least two reasons:

— That for many such workers the 35 hour week is already a reality, and many more are relatively near that goal. Thus views on what it might ''cost'' to move to a shorter working week need to take into account the very large numbers already significantly below the basic 40 hours that still characterises most male manual work.

— That for many manual workers the argument about shorter working time already points to the present practice of non-manual workers (with whom they may be in relatively close contact), and may be seen in part as a matter of reducing discrimination.

* Some 60% of whom are employed in the hospital services.

21

Here we review the salient data, firstly identifying the timing of the falls in the non-manual basic week (as revealed in the proportions shown by the New Earnings Survey to be in particular bands of basic hours). Secondly we emphasise the wider spread of basic weeks found among non-manuals, and the narrow concentration of manual men's basic hours around 40. Thirdly, we estimate by "grossing up" from the New Earnings Survey samples how many full-time employees are on shorter basic weekly hours in the late 1970s compared with the start of the decade.

The first set of tables of "cumulative percentage distributions" of basic hours for non-manual men and women makes clear that the downward shift occurred throughout the first half of the 1970s (see Table 1.13). Thus the proportion of non-manual men with a basic week of 37 hours or less rose from 38.5% in 1970 to 53.5% by 1976; for women the proportions improved from just under 50% on 37 hours or less to 62% by 1976. The process appears to have halted during the period of "social contract" incomes policies (which would explain the stabilisation from 1976 to 1978). Priority attention to raising pay in the late 1970s may explain the lack of movement even by 1979, but the process of reducing the non-manual week is clearly being resumed in 1980-81 (e.g. for the very large group of NHS nursing staff).

Dispersion of Basic Hours—Manual and Non-Manual

The New Earnings Survey tabulates the numbers in its sample recorded as having a particular level of basic normal hours. In this study we concentrate on the dispersion of such hours recorded for full-time workers in the four main categories: manual men; non-manual men; manual women; non-manual women. It is possible to estimate numbers involved (although these can be only broad approximations) by using the "grossing up" factors provided in the survey; these are 119.7 for males and 124.8 for females. Multiplying up the sample numbers by these factors provides an approximate figure for Great Britain.

In the following tables, the pattern revealed is analysed by identifying the normal week corresponding to three key stages in the dispersion; the lowest decile (LD), the median (M), and the highest decile (HD)*. The data for 1978 are contrasted with those for 1970.

* In this context, the *lowest decile* means that one tenth of the category analysed (e.g. manual men) had the same or shorter hours and nine tenths had the same or longer hours; the *median*, that half had the same or shorter hours and half had the same or longer hours; the *highest decile* means that nine tenths had the same or shorter hours and one tenth the same or longer hours.

Table 1.13 Cumulative Percentage Distributions of Normal Basic Hours:[1] Full-Time Adult Non-Manual Men

	1970 %	1971 %	1972 %	1973 %	1974 %	1975 %	1976 %	1977 %	1978 %	1979 %
32 and under	5.2	5.7	6.0	5.6	4.5	5.2	5.7	5.1	5.1	5.3
34 and under	6.4	7.0	7.0	6.8	5.7	6.3	6.8	6.4	6.4	6.6
35 and under	16.3	17.4	17.7	18.5	18.5	19.8	20.7	20.4	20.6	20.6
36 and under	20.4	21.9	22.5	23.6	23.0	25.3	26.1	25.9	26.1	25.6
37 and under	38.5	40.5	40.9	47.9	49.5	51.6	53.5	53.5	53.6	52.2
38 and under	68.8	71.2	71.8	72.9	75.4	74.4	74.8	75.1	75.0	75.0
39 and under	70.9	73.0	73.5	74.7	77.1	75.9	76.1	76.2	76.1	77.0
40 and under	90.3	91.6	92.3	94.3	95.2	93.5	94.5	94.7	95.3	95.8
42 and under	94.6	95.4	95.1	96.2	96.4	95.6	95.7	96.8	96.3	97.7
44 and under	96.6	97.1	96.9	97.5	97.6	96.9	96.8	97.0	97.4	98.6
50 and under	99.0	99.0	90.0	99.0	99.0	99.5	99.5	99.5	99.6	99.6
all hours	100.0	100.0	100.0	100.0	100.0	100.0	100.0	100.0	100.0	100.0

Source: 1979 NES Table 29: equivalent tables in earlier years.

Cumulative Percentage Distributions of Normal Basic Hours:[1] Full-Time Adult Non-Manual Women

	1970 %	1971 %	1972 %	1973 %	1974 %	1975 %	1976 %	1977 %	1978 %	1979 %
32 and under	9.4	9.9	10.6	9.7	8.8	9.6	10.2	8.8	8.7	8.9
34 and under	12.8	13.5	13.5	13.0	12.2	12.9	13.5	12.3	11.9	12.3
35 and under	26.9	20.3	28.5	28.5	29.5	30.4	30.8	20.2	29.9	30.5
36 and under	31.7	33.6	33.7	34.2	35.5	37.4	37.8	37.1	36.7	37.8
37 and under	47.8	49.0	49.6	55.1	56.6	61.1	62.1	62.1	61.8	61.5
38 and under	74.4	76.8	76.1	75.8	77.6	78.8	70.2	70.0	78.7	78.3
39 and under	77.1	79.0	78.1	77.5	79.2	88.2	79.4	79.3	79.8	79.4
40 and under	86.8	88.4	95.4	97.4	98.2	90.0	98.0	90.0	99.1	99.2
42 and under	98.3	99.0	98.9	99.1	99.2	99.7	99.5	99.5	99.7	99.7
44 and under	99.3	99.7	99.4	99.5	99.8	99.9	99.8	99.9	99.9	99.9
50 and under	100.0	100.0	100.0	100.0	100.0	100.0	100.0	100.0	100.0	100.0
all hours	100.0	100.0	100.0	100.0	100.0	100.0	100.0	100.0	100.0	100.0

Source: as above.

[1] Normal basic hours: "Number of hours excluding all overtime and main meal breaks which employee was expected to work in a normal week".

23

Table 1.14 Dispersion of Normal Basic Hours (Full-time Adults)

1978	Manual Men	Manual Women	Non-Manual Men	Non-Manual Women
LD	37 to 38	34 to 35	34 to 35	32 to 34
Median	39 to 40	39 to 40	36 to 37	36 to 37
HD	39 to 40	39 to 40	39 to 40	39 to 40
1970				
LD	38 to 39	34 to 35	34 to 35	32 to 34
Median	39 to 40	39 to 40	37 to 38	37 to 38
HD	41 to 42	39 to 40	39 to 40	41 to 42

Sources: NES 1978 and 1970.

Note: The range shown means *over* the first figure, and *up* to the second.

What is apparent is the narrow spread of normal hours for manual workers. The only shift evident since 1970 is a reduction in the normal week at the upper end of the dispersion to the predominant 40 hours. For both men and women, over 39 and up to 40 hours is the modal group; indeed in 1978 80% of manual men and 70% of manual women were in that category.

By contrast there is a wider spread of basic hours for non-manual workers which is even more marked for the women than for the men. The notable change between 1970 and 1978 is the fall in median hours from over 37 to 38 in 1970 to over 36 to 37 in 1978. The modal group moves similarly. In 1970 and in 1978 nearly half of all non-manual men had normal hours in the two hour range from (over) 36 to 38. But whereas in 1970, 30% were in the range 37 to 38, by 1978 the modal group had shifted down to 36 to 37 hours (27.5% of the total).

If we compare the position of manual and non-manual workers in respect to the length of the normal week, we find close similarity only at the top end of the dispersion. For all categories by 1978 the Highest Decile is effectively the 40 hour week. But at the *median* the normal week for non-manual workers (both men and women) is *three hours less* than for manual workers; this differential has widened since 1970 when it was only two hours. A similar differential is found at the lower end of the dispersion of weekly hours.

Growing Numbers on Shorter Hours

The New Earnings Survey data can also be used to identify both the proportions and (approximately) the numbers of full-time adults whose working week was below a given level in any particular year.

Given the recent emphasis in trade union policy on the achievement of the 35 hour week, it is interesting to identify how many workers are already on a 35 hour or shorter normal week. But the most notable shift has been the substantial increase in the proportion and number of non-manual workers achieving a 37 hour or shorter week.

For the main categories of workers we have been considering the proportion with a normal working week of 35 hours or less grew only modestly in the 1970s. However, a significant proportion of all types of workers apart from manual men are by now on or below the 35 hour week. In particular we should note that about *one in four* non-manual workers enjoy a 35 hour week or less.

Table 1.15   Proportion of Workers* on 35 Hour or Shorter Normal Week

	1970	1978
Non-Manual Women	27.0%	29.8%
Non-Manual Men	16.3%	20.5%
Manual Women	14.1%	16.0%
Manual Men	1.1%	2.0%

* For whom normal hours were recorded. Full-time adults. Source: NES 1970 and 1978.

It is possible to provide an estimate of the approximate number of full-time adult workers that these proportions represent. The method adopted to arrive at the numbers uses the New Earnings Survey samples** in conjunction with employment data to estimate the four main categories:

** It should be noted that for a proportion of the NES returns, notably for non-manual workers, the normal week was not recorded. The earnings data provided for those without specified normal hours (cf NES Table 159) is more characteristic (particularly for non-manual men) of those working shorter than average hours than of those with longer hours of work. For purposes of estimation it is assumed in the text that those without normal hours specified had a similar pattern of normal hours to those whose normal hours were specified. If anything this might involve a slight understatement of the total numbers with relatively short normal hours of work.

25

Table 1.16 1978: Numbers on Normal Weekly Hours of 35 Hours or Less
(Full-time adult workers only)

Non-Manual Women	around	1,065,000
Non-Manual Men	around	900,000
Manual Women	around	250,000
Manual Men	around	135,000
Total	around	2,350,000

On this basis it would seem that nearly two million non-manual adult workers enjoy a 35 hour (or shorter) "normal" week. The total is around half a million more than in 1970; due less to the shift in percentage terms, than the growth in the numbers of non-manual workers since 1970.

But, by contrast, the shift in the case of non-manual workers to a normal working week of *37 hours or less* has been much more marked. By 1978 a *clear majority* of non-manual workers in full-time employment enjoyed a normal week of 37 or fewer hours.

Table 1.17 Proportion of Workers* on 37 Hour or Shorter Normal Week

	1970	1978
Non-Manual Women	47.9%	61.7%
Non-Manual Men	38.5%	53.5%
Manual Women	17.6%	21.6%
Manual Men	4.1%	5.5%

* Full-time adults for whom normal hours were recorded. Source: NES 1970 and 1978.

Once again, it is possible to provide approximate totals for the four main categories, setting out for 1978 the number of full-time adults who can be assumed to have a normal week of 37 hours or less:

Table 1.18 1978: Numbers on Normal Weekly Hours of 37 or Less
(Full-time adult workers only)

Non-Manual Women	around	2,200,000
Non-Manual Men	around	2,355,000
Manual Women	around	340,000
Manual Men	around	380,000
Total approximately		5,275,000

The predominance of non-manual workers is again notable. We estimate *over 4½ million* full-time non-manual workers on a normal basic week of

37 hours or less in 1978. This represents an increase from about 3 million in 1970, stemming from a rising total employment of non-manual workers and a higher proportion enjoying such a short basic week. By contrast the declining total numbers of manual workers, and the limited increase in the percentage of such workers enjoying a basic week as short as 37 hours, makes the numbers of manuals involved little more than in 1970.

Given the hostile reception from employers' organisations to proposals for a shorter working week which were being discussed in the later 1970s, it is surprising that this slightly earlier phenomenon of increasing numbers and proportions of non-manual workers on a comparatively short basic week has gone virtually without comment. Perhaps the phenomenon had not been identified.

It is at least interesting to note that the tendency for basic hours to fall has been accompanied by a rise in non-manual employment. Most of this can be ascribed to longer run occupational trends. But there might be some association with the shift to shorter hours, not least so far as non-manual women workers are concerned—with their associated extremely limited overtime working.

Non-Manual Workers: Total Weekly Hours and Level of Earnings

The wide spread of "basic hours" enjoyed by non-manual workers has already been noted. There is a further feature of the relation between pay costs and working time that is important in this context. Put simply it is that in general the relatively large concentrations of non-manual workers that still have longer basic weeks (notably 40 hours) than the average tend to have *lower than average* earnings. Therefore the "cost" of reducing the basic weekly hours of such workers cannot be read off from overall figures of average earnings of *all* non-manuals.

Once again the data source is the New Earnings Survey, which contains information relating total weekly hours worked and the level of earnings. Given the relatively low incidence of overtime any such table gives broad guidance about earnings and "basic" weeks (thus *most* of those working actual hours of 40 or more can be assumed to be on "basic" hours close to a 40 hour week*).

* Nearly 20% of non-manual men for whom basic hours were specified had a 40 hour basic week.

27

(i) Non-Manual Men

The Table 1.19 below picks up the *main concentrations* of non-manual men grouped by hours worked (sample sizes implying a "population" of less than 80,000 have not been included).** Roughly seven-eighths of all full-time manual men had their weekly hours specified; the group that did not have specified hours had considerably higher weekly earnings than those whose hours were specified. On the evidence of the table that follows one might expect the "unspecified" hours to centre around 35 or less per week.

Table 1.19   Non-Manual Men: Total Hours Worked and Level of Earnings (April 1978)

Number in Sample	Total hours worked	Gross weekly earnings (£)	Assumed hours	Hourly earnings (£)	Hourly earnings as % of av. for all with specified hours*
788	26-28	104.0	(27)	3.85	150
3,564	34-35	112.6	(35)	3.22	125
1,639	35-36	104.1	(36)	2.89	112
6,527	36-37	97.1	(37)	2.62	102
5,716	37-38	102.0	(38)	2.68	104
873	38-39	95.7	(39)	2.45	95
4,469	39-40	87.2	(40)	2.18	85
683	41-42	88.6	(42)	2.11	82
662	43-44	92.3	(44)	2.10	82

* Average hourly earnings for all those with specified hours were £2.57.

Source: NES 1978, Table 159: slight estimation involved in calculating hourly earnings.

A number of points can be made in the light of the data in the table:

i)   For these major concentrations of non-manual men there is a negative correlation between total hours worked and the level of hourly earnings. Those with shorter than average hours secured significantly higher hourly earnings than those with longer hours. Thus, the major group of such men who worked a 35 hour week

** "Grossing up" from the sample size of the NES to the actual "population" is by a factor of approximately 120; thus a sample size of 660/670 would be close to a "population" of 80,000.

28

(34-35) had average hourly earnings nearly 50% higher than the major concentration who worked a 40 hour (39-40) week.*

ii) The lower level of hourly earnings associated with higher levels of total hours worked is so marked that for the largest groups of workers identified in the table the same negative correlation holds true of weekly earnings. The largest concentrations are bunched close to 37 hours, with close to £100 weekly earnings; the 35 hour week concentration had weekly average earnings of £112.60 while the group who worked 40 hours had only average weekly earnings of £87.20.

iii) The table suggests that above 40 hours worked, hourly earnings in 1978 were levelling out at a little above £2; this is broadly true of the men who worked longer hours. (But for the 60,000 or so whose total hours were 48—not shown on the table—the level of hourly earnings was even lower at £1.89).

Occupational analysis of the length of the "basic" week of different categories of non-manual men reveals the particular occupations where an unusually high proportion had a 40 hour (39-40) basic week. These included salesmen, shop assistants, sales supervisory, and shop managers, with 50% or more having a basic 40 hour week; thus, the relatively low paid *distributive trades* are particularly associated with a 40 hour basic week for non-manual men. Male nurses and nurse administrators, and prison officers, had over 90% with a 40 hour basic week. A number of managerial categories, notably works managers and foremen, had a high proportion (typically a third or more) on a 40 hour basic week—doubtless a reflection of their role in managing manual grades with a 40 hour basic week.

In consequence one could not estimate the "cost" of reducing non-manual working hours (actual and basic) from overall average figures of the level of non-manual men's earnings. Most of the higher paid non-manual men are already working an actual working week, and have a basic week, close to (or below) 35 hours. Major groups among those with a longer working week are lower paid, and share more of the characteristics of actual and basic hours of male manual workers.

(ii) Non-Manual Women

A somewhat similar pattern emerges when the earnings associated with different ranges of total hours worked are surveyed for non-manual

*Using the approximate grossing up factor of 120, there were around 425,000 non-manual men working a total of 35 hours, and around 535,000 working a 40 hour week.

women. Since overtime plays an unusually minor role in the earnings of non-manual women (on average only 0.4 overtime hours per week) the information in this case must be very close to "basic" weekly hours.

For women the "grossing up" factor from the sample size to the actual population is approximately 128; thus a sample size of about 625 indicates a population of around 80,000. As before, the table picks out the main concentrations by hours worked:

Table 1.20 Non-Manual Women: Total Hours Worked and Level of Earnings (April 1978)

Number in Sample	Total hours worked	Gross weekly earnings (£)	Assumed hours	Hourly earnings (£)	As % of av. for all with specified hours*
623	24-26	87.3	(25)	3.49	221
990	26-28	89.4	(27)	3.31	209
787	32-34	51.9	(33)	1.57	99
3,761	34-35	55.5	(35)	1.59	101
1,978	35-36	62.0	(36)	1.72	109
5,859	36-37	56.1	(37)	1.52	96
4,089	37-38	53.5	(38)	1.41	89
4,377	39-40	52.9	(40)	1.32	84

* The average hourly earnings for all those with specified hours were £1.58.

Source: NES Table 160.

Some comments may help to interpret the table:

i) The teaching profession—as with men non-manual—largely accounts for the high pay in the concentrations working 24-28 hours. However, unlike the pattern of men's earnings there is no further category of relatively highly paid workers bunched around 35 hours; this may reflect the limited proportion of women in the higher salaried positions.

ii) Hourly earnings for those working 40 hours were 84% of the average for all full-time non-manual women; this is very similar to the relative position of non-manual men working 40 hours (85% of the average).

iii) Gross weekly earnings vary little for the major concentrations working in the various bands of hours between 32 and 40 a week.

iv) Around 90% of all non-manual full-time women workers with hours specified are covered by the table. As in the case of non-manual men, those women workers whose hours were not specified (7% of the

30

total) had considerably higher average earnings than those whose hours were specified.

For non-manual women then, as for non-manual men, longer than average hours worked are associated with lower than average hourly earnings.

Consequently, it is useful once again to identify the particular occupational groups with a longer (typically 40 hours) basic week in 1978. The key categories are the same as for men non-manual workers: saleswomen, sales supervisors, branch managers of shops (around half of the sales personnel are on a 40 hour basic week, and over two-thirds of the branch managers); registered nurses and nurse administrators (around 90% on a 40 hour basic week), and nursing auxiliaries (around 70% on a 40 hour basic week). These categories alone account for a substantial majority of the non-manual women with a 40 hour basic week (as for men, just under a fifth of the total with hours specified had a 40 hour basic week). Consequently, the retail trade and hospital services are particularly important in any exploration of those categories of non-manual workers still on a 40 hour week in the late 1970s—in contrast to the majority enjoying a shorter basic week.

Chapter 3: Other Aspects of Working Time

In this section we review briefly some aspects of the pattern of working time that are of persistent importance, especially in seeking to determine the likely outturn of attempts to reduce working time further. In turn we examine some of the salient features of overtime working, some aspects of shift work, and the trends in annual holidays with pay.

To some extent these aspects of working time have attracted attention and comment in relation to recent discussions as to whether reductions in working time might alleviate unemployment in the medium term. For instance the Department of Employment in the "Gazette" in March and April 1978 examined briefly the potential of reducing the retirement age, reducing normal weekly hours of work, reducing the level of overtime working and increasing annual holiday entitlements.

But any such discussion must be related to evidence of existing patterns, of any trends of change in those patterns, and must attempt some analysis of the conditions under which particular patterns of working time develop.

In Britain a major analysis and survey looking particularly at overtime and shiftworking was published late in 1970 by the National Board for Prices and Incomes. (Report No. 161, "Hours of Work, Overtime and Shiftworking"). No equivalent study of such thoroughness had been attempted before, and many of the Report's findings and comments remain valid since only minor changes have taken place in the 1970s in either overtime patterns or shiftworking. However, there are some aspects of the subject that were not fully discussed in that report, and it is also important to place the situations encountered and analysed in our case study work in the general setting of the most important overall data available.

Overtime

We have already noted the most significant general differences in the actual practice of overtime working, as between manual men and not only non-manual workers but also manual women workers. The only caveat that might be put in is that the New Earnings Survey material, on which our most reliable understanding of overtime is built, does not contain any calculations of the extent of unpaid overtime among higher grade non-manual staff.

It is also appropriate to emphasise the comparatively greater importance of

32

the overtime of *men* manual workers. Data on the average overtime worked in relation to *age* makes the point more clearly:

Table 1.21   Overtime and Age: Full-Time Manual Male Employees

Age range	Av. Weekly Overtime
under 18	2.2
18-20	3.5
21-24	5.2
25-29	6.3
30-39	7.1
40-49	7.1
50-59	5.9
60-64	4.9

Source: 1979 NES.

The highest levels of overtime are worked by men in their 30s and 40s and thus the table must tell us something of worker preferences and attitudes. The NBPI Survey of 1970 commented, in face of similar information, that:

"In our survey of individual workers the high overtime group contained a higher proportion of married men than the low overtime group. Financial commitments and hence the incentive to work overtime tend to be greatest during the earlier years of married life . . . The importance of pay as a reason for overtime is shown by the fact that 87% of the workers in our survey gave no reason other than pay for working overtime". (Op. Cit. Page 25).

The NBPI went on to say that: "Low pay and consequent low hourly earnings have been frequently cited as a major cause of high overtime working. This conclusion was reached by the Donovan Commission." This argument in fact seems unavoidable, but some care is needed in stating it.

The link between comparatively low pay and high overtime may be demonstrated by looking at industrial groups in manufacturing where manual men worked an average of over 8 hours a week in overtime in the survey period in 1979:

Table 1.22 Manufacturing Industries with High Overtime (Manual Men)

	Av. Hourly Earnings excluding overtime pay and hours (p)	Av. Hours of over- time
Manufacturing av.	208.7	6.2
Bread and Flour	165.8	10.6
Insulated Wires, Cables	210.4	9.7
Shop & Office Fittings	180.4	9.6
Food Manufacturing	184.8	9.1
Milk, Milk Products	175.7	9.1
Other Drink	184.5	9.0
Abrasives, Building Materials	195.8	9.0
Electrical Machinery	200.6	8.5
Bacon Curing	181.2	8.4
Fertilisers	209.4	8.3
Fruit, Veg., Products	180.3	8.3
Cocoa, Chocolate	206.1	8.1

Source: 1979 NES.

Only three of the twelve industries with high levels of overtime were close to the manufacturing average level of hourly earnings (none of these were as much as 1% above that average). The others were below, and seven of them were very considerably below with hourly earnings of less than 185p (at least 11 ½ % below the manufacturing average).

Outside manufacturing another sector of high overtime is transport and communications. In the main industries involved with such high overtime, hourly earnings are considerably lower than in manufacturing, but weekly earnings are brought close to or above the manufacturing averages by long hours of work:

Table 1.23 High Overtime Industries: Transport and Communication

	Av. Hourly Earnings excluding overtime pay and hours (p)	Av. Hours of over- time
Sea Transport	193.2	18.2
Road Haulage Contracting	184.6	12.3
Other Road Haulage	187.4	11.7
Railways	178.1	11.0
Road Passenger Transport	181.9	9.7
Postal and Services Telecommunication	183.7	8.4

Source: 1979 NES.

Yet it is important to recognise that there are large numbers of manual men in industries characterised by *low* average levels of overtime working but also by *low* hourly earnings. The main factor at work in these cases is that these are industries or services where female employment exceeds that of male employees. The likely connection here is that the preferences of most women workers are for normal hours without regular use of overtime, as little overtime is worked by the women workers. Thus the work of the men is likely to be a direct adjunct to such working hours, so that recourse to overtime is limited. In manufacturing this pattern is true for clothing (manual men's hourly earnings only 167.9p, average overtime 3.4 hours), footwear (199.1p; 2.3 hours overtime), and hosiery (190.6p; 3.9 hours overtime). In the service trades it is true of the large "miscellaneous services" sector (manual men's hourly earnings 168.2p; 4 hours overtime) and retailing (168p; and 4 hours overtime).

The NBPI Report analysing the extensive and regular use of overtime by employers to meet the normal level of demand thought that:

> "Clearly labour shortages have had a great deal to do with this situation. There can be no doubt that the continuing pressures of generally high demand for labour in the post-war period have been a powerful factor in pushing up overtime levels''. (Op. Cit. Page 20).

But while labour shortages are evidently one reason for overtime working, the experience of the 1970s indicates that they are only a minor part of the rhythm of overtime work. The UK manufacturing industries experienced their most severe post-war recession in 1975-76; yet the average level of overtime for manual men in manufacturing merely moved from 6.3 hours in 1974 to 5.1 hours in 1975, and 5.2 hours in 1976; by 1979 it had returned to 6.2 hours. The shipbuilding industry has typically had high levels of overtime (circa. 8 hours); but in its currently depressed condition it averaged 6.9 hours in the April 1979 NES. For many enterprises, regular overtime is evidently part of the style of operation helping with recruitment and retention.

The 1970 NBPI Report also suggested that for many employers the persistent use of overtime may seem financially more economical than employing a rather larger labour force with little or no overtime. This would certainly be true if low levels of overtime led to increased wastage and higher costs ofrecruitment and training. The evidence suggests that since 1970 the financial calculation has, if anything, tilted further in the direction of overtime working and against additional recruitment. Thus, in 1970 the addition to wages and salaries represented by holiday pay was on average just over 6%; by 1976 it was over 10%. Besides such additional labour costs and associated administrative expenses, unless the employer is

35

able to use additional employment to extend his shift utilisation of plant and capital it may be more economic (per unit of capital) to extend overtime working. (For this reason, as in motor vehicle production, day and night shifts may be preferred to double day shifts).

It would appear also that the porportional increase in pay involved in overtime had fallen in the 1970s. This was a feature particularly of periods of pay policy (such as the "social contract" from 1975 to 1977), since additional pay was not consolidated in a way that raised overtime rates. (At the same time the only element of pay flexibility left the employer was the availability of additional overtime work, so far as timeworkers were concerned). Consequently, although overtime is conventionally thought of as carrying relatively high premia (time and a quarter or time and a third in many agreements for weekday overtime, time and a half for Saturday working, etc.) it can be calculated from the 1979 NES that the average hourly earnings for manual men during overtime working were only 14% of average hourly earnings *excluding* overtime hours and premia. In 1968 the NBPI estimated that overtime pay was 43% above the "basic" hourly rate for manual men (but pointed out this gave an exaggerated impression). Yet in 1979 the appropriate figure was 34% above basic rates and even that represented some recovery from lower levels of effective premium in the years of incomes policy. In other words, during the 1970s the real costs of additional recruitment rose for employers, while the real cost of high levels of overtime (assuming a real workload was provided) fell.

Finally, it is worth noting that non-manual men who worked overtime received even smaller effective premia over their hourly average earnings for non-overtime hours; in 1979 the overtime hours only represented 8% more in hourly earnings terms. Consequently the comment on the relative attractiveness to employers of offering more overtime instead of increasing manning applies with even more force to the relative financial costs involved for non-manual men. Not surprisingly it is also true that the non-manual men who received pay for working overtime were considerably lower paid than the average non-manual full-time man. Those who worked overtime had basic pay of £93 in April 1979, whereas it can be estimated that those who did not work overtime had basic pay of over £108.

'For purposes of illustration' the Department of Employment calculated in its April 1978 article on "Work sharing" that,

> "If half all hours at present worked by manual men in excess of 48 per week were worked instead by additional full-time workers, the unemployment register could be reduced by over 100,000".

But realising such a potential change remains for the future. In the 1970s the trends of costs, and external pressures such as pay policy, were if anything consolidating the persistent use of overtime working.

Footnote   Annual Hours

Any view of working time built up by thinking of overtime as an addition to the "basic" week has to be modified to take account of working time lost. The NES data concentrate on those workers who did work a full week. Other series (such as the six monthly series on occupational pay and hours of manual men in engineering and chemicals) cover all workers who worked in the survey week, and therefore show some element of time lost. Typically, the actual hours worked *less* overtime hours worked indicate a residual working time some 1½ to 2 hours less than the basic week. Examination of the NES samples indicate that each week around 15% of male manual workers and nearly 20% of female manual workers lose some pay due to absence during the week. (Late starting or early finishing was found in the 1968 NES to be a major reason why some pay was lost though it amounted to very few hours work on the part of the workers affected; voluntary absence and uncertified sickness led to loss of pay for nearly 5% of male workers and 8½% of female workers). The pay of non-manual workers is much less affected by stoppages and loss of pay due to absence and in practice we cannot be sure what the average *actual* working hours of non-manual workers were.

In 1975, as an adjunct to an official survey of labour costs, there was a calculation of "average annual hours worked per employee" in manufacturing. The survey was presented in the least useful manner although it distinguished manual and non-manual workers. The non-manual data had no significance since it was based on normal hours and did not adjust for paid absence, while for manuals the information did not distinguish between male and female hours, and included part-time workers. It is possible to make a very approximate calculation, however, for manufacturing. The average annual hours worked by manual employees in 1975 were 1,832. This was some 6% less than the total that would have resulted from all manual workers working without loss of time for the length of the working week recorded in the NES.

Shift Work

The salient features of the occupational balance of shift working have already been given in an earlier section. The main detailed official source linking national statistical sources with empirical studies is again the NBPI Report of 1970 on "Hours of Work, Overtime and Shiftworking".

37

That study showed that in manufacturing (which had been subjected to earlier official surveys on shiftworking) there had been a considerable increase in the proportion of manual workers affected by shiftworking, from around 12 ½ % in 1954 to an estimated 25 % in 1968. (Op. Cit. Page 65). The NBPI's survey of "establishments" required the recording of a shift system if it was worked by one quarter or more of its shiftworkers, so in some cases more than one shift system was recorded. But the following figures indicate the prevalance of particular kinds of shift systems:

Table 1.24

Type of Shift system	% of establishments in which system was used
Continuous 3 shift	36
Permanent night work	34
Double-day	31
Alternating day and night	26
Discontinuous 3 shift	10
Others	5

Source: NBPI Op. Cit. Page 58.

Many commentators assumed that the proportion of manufacturing workers employed on one or other shift system would continue to increase. But in the 1970s, and on the evidence of the NES survey returns on numbers receiving shift premia, this does not appear to have happened. Thus in 1970 the NES identified 27 % of full-time manual men as receiving such premia; in 1979 the figure was 25.5 %. This overall stabilisation of the proportion involved conceals some important changes within sectors, however it does suggest that lower levels of demand in some industries may have played a part. The NBPI in 1970 surveyed firms which had abandoned shiftwork and found that two-fifths of these cited "fall in product demand" as the main reason.

So far as manual women are concerned, 7 % were recorded as receiving shift payments of 1970 and the proportion was unchanged in 1979. These estimates appear low in the light of collective agreements (as in textiles) providing for enhanced rates for double-shift workers; it may be that there are problems of interpretation as to what constitutes a shift premium,* and

* Thus, the cotton spinning and weaving agreement provides that "where double shifts are operated on a five day basis, the normal working week is 37 ½ hours paid at the normal piece or hourly rate. Rates for a 37 ½ hour double shift week are normally 5.6% higher than the rates of a 40 hour single shift week''.
(Department of Employment, Time Rates of Wages, 1978, page 65).

38

that some shift work is not necessarily recorded in answering the question on payment of shift premia. Protective legislation to some extent limits the employment of women workers in the factory trades on shiftwork, but this is subject to a widespread system of securing "exemptions" with the authorisation of the inspectorate. On the latest information just over 200,000 women workers in manufacturing were covered by such exemptions.

So far as manual men in the engineering and allied industries are concerned the NES indicates a fall in shiftworking in the 1975 recession followed by very little move to restore previous levels of shiftworking:

Table 1.25 Manual Men Receiving Shift Premia in the Engineering
            Industries   (% of total)

	1970	1974	1975	1979
Mechanical Engineering	22.2	13.1	13.6	13.7
Electrical Engineering	23.9	18.2	16.9	16.4
Shipbuilding	13.8	8.4	10.6	9.9
Vehicles	34.7	28.5	25.2	29.6

Source: NES.

But by contrast there has been a proportional increase in shiftworking (that has to be set in the context of a major fall in employment) in the textiles sector (rising from 28% in 1970 to 37% in 1978, but falling to 35% in 1979). The food and drink industries have also shown a growth in shiftworking for manual men (rising from 25% receiving premia in 1970 to 33% in 1979).

Of course, the capital intensive continuous process industries continue to show high levels of shift working by manual men:

Table 1.26 Manual Men Receiving Shift Premia, 1979

General Chemicals	41.0%
Iron and Steel (General)	62.1%
Coal and Petrol. Products	40.6%
Man-Made Fibres	61.0%
Carpets	49.6%
Glass	46.2%
Rubber	54.1%

Source: 1979 NES.

In this connection the NBPI made the important observation that it was "difficult to avoid some overtime given a normal week of 40 hours" where continuous four-crew three-shift working operated and 168 hours a week had to be covered. This is another way of saying that the handling of this key shift pattern had not adapted to the nominal fall in the basic week in the 1960s. Since the NBPI Report the problem has been made more acute by the extension of annual holiday provision (a feature of the 1970s discussed in the next section), and this is a matter that features in particular case studies discussed later in this report.

Outside manufacturing the main sectors heavily affected by shift work, apart from coal mining and the production industries, are transport and health services. In these cases it is not capital intensity but the personal and social needs that the services cater for that dictate large scale shift work. Nearly two-thirds of manual men in road passenger transport and in railway employment are in receipt of shift premia. In the health services, and this is virtually unique, all the main categories of employee show comparatively high proportions of shift work:

Table 1.27

Medical and Dental Services	Percentage Receiving Shift Premia 1979
Manual Men	44.1%
Non-Manual Men	22.0%
Manual Women	42.1%
Non-Manual Women	42.4%

Source: 1979 NES.

The issues posed by adapting shift work to shorter basic weekly hours therefore affect very large numbers of workers in these major public services, as well as the familiar areas of industrial shift work. Indeed, it was the health service in particular that raised this question at the end of the 1970s, as the result of an agreement to move from a 40 to a 37½ hour basic week for nursing staff.

Finally, the subject of the premia paid for shift work is a complex one in its own right. Accordingly it is dealt with in a separate *Appendix* to this part of the report. For manual men on shift work in manufacturing shift premia account on average for a 16% addition to average earnings less overtime pay; outside manufacturing the premia only add some 11% to such earnings.

Trends in Annual Holidays With Pay

Most of the recent discussions on working time have concentrated on the impact of reductions in the normal basic week. However working time includes changes in both the working life and the working year. One important aspect of the latter is a workers entitlement to a basic paid annual holiday. Unfortunately the official data on this aspect of working time is unsatisfactory and only gives a partial view of the true situation. Most of the data is restricted to manual workers and amongst them is only collected for the major national agreements of various types. Moreover the one source that covers all categories of worker, the New Earnings Survey (NES), is limited to the two years 1970 and 1974. In these circumstances it is virtually impossible to construct a comprehensive analysis of the pattern of paid annual holiday entitlements.

Despite these reservations about the adequacy of the basic official data, the level of paid annual holiday entitlements together with changes in their incidence are an important aspect of any analysis of the overall pattern of working time. Thus although the data is unsatisfactory, some of the overall trends and patterns revealed may be sufficiently reliable to provide some valid indicators, that can act as proxies for the overall picture. We examine the information contained in the two main official sources; namely, the manual worker data derived from 'Time Rates of Wages and Hours of Work', and the limited NES returns for all categories of worker.

(i) Manual Workers Covered by National Agreements

Table 1.28 shows for the period 1951-1979 the percentage of manual workers who were entitled to basic annual paid holidays within given ranges. Also shown is the percentage of workers covered by agreements which contain clauses specifying additional holidays for length of service* and an estimate of the average basic holiday entitlement for all manual workers. The data is derived from information published in 'Time Rates of Wages and Hours of Work' and as such refers to the terms and conditions of employment determined by national agreements or by statutory orders under the Wages Councils Acts and the Agricultural Wages Acts. Thus it takes no account of company or local agreements. Moreover, the data excludes any entitlement to public or customary holidays.

The main points from Table 1.28 are:

i) By 1955 holiday entitlements of less than two weeks had virtually disappeared. The predominant pattern for the vast majority (96%) of manual workers was two weeks. This pattern persisted until 1960.

ii) During the 1960s, particularly in the latter half, there was a steady upward drift in holiday entitlements towards the establishment of three weeks as the dominant pattern. Thus, whereas in 1960 97% of

* It should be noted that the basic annual holiday data excludes the impact of service related holidays.

41

Table 1.28 Percentages of manual workers with specified holiday entitlements

	1 week %	Between 1 week and 2 weeks %	2 weeks %	Bewteen 2 weeks and 3 weeks %	3 weeks %	Between 3 weeks[1] and 4 weeks %	4 weeks %	% covered by agreements which provide additional length of service holidays %	Average[2] holiday weeks
1951	28	3	66	2	1	—	—	4	1.7
1955	—	1	96	2	1	—	—	9	2.0
1963	—	—	97	1	2	—	—	9	2.0
1965	—	—	75	22	3	—	—	28	2.1
1966	—	—	63	33	4	—	—	27	2.2
1967	—	—	60	34	6	—	—	27	2.2
1968	—	—	56	34	10	—	—	27	2.3
1969	—	—	50	35	14	1	—	30	2.3
1970	—	—	41	7	49	3	—	25	2.6
1971	—	—	28	5	63	4	—	17	2.7
1972	—	—	8	16	39	33	4	12	3.0
1973	—	—	1	2	38	52	7	19	3.3
1974	—	—	1	1	30	40	29	20	3.5
1975	—	—	1	1	17	51	30	26	3.5
1976	—	—	—	1	18	47	34	32	3.6
1977	—	—	—	1	18	47	34	32	3.6
1978	—	—	—	1	17	47	35	36	3.6
1979[3]	—	—	—	1	14	48	37	36	3.6

Source: British Labour Statistics; Historical Abstract, Table 34. British Labour Statistics; Year Book 1976, Table 48. Time Rates of Wages and Hours of Work, Appendix III.

[1] Prior to 1969 three weeks and over was the highest range shown. However since the 1969 date shows that there was only one per cent of workers covered by agreements which specified holidays of over three weeks the discontinuity in the data is only of marginal relevance.

[2] The average has been calculated by reference to the mid-point of the relevant ranges. Thus although the results are given to one decimal point too much weight should not be attached to them. The main purpose of the figures is to illustrate the overall trend.

[3] Prior to 1979 the date refers to the year ending December, from that date it refers to the year ending April.

manual workers had an annual holiday entitlement of two weeks this proportion fell to 41% in 1970. Conversely entitlement to three weeks holiday increased from 2% of manual workers to 49% over the same period.

iii) Throughout the 1970s there was a further upward shift in the level of holiday entitlements. Although the major part of this occurred prior to 1975, after which it was inhibited by the constraints of pay policy, by 1979 entitlement to a holiday of less than three weeks had been virtually eliminated while the percentage of workers covered by the three week category had declined to 14%. In contrast 48% of manual workers were entitled to a holiday of over three and under four weeks and a further 7% were entitled to four weeks and over.

iv) Since 1951 there has been a significant increase in the proportion of workers covered by agreements which provide for additional service related holidays. This proportion rose from 4% in 1951 to 30% in 1969. Subsequently there was a decline to 12% in 1972, however the former peak was rapidly re-established and had been surpassed by 1979.

v) On average over the whole period 1951 to 1979 there has been an increase of approximately two weeks in the average annual holiday entitlement of all manual workers. A significant part of this change was concentrated in the period 1969 to 1975 with very little change occurring since.

It is also interesting to note that the increase in holiday entitlements has occurred independently of reductions in normal basic weekly hours. For the major part of the manual labour force the reduction in normal basic hours took place during the late 1950s and mid 1960s, whereas the increase in holiday entitlement was well established prior to this period and has continued since. Thus, viewed in the context of annual hours, the past three decades are characterised by an almost continuous decline in the length of the basic working year which is derived from both the reduction in the normal basic week and increases in annual basic holiday entitlements. Indeed it can be calculated that the increase in the average holiday entitlements of manual workers since 1951 is equivalent to a 1.5 hour reduction in the normal basic weekly hours.

The data collected by the Department of Employment does not indicate why there was a reduction in the proportion of workers covered by service related holidays between 1969 and 1972. However it can be surmised that there was some 'trade off' between the basic and service related elements of the annual holiday entitlement, the latter being surrendered in exchange for increases in the former. Even if this assumption is true the period over which it occurred was relatively short-lived, moreover it does not explain the subsequent rapid re-establishment of the coverage of service related holidays. This could arise from the reintroduction of such holidays in areas where they had previously existed, their extension to new groups of workers, or some combination of the two. Another problem with the Department of Employment's data is that they give no indication of the extent to which service related holidays affect the average level of holiday entitlements. However there is some limited data on this aspect of holidays in the NES data, and this, together with the information on the total annual holiday entitlement, is examined in the next section.

(ii) The New Earnings Survey Data

The NES is of limited use as a means of assessing trends in holiday entitlements since it is only available for two years, 1970 and 1974. Moreover even with respect to this restricted period problems arise from differences in the question asked in each of these two years and deficiencies in the 1974 sample. The latter was a consequence of reorganisation in Local Authorities and the National Health Service which led to a serious under-representation of workers in these areas. Despite these reservations the NES is practically the only reliable source of information on the holiday entitlements of non-manual workers and as such provides some insights, albeit of a limited nature, into the overall pattern of paid holiday entitlements for all workers.

Unlike the data in the previous section the NES information covers both manual and non-manual workers according to their sex. In addition it includes both the impact of basic annual entitlements and service related holidays*. Thus, both in terms of the type of worker covered and the definition of the annual holiday entitlement, the NES data are not compatible with that used in the previous section. However, for 1970 only, service related holidays are separately recorded, thus for that year it is possible to identify the impact of this element of total holiday entitlements. Before examining this factor it is helpful to look at the overall patterns for 1970 and 1974, in particular the changes that occurred between these two dates.

(a) Change 1970-1974

Table 1.29 shows the proportion of full-time adult male and female manual and non-manual workers whose paid annual holiday entitlement fell within given ranges in April 1970 and April 1974. The 1974 data are given on two bases, firstly as published by the Department of Employment, secondly, adjusted to take account of the known underrecording in that year.

* Excluding public or customary holidays.

44

Table 1.29 Percentage of Workers With Annual Holiday Entitlements by Range: April 1970 and April 1974

(a) Full-time adult manual men

Weeks[1]	1970 %	1974 %	% point change
0–2	14.8	4.3	– 10.5
2–3	64.3	41.2	– 23.0
3–4	17.2	44.5	+ 27.3
4–5	2.8	9.1	+ 6.3
5–6	0.3	0.5	+ 0.2
over 6	0.4	0.2	– 0.2
Average[5]	2.7 Wks.	3.4 Wks.	

(b) Full-time adult non-manual men

Weeks[1]	1970 %	1974[2] %	% point change[3]
0–2	3.8	2.5 (2.4)	– 1.3
2–3	30.2	22.8 (22.3)	– 7.4
3–4	35.1	41.8 (40.9)	+ 6.7
4–5	16.8	19.4 (19.0)	+ 2.6
5–6	4.3	5.9 (5.8)	+ 1.6
over 6	9.6	7.6 (9.6)	– 2.0
Average[5]	4.0 Wks.	4.3 Wks. (4.4 Wks.)	

(c) Full-time adult manual women

Weeks[1]	1970 %	1974 %	% point change
0–2	15.0	7.1	– 7.9
2–3	69.5	42.0	– 27.5
3–4	12.4	47.7	+ 35.3
4–5	2.1	2.2	+ 0.1
5–6	0.3	0.4	+ 0.1
over 6	0.4	0.9	+ 0.5
Average[5]	2.7 Wks.	3.3 Wks.	

(d) Full-time adult non-manual women

Weeks[1]	1970 %	1974[2] %	% point change[3]
0–2	8.6	5.1 (5.0)	– 3.5
2–3	39.9	35.8 (35.4)	– 4.1
3–4	27.3	36.0 (35.6)	+ 8.7
4–5	9.0	10.1 (10.0)	+ 1.1
5–6	3.6	3.1 (3.1)	– 0.5
over 6	11.0	10.0[4] (11.0)	– 1.0
Average[5]	3.9 Wks.	4.0 Wks. (4.1 Wks.)	

[1] 2–3 weeks means over two weeks up to and including three weeks.
[2,3] Figures in brackets refer to date adjusted to take account of the Department of Employment's contention that the reduction in the over six weeks category between 1970 and 1974 is 'spurious'.
[4] Affected by underrecording in Local government and the NHS.
[5] A weighted average based on the data in the 1970 and 1974 NES's.

Unfortunately because of differences in the definition of holiday entitlements between Tables 1.28 and 1.29 it is not possible to make direct comparisons between them. However, the manual worker data in Table 1.29 confirm the trend shown in Table 1.28, namely a significant increase in holiday entitlement between 1970 and 1974. Additional points worth noting from Table 1.29 are:

i) There are marked differences in the pattern of holiday entitlements for manual and non-manual workers. Thus in 1970 just under 80% of manual men had a holiday entitlement of three weeks or less whereas less than 35% of non-manual men were in this position.

ii) A similar pattern is evident in 1974, albeit at a higher absolute level. Thus whereas the proportion of manual men with holiday entitlements of three weeks or less had fallen to under 45% the figure for non-manual men had fallen to under 25%.

iii) Manual workers' holidays tend to be concentrated within a considerably narrower range than those for non-manual workers. Thus, in 1974, whereas over 15% of non-manual men had holidays of over five weeks this proportion fell to less than 1% in the case of manual men.

iv) There is some evidence to show that the gap between manual and non-manual workers annual holiday entitlements narrowed over the period April 1970 to April 1974. On average the holiday entitlement for manual men increased by 0.7 weeks compared to an average increase of 0.4 weeks for non-manual men.

On the basis of the available data it is not possible to say whether the trends shown in Table 1.29 are representative of those prior to 1970 or after 1974. For manual workers the data in Table 1.28 will provide a reasonably reliable indicator of the main trends. However, given the indication of a differential movement between the experience of manual and non-manual workers, this is not necessarily the case for non-manual workers. The most that can be said is that it is probable that both manual and non-manual workers were equally subject to the restraints imposed by incomes policy. Thus the trends shown in Table 1.29 will probably have come to a halt in 1975 for both the main types of worker. Thus, as an approximate 'rule of thumb' it is possible to argue that the average non-manual man's holiday exceeds that of his manual counterpart by one week, with slightly less (0.7 weeks) difference for the female comparison.

(b) **Service Related Holidays**

The NES data included the impact of service related holidays, but only for 1970. It is worth briefly summarising the information gathered:

i) Over 70% of non-manual men and nearly 80% of manual men were not in receipt of service related holidays. Nearly 82% of non-manual women and over 85% of manual women workers also lacked any such entitlement.

ii) For most workers who were in receipt of service related holidays four or five additional days was the most frequent pattern.

The overall significance of service related holidays is therefore small (an average of approximately one additional day a year). Table 1.28 showed a decline in the proportion of manual workers in receipt of service related holidays over the period 1969 to 1972, but this was subsequently followed by a rapid restoration of the previous position. (It has already been suggested that this probably represented some temporary 'trading off' against a general extension of holiday entitlement).

"Public Holidays"

Up to the 1970s most workers were entitled in addition to their ordinary holidays to six paid public holidays a year. In the 1970s two additional days were granted; New Year's Day (in Scotland, Christmas Day) and a May holiday.

Assessment

For manual workers the evidence is that an important further advance in annual holidays developed in the 1970s. In addition all workers secured two further public holidays. There may have been some narrowing of the difference in holiday entitlement typical of non-manual as compared to manual workers, but a differentiation (of approximately a week) remains. More recently, private management salary surveys indicate a rising proportion of business executives in 1979 enjoying holidays in excess of 25 days (five weeks). *This may be expected to strengthen pressure for a further lengthening of non-manual holiday entitlements in the next stage.* Meanwhile the general picture is one of a relatively slow but persistent upward shift in annual paid holidays. However it has taken 30 years for this process to have (for manual workers) an effect equivalent to a reduction of approximately two hours in the basic week.

THE STRUCTURE OF SHIFT AND 'ABNORMAL' HOURS PREMIA
BY MAJOR COLLECTIVE AGREEMENTS

Introduction

This note examines some broad features of the structure of premium payments for 'abnormal' hours and shift working. It does not examine the average money payment nor the number of workers in receipt of such payments, rather it analyses the prevalence of the various types of payments, the main methods of calculation, and variations in their level according to the day in the week or time of day.

The analysis is based on the information contained in the Department of Employment's publication "Time Rates of Wages and Hours of Work; April 1978". This publication covers over two hundred major national agreements the majority of which apply to manual workers. Approximately 70% of these agreements mentioned provisions for various types of payment for 'abnormal' hours, that is shift premia, weekend payments, unsocial hours payments and night work allowances. One drawback associated with the use of the "Time Rates and Hours of Work" data is that it is a summary of the main points in each agreement and as such either excludes or only partially covers important details. Despite this reservation the data is sufficient to obtain an overall picture of the structure of 'abnormal' hours payments in the United Kingdom.

Types of Payment

The relative importance of the various types of shift and 'abnormal' hours payments according to the number of agreements in which they are mentioned is shown in Table 1.30.

Table 1.30 Types of 'abnormal' hours payment by broad headings[1]
(percentages of those mentioning such payments)

	%
Nights	55.3
Unsocial Hours	2.9
Shift Systems	46.5
Weekends[2]	20.6

[1] Some agreements list payments under more than one heading.
[2] Includes both shift premia at weekends where they differ from Monday to Friday premia and payments to other workers not in receipt of shift premia on week days.

The most frequently mentioned type of payment is that for night work, followed by shift premia and weekend premia. The remaining category, unsocial hours, is only mentioned in a small proportion of cases and on closer examination is virtually indistinguishable from what in other agreements is called night allowance.

Indeed on closer examination many of the distinctions between the various main headings are more a matter of wording than fact. Various payments listed as night work or night allowances can operate as the basis of payment for shift systems and are listed as such in other agreements. For example, for the agreement for Ready Mixed Concrete Industry—Great Britain, eligibility for *night work premia* is defined as:

"Workers whose hours of duty entail employment between 7.00 p.m. and 6.00 a.m. are paid at the rate of time-and-one-third for all time worked between these hours".

Whereas in the Knitting Industries—Midlands agreement, eligibility for *shift premia* is described as:

"The agreement makes provision for single, double and three-shift working. For hours worked between 8.00 p.m. and 6.00 a.m. a premium of 20p per hour is paid".

In practice it is difficult to see any difference between these two types of payment except the heading under which they are listed. A stricture that applies to a significant number of the other agreements used in this analysis.

Despite what has been said in the previous paragraph there is one type of payment that can be clearly separated out; namely payments to regular night shift workers, that is workers who in most cases are on permanent nights and not shift workers whose rota includes nights. Payments for regular night workers account for approximately 72% of those classified as nights in Table 1.30 or 40% of the total mentioned.

Method of Calculation

In broad terms there are two main methods of calculating shift and 'abnormal' hours premia, a fixed money supplement or a percentage payment. In either case these can be based upon pay per hour, shift, week or year. On the basis of the headings used in Table 1.30 the relative importance within each heading of the two main methods of calculation is shown in Table 1.31.

Table 1.31 Method of Calculating Premia[1] (percentages within each type)

	Fixed Money %	Percentage payment %	Total %
Nights	28.3	71.7	100.0
Unsocial Hours	20.0	80.0	100.0
Shift Systems	61.3	38.7	100.0
Weekends[2]	8.6	91.4	100.0
All types[3]	36.7	63.3	100.0

[1] and [2] see Table 1.30
[3] Excluding six agreements where both methods of calculation were used.

Clearly in most cases the percentage method of payment is more popular than the fixed method, although for shift systems the reverse is the case. As in Table 1.30 the classification nights includes regular or permanent night workers; since payment on a percentage basis is more prevalent for these workers than other workers, it affects both the percentage distribution for nights and all types. If permanent night shift workers are excluded the proportion of all types on fixed money premia increases to approximately 42% while that for percentage payments falls to 58%.

Premia By Day in the Week

In a number of cases the method of calculating the premium payment for 'abnormal' hours changes at weekends and/or the level of payment is enhanced. Effectively this involves weighting the relative unsocialness of days in the week. Approximately 30% of the agreements mentioning shift premia also list different arrangements for weekend work. In addition a number of agreements, particularly in retail distribution, where normal hours are spread over a six or seven day week, specify an enhanced rate for Saturday and Sunday working. In total agreements where premia are differentiated by the day of the week account for approximately 21% of those where 'abnormal' hours payment are specified. Table 1.32 is based upon those agreements where weekend premia are mentioned and shows the percentage in which the basis of calculation is the same as on Monday to Friday, differs from that on Monday to Friday, and where only weekend premia are specified.

Table 1.32 Comparison of the Method of Calculating Weekend Premia (as percentage of agreements where weekend premia were specified)

	%
Same basis as Monday to Friday	34.3
Different basis from Monday to Friday	42.9
Weekend Premia only	22.8

Clearly in the majority of cases where there are weekend premia in addition to Monday to Friday premia for 'abnormal' hours there is a change in the method of calculating the premia at weekends. (If those agreements which only mention weekend premia are excluded the percentages are, same basis 44.4% different basis 56.6%). Moreover, in all cases this represents a change from a fixed money premia to a proportional payment. Put another way, whereas on Monday to Friday just over half the agreements where both a weekend and weekday premia for 'abnormal' hours are mentioned use a flat-rate money system, this proportion falls to one-ninth at weekends.

Premia by Time of Day

Premia payments for 'abnormal' hours by time of day can be sub-divided into two broad headings. Firstly those where a band of hours attracts a premium payment for every hour worked within it. In some cases this simply entails one rate for all the relevant hours, in others it is more complex and groups of hours with different premium rates are specified. Secondly those where different premia are associated with different shifts. Since all the shift systems used in this analysis do not mention more than three shifts a day this manifests itself as either all shifts paid at different rates of premia or two of the daily shifts paid at the same rate and the third at a different rate. Approximately 22% of the agreements used in this analysis differentiate premia by the time of day, and the proportions of these where payment is according to a band of hours or by shift worked are shown in Table 1.33.

Table 1.33 Premia by Time of Day according to Type (as percentages of agreements where mentioned)

	%
Premia related to:	
Band of hours[1]	44.7
Shift worked	55.3
Two the same, one different	26.3
All different[2]	29.0

[1] Includes unsociable hours, shift and night allowances (where appropriate)
[2] Includes both 2 shift and 3 shift systems.

From Table 1.33 it can be seen that there is a preference for payments varying according to the shift worked. Within the latter there is a small bias in favour of premia which vary from shift to shift. In all cases where different shifts attract different rates of payment the largest premia are payable on the night shift. Where three levels of payment are operative the lowest payment goes to the morning shift (in a few instances this shift is not given a premia) and the next highest to the afternoon shift, and that for night shift is the largest.

In a few agreements the differentiation by time of day also applies to weekend shifts. In general work on a Sunday is paid at a higher rate, however, there are some variations. For example, work on Saturday nights being paid at a higher rate than work on a Sunday night or weekend premiums not becoming operative until the second shift on Saturday. It is also worth noticing that a quarter of those agreements where premia are differentiated by time of day also differentiate according to the day of the week.

Systems in which premia are related to the shift worked often use a common premium payments structure. Thus in an agreement where double day, alternating day and night and continuous three shift working are specified, the double day shift would attract the appropriate premia for the morning and afternoon shifts, alternate day and nights would get the payment for night work while in three shift working all the premia would be payable.

Payment for 'abnormal' hours by time of day or time of the shift only directly applies to around half the agreements where shift payments are mentioned, the remainder usually link any premia to the type of shift. In practice this may give a similar result to time of day based systems since those shift systems which cover the highest proportion of 'abnormal' hours attract the largest payment. Thus in general the level of premium rises as one moves from double day shifts through alternate day and nights to three shift systems. Also there is some evidence that additional payments are made according to the speed of rotation between shifts.* That is in those cases information is given for some agreements and not others, a factor which undermines further analysis. However, it is worth drawing attention to four further points although the basic data is incomplete.

Other Factors

As stated previously the "Time Rates and Hours of Work" data can exclude important details which would help to clarify further features of the shift work systems operative in the United Kingdom. Thus in some cases information is given for some agreements and not others a factor which undermines further analysis. However, it is worth drawing attention to four further points although the basic data is incomplete.

a) **Hours.** In most cases hours for shift workers are not separately identified, however where they are they indicate that time spent at work to complete the normal basic week is less than that for their day

---

* The main exception to this is the regular or permament night shift.

work counterparts.* Whereas a day worker's hours are usually defined as 40 exclusive of meal breaks (effectively in a five day week this entails a weekly attendance of 45 hours) shift workers hours are 40 including meal breaks or less frequently 40 plus a paid meal break and 37½ excluding meal breaks.**

b) **Consolidation for overtime.** In the majority of cases the various 'abnormal' hours payments are not consolidated for the calculation of overtime payments. There are a few exceptions to this, for example, the agreement for Heating Ventilating and Domestic Engineering states that for night workers:

"The basic rate for men who work at least five consecutive nights on night shifts is one-and-a-quarter times the normal pay, any overtime being calculated on this enhanced rate''.

c) **Relationships of shift premia to basic rates.** In the majority of cases shift premia calculated on a proportional basis use an individual's basic rate as the starting point. However, with the fixed money method of calculation there is usually only one premium rate for all grades. There are a couple of agreements which specify different fixed money premia according to grade, but even here it is usually one rate for operatives and another for craftsmen.

d) **Variations in the width of the 'abnormal' hours band.** In general the majority of agreements specify a period within the range 7.00-8.00 p.m. to 6.00 a.m. However there is no standard pattern and the starting point ranges from 3.00 p.m. to 10.00 p.m. while the finishing time ranges from 5.30 a.m. to 8.00 a.m.

Concluding Comments

There are a wide variety of ways of compensating for 'abnormal' hours working. The most common methods are a flat-rate money or proportional payment which is based on hours worked or less frequently on each working week. However a significant minority of agreements specify more complex arrangements which either weight the day in the week and/or the

---

* A check on more detailed data shows that in many cases where hours for shift workers are not separately identified their working week includes a paid meal break of between 20 and 30 minutes. For example, Gas Supply—Great Britain.

** This arrangement appears to be a direct consequence of the convenient fact that a working day divides into three eight hour shifts and not any conscious move to reduce working hours.

hours in a day. The overall impression is that the determination of premia for 'abnormal' hours is influenced by factors which are relevant to a particular group of workers and the industry in which they are employed and that these can be dealt with in a variety of ways. To take one example, the choice between a fixed or proportional method for calculating shift premia. It can be argued that 'abnormal' hours are just as unsocial for all workers and that any premium should be the same for everybody, on the other hand this will affect pay differentials and may be opposed by craftsmen. Clearly this is a matter that can be, and has been, resolved in different ways according to the circumstances affecting each agreement.

Although this paper has concentrated on an analysis of the data in "Time Rates of Wages and Hours of Work", the Unit does have some data on company agreements which provide useful additional insights into the structure of 'abnormal' hours payments in the United Kingdom. Certainly these company agreements are not a comprehensive sample, however, they do indicate that there is a significant degree of flexibility associated with decisions about the appropriate structure of 'abnormal' hours payments and draw attention to a number of points which are not apparent from the Department of Employment data. Thus it is helpful to highlight some of the main points that can be extracted from them, namely that:

a)   Virtually all specify a paid meal break for shift workers of between 20 and 30 minutes. Often there is no specified time for it to be taken and a form of words, such as "all shift employees have a 30 minute paid meal break which is taken as operational requirements allow", is used.

b)   A greater proportion consolidate shift premia for the purposes of calculating overtime premia than is apparent from the Time Rates data.

c)   In a number of cases where the method of calculating 'abnormal' hours changes from a weekday flat-rate money payment to a proportional weekend payment, the latter is calculated on the basic hourly rate plus the weekday shift premia.

d)   Whereas the Time Rates data indicates very few agreements where flat-rate money payments vary according to grade this is more frequent in company agreements.

e)   In the public sector there are often separate shift work allowances for white collar workers.

f)   In shift systems which entail working an average week throughout the shift cycle longer than the normal basic week, two main methods of compensation are used. Either payment for the additional hours at overtime rates or the granting of additional time-off (lieu days). An example of the latter is a four week shift cycle containing three weeks of 40 hours and one of 48 hours where 13 lieu days a year are available to each worker.

g) Company agreements often specify complex structures of 'abnormal' hours compensation. Combining banded hours payments and differential shift payments, premia weighted according to type of shift and banded hours payments, extending the weekend premia to include the Friday night shift, and specifying half a dozen or more premia for shift systems according to the number of shifts worked and the speed of rotation.

h) In some cases the workers have been influential in deciding the length of the daily shift and the pattern of hours worked. In one case groups of workers are required to provide cover for a given period of time, the exact arrangements over how this is done being entirely the responsibility of the workers concerned.

Clearly the structure of 'abnormal' hours payments is extremely flexible and as such provides ample scope for bargaining and adaption to the circumstances of each case.

PART 2　GENERAL ECONOMIC AND WORKING TIME TRENDS AT INDUSTRY AND CASE STUDY LEVEL

Chapter 4　Working Time Patterns in Six Selected Industries

Introduction

This part of the report brings together and comments on the analytical work carried out at *industry* level and the more detailed findings derived from the industrial case studies.

In order to clarify this data we have grouped the Distribution, National Health Service and Road Passenger Transport industry studies together with the appropriate case studies in the first half of this part. In sum this provides an indication of working time patterns and possibilities in typical *service* sector industries. In the second half of this part we have grouped Electrical Engineering, Chemicals and Vehicles, again with the requisite case studies, to provide a similar picture with respect to typically *manufacturing* sector industries.

Located at the end of this part is a section drawing out the lessons for collective bargainers.

Methodology: Industries Studies

The industrial sectors chosen: Chemicals, Electrical, Retailing, Motors, Bus Transport and the National Health Service can be seen to reflect a broad cross section of the aggregate labour/capital mix which is to be found in the UK economy. Moreover, the variety of employment forms covered do provide reasonable comparisons as between high and low technology industries, male dominated and female dominated workforces, public and private sector ownership, and the secondary and tertiary sectors of the economy.

In addition, all of the industries chosen display a variety of shiftwork systems and embrace an equally diverse range of collective bargaining structures.

The industry studies necessarily rest on published data, supplemented in some cases by data from major organisations and authoritative studies and reports on aspects of industrial organisation. The time span over which the sector is studied is partly a function of availability of data (e.g. the detailed New Earnings Survey material only since 1968).

Inevitably some sectors are better served with regard to official data coverage (it should be noted that where extensive data has been gathered, e.g. in the NHS and Road Transport a fuller exposition of trends can be found in unpublished papers) however insofar as it has proved possible we attempted to cover the following broad headings in our analysis:

— The key features of industrial organisation e.g. size of firm, market concentration, general economic performance;

— the collective bargaining structure which characterised the industry;

— patterns of working time, e.g. shift and part-time labour utilisation manual and non-manual distinctions.

One consequence of the wide spread of industries chosen for study is the lack of commonality insofar as data sources are concerned. Only the NES provides a common data source. Accordingly it is impossible to present the data in the industry studies in a uniform manner with regard to either coverage or timescale. Insofar as it has proved possible we have attempted to follow broadly the same ordering of data in the final version of the industry studies. Some allowance must, however, be made for inevitable deviations.

The industry studies are intended to offer a general introduction to the more specific detail of the company and plant level case studies. They also help to establish how far case studies correspond to the general features of the industry. Ideally, there should be an inter-action between the identification and analysis of broad industrial trends with the material generated at case study level.

Case Study Methods

In order to provide a sharper focus on, and cross checking of the constraints and potentialities identified in our macro-level analysis, the research team carried out a number of case studies pitched at plant level. As far as possible, at least two case studies per sector were attempted. Table 2.1 shows the key characteristics of the case studies and their sectoral location.

Table 2.1 Case Studies by Sector and Industry

Service Sector		
Retail Distribution		
Case Study 1	Midlands	Large co-operative retail organisation, food and non-food operations
Case Study 2	North West England	Independent multiple operating chain of department stores

Continued on page 58

Table 2.1—*continued*

Health Services

Case Study 3	South Wales	Medium sized hospital—all hospital specialities except obstetrics, gynaecology and paediatrics

Public Services: Bus Passenger Transport

Case Study 4		Post Office Engineering Agreement on reduced working time.

Manufacturing Sector

Electrical Engineering

Case Study 5	South East England	Medium sized company, part of UK MNC*. High technology electronics, mostly batch production
Case Study 6	Scotland	Small company, wholly owned by US MNC* low technology electronics mixed production
Case Study 7	Midlands	Large plant, part of large UK MNC*. Low technology electrical engineering

Chemicals

Case Study 8	South West England	Single site, medium size company jointly owned by US MNC. Heavy chemical production continuous process
Case Study 9	Midlands	Pharmaceutical company large sized, part of large UK MNC batch production
Case Study 10	Midlands	Large complex, wholly owned by US MNC heavy chemical production continuous process.

Motor Vehicles: Manufacturing

Case Study 11		US owned MNC
Plant A	South East England	Large complex—volume production sub-assembly and final assembly
Plant B	South Wales	Small complex—volume production sub-assembly
Case Study 12		UK owned MNC
Plant A	Midlands	Large complex—volume production sub-assembly and body production
Plant B	Midlands	Large complex—volume production final assembly and power train operations.

* Multi-national company.

The case studies carried out were chosen to facilitate comparisons of working time organisation in both publicly and privately owned enterprises. The selection was made to ensure a wide variety of enterprises by size and method of production and similarly to confront differing types of working time organisation. In every case, the enterprise studied was trade union organised, and it should be noted that a variety of individual unions, and consequently their particular approach to issues of work time organisation, were covered by the research.

In sum the case studies set out:

a)   To try to understand the rationale for present work time patterns, including shift and overtime patterns, and breaktime patterns, in terms of the nature of the production process, the tasks involved, the market for the product, the nature of the labour input demanded and/or supplied. Also to understand the technical, economic, social and cultural reasons for different patterns within the establishment and to understand the interrelationships of these different patterns.

b)   To establish the premia paid for different patterns.

c)   To understand and evaluate perceived problems, or disadvantages (if any), associated with present patterns and to quantify these where possible.

and regarding *Changes* in Patterns and Durations of Working Time

d)   To try to understand management and employee preferences with respect to forms of reduction in working time—particularly with respect to a shorter working week and a shorter working year.

e)   To examine the organisational consequences of proposed forms of shorter working time—including the possible rearrangement of patterns of working time—and the output and employment effects of these.

f)   To look at the effects on costs, particularly labour costs, of changes.

g)   To look at the value of any benefits (elimination of disadvantages) resulting from changes.

h)   To identify potential 'least cost' solutions.

Data was gathered by means of semi-structured interviews with key representatives of management and trade unions at site level. Although a common 'core' of questions were utilised for both sets of interviews, differences in terms of access to basic information and experience at the particular site varied considerably between individuals. Hence, comparisons of either management or trade union responses across case studies are rendered problematic.

The main difficulties encountered were familiar ones to researchers at this end of the industrial spectrum, namely problems of access to key individuals and critical data, and the constraints imposed upon a consistent approach to data collection by both the differing degrees of access granted and the very diversity of the type and style of enterprises chosen. In only one instance did we encounter any difficulty at all in gaining the confidence of the local trade union representatives. As far as members of management were concerned, however, their willingness to disclose information on potential working time reduction was inversely correlated with their perception of the issue as a current or likely future bargaining demand. It tended to be much better later in the life of the project when a significant National Agreement on hours had been made. The one exception to this appears to be in the health service where managers are to some extent faced with a 'fait accompli' on reduced working time for nurses (the 37½ hour week being agreed should be implemented on or before April 1981).

A further difficulty which has to be weighed carefully by both the academic researcher and potential bargainers stems from the economic, and to a lesser extent the political, environment within which case study participants formed their assessments and gave their answers to our questions on the scope for reducing working time. It was clear that at the time that our fieldwork was carried out all the enterprises examined were feeling the general effects of the recession which tended to produce negative responses from both management and trade unionists as to the short term scope and desirability of reducing working time. It should also be noted that there was considerably less *political* interest, particularly on the part of the trade unions, in the subject, rather a much greater practical interest—e.g. in its implications for the organisation of work. The methodological problem which this gives rise to lies in the analytical need to distinguish, after the main bulk of the case study work has been completed, between those responses which are genuinely negative on the *scope* for reduced working time and those that are heavily (and possibly only in the short term) influenced by immediate economic or political considerations (political in the small 'p' sense as related to the balance of power in local collective bargaining) which produce a pragmatic negativity on the *desirablility* of embarking upon a bargained programme of reduced working time. Accordingly in the following reports of the case studies some attempt is made to allow for the economic and political context which informed the particular responses under scrutiny.

Case Study Objectives

Initially, we defined our case studies as having two objectives: firstly, to increase our knowledge of the key elements controlling the present systems of work time management at selected enterprises and secondly, by checking these key control elements against potential shorter working time options, to begin to build a more comprehensive analysis of either the *limiting* or *sponsoring* factors which are likely to characterise the change process in prospect.

The case studies, then, play an essential role. Given that we cannot understand the effects of change except a "change in relation to what exists now", it is important to understand the nature of this present context, so that our first objective is:

> To try to understand the rationale for present work time patterns, including shift and overtime patterns, and break time patterns (both formal and informal).

> *In terms* of the nature of the production process, the tasks involved, the management system, the market for the product, the labour input demanded and/or supplied and as subject to other economic, technical, social and cultural variables.

Our intention is to try to explain not only differences within an establishment—e.g. across different sections, different skills and functions, different socio-technical systems, but also differences between establishments on the basis of the above mentioned variables.

Through our case studies we have sought to examine two forms of reactions—those which are (technically, and organisationally) *possible* and those which are *likely*. We must necessarily assume a "cost of minimising" management strategy such that in those instances where reductions in "negotiated hours" or work entail a reduction in "actual hours" of work (not necessarily the case since a successful cost minimising strategy might involve buying off the reduction in "negotiated hours" by an extension of overtime) management will be seeking to offset reductions in labour supply by various attempts to increase labour productivity, and by making more efficient use of available resources.

Alongside any cost minimising strategies deployed by management we have also to consider the range of employment effect strategies which can be expected to populate the trade union response. It cannot, for example, be assumed that at plant level groups of trade unionists will necessarily view reductions in working time as a direct lever to additional employment opportunities at their place of work. Experiences dating from the mid-1960s to the early 1970s for example suggests that in cases of significant "step-like" reductions of working time these were tied to significant changes in the deployment of and intensity of the existing labour effort—i.e. were part of wide ranging "productivity deals".*

It is precisely because of the existence of these strategies and the perceived effects of previous reductions in working time, that we consider suggestions of a simple one to one relationship between a reduction in working time and the employment effect to be over-simplified and not supportable.

What the case studies enable us to do is to evaluate in some detail the potential for an individual enterprise to "absorb" possible reductions in working time without any significant increase in employment. Since this ability (or otherwise) to absorb will depend, in the main, on the extent to which any reduction in basic hours can be offset, either by increasing overtime or labour productivity, or by accepting a reduction in output (and that any of these offsets will have profound bargaining implications at plant level), it follows that a thorough grasp of the factors limiting absorption at plant level is an essential pre-condition for successful efficiency bargaining either to maintain or increase employment alongside an objective of reducing actual hours worked.

Whilst the case studies can do more no than predict possible and probable changes within the limited circumstances examined, they are intended, and this can be seen as their third objective, to form a link between the more abstract analysis of working time depicted in the industry studies and the hard reality of the individual bargainer's domain—i.e. the enterprise, where abstract notions have to be forced into acceptable bargaining priorities and strategies. To facilitate this "identification" process in what follows we position the appropriate case studies directly after each industry study.

* See, for example, "Shift Working in the Motor Industry", NEDO 1974.

INDUSTRY STUDY

The Structure of the Retail Industry

The retail trades comprise Minimum List Headings 820 and 821; 'Retail Distribution of Food and Drink' and 'other Retail Distribution' respectively. This study suggests that the division between food and other retailing is reflected in the patterns of both sales, outlets, employment and working time and is fundamental in understanding the industry. However, these headings are also broken down into a number of sub-sectors: food and drink into (1) grocery and provisions, and (2) other food; other retail distribution into (1) confectionery, tobacco and newspapers (2) clothing and footwear (3) household goods (4) other non-food goods, and (5) general stores. These sub-sectors are considered below with reference to consumers' expenditure and retail sales, but first it is necessary to examine the difficulties presented by the standard definitions.

The problems are best illustrated by comparing the scope of the Business Statistics Office (BSO) and Distributive Industry Training Board (DITB). First, there is no clear distinction between the retail and wholesale trades. Some DITB retail categories such as paper, solid fuel, building materials and motor accessories are classified as wholesale by the BSO, while the DITB has itself recorded a significant number of distributors changing their status from retail to wholesale or vice versa. The former tend to be firms with an average size of more than 250 employees dealing in engineering products, hardware or clothing and textiles; the latter firms employ an average of 150 workers and are now retailing products such as solid fuels, tobacco and newspapers or radio and television apparatus.

Secondly, the DITB excludes the traditional specialist retailers—butchers, bakers, fishmongers and greengrocers in 820.2, the hire and repair businesses (except TV and radio) in 821.3, and the florists and nurserymen classified under 821.4. These are predominantly small independent concerns, indeed statutory returns to the DITB for statistical and levy purposes specifically exclude employers with less than ten staff or an annual payroll of less than £15,000.

Third, and closely related, there are discrepancies regarding the definitions which should be applied within the industry. The clearest case is that of multiples, whom the BSO define to have at least ten branches while the Board impose no limit. More seriously, DITB 'employers' (due to group registrations) often comprise more than one of the BSO's organisations, making comparisons extremely tortuous.*

* DITB Statistical Report, 1977/8, pp.1-3 and Appendix 1.

The varying definitions employed in the available data inevitably raise the question of the proper scope for study of working time in retail distribution. Essentially, the statistical base includes the whole industry; however discussion of organisational, employment and working time issues is generally confined to the main areas comprehended by the DITB—the larger (multiple) retailers in the chief consumer sectors. Coincidentally, these form the realistic constituency of potential trade union membership, for (discounting newspaper boys and Saturday only sales staff) experience proves that persons employed in the small independently owned shops, market stalls etc., are not a fruitful field for trade union recruitment.* The larger employers then, are also more likely to come under one of the industry's major collective agreements, or alternatively to observe the awards of the several wages councils for the retail distributive trades. These are themselves organised upon the basis of the industry's sub-sector, notably food and groceries and the sub-divisions of the non-food sector.

Consumer Spending and Retail Sales

In general terms, the most important influence upon a distributor's economic performance—and by implication upon industrial organisation and employment—is the level of consumers' expenditure and retail sales. This in turn is dependent upon a number of factors, chief among them trends in demographic and social structure, real disposable income and the personal savings ratio.

The salient feature of British demographic trends in recent years has been the overall stability in population levels, within which can be observed a growing population of elderly retired persons offset (until very recently) by a declining birth rate. Although this could have meant a contracting market, it has been more than compensated for by the emergence of adolescents as a discrete and increasingly valuable market, particularly in areas such as clothing and consumer durables. There has also been a growth in the working population, principally the result of increased female participation rates. This has permeated through to new shopping patterns, characterised by dependence upon occasional (often weekly) bulk purchasing for the family, topped up by lunch-hour and evening visits to local shops. Within the industry these trends manifested themselves in the rapid growth of large sales units, extended opening hours and new employment and working patterns.

* USDAW Report of Investigation into Membership Recruitment and Losses (1965).

But if demographic and social structure determine the form of retail distribution, its day-to-day content is the product of more tangible economic forces. Table 2.2 shows that the steady rise in real personal disposable income (PDI) throughout the 1960s came to an abrupt halt in 1974-75, after which it declined 1.5% to a low of £73.6 billion in 1977 only to rise again to a new peak in 1979, some 9% above 1974 levels.

Britain is unusual in that the personal savings ratio has risen broadly in line with inflation, doubling from between 7½ and 9 per cent in the 1960s to the present level of over 15%. However, it is noticeable that the largest rises have come during the cyclical peaks around 1973-74 and 1978-79, which means that the retail trades have not fully benefited from the rises in PDI associated with these periods. Thus real consumers' expenditure fell sharply in 1974 following an era of regular growth, since when it has paralleled the cyclical trends in personal income and savings. However, the latter's rise confined the 1979 peak in consumers' expenditure to only 6% above the 1973 figure and barely 10% above the 1977 low of £63.3 billion.

The 1970s were therefore turbulent years for the retail trades; the accustomed growth in consumer spending was suddenly reversed in 1974 and subsequently the industry as a whole has experienced fluctuating and often weak demand. This has bred a new atmosphere of insecurity and unpredictability while stimulating far-reaching changes in industrial organisation. Yet these tendencies have received different manifestations among the industry's sub-sectors due in large measure to varying movements in the components of consumer's expenditure.

Looking at the main retail elements it is apparent that since the early 1970s demographic trends have ensured a generally static demand for food and over the decade as a whole food purchases have fallen from 20% to 18% of total consumer spending. There is a very different picture however, in the semi- and non-food sectors. Expenditure on alcohol and tobacco has moved exactly in line with PDI, but the chief non-food items have reflected trends in real consumers' expenditure. Again the influence of population levels and social trends are apparent as spending on clothing and footwear has remained a steady 8% of total expenditure, while purchases of durable household goods have risen particularly fast overall, although subject to violent fluctuations in demand.

Two main trends can thus be isolated in consumer spending during the 1970s: a generally stagnant food and grocery market, contrasted with a volatile but in total growing demand for non-food goods, subject in different degrees to cyclical economic trends and changing expenditure

Table 2.2 Personal Disposable Income, Consumers' Expenditure and Retail Prices 1975 = 100; 1975 prices

Year	Real personal disposable income £m	Index	Personal saving ratio[1] %	Real Consumers' expenditure £m	Index
1969					
1970	63,352	84.8	9.0	57,676	90.5
1971	64,585	86.4	7.8	59,557	93.5
1972	69,597	93.1	9.5	62,999	98.9
1973	74,069	99.1	11.0	65,911	103.5
1974	75,051	100.4	14.2	64,418	101.1
1975	74,707	100.0	14.7	63,704	100.0
1976	74,773	100.1	14.6	63,852	100.2
1977	73,560	98.5	13.9	63,313	99.4
1978	78,682	105.3	15.2	66,728	104.7
1979[2]	61,427	109.6	15.5	51,926	109.1

Components of Consumers' Expenditure

Year	Food Index	%	Alcohol and tobacco Index	%	Clothing including footwear Index	%	Durable household goods Index	%	of which: Index of retail prices	Total food Index	Total non-food
1969									51.0	45.3	53.1
1970									54.2	48.5	56.3
1971	100.4	20.3	85.7	10.9	91.1	7.9	76.0	4.1	59.3	53.9	61.4
1972	99.6	19.1	91.5	11.0	96.0	7.9	93.4	4.7	63.6	58.6	63.3
1973	101.1	18.5	101.2	11.7	100.2	7.9	106.2	5.2	69.4	67.5	70.1
1974	100.2	18.8	102.3	12.1	98.8	7.9	101.2	5.0	80.5	79.6	80.8
1975	100.0	19.0	100.0	11.9	100.0	8.1	100.0	5.0	100.0	100.0	100.0
1976	101.0	19.1	100.8	12.0	100.5	8.1	105.7	5.3	116.5	120.0	115.6
1977	99.8	19.0	98.1	11.8	98.6	8.1	98.5	5.0	135.0	142.8	132.8
1978	102.0	18.5	106.3	12.9	105.6	8.2	107.3	5.1	146.2	152.9	144.3
1979[2]	104.0	18.1	110.3	12.1	109.5	8.1	115.5	5.3	165.8	171.3	164.3

Source: Economic Trends February, 1980.
Notes: [1] Personal savings as a percentage of personal disposable income.
  [2] For all columns except the RPI, the 1979 figures are for the first three quarters; the index is based on a comparison with 1978 figures for the same period.

patterns. Comparative rates of inflation may have encouraged these developments; note the price index for food rising appreciably faster than that for non-food items, especially since Britain's accession to the EEC.

The effect upon the industry of differential movements in consumers' expenditure can be readily traced in Table 2.3 (i), the volume of retail sales 1971-77. Most noticeable is the stagnation and later decline in sales from food shops which stood at the same level in 1975 as 1971. All non-food shops experienced a drop in sales for the first time in 1974, thereafter vacillating and falling to 1977. However, developments in industrial organisation are already evident in the increased market share of mail order houses. These shifts can be examined in greater detail in Table 2.3 (ii) which re-allocates and re-bases the same and later data according to the BSO's revised categories used in the new series of annual inquiries into retailing. These replace the periodic census of distribution and provide more realistic breakdown of the industry's sub-sectors, based essentially upon the type of shop rather than its characteristic product.

First, examining non-food retailers, it is clear that in addition to suffering a sales reversal in 1974, they have also failed to benefit from the renewed growth in consumer spending on non-food goods after 1977. Among specialist clothing and footwear retailers the shortfall has been less significant, with a gap between actual and potential sales (i.e. consumers' expenditure) of only some 3 or 4 per cent in 1979. Yet the situation for household goods retailers (12.5% gap and only 3% up in volume terms since 1976) is more worrying, while for other non-food retailers (principally chemists, off-licences and tobacconists) it has been catastrophic, the volume of sales falling some 13% between 1976 and 1979. Overall the market share of all non-food retailers, which rose from just 37 to over 39 per cent in the period 1971-76 has since fallen back to 37.5% with total sales down over 2.5%.

The explanation for the declining non-food market lies in developments among food retailers, and more particularly, the rapid growth in the market share of mixed retail business. The early 1970s witnessed a prolonged fall in the sales of (specialist) food retailers, down nearly 20% by 1977; their market share down 8% by 1976, but barely 1% thereafter. This was accompanied by a spectacular advance on the part of mixed retail businesses, their sales rising over 25% by 1976 and market share increasing from 21 to nearly 30 per cent in the whole period 1971-79.

In short the large mixed distribution already firmly based in supermarkets, began to squeeze the peripheral food retailers as margins were cut in a stagnant market. As that process has now been carried to extremes and with

Table 2.3(i) Volume of Retail Sales (Old Categories): Index numbers of the value of sales per week (average 1971 prices) 1971 = 100

	Sales in 1971 (£m)	1971	1972	1973	1974	1975	1976	1977
Food Shops	6,866	100	101.6	101.6	102.4	100.0	98.7	94.8
Clothing and Footwear Shops	2,436	100	104.0	108.0	106.0	106.0	106.0	105.0
Durable Goods Shops	1,897	100	113.0	127.0	122.0	119.0	122.0	119.0
Mail Order Houses	633	100	119.0	136.0	138.0	130.0	148.0	133.0
Other Non-Food Shops	4,464	100	106.0	114.0	112.0	108.0	123.0	106.0
Total Retail Shops	16,296	100	105.3	110.3	109.0	106.7	106.5	103.6

Source: Trade and Industry.

Table 2.3(ii) Volume of Retail Sales (New Categories) Index numbers of the value of sales per week (average 1976 prices) 1976 = 100

Sales in	All retailers	Food retailers	Mixed retail businesses	Non-food retailers total	Clothing and footwear retailers	Household goods retailers	Other non-food retailers
1976- (£ million)	33,616	11,369	9,045	13,202	3,384	4,745	5,073
1971	94.0	116.4	73.3	88.9	101	79	90
1972	98.7	115.6	81.5	95.8	105	89	96
1973	103.1	112.0	90.2	104.2	106	101	105
1974	101.9	110.0	91.6	102.0	103	99	104
1975	100.1	104.2	95.7	99.5	101	97	101
1976	100.0	100.0	100.0	100.0	100	100	100
1977	97.5	97.1	100.8	95.6	98	94	95
1978	100.9	98.4	107.8	98.3	103	101	93
1979	102.0	98.3	113.5	97.4	106	103	87

Source: British Business, 14th March 1980. Further information from the Department of Trade and Industry.

the volume of food retailers sales stabilising in recent years, the major mixed multiples have begun using the high volume "sundry consumables" (alcohol, tobacco and pharmaceuticals) as a springboard for a further advance into the non-food sector proper. The effects are already being felt by household goods retailers, whose high values mass produced electrical and mechancial goods are especially vulnerable to price cutting.

The Growth of Oligopoly

The economics of this process are fairly clear. Since the development of supermarket chains in the 1960s, the retail distribution of food has been increasingly concentrated in the hands of a few major distributors, until today over 90 per cent of UK groceries are sold by a mere 18 retail groups, more than three-quarters by the largest nine and exactly half by the four market leaders. In descending order these are the Co-op grocers (17.4%), Tesco (13.6%), Sainsbury (11.9%) and Asda (7.3%).*

In a static market increased profitably in food retailing depends upon either an improvement in net margins, a decline in the cost of capital, or a growth in volume. As competition and economic conditions have prevented the first two, large food retailers have inevitably concentrated upon increasing the size of their operations in order to maximise scale economies. The lower unit costs which resulted from bulk-buying for distribution through an integrated network of outlets have allowed the large organisations to wage a price war upon the smaller businesses, thus, increasing their market share.

Able to capitalise upon a very high stock turnover, the major companies with their greater net cash flow and their consequent ability to finance the increased working capital necessitated by rapid price inflation, have been able to significantly increase their level of capital investment. The still larger stores which are now appearing have permitted the oligopolists to make further scale economies and also cut wage costs, which formed around 63% of total operating costs in the early 1970s. The result is the continual strengthening of the financial and market position of the dominant distributors.**

This process has now been pushed to extremes following Tesco's price cutting war in 1977 as profit margins on "dry groceries" (i.e. canned and packaged goods) now average only 9%—which is not particularly rewarding—with meat and vegetables only slightly better at around 13%.

* Sunday Times, 2 March 1980, p.63 quoting AGB Research. Much of this section is taken from this article, entitled 'Where will you be shopping in 1984?'.

** NEDO: Profitability and liquidity in the Distributive Trades (1975)

Moreover, the near-monopoly power of the large multiples has enabled them to pass a high proportion of the costs of price cutting onto the food manufacturers. By pressurising them into further discounts for bulk buying and keeping a product before the housewife's eyes, the grocers have pushed down food manufacturers' profit margins from 5.25% in 1972 to just 3.7% last year.*

As competitive pressure in retail food becomes more intense the oligopolists have begun to turn elsewhere for profits and using the drawing power of cheap food and "sundry consumables", they have crossed the divide into the non-food sector where margins are considerably higher. For example, the margins on volume goods like motor accessories, paint and do-it-yourself products, clothing and electrical goods are all between 25% and 28%.

Non-food retailers have been vulnerable to this attack on a number of counts. Although their wages bill forms only just over half of operating costs, the smaller size and weak financial structure of non-food businesses places them at a serious competitive disadvantage. Consumer durables have a significantly higher unit cost and lower stock turn ratio than food products while credit sales are of much greater importance. For a given size cash flow is consequently lower and non-food distributors therefore operate with a higher assets/liabilities ratio than food retailers. This in turn lessens their potential for capital investment, which has inevitably been guarded as the long lead times are dangerous, given that sudden changes in cashflow (all too frequent in the 1970s) can severely strain liquidity.

The chief weapon in the multiple grocers' attack upon the non-food sector has been the new superstores, which sell a wide range of both food and non-food consumer goods, but with variety limited to the house brand and one or two market leaders. Lower margins in the food sector are thus compensated for by higher profits in other areas. Superstores by current definition are those with a net selling area of at least 25,000 square feet and parking for hundreds of cars, as they are usually situated on the edge of towns by main roads (a small town needs only one superstore). At present there are about 200 dotted throughout Britain and trade estimates suggests there is room for another 300. Asda is moving south in search of these key sites. Sainsbury is moving northwards and Tesco is simply expanding all over—at the expense of the Co-op's, smaller chains and local independents. The battle for future business is now being fought less at the checkout (for monopoly pricing is uniform) than in council planning offices around the country.

Reaping maximum scale economies and monopolising local markets, superstores are highly profitable. Asda (owned by Associated Dairies) is the most striking example. It has only 72 shops, but these include 52

* Sunday Times, ibid.

70

superstores and the company's profits have jumped almost tenfold over 7 years to around £35 million per year. Fine-fare (a subsidiary of Associated British Foods) is more typical: its 684 stores include 33 superstores, yet these provide more than one-third of its business, moreover they are operating on better profit margins than the older smaller units that the oligopolists are now dispensing with. However, those that remain in competition with other high street traders still operate fierce price-cutting. Tesco, for example, maintains five different price lists, one for its superstores and the others related to size and turnover of the shop. When Asda launched its latest round of cuts, Tesco matched them —but only in the branches in direct competition with Asda Stores.

The implication of this analysis for the medium-term future of the retail distribution industry are immense. Supermarkets are now chewing away at the independents' share of the UK grocery trade by around 3% a year and estimates suggest that by 1984-85 'jumbo marts' may approach saturation point. The rest of the grocery trade is likely to be limited to the small, convenient and rather expensive shops prepared to remain open long after the superstores. "Other food" (particularly fresh meat, fruit and vegetables) and "sundry consumables" will become increasingly dominated by the large multiples. Non-food retailers will probably be confined to (larger) department stores and specialist shops that can survive without the profits derived from the sale of the mass produced high-volume consumer durables which the massive mixed retail businesses will increasingly monopolise.

The contemporary history of retail distribution is therefore the consolidation of oligopoly and while this may be fine for the consumer who is part of a nuclear family owning a car and deep-freeze, (note the congruence with advertisers' stereotypes) it is a less exciting prospect for those poor, single, isolated or immobile.

Bargaining Structure

The retail industry as a whole is dominated by industry level bargaining of two types. Firstly, collective agreements covering large sectors of industry such as the Wholesale grocery and provisions trade JIC (E&W), Retail multiple grocery and provision trade, JC, Retail Co-operative Societies, Retail Pharmacy NJIC. Secondly, wages board orders covering broadly defined sectors such as Retail Food, Retail Bread and Flour, Confectionery, Retail drapery, outfitting and footwear, and Retail furnishing and allied trades. Recently there have been moves to rationalise the structure of the latter by amalgamating some ten separate Wage Councils into two main bodies covering Retail Food and Retail Non-Food. In addition there are a limited number of company agreements.

The relative coverage of the two main types of national level bargaining is problematical, however, a recent survey (CIR Report 89) found that only 37% of employees were covered by collective agreements. Moreover, it concluded that outside the areas already covered by collective agreements the scope for the growth of bargaining was limited and that wages councils were likely to continue to have a role for the foreseeable future.

The importance of national level bargaining can be attributed to a number of factors which act either individually or in conjunction with each other. The main ones are, firstly, the low level of unionisation, secondly, the relatively small size of a significant proportion of the employment units, thirdly, the high percentage of female and part-time labour, and finally the high rates of labour turnover. In these circumstances it is difficult to build up the membership base which allows the development of effective plant and company level bargaining. However, it is important to remember that within this overall pattern there are some relatively strong islands of trade union membership and influence. Thus one of the main unions in this industry, USDAW, is heavily represented in the Co-operative Retail Societies and has obtained a closed shop agreement. Similary closed shop arrangments exist in other large companies such as Tesco.

This concentration of membership in specific areas gives a clue to one of the main bargaining tactics in this country. Namely, an improvement in the terms and conditions of employment in those agreements where the unions are strongly organised, which are gradually extended throughout the industry until, after some time-lags, they are implemented in the wages council sector. Certainly this scenario helps to explain why, in an industry that normally has been among the last to concede changes in working hours,* it should be one of the front runners at the present time. It is doubtful whether the employers' side to the recent Multiple Grocery Agreement conceding a 39 hour week from November, 1980 would have given their consent unless they were fairly certain that the unions would, fairly rapidly, extend such arrangements throughout the whole industry. Moreover, it is interesting to note that this is an industry where the large firms have learnt to utilise different patterns of working time and the flexible use of labour to maintain their competitive advantage. Thus they are undoubtedly quite confident that they can continue to do so in the immediate future.

General Employment Trends

The most notable general features of the manpower structure of the retail sector are the dominance of female employees and the high proportion of

* The 40 hour week was not sanctioned by all distribution Wages Councils until 1973.

part-time workers. The Census of Distribution shows that in total the labour force increased by some 15% between 1961 and 1976. Within this increase female employment increased from 62% of the total to 66%. This aggregate, however, masks the profound switch from full-time to part-time working. For example, in 1961 28% of paid employees worked part-time by 1976 this had risen to 46%. The latest annual census of employment shows that by June 1977 part-time employment accounted for 19% of all male employment and 54% of all female employment in the sector.

The shift in favour of part-time employees has given rise to the illusion that the absolute workforce in the sector has grown in recent years. However, if part-time employees are converted to whole time equivalents (treating a part-timer as being equal to 0.4 of a full-time worker) then it can be seen from the census of distribution that over the decade 1966-76 that the whole time equivalent total declined from 1.9 million to 1.6 million a fall of some 15%. More recent data from the annual census of employment suggests that between 1975 and 1977 this decline slowed down largely as a result of a small increase in the whole time equivalent male workforce over the period. Care should be exercised in placing undue emphasis on these results covering just three years, however, it is of interest that a fall in female employment both part-time and full-time is also shown.

Unfortunately, reliable data on employment by type of retail outlet is constrained by the degree of aggregation to be found in the census of distribution—which lumps "all persons engaged" to include full-time, part-time and working proprietors and their families—and the fact that the more recent retailing inquiry run by the Department of Trade has both regrouped some types of retail outlet and appears to be maintaining the practice of not disaggregating "all persons engaged". This being said, comparing 1977 census data with the provisional inquiry results for 1978 suggests that significant falls in employment were recorded in grocery and provisions, other food, and clothing and footwear shops. A much slower fall would seem to be the case for confectionery, tobacconist and newsagent shops, whilst household goods shops appear to have maintained their employment share.

Future Changes in Employment

In 1974 the Retail Distribution EDC made the following comments:

para 5.9: 'Changes in the structure of retailing are likely to accelerate the trend to an increased number of employees per outlet in most sectors of retailing and the industry's heavy reliance on part-timers is likely to continue . . . The dependence on part-time workers would accelerate should there be any change in the law to bring an extension of shopping hours'.*

* Retail Distribution EDC.

Evidence adduced from our case studies suggests that the latter comment on the use of part-time workers particularly has proved to be the case. However, whilst we would agree that the drive for economies of scale continued with the steady incremental lengthening of trading hours will continue to provide the major forces acting upon the sector's demand for labour in the immediate future, in the medium to long-term the influence of technology is likely to have a further significant impact. It is to this possibility that we now turn.

Technological Change*

Much attention has recently been focussed on the introduction of "laser scanning checkouts" into the retail, and particularly the grocery and provisions' trade. These checkouts are capable of scanning each item as it passes the till for a printed "bar code", interpreting this information into the current price for the item, and printing out a detailed receipt far faster than could be done via conventional manual operations. In addition the checkout is able to store information about goods passing out of the store, and thus it can play an important role in the management of stock control.

The new technology has significant implications for the retail industry's future demand for labour, and indeed its manufacturers "sell" it very much, although not entirely, on the basis of the labour savings it makes possible. These savings come from various sources:

1) from the increased speed of operation of the checkout. A given number of customers per hour can be dealt with by a small number of checkouts, without any increase in the length of queues.

2) from providing a means of identifying the most efficient number of checkouts (to reduce queues and to keep the checkouts in continuous operation) to have open at any one time. For each checkout the computer within the system can give precise information on the number of customers, sales volume, what is sold, etc., and optimum manning levels can thus be more closely calculated. In addition, the system gives management the ability to screen checkout operators through computer analysis of their performance and to identify those who are "underperforming".

3) from cutting the number of staff neeeded for such jobs as individual price labelling of every item. The bar code will have already been printed onto the packet by the manufacturer.

* Much of the information herein is drawn from "Electronic Revolution in the High Street" Financial Times 12.11.79 p.29 and "Start of a Supermarket Laser Checkout Revolution" Financial Times 12.10.79 p.31.

4)   from cutting the number of staff needed for counting stocks as part of the process of stock control. Up until now the most effective method of keeping track of what happens to goods within the store has also been the slowest and most labour intensive, that of "counting the tins on the shelf", now the checkout monitors all outgoings and alerts management accordingly.

NCR and US computer manufacturers estimate that the "hard savings"—essentially savings from reduced labour costs—of a typical UK supermarket will be equal to rather more than 1% of annual sales, after costs have been met, and in the US supermarket chains using the new technology are reporting productivity increases of up to 40%.

Thus the new technology implies, all things being equal, a substantial reduction in numbers employed in the retailing sector, along with a significant enhancement of productivity. Retailing companies hope that the high rate of labour turnover in the industry will enable the reduction in jobs to be achieved without forced redundancies, whilst the unions, in a traditionally low paying industry, appear to be formulating a response to take advantage of the dramatic productivity increases made possible, and by means of a "productivity deal" to substantially raise levels of pay.

The Hours of Work of Full-Time Staff

It is apparent from the above analyses of industrial structure and man-power trends that there are significant differences between the food and non-food sectors of the retail distribution industry. Table 2.4 therefore gives the averages and distributions of total weekly hours for full-time male and female, manual and non-manual workers in both MLH 820 and MLH 821 at three year intervals during the past decade. However, it is limited in that the New Earnings Survey does not report figures for juveniles (a significant element in the retail trade workforce) or for those absent at any time during the survey week—a proportion which may vary between different employment groups.

When the distribution of hours of male and female part-timers is compared some considerable differences are revealed. Nearly half (48.6%) of male part-timers work not more than 9 hours per week, whilst less than a quarter (23%) of female part-timers do so (of whom the vast majority—probably Saturday only staff—work between 7 and 9 hours). On the other hand nearly half the female part-timers (46%) have a working week of between 19 and 24 hours compared to only 17% of male part-timers.

Table 2.4 Average and Distributions of Total Weekly Hours in the Retail Distribution Industries, 1970-79
Full-time adults, not affected by absence.

(i) Men

Percentage with total hours on the range

April	Manual							Non-Manual						
	30 to 34	34 to 39	39 to 40	40 to 45	45 to 50	over 50	aver. age	30 to 34	34 to 39	39 to 40	40 to 45	45 to 50	over 50	aver. age
MLH 820 — Retail Distribution of Food and Drink														
1970	1.1	3.0	17.5	25.5	27.5	24.0	46.7	0.4	11.3	26.0	42.0	14.4	5.8	42.7
1973	0.2	2.0	25.0	21.8	21.4	29.7	47.3	0.7	10.4	39.5	27.6	15.3	6.5	42.9
1976	0.5	2.8	35.4	19.3	17.9	23.9	45.9	0.4	15.1	48.8	20.0	10.0	6.0	41.7
1979	0.8	3.4	38.3	16.4	20.5	20.7	45.5	0.2	14.1	54.0	16.4	11.1	4.2	41.5
MLH 821 — Other Retail Distribution														
1970	0.6	8.5	32.8	25.9	16.1	14.9	44.1	0.3	25.5	31.0	34.8	6.1	3.9	41.0
1973	0.3	9.0	41.0	22.0	13.2	14.5	44.0	0.7	30.0	41.4	19.2	5.8	2.9	40.5
1976	0.7	12.9	46.8	18.8	11.3	9.5	42.6	0.7	35.3	42.8	15.6	3.4	2.2	40.0
1979	0.4	16.0	43.2	19.9	10.7	9.8	42.9	0.5	40.7	40.1	12.6	4.0	2.0	39.7

Table 2.4—*continued*

(ii) Women

Percentage with total hours on the range

April	Manual							Non-Manual						
	30 to 34	34 to 39	39 to 40	40 to 45	45 to 50	over 50	aver. age	30 to 34	34 to 39	39 to 40	40 to 45	45 to 50	over 50	aver. age
MLH 820—Retail Distribution of Food and Drink														
1970	14.6	12.4	35.8	25.6	4.4	2.2	39.0	8.8	19.9	31.7	36.6	2.4	0.6	39.7
1973	14.3	17.9	47.6	15.5	3.6	1.2	39.1	10.3	16.8	50.2	16.1	3.7	3.0	39.8
1976	9.1	23.8	50.0	12.5	2.2	2.2	39.5	8.9	22.6	56.8	8.7	1.7	1.3	39.1
1979	8.8	27.9	39.7	11.8	8.8	3.0	39.9	7.6	21.7	58.6	9.8	1.6	0.7	39.2
MLH 821—Other Retail Distribution														
1970	6.9	30.2	39.9	16.3	3.5	0.3	38.8	5.0	41.0	31.1	21.0	1.5	0.4	39.1
1973	8.3	37.4	41.1	9.9	2.5	0.9	38.9	3.7	40.9	41.6	10.3	2.3	1.3	39.2
1976	6.4	48.8	40.4	3.2	1.2	0.0	38.3	5.3	50.7	38.2	4.8	0.9	0.2	38.3
1979	5.6	51.6	31.8	8.1	1.9	0.5	38.6	4.9	55.5	33.7	4.3	1.2	0.4	38.3

Source: New Earnings Survey data supplied by the Department of Employment.

This suggests that part-time employment is sought for different reasons by men and women. The shorter hours of male part-timers might well be indicative that for them part-time work is a second source of income, and that indeed only limited time is available for a second job (e.g. on a Saturday, or in the evening). Part-time females (Saturday girls excluded) appear to have a part-time job that is, by contrast, approximately a half time job.

This can be seen from the fact that 71% of females worked no more than 20 hours a week. This level is likely to have suited both employers—(the cut off level for the operation of most Employment Legislation was at that time 21 hours) and also employees who—on the then average wage for the industry of 37.5p per hour—remained below the £460 limit per year, or £8.84 per week, beyond which married women would have paid income tax on their earnings. The fact that many employees might have made a conscious decision to adjust their hours according to this constraint is shown by the fact that the earnings limit would have been reached on 23.5 hours per week, and that there is a sharp drop in the proportion working more than 24 hours per week. However, given employer preferences, the desire to avoid the constraints of Employment Legislation are likely to have been dominant.

Overall we can observe a progressive fall in the sample numbers of full-time manual workers, who comprise such occupations as storekeepers, packers, market and warehouse porters, drivers and cleaners: down some 20% throughout the industry during the past decade. As one might expect, there is a higher proportion of manual workers in the food sector (around one-third) than in non-food areas, where the percentage has declined from 25 to just over 20% since 1970. Moreover, manual labour is increasingly the province of men, in the food sector the proportion of full-time women dropping from 16 to 12% and in the non-food sector from 35 to 24% between 1970 and 1979.

By contrast the sample number of non-manual workers was at roughly the same level at the beginning and end of the decade in both sides of the retail industry. These employees include administrative, clerical and secretarial staff, sales personnel, shop assistants, shelf fillers and checkout operators. Although there has been some transfer of work from women to men in the non-food divisions, women have generally accounted for around 35% of the full-time non-manual workforce throughout the industry.

Hours of Work of Part-timers

As part of its inquiry into the Wages Councils sector of Retail Distribution the CIR conducted a survey in 1973 of the hours worked by part-time

78

employees within the industry. The CIR sample included all employees, both male and female, juvenile and adult. Thus, for that part of the industry covered by their report, the CIR's data provides far more useful comparisons than does that of the New Earnings Survey which covers only adult female workers who pay insurance contributions. The results are presented in the Table below:

Table 2.5   Hours Worked by Part-Timers in Retail Distribution

percentages

	Hours									
	1-3	4-6	7-9	10-12	13-15	16-18	19-21	22-24	25-27	28-30
Male	1.4	14.0	32.2	14.4	5.8	12.5	10.1	6.4	0.5	1.6
Female	0.3	3.8	18.7	6.6	7.3	9.1	25.0	20.6	6.1	2.5

RETAIL DISTRIBUTION

CASE STUDIES

Case Study 1

Introduction

The organisation investigated was a large Co-operative Retail Society situated in the Midlands. Considerable assistance was given to the researcher by both central and local management. The trade union concerned (USDAW) provided co-operation in various retail outlets, in the administrative offices and in the dairy operation. In what follows attention is focussed on working time organisation in the retail operations of the Society, but details of our findings relating to clerical, administrative and dairy workers can be found in the fuller unpublished version of this case study.

Economic Context

Whilst subject to the market forces already noted in the industry level analysis it is worthwhile noting that this particular Co-operative Society, by comparison with many of its counterparts elsewhere in the country, had largely withstood the competitive pressures of the multiples. It was regarded as a vigorous example of what a large co-operative organisation could achieve given the right management, structure and levels of customer support.

The Structure of the Society

Concentrating only on the retail outlets operated by the Society reveals considerable diversity both in style and size of shop. This is summarised in the following table which also provides an indication of the normal trading hours operated by broad category of outlet.

The number of stores by the categories listed in Table 2.6, together with the numbers of employees in each category is given in Table 2.7.

Trading hours are settled at group level for each type of store although individual store managers can vary hours by the odd half-hour or hour at their discretion, e.g. to pick up local early morning trade, and where late evening opening is involved, cut out that which is not proving worth-while—e.g. cut one hour of late Thursday opening.

80

Table 2.6

Types of Stores	Trading Hours
Department Stores —predominantly non-food—carrying a wide range of non-food merchandise.	5 day trading (closing day determined by local custom), except the store in City Centre shopping complex, which is 6 day trading, and at a sea-side resort which has 6 day opening during summer holiday period—9.00 a.m.–6.00 p.m. opening with late night opening night opening e.g. pre-Christmas peak only.
Superstores —Food and non-food sales—minimum of 25,000 sq.ft. of selling space—car parking space—usually on outskirts of conurbation—cut prices, low margin, high turnover, no dividends. **Price Fighter Branches** —minimum of 10,000 sq.ft. of selling space—minimum turnover of £5,000 per week—large range of cut prices, no dividends—aimed at improving trade penetration in selected geographical areas.	6 day trading Monday–Wednesday Thursday & Friday 9.00 a.m.–6.00 p.m.; Saturday 9.00 a.m.–8.00 p.m.; 9.00 a.m.–5.00 p.m.
Supermarkets —predominantly food sales—minimum of 5,000 sq.ft. of selling space—self selection.	5 day trading normally closed Mondays (but cf local customs). Monday–Thursday 9.00 a.m.–6.00 p.m.; Friday 9.00 a.m.–7.00 p.m.; Saturday 9.00 a.m.–5.00 p.m.

Continued—page 82

81

Table 2.6—*continued*

Non-Food Branches
—small specialist type shops—e.g. shoes, "do-it-yourself" etc.

Self-Service Stores
—predominantly food sales—less than 5,000 sq.ft. of selling space—self-selection. Self-Service (incl.).

Handi Stores
—lower turnover, c.£2,500 per week, higher margins (prices)
—in areas (usually villages) where competition is not great, and where the store is geographically difficult to service.

Traditional Stores
—predominantly food (butchery, wines & spirits only) sales
—less than 5,000 sq.ft. of selling space—counter service.

5 day trading
could be 5 full days or 4 full days and e.g. Wednesday and Friday mornings, close for lunch one or one and a quarter hours—40 hour trading week.

Table 2.7   Distribution of Stores and Employment by category

| Type of Store | No. of Stores in category | No. of Persons employed | | | | Av. no. of Persons employed per store |
| | | Male | | Female | | |
		FT	PT	FT	PT	
Department Stores						
5 day trading (excl. food depts)	9	154	22	223	203	67
5 day trading (food depts only)	7	38	9	66	92	29
6 day trading (no food depts)	1	48	3	71	59	—
Superstores	1	23	12	21	119	—
Price Fighters	10	82	23	80	285	47
Supermarkets	19	99	24	67	283	25
Traditional Stores Self-Service, Handi-Stores, etc (40 hr. trading)	98	158	61	114	454	—
Totals	145	602	154	642	1,495	
TOTAL FT + PT			2,893			
Part-time males as % of male employment			20.4%			
Part-time females as % of female employment			70.0%			
Part-time as % of all employment			57.0%			

Regulations of Terms and Conditions of Employment

Historically the Union of Shop Distributive and Allied Workers (USDAW) has had a membership agreement with Co-operative Retail Societies, which to all intents and purposes has operated as a post-entry closed shop agreement granting recognition and sole bargaining rights. As wages and salaries and principal conditions of employment are negotiated nationally it is thought unlikely that any significant changes in working time could be bargained locally. However, if a national agreement for example specified a reduction in basic hours, although guidance may also be issued centrally, the actual implementation of such a reduction would probably be subject to local bargaining.

Present Working Time Patterns

Hours of work of selling staff are conditioned by the opening hours of stores. Full-timers work a 40 hour week, with one hour unpaid lunch break.

CHART 1 Full-time and Part-time Staff by Hours Worked and Type of Store

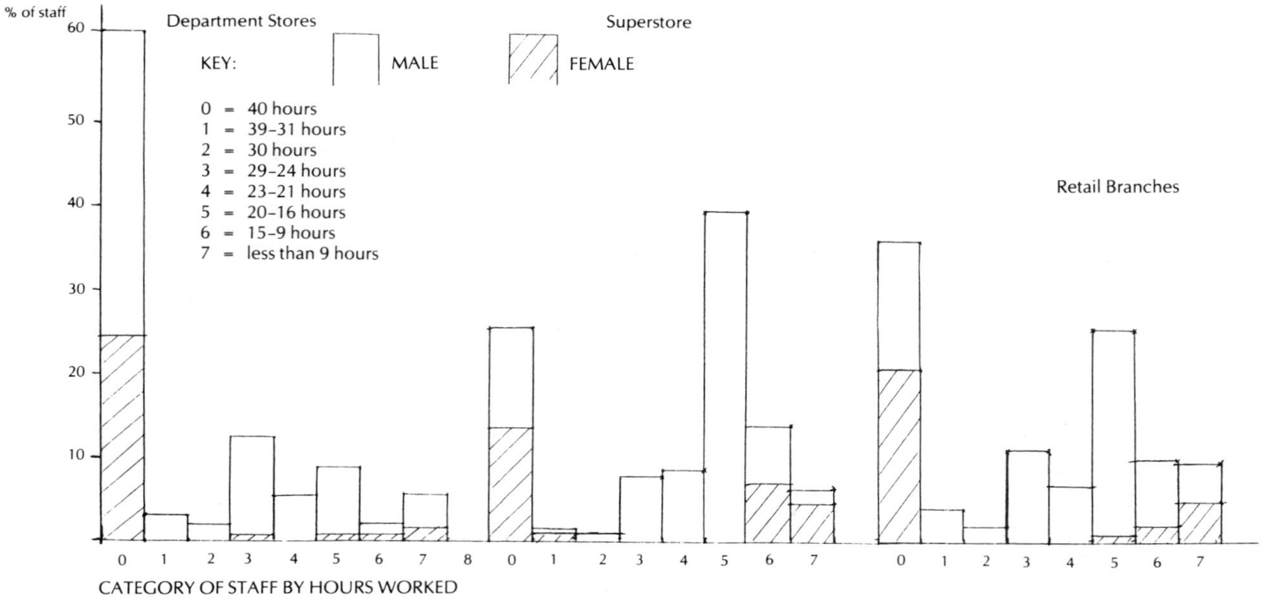
% of staff
60
50
40
30
20
10
Department Stores
Superstore
Retail Branches
KEY:
MALE
FEMALE
0 = 40 hours
1 = 39–31 hours
2 = 30 hours
3 = 29–24 hours
4 = 23–21 hours
5 = 20–16 hours
6 = 15–9 hours
7 = less than 9 hours
0 1 2 3 4 5 6 7 8 0 1 2 3 4 5 6 7 0 1 2 3 4 5 6 7
CATEGORY OF STAFF BY HOURS WORKED

In the smaller self-service stores and supermarkets this is based upon five full days per week (e.g. Tuesday to Saturday, or Monday to Saturday with Wednesday off), or on a four days and two half days (e.g. with Wednesday and Saturday afternoons off), according to area custom for opening and closing.

In the larger stores, including the superstore, where there is six day opening 8.30 a.m. to 5.30 p.m. with late night shopping on two, or at the superstore three, nights per week, until 8.00 p.m., systems of staggered hours are worked by full-timers, including management. Full-timers work on a rota, giving in week 1: Tuesday to Saturday working with one late night, in week 2: Monday to Friday working with one late night. Thus every other week there is a three day weekend. Saturday working attracts the 20% premium.

Saturday working is determined by a rota system and one of several systems might operate according to geographical area. Under a "straight Rota" every six weeks Saturday and the following Monday are not worked, this giving the advantage of a long weekend.

Another rota system provides for every other Saturday off.

Where the pattern of trade is fairly constant—as in a large inner city shopping centre—the rota day off moves one day each week.

Full-timers cover the late night openings but no full-timer will work more than one late night per week. Late night working is rewarded by *time off in lieu*, usually at the start of another day, but time off can be taken on more than one day. The group has no hard and fast rules on the management of time off in lieu, feeling that to permit individual flexibility promotes good industrial relations.

Managerial cover outside the normal 40 hours of the store manager is provided by deputy managers. Rotas are staggered to permit this.

Overtime apparently for any grade of staff is only worked under very exceptional circumstances.

Part-Time Working

Chart 1 shows the Society's employees distributed according to type of store and category of hours worked. It can be seen that in department stores full-time workers account for some 60% of staff. By comparison in the society's superstore only 25% of the staff are full-timers whilst in other retail branches the full-time complement reaches 35% of staff.

Notwithstanding this and the evidence in Table 2.7, headquarters management at the Society claimed that they made comparatively little use of part-time labour. However, from the evidence it would seem that this is really only the case for the deployment of staff in department stores, where the arguments that the selling skills required making it imperative to retain a predominantly full-time stable workforce do have some validity. This is clearly far less true of supermarkets and self-service stores and it is therefore unsurprising that management at the society's superstore claimed that changing trading patterns meant that there was increasingly no reason to use full-timers except for those jobs requiring continuity—i.e. the management function. Out of some 130 employees at the store, only 40 including the management team were full-timers, whilst out of 34 check-out operators only five, including two supervisors, worked full-time. A new, and growing, tendency is the use of part-timers as supervisors.

At the store, in addition to Saturday workers, three "shifts" of part-timers could be identified—working, approximately, from 9.00 a.m. to 1.00 p.m., 1.00 p.m. to 5.00 p.m. and 4.00 p.m. to 8.00 p.m. Additional flexibility of staffing was achieved by part-timers being prepared, given a minimum of a week's notice, to make adjustments to their schedules. In this way, in particular, staff holidays could be covered.

In general terms Society policy is to staff up stores to cope with "normal" levels of trading with full-timers. Manning levels are then supplemented by part-timers. Some part-timers will be used to cover trading peaks occurring towards the end of the week. Such part-timers will work Saturdays only. Fridays and Saturdays, or perhaps a half day on Thursday, and Friday and Saturday. At certain stores a "twilight shift" is employed working from 5.00 p.m. to 8.00-9.00 p.m. Those employed are frequently married women. The shift is used both to provide selling staff during late opening, and to provide staff to fill shelves in preparation for the subsequent day's trading, thus relieving normal selling staff.

A limited use is made of part-time staff to cover the lunch breaks of full-timers. However, such a system is only adopted in those areas where trading peaks are such that the system of staggering lunch breaks does not provide adequate cover. Hours of work of such part-time staff are from 11.00 a.m. to 2.00-3.00 p.m.

As Chart 1 shows weekly hours of work of part-timers usually lie in the 16-20 hours range, i.e. category 5. Society "policy" is to suggest that part-timers aim for about 16 hours work per week, and they point to the economic advantages of this both for the employee and the employer. Principally, these revolve around the £19.50 (= approximately 16 × average hourly rate) earnings limit above which National Insurance contributions are payable. On earnings above that level the employer pays the equivalent of two hours pay in contributions, whilst for the employee the gains after deductions from additional hours are very marginal. Keeping earnings, and thus hours, within the £19.50 limit means that the Society "gets the labour hours for which we are paying".

To summarise, it is important that a distinction be drawn between patterns of working time current at the Society's department stores, compared with its predominantly food-based supermarkets and self-service stores. In the former where specialist dry goods are sold elements of sales "skills" are still sufficiently valued to require a predominantly full-time staff. Where, however, self-service has de-skilled the selling operation the need for full-time staff diminishes dramatically. Moreover, where trading hours are extended e.g. on Friday and Saturday evening the flexibility of part-time staff is clearly of considerable value. It would seem reasonable to conclude that as more and more "dry goods" and specialist items are put on sale in supermarkets that the unit cost pressure on the society to change its full-time—part-time mix in its department stores will intensify in favour of a reduction in full-timers.

The Potential for reduction in Working Time

Although it was claimed that labour utilisation in the larger stores was already highly efficient it was, nevertheless, suggested that a 12½% reduction in hours which the 35 hour week would imply for full-timers would only require marginal compensation via changed manning. It was argued that the majority of large stores could already cope with a 38 hour week without manning changes.

A reduction to a 35 hour week would require the labour force to be supplemented, but this supplement would probably take the form of an increase in the part-time component in the labour force. Whilst such forms of reduced working weeks as the "nine days fortnight" might be possible (if there were sufficient numbers of employees for it to be operationalised), it was felt to supplement via part-timers would: a) be cheaper, and b) provide for greater flexibility in readjusting manning levels. However, the net increase in part-time staff levels was felt to be marginal.

On the other hand, a 35 hour week would probably necessitate an increase in the number of supervisory staff required. Since supervisory functions were felt not to be suitable for part-timers—although part-time supervisors were employed in some stores—a reduction in the man hours offered by present supervisors would require that their numbers be increased. In addition the system of staggered hours of work worked by such staff would necessarily have to be extended to provide full supervisory cover. It was, however, stressed that the increase in full-time (supervisory) staff would, in terms of actual numbers involved, be very small.

Response in Smaller Stores

In smaller stores the first response would be to look more closely at opening times.

Small stores tend to be open at present for 40 hours per week (9.00 a.m. to 6.00 p.m. Tuesday to Saturday with a one hour closure for lunch). However, it was suggested that "the reason why such stores are kept open is because the staff are paid for 40 hours", and thus that the response to a shorter working week would be to "cut down trading hours where possible". Forms of reductions of trading hours would include earlier closing in the evening (5.00 p.m. closing on Tuesdays, Wednesdays and Saturdays was considered feasible), or the introduction of an additional half day closing.

Staggering the hours of work of full-timers was not considered possible, primarily because full supervision cover could not be provided by this means. Such considerations would also militate against the use of part-time labour to supplement the workforce.

Other Forms of Shorter Working Time and Other Responses

It was felt that increased holiday entitlements would be a less costly form of shorter working time, particularly if these could be arranged to release people at periods of below peak trading. Otherwise where necessary, the Society practice of taking on temporary labour to cover holiday breaks could be extended.

It was pointed out that the last increase in holiday entitlements was absorbed without any need to supplement the labour force.

It was suggested that the introduction of a shorter working week might have a negative effect upon an employer's willingness to grant "day release" to trainee staff, particularly to the extent that the employer was dubious about the material benefits accruing from day release. By cutting down on day release granted a reduction in working time might be absorbed, and this option might be less costly, even if it were to mean losing part of a training grant. *

* This absorption option would seem to be less viable in the case of the Society's department store given their stress on the need for a skilled sales force in such stores.

Case Study 1

Summary of Key Points Emerging

— The organisation studied made extensive use of part-time labour, this was however differentiated by type of store. In the non-food department store greater emphasis was placed on preserving a skilled full-time sales force, whereas in the supermarkets and more traditional food store part-time females in particular dominated the employment categories;

— No labour market constraints were identified with respect to the supply of part-time labour, indeed such was its availability that a form of part-time 'shift' working could be seen to be operating in the very big supermarkets;

— Increases in opening hours were met by increased utilisation of part-timers, and it was considered most likely that any reduction in basic hours would similarly be absorbed through increased deployment of part-time workers;

— The management attempted to maintain the number of hours put in by part-timers below the level at which national insurance contributions became payable—at the time of the study around 16 hours per week represented the cut off point. This did not however appear to constitute a significant pressure on either the *external* or *internal* labour markets;

— It would seem that, as the trend towards greater scale economies in retailing further pushes both the extent of opening hours and the practice of mixing food, dry and specialist goods all under one roof, the pressure on the Society to adjust its labour force mix in favour of part-timers will intensify.

Case Study 2

Introduction

The data provided in this case study is seriously constrained by the fact that it was in the main drawn from one interview with the Personnel Director of the organisation under study. Subsequent access was refused to the researcher. We include our consequently restricted findings to provide a limited contrast to the more detailed material provided in case study 1.

The organisation studied in case study 2 owned some 22 department stores distributed throughout England and Wales. The largest stores operated comprised some 500-600 employees, medium sized stores were defined as those with around 200 employees and small stores in the group typically employed between 75-100 workers.

Settlements of Terms and Conditions of Employment

The group was one of the first to recognise USDAW for bargaining purposes. Bargaining takes place on all contractual terms and conditions of employment, including hours of work, at company level; and the Retail Drapery and Outfitting Wages Council is the relevant statutory determinant of pay and conditions for employees of the group. Bargained terms and conditions however exceed the Wages Council minima on all important matters.

Trading Hours

Six day opening is now universal within the group but trading hours within each day are determined by local competition, and by the general pattern of the relevant region. However:

All stores open Monday to Friday   9.00 a.m.-5.30 p.m.
Saturday   9.00 a.m.-6.00 p.m.

Certain large stores might open two evenings per week (including Saturday) until 5.00 p.m. or 6.30 p.m. (usually until 6.00 p.m.).

Company policy is to operate "sensible trading hours" and in the recent past this has led, if anything, to a small reduction in trading hours, the economic justification of the last half-hour being examined and a consequent move from 6.30 p.m. to 6.00 p.m. "late" opening. In the pre-Christmas period late opening, until 7.00 p.m., operates in the largest store in the group for a limited number of nights per week. Notwithstanding this, opening hours are considered by the company to be non-negotiable—because they do not form part of contractual terms of employment. However, the union would normally be informed and consulted on any proposed change in trading hours.

Patterns and Hours of Work—Full-Time Staff

Full-time staff start work 10 minutes before opening time, at 8.50 a.m., and finish some 15 minutes after closing time, at the completion of "cashing up". Within this period they have a lunch break of one hour, plus a morning and an afternoon break each of 20 minutes. All breaks are unpaid, so that the normal working day Monday to Friday ranges from 7¼ to 7¾ hours, depending on closing time. However, during periods of low trading activity staff are permitted time within paid working hours to do their own

90

shopping within the store, to visit the store hairdressing salon, chiropodist, etc., (if these facilities exist).

Full-timers work five days per week. Saturday working is determined by a rota system, all full-timers being obliged to work some Saturdays but on a rota permitting between one Saturday in six and one Saturday in two off. Within the constraints set by the need to maintain staffing levels rotas are determined as far as possible to fit personal preferences. It was suggested that alternate Saturdays off were by no means universally sought, and that, e.g. a married woman might prefer her day off during the week, when her family were out of the way.

Average weekly hours are approximately 37½ per week, averaged over two weeks. Those working late one week, i.e. until 6.30 or 7.00 p.m. are rewarded by time off in lieu in the following week. Saturday working attracts an unsocial hours payment, and so can be considered a form of shift working.

As from 1979 overtime is payable for hours worked in excess of 38 rather than 40. Overtime is however, normally only worked in the pre-Christmas period. Work on "customary days" (entitled days off as prescribed by Wages Council Order) also attracts overtime pay. (Such pay is calculated as a percentage on top of a notional hourly rate for a 40 hour week).

Patterns and Hours of Work—Part-Time Workers

Over the whole group part-timers account for some 25-30% of the weekly wage bill. This suggests some 50-60% of employees are part-timers. However, the proportion will vary between stores and areas, and is also subject to seasonal fluctuation. Four types of part-timers can be identified:

a)   Part-timers covering lunch times
b)   Part-timers covering "days off" of full-timers
c)   Part-timers covering "peak days"
d)   Part-timers covering "peak periods".

With reference to type (a) part-timers:

Lunch breaks for full-timers are staggered over a three hour period from 11.30 a.m. to 2.30 p.m., with one-third of full-timers off at any one time. To provide cover for those taking a break, and also to provide cover for the high level of trading occurring over the lunch time peak, a relief staff of part-timers is employed. Such staff work three hours per day, usually for five days per week. It was remarked that such a shift provided opportunities for work, e.g. for married women with school age families, who would be available only during the middle part of the day.

With reference to type (b) part-timers:

Part-timers working full days, or nearly full days (e.g. from 10.00 a.m. to 4.00 p.m.) but less than five days per week are used to cover for full-timers who are on their "rota day off". More complete cover will be required for peak trading days, towards the end of the week, than for slacker days, towards the beginning of the week, and thus the number of such part-timers working on any one day will vary. The number of days worked by such part-timers will vary from person to person. However, it is group policy that such part-timers must include Saturdays on their rota.

Regarding type (c) part-timers:

The peak trading day is Saturday and additonal "Saturdays only" staff are recruited to cover this peak of activity. Such employment might typically serve as a training period for certain school students who, on leaving school, move into retailing.

With reference to type (d) part-timers:

For peak trading period before Christmas a certain number of temporary full-timers are hired. Similarly in the summer particularly in those areas where annual holidays tend to be concentrated together temporary full-timers (often students) are recruited to cover for holiday absences of permanent staff.

No one particular type of part-timer can be identified; each pattern of work demanded will produce its own type offering him/herself. However, the opportunities in part-time work for providing a second career for, particularly, married women were stressed, as were the possibilities offered to the newly retired. In such a way the experience of both types could be retained in the industry.

The group has no particular hiring policy, beyond preferring experience and valuing enthusiasm, for part-timers other than the demand for flexibility. Thus, whilst a potential employee will offer a certain number of days availability during the week the store reserves the right to specify the days of the week worked. As was stated above part-timers in category (b) above are required to include Saturdays in their rota. In addition, as staffing requirements for the following week are planned out each Monday, it might occasionally be found necessary to temporarily change one of the days of work of such a part-timer. Such changes are made in agreement with the individual concerned, who will have a minimum of a week's notice of the change. The possibility of such alterations in their work schedules does enhance the flexibility of this category of part-timers.

92

It is the ability to offer such a flexible supply that makes part-time labour so attractive. Particularly significant is the contribution of those who compose a sort of "task force", who are very mobile and can be switched from department to department as the level of trading activity varies and cover is required.

The flexibility of the part-timer itself was held to explain the secular trend towards the substitution of part-time for full-time labour. However, the £6 day policy was seen as having a disproportionate cost effect on retail wages and probably stimulated a remix, since whilst part-timers are no less expensive on an hourly basis they are more flexible, and thus can be employed in a more cost effective manner.

The Potential for Reducing Working Time

Given the limitations of our inquiry only brief comments are possible here. It is, however, significant that management expressed little doubt as to their ability to accommodate a reduction in the working week because of the flexibility inherent in the full-time/part-time mix of their labour force. It was clear too that their confidence was bolstered by a certain anticipation of yet further flexibility and productivity gains from the introduction of new technology into their stores.

35 Hour Week

Given the present working week of approximately 37½ hours and the present arrangement of patterns of working time, it was felt that should the 35 hour week, as a shorter working week, be conceded, it could be accommodated within present staffing levels, for it was argued that it would require not more than a half-hour reduction of the working day for full-time staff.

It was felt that this could be coped with by staggering starting and finishing times, so that some employees arrived at the traditional time and finished early, whilst others arrived slightly later and finished at the traditional time. Given the low level of trading activity early in the morning, a considerably lower level of staff, first thing, would be acceptable, and it is anticipated that in this sense this system of staggering would be asymmetrical.

Given the introduction of new (electronic) technology, reducing the work involved in chasing up and thus freeing staff at the end of the day, a slight reduction in staff available at the end of the day was thought to be manageable.

Given the trading hours policy of the group, which did not envisage the need for any significant change in trading hours (in the absence of a universal shift in behaviour), an approach linking shorter hours to e.g. extended opening was not pursued.

It was felt that with respect to changes in patterns and durations of working time, more significant for employees had been the shift from 5½ to 5 day working, which had provided a useful block of additional time-off. This change had been effected in the late 1950s and the group had been amongst the first to introduce such a working week.

Case Study 2

Summary of Key Points Emerging

— Bargaining was carried out at company level, however, some scope for local bargaining, e.g. regarding the deployment of staff within the working day could be identified. Management did not, however, consider opening hours to be a valid subject for collective bargaining.

— Extensive use was made of part-time employees, four main categories were identified covering lunch times; covering 'days off' for full-timers, covering 'peak days' and covering 'peak periods'.

— The ease with which part-time labour could be both recruited and deployed gave the company ample labour flexibility to meet short run fluctuations in trading patterns. In this sense neither *external* or *internal* labour market constraints could be identified.

— It was felt that any reduction in working time e.g. a 35 hour week could be absorbed simply by using existing labour more flexibly, i.e. staggering starting and finishing times across opening hours.

INDUSTRY STUDY

The Current Situation in the Health Service

Health and Personal Social Services (PSS) forms a vast bureaucratic organisation and while decisions about actual levels of employment and service are taken by local administrators, the NHS is centrally guided and financed and therefore subject to the vagaries of government spending policy. Thus the NHS benefited from a steady increase in expenditure during the 1960s and early 1970s. Before the public spending cuts of 1976, volume expenditure at constant prices was about one-third higher than a decade earlier. But with only a temporary respite during 1978-79, the succeeding years have witnessed a real and increasing decline in the cost of the NHS already down 3% by 1977-78. The half of one per cent real increase in the current financial year entails yet another relative fall for according to the last Secretary of State, "health services' current expenditure needs to grow at about 1 per cent a year merely to allow for demographic change and the spread of improved medical techniques". (Table 2.8).

The rise in spending was accompanied by a similar rate of growth in employment and the NHS now employs over one million people in the UK. It is extremely labour intensive and wages and salaries account for at least 70% of health service costs. Expenditure cuts have therefore had a marked effect upon job opportunities and the New Earnings Survey (NES) suggests that full-time adult employment in medical and dental services may have declined by as much as 4½% between April 1976 and 1979. Meanwhile the growth in part-time employment—defined as those working less than the normal whole-time hours, consisting mostly of women and now forming over one-third of the total labour force—has been severely curtailed. At the same time in order to maintain services managers have been making rigorous attempts to improve the utilisation of the remaining staff by increasing flexibility and efficiency. This has occasionally led to industrial disputes among ancillary and maintenance workers, worried at the threat to traditional patterns of overtime work and at the consequent loss of pay. Recently, for example, at the Charing Cross and Royal Liverpool Hospitals.

There have also been continuing demands from other groups of workers for a reduction in the very long hours traditionally worked by full-time staff in the medical and dental services. In 1979, as in 1970, nearly 40% of male and 10% of female manual employees worked more than 45 hours per week, while among the non-manual staff well over half the men and two-thirds of women had total weekly hours of at least 38. Moreover after some

Table 2.8 NHS Employment and Expenditure 1959/60—1978/79: Great Britain   Expenditure indices at 1975 prices[1]
1971 = 100

Year	NHS Staff	Total NHS and PSS Expenditure[2]		Hospital Current Expenditure[3]		Hospital Capital Expenditure	
		At Constant (1975) Prices Index	To Hospital Services %	At constant (1975) Prices Index	Of total NHS/PSS Costs %	At constant (1975) Prices Index	Of total NHS/PSS Costs %
1959/60		53.5	54.4	54.5	51.4	25.0	3.0
1963/64		63.9	55.9	64.3	50.7	53.0	5.2
1967/68	753,486	79.8	56.0	78.3	49.4	82.6	6.6
1969/70	778,998	87.5	55.7	85.8	40.4	86.8	6.3
1971/72	799,673	100.0	56.7	100.0	50.4	100.0	6.3
1972/73	831,753	107.2	56.7	106.0	49.8	116.4	6.9
1973/74	843,119	113.9	55.9	110.3	48.8	128.0	7.1
1974/75	859,468	124.1	55.8	122.0	49.5	122.7	6.3
1975/76	914,068	134.5	56.1	133.3	50.0	130.0	6.1
1976/77	945,977	133.6	55.5	132.2	49.9	118.8	5.6
1977/78	970,900	131.1	55.2	131.6	50.6	95.4	4.6
1978/79		137.0	54.4	134.8	49.6	103.3	4.8

Source: Royal Commission, Tables 12.1 E9, E10.
Notes: [1] Current prices have been deflated by the index of total domestic expenditure at constant 1975 prices.
[2] The total cost of services from all sources of finance including charges to persons using the service.
[3] At reorganisation on 1 April 1974 executive council administration, local authority and school health services were transferred to what became termed 'hospitals and community health services'. Their average proportion of total NHS and PSS expenditure 1970-74 (7.2%) has been subtracted from the hospital current account in succeeding years.

improvement during the early seventies, the situation has deteriorated in recent years and in all labour intensive groups falls in employment have been reflected by an increase in working time.

Among the white collar occupations the calls for a shorter week have come mainly from medical care staff. There is a growing undercurrent of discontent among junior hospital doctors who are regularly subject to 1 in 2 and 1 in 3 night shift patterns with the overtime paid at only three-tenths normal rate. Nurses and midwives, on the other hand, work little overtime but they are the only significant group of non-manual women to undertake shiftworking at nights and weekends, while their basic week has always been one of the longest. It was not until 1972 that the basic hours of nurses and midwives fell from 42 to 40 and they are only now implementing an agreement to reduce the standard week from 40 to 37½ hours by 1 April 1981.

In an organisation whose employees are distributed among nearly 2,750 hospitals and innumerable clinics and general practices throughout the UK, the 'average' is a somewhat meaningless concept. There are vast disparities in regional resources distribution and significant differences in the type of demand and quality of service even between adjacent districts. It was necessary therefore, to confine our study to the central institutions and consider only hospitals, where 70% of NHS expenditure and about 80% of its manpower are concentrated.

Capacity Utilisation in Hospitals

The key to hospital work time management is capacity utilisation and we must now examine this in some detail before passing on to employment issues. In 1948 the NHS inherited more than 3,000 old, poorly distributed and often ill-equipped hospitals. A central feature of the modernisation policy in the 1960s and early 1970s was therefore the closure of many small, isolated units and the running down of the huge Victorian mental institutions. By 1973 over 350 hospitals had been shut including more than 250 units with less than 50 beds and there remained no psychiatric hospitals with over 2,000 beds.

This was offset by a substantial building and renovation programme and the centralisation of new and remaining institutions into the system of DGHs* and supporting units. Thus between 1959 and 1973 capital expenditure on hospitals increased five-fold in real terms, its share of the total NHS and PSS budget doubled to over 7 per cent, and more than 60 new hospitals were opened with between 250 and 1,000 beds. However, while hospital current expenditure has continued to account for half

* District General Hospitals.

97

the total budget, the building programme bore an early and disproportionate share of public spending cuts with the result that reduced capital
expenditure is now concentrated upon upgrading and extending existing
facilities. At the same time there have been further closures of
small, 'uneconomic' hospitals.

The effects of hospital rationalisation are reflected in the number of
allocated beds, so that although beds in medium sized hospitals (250-999
beds) rose by nearly 54,000 (or over 20%) in the years to 1974 they were
more than halved in large hospitals and are now quickly disappearing
from smaller institutions, with less than 250 beds. Overall the
number of allocated beds fell by around 12% and at an increasingly rapid
rate before 1976 and this resulted in a 15% fall in the average number of
(staffed) beds available daily. After the shortages of trained personnel are
accounted for, this meant a 20% decline in the number of beds occupied
daily during the same period. (Table 2.9).

During the 1960s the proportion of available beds occupied daily fell by
around 4% yet at the same time the hospital service was able to treat a
growing number of in-patients, annual discharges and deaths increasing by
over 1½ million or one-third again. This was achieved by an improvement
in capacity utilisation that took two inter-related forms: shortening the
average length of stay of in-patients and substantially increasing the
number of 'day-patients'. In the first instance improvements in medical
techniques and better nursing led to a steady fall—at the rate of one day
per year—in the average length of stay in all hospital beds, until by the end
of the sixties it was down to 25 days and to just over 10 days in acute
specialities, which declined at only half the general rate. Because of their
shorter stay these units experienced the most rapid rise in annual patient
throughput (ie, discharges and deaths per available bed per year), which
rose from 20 to 25 during the decade.

However there has been no significant increase in the number of in-
patients treated annually since 1970 and the situation is noticeably worse in
the acute wards (in which we are primarily interested), where average
length of stay declined only marginally after 1970 and throughput, which
fell in 1973 and 1975, was at the same level in the latter year as in 1971.
Unable to significantly increase in-patient flow any longer by improved or
more intensive medical care, acute specialities began to rely upon treating
minor and post-operative patients as 'day cases', so removing non-essential
users from scarce hospital beds. Between 1972 and 1976 day case attendances rose by over 50% to 540,000, but although out-patient demand was
slowly falling, this did not prevent waiting lists from rising more than
25% to 686,000 during the same period.

98

Table 2.9 NHS Hospital Facilities and Patient Flow, 1959–1977

Year	NHS Hospitals Number	Average available daily All specialities Thousands	Average occupied daily All specialities Thousands	Percentage of available beds occupied All specialities Percentage	Non-psych.[2]
Great Britain					
1959	3,027	540	467	86.5	
1963	2,953	529	457	86.4	77.5
1967	2,885	524	444	84.7	76.0
1969	2,857	518	435	84.0	74.9
1971	2,760	508	421	82.9	73.3
1972	2,748	501	415	82.8	73.1
1973	2,724	491	400	81.5	71.4
1974	2,736	483	393	81.4	71.7
1975	2,684	473	382	80.8	70.2
1976	2,657	468	380	81.2	70.1
1977	2,655	459	375	81.7	71.9

Continued on page 100

99

Table 2.9—*continued*

	Discharge and Deaths					Attendances		
	Number	Per available bed		Average length of stay[1]		Day care	Out-patient[3]	Waiting list
	All specialities	All specialities	Non-psych.	All speclts.	Non-psych.	Non-psychiatric excluding UTD[2]		
	Thousands	Rate		Days		Thousands		
1959	4,554	8.4		37.6	15.6		32,511	503
1963	5,188	9.8	20.9	32.2	13.6		34,653	572
1967	5,669	10.8	23.0	28.4	11.9		35,543	595
1969	5,975	11.5	24.5	26.3	11.1		36,966	559
1971	6,207	12.2	25.7	74.5	10.3			
1972	6,278	12.5	26.1	23.9	10.2	355	36,763	547
1973	6,158	12.5	25.9	23.4	10.0	396	36,878	591
1974	6,219	12.9	26.3	22.7	9.9	438	36,895	596
1975	5,994	12.7	25.7	22.9	9.9	411	34,371	667
1976	6,294	13.4	27.1	21.6	9.5	540	35,907	686
1977	6,391	13.9	28.0	20.9	9.2	617	36,732	679

Source: Health and Personal Social Services Statistics (various editions).

Notes: [1] England and Wales 1959-69; England 1971-77;
[2] Non-psychiatric specialities excluding geriatrics and units for younger disabled. (UTD) This group therefore comprehends all acute specialities and is responsible for over 95% of all day case and out-patient attendances and a similar proportion of the waiting list.
[3] Excluding all accident and emergency work.

100

Management's response to the spending cuts has been another attempt to improve utilisation in a system that was evidently already approaching its limits under the current organisation. Thus the years since 1976 have seen further moves towards raising in-patient flow, but it is apparent that the increases in 1977 (the last year for which figures are available) were only a fraction of those achieved during the 1960s. There must then, be doubts as to how much further this process can be pushed, for the human metabolism does impose certain limits.

The pressure is inevitably more intense in the acute specialities than in long-stay hospitals, where day and out-patient cases are rare and the problem tends to be one of accommodation rather than cure. However with the day-patient system now firmly established in the predominantly acute DGH's, any improvement in capacity utilisation can only come from better medical care, and, significantly, from an increase in the proportion of available beds that are occupied daily. Now these are essentially problems of work organisation and staff availability; thus there is a strong case for an investigation of the acknowledged inefficiencies of labour utilisation in the NHS. Given the current constraints upon employment, this must necessarily concentrate upon the efficiency of present working time patterns.

Manpower Structure

In a large inter-dependent organisation like the NHS, labour utilisation is far from uniform and in order to isolate the crucial areas we need to make sense of the manpower structure and labour markets. This is not simple, for with the exception of doctors and dentists collective bargaining is conducted in eight functional Whitley Councils, while there are at least ten or twelve main occupational groups in the hospital service with innumerable sub-divisions according to speciality, training or trade. Nevertheless, these may be aggregated into three major categories according to their relation to the delivery of service. These are:

1)   Medical Care, i.e., doctors, nurses and midwives.

2)   Support and service, i.e., professional and technical, and administrative and clerical staff.

3)   Ancillary and Estate, i.e., ancillary, works and maintenance staff.

The most significant difference between these categories is that the first two are composed entirely of non-manual workers, while the latter (apart from works staff and supervisors) are almost exclusively manual employees. However, there are also considerable variations in the proportions of female, part-time and trained staff both between and within each category. This in turn ensures a number of different labour markets. (Table 2.10).

101

Table 2.10 NHS Employment Trends and Distribution 1959-1977

Category of staff	Index of employment (w.t.e. 1974 = 100)											No. of staff UK[1]	Percnt. of total[2]	Percnt. based in hospitals[3]
	1959	1963	1967	1969	1971	1972	1973	1974	1975	1976	1977	1977	1977	1974
Doctors	59.4	66.6	75.6	81.6	88.5	93.3	97.5	100	104.6	107.5	110.4	67,200	6.7	52.3
Nurses and Midwives	67.4	71.5	82.4	84.7	90.7	96.5	98.1	100	108.6	112.4	112.7	430,500	43.0	89.3
Professional and Tech.	54.7	63.7	76.9	83.5	92.6	97.6	102.4	100	107.9	120.6	124.5	64,700	6.5	85.9
Administrative and Clerical	50.9	58.5	68.2	73.1	80.9	86.3	92.9	100	111.6	119.4	120.0	123,200	12.3	67.8
Ancillary Staff		95.1	102.0	100.9	104.3	104.4	101.7	100	103.3	106.6	106.0	219,700	21.9	97.7
Works and Maintenance		86.7	88.9	90.7	96.4	99.5	97.3	100	108.0	110.1	113.3	31,600	3.2	89.9

Source: Royal Commission, Table 12.2; "Staffing of the NHS (England)" Table 4; Health and Personal Social Services Statistics (various).

Notes: [1] Whole time equivalents.

[2] The column does not sum to 100 as various small groups have been omitted, notably dentists other practitioners and ambulancemen, with whom this study is not concerned.

[3] Derived from figures for England and Wales.

Medical Care Staff

Medical care requires a high degree of skill and hence long periods of training, doctors spending at least six years at university medical school, nurses and midwives two or three years under training. The availability of staff is therefore governed in some measure by the output of training institutions; however the skills learned there are readily transferable, either outside the NHS or between hospital and community within the health services. The supply of staff to hospitals then, is additionally dependent not only upon pay, but also upon the reputation of a particular department, accommodation and morale forming important factors in labour turnover. There is thus a national (and international) market for qualified medical care staff and the hospital service has experienced shortages of doctors and nurses at times of relatively low pay, in less favoured regions and units, and in particular 'unattractive' specialities such as psychiatry and geriatrics.

Apart from their training, pay and status, the principal differences between doctors and nurses lie in the proportions of female and part-time staff. Each of these constitutes about one-fifth of medical manpower in hospitals, but in contrast nearly 90% of nurses and midwives are women. This means that marriage and childbearing entail a continual loss of skilled staff and nursing has therefore been in the vanguard of the movement towards part-time female employment, until by 1977 almost 40% of nurses and midwives worked part-time. Thus while medicine is a predominantly full-time male profession and highly careerist, nursing is almost entirely female and increasingly part-time orientated.

Nursing has consequently developed a segmented manpower structure and labour market, based upon contract and qualification. At the top appear the registered and enrolled nurses represented by the Royal College of Nursing (RCN), their full-time complement particularly the senior staff, operating in a competitive national market. In the middle come student and pupil nurses training for the respective qualification, nearly all of whom are full-time. Finally at the bottom lie the unqualified nursing auxiliaries (non-psychiatric) and assistants (psychiatric), who have the largest part-time element and are organised by trade unions. They were (unfairly) considered by the Clegg Commission as "much more closely akin to ancillary staff than to the job of a qualified nurse" and their part-time members are often treated as little better than casual labour. This is encouraged by their presence in the local labour market for married women, which is in part determined by such mundane factors as public transport and school hours and holidays.

Support and Service Staff

Support and service staff can be divided into three types according to their appropriate Whitley Council. Groups bargaining under Professional and

Technical (A) include the remedial and therapeutic professions supplementary to medicine together with hospital scientific/diagnostic back-up staff. In Professional and Technical (B) are found medical, dental and pharmaceutical technicians and auxiliaries; while the Administrative and Clerical council also comprehends large numbers of secretaries, typists and other office machine operators. They all fall into two distinct labour markets.

The scientific and remedial professions are similar in character to doctors and nurses respectively, but being at one step removed, suffer from inadequate pay and status. Consequently there are again shortages in certain regions and specialities and the training of therapists has yet to receive the attention accorded to nurses and midwives. There is thus a parallel growth in unqualified employment and 'helpers' figure prominently in remedial manpower tables.

On the other hand technical and office staff need only a general education and readily acquired scientific or typing skills, and where necessary, additional training is generally given on-the-job. These groups are therefore firmly based in the local labour market, with only the senior administrators—who now have a graduate training scheme—moving between regions. Unlike the remedial professions which are rarely found outside the NHS, office and laboratory work is universal and there have been frequent complaints of settled staff leaving either for better paid jobs outside the health service, or, in the case of dental technicians, because there is no career structure. Not surprisingly, three quarters of administrative and clerical employment is female and staffing problems have again led to a growth in part-time workers, who now form nearly 30 per cent of the total number.

Ancillary and Estate Staff

Ancillary and maintenance staff are employed in an extremely wide range of services: DHSS manpower tables identify at least 15 major occupations, while the Ancillary Staffs Whitley Council handbook defines scores of sub-divisions, grouped into 18 different pay grades according to skill and responsibility. Nevertheless they can be divided into three main types:

1) Employees concerned with the upkeep of facilities, for example gardeners, laundry workers, maintenance and building operatives.

2) Workers employed primarily in supporting patient services, including domestics, ward orderlies and operating department staff.

3) Those engaged in servicing both hospital staff and patients, such as catering staff, porters and telephonists.

Overall two-thirds of ancillary employment is female, but the proportion of men and women differs greatly within each category. Some groups like porters, gardeners and maintenance staff have historically been an almost exclusively male preserve; others such as telephonists, laundry workers and domestics are predominantly female; while one or two occupations, catering in particular, employ both men and women. These divisions are overlaid by significant variations in the extent of part-time employment. As a whole 46% of ancillary workers are part-time, but although they include well over half the domestic staff, the facility-based occupations have generally remained bastions of full-time employment, with the service occupations lying somewhere in between. In short, and with some exceptions, there are an increasing proportion of female and part-time ancillary workers as one moves from the facility through the service to the patient-based occupations.

Despite these differences, there are a number of important factors common to all manual workers in the NHS. First, as there are few promotion prospects and the health service encourages a special loyalty from its employees, ancillary and maintenance workers tend to be elderly, often with very long lengths of service. In 1970 around 70% of ancillary staff (male and female, full- and part-time) were over 40 years old, while more than 40% of full-time and nearly 30% of part-time staff had worked in the same hospital for at least five years. (NBPI Report No. 166). Secondly, nearly all ancillary occupations are unskilled, many of them are labour intensive and the little training is always given on-the-job. As a result the hospital service contains large concentrations of workers who are among the lowest paid in the country, average weekly earnings of male ancillary workers standing at only about three-quarters of those of male manual workers in general. It follows, thirdly, that ancillary and maintenance staff are recruited from the local labour market and while there have been shortages in some areas (notably the South-East) during cyclical peaks, there will be no lack of staff in the foreseeable future.

Trends in Employment and Wage Costs

The improvements in capacity utilisation deriving from faster turnover and more intensive care have inevitably increased the workload of the hospital service and hence the demand for staff. However both the rising numbers in NHS employment—one-third higher in 1977 than a decade earlier— and the recent retrenchment have not been equally distributed between the major categories of staff.

Advances in medical techniques have generated many new tasks, making the jobs of doctors and nurses far more complex and demanding, whilst the increases in patient flow have affected these 'front-line' employees first. In short, the labour input required from medical care staff seems to have increased greatly in both size and content; however the steady 3% annual growth in the number of doctors and a similar, though more erratic rise in the supply of nurses, have been insufficient to prevent shortages. In the case of nurses the (professionally defined) deficiency was at high as 20 per cent in the years before the Halsbury award of 1974 and it is still 10 per cent even now. (Table 2.10).

Medical staff then, are the health service's most valuable asset, yet a sizeable element in the workload of both doctors and nurses has been of a non-clinical or non-curative variety. Doctors, for example, may spend much of their time in teaching, administration or routine scientific tests; while many nurses are sometimes engaged in record keeping and simple domestic chores. The central feature of hospital manpower policy has therefore been to release trained medical care staff from these extraneous tasks, allowing them to concentrate upon their central clinical and curative functions.

Thus within the ward system we can observe first, the creation of a new occupation of 'clinical nurse' to assist doctors in operating theatres and intensive care units. Second, the rapid growth in reliance upon unqualified nurses for the routine tasks of patient feeding, washing and medication. And third, the development of ward 'housekeeping schemes' in which domestic and ward orderlies perform elementary 'patient contact' functions, such as bed-making, once undertaken by nurses. (Table 2.11).

This tendency towards the concentration of skills and the relief of medical care staff has also been reflected in other manpower categories. Thus the fastest growing groups among NHS employees have been the support and service staff, both professional and technical and administrative and clerical manpower more than doubling between 1959 and the mid-1970s. The growth of the scientific and technical classes, and the emergence in their own right of the professions supplementary to medicine, have relieved medical staff of peripheral parts of their diagnostic and remedial functions. Indeed, until 1976 the growth rate of professional and technical manpower was increasing annually and numbers had risen to well over fifty thousand. Administrative and clerical staff have increased less regularly, much of the growth concentrated in the years surrounding NHS reorganisation in 1974. However much of the criticism this engendered was misinformed as many clerical staff are employed to assist organisation in operational units (ward clerks for example) and medical secretaries provide invaluable help for doctors. Moreover the growth of personnel, planning and training services has done much to improve efficiency in the health service. Hence the growth in support, service and some ancillary occupations may be viewed as an effective increase in the number of medical care staff.

Table 2.11 Hospital Nursing Staff: Analysis by Grade and Contract, 1971-1979

England Year	Total (whole time equv.)	Percent. of all nursing staff	Index		Percent. of part-time staff (number)	Total w.t.e. ÷ number (per cent)
			Full-time	Part-time		
Registered Nurses						
1971	74,520	32.0	100.0	100.0	35.6	84.8
1973	76,057	30.2	101.2	103.4	36.2	84.9
1975	83,329	29.7	109.8	119.8	37.7	83.7
1977	89,643	31.2	122.2	118.2	34.9	84.5
1979[1]		(35.5)	126.1	123.5	34.8	
Enrolled Nurses						
1971	35,898	15.4	100.0	100.0	44.7	85.1
1973	39,327	15.6	110.4	105.7	43.6	86.1
1975	44,480	15.8	123.7	125.4	45.0	84.7
1977	50,527	17.7	148.4	128.4	41.1	85.9
1979[1]		(18.1)	165.8	141.7	40.9	
Nursing Auxiliaries and Assistants						
1971	54,559	23.5	100.0	100.0	67.4	75.5
1973	62,590	24.9	112.8	114.2	67.8	76.1
1975	77,003	27.4	136.2	147.3	69.1	74.2
1977	73,484	25.7	135.5	134.9	67.3	75.3
1979[1]		(28.2)	140.0	123.8	64.6	
Student and Pupil Nurses						
1971	67,970	25.1	Less than 2 per cent of student and pupil nurses are part-timers. This section is therefore omitted.			
1973	74,207	25.4				
1975	76,264	23.0				
1977	74,053	25.7				
1979[1]		(18.2)				

Source: Health and Personal Social Services Statistics for England, 1978; Standing Commission on Pay Comparability, Report No. 3, Nurses and Midwives, Table 1.

Note: [1] The 1979 figures are derived from the Clegg Commission Report and are originally for Great Britain. Problems of conversion factors and definitions mean they should be treated with care. The 1979 percentage of all nursing staff is therefore for numbers not w.t.e.'s. The difference is usually small.

Ancillary, works and maintenance staff, particularly the former, have been the slowest growing occupational categories within the NHS and there are several explanations for this:

1) The employment of many groups is facility based and the number of hospitals and beds has been steadily declining.

2) An increasing proportion of hospital facilities are now being devoted to geriatric and psychiatric units, which require lower ancillary manning levels.

3) Technological innovation and new methods of work organisation, especially in the more capital intensive laundry and catering departments, have lessened the demand for staff.

4) The introduction of productivity schemes following the NBPI Reports of 1968 and 1970 noticeably restricted employment opportunities until incomes policy put a halt to new schemes after 1975.

5) Ward orderlies and some operating department staff are being progressively transferred to the nursing auxiliary grades.

Thus in spite of an increase in the numbers of domestic and maintenance staff, the overall employment of ancillary staff barely grew at all during the decade to 1977 and both ancillary and maintenance manpower fell sharply during the mini-boom of 1973. (Table 2.12).

Indeed there is a strong counter-cyclical pattern to full-time manual employment in the NHS. During periods of peak economic activity wage rates have fallen even further behind the private sector and with the rise in alternative employment opportunities, staff have been attracted elsewhere; ancillary manpower falling in the years 1962-63, 1967-68, 1972-73 and 1978-79. Yet the deterioration in relative pay soon leads to substantial wage demands, committees of enquiry, and an eventual restoration of the comparative position. However by the time the new rates have been recommended (1970, 1974, 1979) the economy is again in a downturn, so the restriction of private sector employment and the renewed attractions of NHS pay and job security drive manual workers back into the hospital service. It is some measure of the decline in overall manpower requirements that the increase in employment has become less with each succeeding cycle. Between September 1970 and 1971 the number of hospital ancillary staff rose by nearly ten thousand, in 1974-75 by barely five thousand, while in the current year it is probably declining.

Within each occupational category the effect of the expenditure cuts since 1976 has been to intensify the process of concentration upon essentials. Thus the growth in the number of hospital doctors continues unabated, but nursing manpower is stable or declining; the increase in professional

108

Table 2.12   NHS Ancillary and Estate Staff: Analysis by Occupation 1971-1977

Year	Number	Whole time equiv.	w.t.e. index	w.t.e. as % of numbers	Number	Whole time equiv.	w.t.e. index	w.t.e. as % of numbers
	MAINTENANCE STAFF				**PORTERS**			
1971	17,600	17,513	100.0	99.5	20,468	19,983	100.0	97.6
1973	17,114	17,045	97.3	99.6	20,749	20,227	101.2	97.5
1975	19,189	19,100	109.1	99.5	19,559	19,110	95.6	97.7
1977	19,907	19,875	113.5	99.5	24,677	24,178	121.0	98.0
	LAUNDRY				**CATERING**			
1971	12,417	11,268	100.0	90.7	36,683	32,572	100.0	88.8
1973	10,750	9,736	86.5	90.6	36,143	31,494	96.7	87.1
1975	10,057	8,991	79.8	89.4	34,714	29,270	89.9	84.3
1977	10,044	9,086	80.6	90.5	36,418	30,500	93.0	83.2
	DOMESTIC				**WARD ORDERLY**			
1971	79,513	61,028	100.0	76.8	16,190	13,829	100.0	85.4
1973	84,979	63,207	103.6	74.4	13,125	10,942	79.1	82.4
1975	92,476	65,690	107.6	71.0	13,620	10,645	77.0	78.2
1977	98,479	68,088	114.0	69.1	14,759	11,855	75.2	80.3

Source: Health and Personal Social Services Statistics, for England; (1978).

General Note: In some cases the rising numbers between 1975 and 1977 may be an illusion. In 1975 (probably as a result of reorganisation), there were 15,820 "staff without a specific ASC grade or, . . . grade not known". The figure is usually around six to eight thousand. Thus the reallocation of staff from local authorities might be a significant element in the 1975-77 employment increase.

and technical staff barely slowed, although administrative and clerical employment is hardly growing at all; ancillary manpower is in decline while maintenance staff have surged forward. In each case it is the smaller group which has expanded so in contrast to the 1960s, when the hospital service became more labour intensive—wages and salaries rising from sixty to seventy per cent of hospital maintenance expenditure—the 1970s have seen a levelling off and, since 1975-76, a decline in the proportion of hospital spending devoted to manpower, which is now down to less than two-thirds.

This has been accompanied by a relative shift in wage costs towards the vital medical professions, their scientific and technical auxiliaries and maintenance staff; and away from the more personal, labour intensive nursing, office and ancillary services where manpower can be more easily stretched; helped in the case of ancillary staff by the revival of productivity schemes. As the hospital service has tended to become more capital intensive as a whole, so spending has been increasingly shifting towards the services with a technological interface between operator and delivery. Thus between 1975-76 and 1977-78 the proportion of hospital services revenue expenditure directed to medical and dental staff services fell from 9.3% to 8.7%, but professional and technical rose from 8.4% to 8.6%; administration and records expenditure stabilised around 7%, while nursing staff services declined by one per cent to 32.4%; and in the manual sector ancillary costs continued their steady fall to just over 20 per cent, although estate management jumped to 12 per cent as the importance of reducing the vast maintenance backlog becomes daily more evident. (Source: NHS Annual Accounts).

Public spending cuts have not only created differential employment trends between and within the main staff categories, but they have also entailed a revision of manpower structure within each occupational group. The principal trend has been a decline in the relative proportion of part-time and unqualified staff, the former demonstrated by the fact that whole-time equivalents as a proportion of total numbers are no longer falling at anything like the rate of the 1960s and early 1970s. In the face of severe employment constraints, health authorities are concentrating upon a full complement to full-time and trained staff.

This has been particularly apparent among nurses and midwives and in several of the ancillary occupations. Between September 1975 and March 1979 the numbers of qualified nurses continued to increase, but those of unqualified staff fell sharply. Moreover among all groups the proportion of part-time employees declined but, significantly, the rate of decline for registered nurses was only half that experienced by auxiliaries and assistants. There is a slightly different picture among ancillary workers and although there are no comparable figures after 1975, the changes from 1974 when manpower was already tight, are suggestive. In the relatively capital intensive departments such as laundry and catering the trend towards part-time employment appears to have continued, but in the labour intensive areas such as portering and domestic services it has been halted or reversed. In short, in all the ward based occupations (and porters may be included here) there has been a marked concentration upon trained personnel and a significant shift in manpower structure back towards full-time employment. (Tables 2.11 and 2.12).

The Organisation of Working Time

These developments have important implications for labour utilisation and working time for it is in precisely these groups—doctors, nurses and midwives, and ancillary staff—that the basic problems of hospital work-time management occur and upon whom we shall henceforth concentrate. The fundamental fact about hospital working time is that representatives of all staff groups who may be needed in a ward must either be present or on call 24 hours a day, 365 days a year. Regular shift work is therefore a necessity and among full-time medical care staff there has developed a more or less universal system of alternative days and continuous night shifts. A pattern also found among many full-time ancillary workers, although permanent days with high overtime remain in the majority and rotating shifts are also common.

However, while 'patient contact' staff must be permanently available, their labour input need not be regular, either in quantity or quality. Hospital wards function according to the dictates of the 'in-patient day', under which all is subsumed to the medical rounds on weekday mornings and to operations and clinical tests which normally occur after midday. The demand for different types of staff therefore varies according to the time of day and week. Medical staff and trained nurses are predominantly required during the day, especially in the afternoon for clinical tasks, but there must also be a sufficient presence at night and weekends. On the other hand unqualified nurses and the various ancillary groups are employed mainly in the mornings, early afternoon and evenings for cleaning wards and patients and delivering meals and medication, only a skeleton cover being required at night.

In these circumstances part-time staff are of great utility to the hospital service, for they can be grafted onto the full-time complement of the main shift patterns as and when the in-patient day requires peaks of particular types of labour input. Thus there are fairly high proportions of part-time patient contact staff to cope with the routine duties of the morning and

111

evening periods (about a quarter in the case of nurses); comparatively few in the afternoon when full-time employees overlap and trained staff predominate; but among nurses in particular as much as half the night shift may be manned by part-timers working two or three nights a week. The reduction in part-time and unqualified staff may therefore pose serious problems regarding the maintenance of shift patterns.

Among both nurses and patient-based ancillary staff there is a strong correlation between the proportions receiving overtime payments and shift premia and this is directly related to the number of staff: the higher the level of employment, the greater the percentage within the shift pattern. This suggests that in times of labour shortage shift systems collapse back into the situation observed in the NBPI Reports, of extended days, high overtime and a large proportion of workers (nurses in 37% of acute hospitals in 1976) enduring split duties. This also appears to be the case with personnel service based ancillary staff, although only after a time lag of as much as a year. However there is again a different pattern for facility based manual workers where the work is quantity rather than time dependent. Here a fall in the number of full-time maintenance staff results in a rise in both overtime *and* shiftwork.

With the patterns of labour utilisation established, we are now in a postition to identify the chief constraints and possibilities for shorter working time. As the above analysis implies, the constraints principally revolve around the availability of staff, especially the provision of adequate cover by qualified nurses at nights and weekends. Current employment restrictions mean that there is now evidence of auxiliary nurses being left in charge of wards at these times, as qualified staff are stretched to the limit under the present organisation. Clearly in areas where SRNs are in very short supply the reduction in nurses' basic hours to 37½ may lead to further and perhaps dangerous de-skilling, otherwise there is a very real possibility that if badly managed, it would result in a large overtime leakage and the break up of shift systems.

Indeed this was the experience of male nursing staff (figures for women are unavailable) after the 40 hour week was introduced on 1st January 1972. At a time when the employment of male nurses was rising slightly, the year to April 1972 witnessed a 5% jump in the proportion working overtime, a fall in the percentage receiving shift premia and a half an hour rise in average overtime with still greater increases for certain groups. It was not until the Halsbury award revived employment again in 1975-76 that the reduction in the basic week was reflected by a fall in total hours from 43 to 41 and a return to levels of shift and overtime working similar to those early in the decade. (Source: NES).

112

Yet the constraints only appear daunting if the current shift pattern is seen as immutable. It is evident that in hospital wards the proportion of full-time, part-time, qualified, student and auxiliary nurses differs greatly according to the time of day and week. The permutation of these five variables is therefore the key to labour and hence capacity utilisation, and at present there is an obvious disequilibrium in the four-hour afternoon overlap. As it is justified for teaching purposes this is the time when qualified and student nurses reach their peak manning levels, but at which part-time staff, particularly auxiliaries, are at their lowest level. Consequently some nursing officers are considering a significant shortening of this overlap as well as the employment of more unqualified staff. However other progressive and adequately staffed authorities are already bargaining over the flexibility necessary for a thorough reorganisation of working time patterns, (including the permanent night shift), in the context of an overall reduction in total weekly hours. It is too early to forecast the general outcome, but there are clearly immense possibilities for shorter working time in hospital wards.

We say 'hospital wards' because the patient-based ancillary staff appear to come into this category rather than behaving as other ancillary groups. In the facility and service-based occupations shift systems and part-time employment are certainly important: however the fundamental working time issues are productivity schemes and the consequent threat to earnings now commonly derived from anything up to ten or more hours rostered overtime and bolstered by a collusive work culture. Although published evidence is scarce and dated, the experience of the early seventies is still revealing, as it suggests first, that incentive schemes are more prevalent among male and facility-based employees, than female domestic staff; and secondly, that they are effective in reducing the proportion of men and women working both overtime and shifts.

Whatever the potential earnings (and efficiency benefits, which may be considerable) it is the perceived threat to jobs and the loss of these payments, (particularly for men, who are relatively less well paid) that engenders distrust. Moreover this can only heighten fear and suspicion when the reform of long established work cultures, largely self-regulated by an elderly unskilled workforce, frequently involves root and branch upheaval. The re-introduction of productivity schemes, particularly when they entail combining several groups with previously differing practices, is therefore proving a severe test of labour relations in the NHS. This is true both for the largely in-bred management who had modern manpower planning and work organisation techniques thrust upon them during the last decade; and also for the trade unions, particularly NUPE and COHSE, who have only recently begun to exercise their potential power and in many cases now find themselves holding the initiative.

NATIONAL HEALTH SERVICE

CASE STUDY

Case Study 3

Introduction

The hospital utilised for this case study was chosen as representative of a medium sized general hospital located in an industrial town in South Wales. The original hospital buildings were opened in 1902. Since that time certain other buildings have been added, and the hospital is currently on the verge of a two year building programme which will increase the number of beds available from the present 310 to a total of 493.

With the exception of maternity, gynaecology and orthopaedics, the hospital offers the full range of normal hospital specialities. It is worthwhile noting, however, that the planned development of the hospital will result in a substantial increase in the number of geriatric beds.

The Area Health Authority which ultimately administers the hospital is divided into two Districts: North and South. The case study is situated in the South district which serves a population of just over 300,000.

Full access was given by management both at district AHA and at the hospital. During the time when the fieldwork was carried out two internal exercises were being run which related to working time organisation for the portering and nursing staffs. Since this generated rather more hard data than is generally available, we have concentrated on these two groups of staff for the purpose of this case study report.

It is significant that the management at the hospital expressed considerable interest and support for our research. They themselves acknowledged that in the next two to three years they would face increasing social pressure for shorter working time.* Hence, their own need to gather information as to the possibilities and types of working patterns which may provide shorter working time options for the future. It was also made clear to us that they were about to embark upon a manpower planning exercise spread over the next two years in readiness for the opening of the last stage of the hospital development which will bring about considerable additions to the number of beds available. If we add to these circumstances the tighter fiscal regime facing NHS adminstrators and manpower planners we can begin to see the parameters which will shape both absolute manning levels and the organisation of working time at the hospital.

* Particularly in the light of the agreement to implement a 37½ hour basic week for nurses by April 1981.

114

The Regulation and Terms and Conditions of Employment

As with all NHS establishments the hospital exhibited a variety of individual bargaining groups ranged across the medical, para-medical and ancillary staffs. In most cases groups within these broad categories were subject to national, e.g. Whitley Council agreements. However, some scope for interpretation at local level existed, although the extent to which this translated into formal bargaining on site depended very much on the strength and nature of the union organisation. It should be noted however that in part as a repercussion of the tightening of the NHS's finances and partly as a result of management's perceived need to exercise a greater control over the utilisation of labour, a number of bonus schemes have been negotiated locally. In the main these applied only to groups of ancillary workers. Whilst the fieldwork was being undertaken a bonus scheme was in fact being discussed with the porters, who as we shall see were resisting the prospect strongly. The rostering of individual groups, e.g. nurses and porters, although operating within the framework of national agreements clearly went through an informal system on site which was akin to a bargaining process. Occasionally if a difficulty arose and the union were more directly involved, then more formal bargaining about working time organisation resulted.

To all intents and purposes the hospital was 100% trade union organised, although no closed shop agreement existed. As may be expected NUPE and COHSE dominated, but a range of other unions had small pockets of membership on site. Although this multi-union situation has given rise to some tension between unions, notably COHSE and NUPE, industrial relations at the hospital are generally held to be good. Management at the hospital tend to attribute this to the size of the organisation and the relative informality with which relationships between management and unions are conducted. By comparison with the other major hospital in the area, situated some half a mile away, the industrial relations climate at the case study was healthy and relatively free of tension.

Present Working Time Patterns

Working time patterns at a hospital are determined by a complex mix of factors, but crucial to the basic structure which emerges are the following:

— the concept of the 'patient day'; this in effect ranges from about 6.00 a.m. to about 5.00 p.m. during these hours a whole range of inter-locking tasks involving ancillary, para-medical and medical staffs have to be filled.

— the optimisation of patient care further determines the priorities of these tasks—hence morning ward rounds, where consultants and

115

their teams review, diagnose and plan their involvement with patients have become institutionalised. These commence at around 8.30 a.m. and hence cleaning, washing and feeding patients all have to be carried out prior to this time.

— the need to provide a service 24 hours per day 365 days per year. Although some of the workload is foreseeable and some planning of hospital "throughput" is thus possible, it is impossible to fully pre-plan and schedule the utilisation of capital and labour resources.

At the case study hospital the sanctity of patient care and the importance of the patient day were stressed repeatedly to us. In this context, the reduction of working hours to 37½ per week was seen as posing a major difficulty.

Table 2.13 shows the manpower levels at the case study hospital, whilst Table 2.14 shows the basic hours of work for the main ancillary and para-medical groups investigated. It should be noted that porters and nurses are excluded from this latter table as they are treated in more detail later in this report.

Table 2.13   Manpower Structure at the Hospital

	Whole-time (w.t.)	Part-time (p.t.)	Total	Whole-time equivalent (w.t.e.)
Medical	27	6	33	32
Nursing	108	135	243	192
Ancillary	188	92	280	249
Professional and Technical	40	21	61	51
Administration	34	16	50	44
Total	397	270	667	572

It can be seen from Table 2.13 that part-time working accounts for around 40% of employment and is particularly significant amongst the nursing grades where it accounts for around 55% of total employment.

Table 2.14 shows that, in the main, ancillary staffs have a contractual 40 hour week spread normally over 5 days. Where a 7 day service is necessary, e.g. in catering, staff are rostered to provide the appropriate cover. Within the patterns displayed in Table 2.14 considerable use is made (with the exception of the Building, Engineering and Gardening Departments) of part-time workers (more details are given in the full report attached as an Appendix) to provide for the shortfall of staff during the ordinary weekdays and at the weekends.

Table 2.14 Basic Working Time Patterns Main Ancillary and
Para-Medical Groups (excluding Porters)

Laundry	40 hour × 5 day basic: 7.00 a.m.–3.30 p.m. Wash House 7.30 a.m.–4.00 p.m. Finishing Dept. 8.00 a.m.–4.00 p.m. Supervisory Staff
Gardening Department	40 hours × 5 day basic: 7.30 a.m.–4.00 p.m.
Domestic Services	40 hour × 5 day or 36 hours × 6 days Domestic Assistants 7.30 a.m.–1.30 p.m. (6 days) Ward Orderlies 7.30 a.m.–4.00 p.m. (5 days) Housekeepers 7.30 a.m.–4.00 p.m. (5 days)
Linen Services	40 hours × 5 days 8.00 a.m.–4.30 p.m.
Catering Services	40 hours × 5 days (NB 7 day service) Basic day shift commences 6.00 a.m. finishes 9.00 p.m. staff are rostered full-time for 40 hours within these times
Medical Records	37 hours × 5 days 8.45 a.m.–5.15 p.m. Monday–Thursday 8.45 a.m.–4.45 p.m. Friday
Building Department	40 hours × 5 days 8.00 a.m.–4.30 p.m.
Physiotherapy	36 hours × 5 days 9.00 a.m.–5.00 p.m.
Engineering Department	40 hours × 5 days 8.00 a.m.–4.30 p.m.

Shift Working

As already noted, the continuous nature of the hospital service necessitates
extensive shift working. At the case study only the Gardening and Linen
Service* Departments could be identified amongst the ancillary categories
as operating a basic day working pattern without some provision either for
weekend working or "on call" for nights.

* Prior to 1972 linen services worked on Saturday morning as part of the
basic weekly hours. They now work extra hard on Friday to provide
sufficient linen for the weekend.

Amongst the other departments the Laundry, Medical Records, Domestic Services, and Building Services did not operate shifts as such but all made provision for weekend working. The Catering Department, Engineering Department, Porters and Nurses all operated formal shift systems.

Overtime

Overtime worked varied amongst ancillary departments, where it made a significant impact among Porters, Kitchen Staff, Building, and Engineering shift workers. It appeared to be related to a) the male predominance in these grades; b) to the low basic pay received, and c) of the difficulties of attracting skilled labour (particularly in the case of Building, Engineering and Kitchen Staff). Where departments were predominantly female overtime tended to be very low—the laundry, where weekend working was common, was the only exception noted.

This being said, it was clear that the institutionalisation of overtime—it is contractual for both porters and shift engineering workers—has created both a major obstacle to the introduction of shorter working time and an indication of how potent such an exercise would be in employment creation terms. In these male dominated grades both management and workers are "locked in" to a high overtime system. The key in both cases would appear to be the low basic wages paid. For the worker this necessitates overtime in order to earn a living wage, whilst for the management it drastically reduces labour market appeal which can only be offset by the offer of additional earnings through overtime. *

We turn now to consider in more detail the working time organisation and potential for shorter working time amongst the Porters and Nursing staff at the hospital.

Structure of Nursing Employment and Working Patterns

The nursing establishment at the case study at the end of 1979 numbered 295 including 96 student nurses. It can be seen from the accompanying table that part-time employees represented some 42% of the total nursing stock (excluding student nurses who operate on a full-time basis).

* This is precisely what happens—management stress overtime availability in all of their recruitment literature for jobs in these departments.

Table 2.15 Distribution of Nursing Staff by Main Working Time Pattern

	Working Time	Number of Staff
Day Staff		
Full-Time	7.45–4.30	40
	12.30–9.00	40
Part-Time	7.45–2.15	63 (44 w.t.e.)
	2.30–9.00	
Night Staff		
Full-Time	8.45–7.50	18
Part-Time	8.45–7.50	67 (39.5 w.t.e.)

A typical shift pattern for full-time staff over a 7 day period might comprise 3 early shifts, 2 late shifts and 2 days off.* Nurses are rostered for 7 days irrespective of weekends, the roster being the responsibility of the individual ward sister. Typical part-time day shifts tend to produce either a 32 hour week of 4 days at 8 hours, or a 30 hour week of 5 days at 6 hours.

Although sickness absence is not held to be a severe problem amongst the nursing staff, there is a high annual turnover. In the main this was attributed to the normal training development of nurses and domestic commitments (only 2 male nurses are on the establishment, hence the staffing levels are particularly susceptible to changes in the individual's domestic circumstances).

There is a marked shortage of fully trained nursing staff available to the hospital. The majority of nurses are drawn from the immediate vicinity of the hospital or from nearby towns well served by local buses. This fairly strictly demarcated local labour market tends to accentuate the shortage of trained staff. There does not appear to be a shortage of untrained nursing auxiliaries (we were told that these were in almost unlimited supply). The distribution of nurses by level of training is shown in Table 2.16.

Table 2.16 Distribution of Nursing Staff by Qualifications

Grade	Number of Staff
Senior Nursing Officer	1
Nursing Officer	5
Sister, full-time	25
Sister, part-time	3 (1.6 w.t.e.)
Staff Nurses State Registered (SRN)	FT 19
Staff Nurses State Registered (SRN)	PT 32 (17.8)
State Enrolled Nurses (SEN's)	FT 28
State Enrolled Nurses (SEN's)	PT 29 (19.1)
Nursing Auxiliaries	FT 18
Nursing Auxiliaries	PT 64 (43.8)

* It would seem that attempts are made to provide days off on consecutive days, but there is no guarantee of this.

It can be seen that some 40% of the nursing establishment have at least an SRN qualification. However almost as many—36% have no formal qualifications at all, i.e. are nursing auxiliaries. Moreover, at *levels below ward sister* (where it is exceptional to find part-time working) it is apparent that the case study hospital is heavily dependent upon part-time nurses (55% of the whole-time equivalent workforce is made up of part-timers). Very little overtime appears to be worked amongst the nurses. As already stated, where male nurses are to be found in greater proportions, e.g. psychiatric hospitals overtime is a much more common feature of the working time pattern. In all probability this reflects an increased willingness on behalf of male nurses to work overtime deriving both from traditional male cultural perceptions of overtime and the slightly more pressing need for male wage maximisation. In all events there would appear to be no overtime constraints on shortening the working time of nurses at the case study hospital.

Since it has been agreed that a 37½ hour week for nursing staff shall be implemented on or before April 1981, Senior Nursing Officers and their staff have been engaged in analysing the impact of such a change in manpower and efficiency items. At the case study a preliminary exercise based upon the funded nursing establishment at 31st December 1979, has been carried out. This revealed that a reduction to 37½ hours per week was equivalent to a loss of some 13 nurses (trainees were excluded for the purposes of the calculation) made up on w.t.e. of 2 sisters, 3 staff nurses; 3 SEN's and 4 nursing auxiliaries (time lost in other grades amounted to 1 w.t.e. nurse).

As previously mentioned, however, the second part of the exercise being carried out at hospital level is an equivalent of how much, and where this prospective loss of nursing hours could be "absorbed" by what would in effect either involve increases in nursing "productivity" (i.e. fewer nursing hours achieving the same quantity and quality of service as currently) or reductions in the standard of patient care. Since this latter is generally deemed sacrosanct by both administrators and nurses alike, it follows that cost minimising strategies (an inevitability given the current regime of tight fiscal control on the NHS) are likely to lead to a concentration on the possibilities of increasing nursing "productivity". Whilst the precise limitations of such a strategy are not clear at present, a number of factors do stand out. These suggest that increases in nursing productivity in order to self finance shorter hours may be difficult to achieve without either damaging patient care, or creating further industrial relations difficulties both within the establishment and in terms of the relationship of this group with other, ancillary workers. Considering the rigidity of the labour market for qualified nursing staff, it may prove difficult to replace, for example, the 2 sisters and 3 staff nurses implied by the reduction to 37½ hours per week. Hence, even if additional cash was found to entirely replace the nursing hours lost by such a reduction, the supply of qualified staff may not be adequate. In such a situation the hospital could either lower the skill level of its replacement—by employing more SEN's, or, attempt to plug the gap by employing more part-time trained nurses (the fact that 3 sisters at the case study worked part-time suggests that such a practice is already being found necessary to fill certain key skilled posts). The recent Clegg award which gave fairly substantial increases to ward sisters may make some impact here, but it must be recognised that unless the supply of well qualified nurses improves, attempts to replace lost, skilled nursing hours are likely to be heavily constrained, with, it would seem, damaging consequences for patient care.

The Porters' Working Patterns and Reduced Working Time Potential

The portering system at the hospital as will be seen is strongly hierarchical. This in itself is not unusual but would appear to give rise to some unusual effects in terms of effective working time.

There are thirty one porters at the case study site split into four main groupings with a head porter. The top tier are chargehand porters who operate at the gate. Below these are found lodge porters. The next tier are shift porters and the bottom group which comprises just over half of the total numbers of porters, are distributed amongst a number of general portering functions.

The porters are 100% trade union organised with the upper tiers tending to belong to COHSE, whilst the lower tier tend to favour NUPE.

The accompanying table details the type of shift operated together with the length of service and age of the porters. It can be seen that length of service is an important determinant insofar as upward mobility is concerned but is also directly correlated with the incidence of days lost through sickness or other forms of absence.

Currently the Management Services Team are studying the portering system at the hospital since unit costs are said to be higher for porters than at any other hospital in the country.* Over the last year days lost total some 24% of days available; at the same time, as can also be seen from the accompanying table, very high levels of overtime are worked. This overtime is of a contractual nature and, as the head porter stated, is in fact used as a recruitment tactic. This latter ploy is necessary in view of the low basic rate.

* Detailed inter-hospital cost comparison show this to be the case.

121

Table 2.17   Porters by Shift, Age, Service, Basic Rate and Sickness

PORTER	Age	Service years	Shift	Basic £	Sick Days April 1978- April 1979
Head	42	6	Rotary	49.22	53
Gate (CH)	41	13	Rotary	43.42	52
Gate (CH)	49	18	Rotary	43.42	52
Gate (CH)	63	17	Rotary	43.42	130
Gate (CH)	31	10	Rotary	42.78	48
Lodge	25	7	Rotary	42.78	
Lodge	38	6	Rotary	42.78	3
Lodge	39	9	Rotary	42.78	39
Shift	34	5	ALT	42.18	91
Shift	30	5	ALT	42.18	33
Shift	25	4	ALT	42.13	9
Shift	44	5	ALT	42.18	1
Pharmacy	28	10	8-5	42.78	2
Laundry	31	7	8-4.30	42.78	41
Laundry	20	4	8-4.30	42.78	2
General	33	11	8-4.30	42.18	13
General	22	2	8-5	42.18	13
General	51	0.4	8-4.30	42.18	
General	17	0.4	8-4.30	42.18	
Pool	56	3	8-4.30	42.18	9
Pool	20	1	8-4.30	42.18	15
Pool	22	0.3	8-4.30	42.18	
Pool	59	0.1	8-4.30	42.18	
Incinerator	56	3	8-4.30	42.18	18
Eye Theatre	22	4	8-5	42.18	52
Stores	52	0.5	8-4.30	42.78	
Theatre	20	0.4	8-4.30	42.18	
Night	51	0.1	10-6	49.05	
Mortuary	52	2	8.30-5	43.42	46
Mortuary	21	0.1	8.30-5	43.42	

There are grounds to suspect that amongst the upper tiers of the group, sickness absence is operated on a collusive basis to ensure that cover is provided by a workmate who is on a rest day or a day off, thereby attracting an extra premium payment to provide the cover. The degree of tension that this brings about can be witnessed by one particular recent event, whereby a senior porter was dismissed for fraudulent time keeping (involving leaving his post in the early hours of the morning). In addition, management attempts to "buy out" contractual overtime by means of a bonus system have been strongly resisted by NUPE porters who allegedly prefer high levels of rostered overtime. According to the head porter contractual overtime is seen to be somehow safe although not guaranteed. Whereas a bonus scheme is viewed with suspicion as a possible means of reducing manning.*

There is no doubt that the hospital is in a particularly difficult situation here since the high levels of contractural overtime are impinging upon the basic utilisation of working time and maybe contributing to the high levels of days absent. At the same time the very low basic pay is wholly underpinning these repercussions. The head porter estimated that the removal of overtime would create a demand for ten extra porters. In the last six years the number of staff has increased from twenty six to thirty one but during that time overtime has been either stable or has increased. In particular in the last three years increasing holiday entitlement has not lead to extra staff but has led to increased overtime. It is not known to what extent increased overtime working has also formed part of a collective bargaining response to the restraints of incomes policy.

The head porter was critical of the general position of his staff not simply from the point of view of low pay but also because of the lack of training facilities, the lack of proper induction training, the fact that porters were the last in line as far as communication was concerned and their general overall low status.

In view of this it is hardly surprising that the portering system draws upon the lower end of the local labour market and receives problems of low motivation as a result. One possible unquantified benefit from reduced working time for porters may be an enhanced supply of labour of better quality.

As can be seen from the accompanying table, overtime tends to be rostered for porters and anywhere between eight and sixteen hours a week is common. Higher levels of overtime tend to be associated with the upper levels within the hierarchy. Although there are some exceptions to this, e.g. the Incinerator Porter works a seventy hour week made up of ten hours a day for seven days without breaks. In view of this exceptionally high level of contractual overtime and the fact that 25% of effective working days in any one year are being reduced through absence, it is difficult to believe that improved utilisation through shorter working time would not ultimately prove cost effective. What the case study has established so far are the institutional constraints built up through the maintenance of a grossly underpaid service and the rigidity of the collective response from the workforce which key sectors at least have evolved, i.e. the complex system of "alternative" work time patterns to secure a living wage.

* Supported by the NUPE Divisional Officer.

Table 2.18 Typical Two-Week Roster for Various Grades of Porter

	Sun.	Mon.	Tues.	Wed.	Thurs.	Fri.	Sat.	Sun.	Mon.	Tues.	Wed.	Thurs.	Fri.	Sat.
Shift	RD	1-9.30	1-9.30	1-9.30	1-10	1-10	2-10 (51.5)	2-10	7.15-3.15	7.15-3.15	7.15-3.15	7.15-3.15	1-10	2-10 (56)
Shift	2-10	7.15-3.15	7.15-3.15	7.15-3.15	7.15-3.15	7.15-3.15	7-1 (54)	RD	1-9.30	1-9.30	1-9.30	1-10	1-10	7-1 (49.5)
Pharmacy	RD	8.30-5.00	8.30-5.00	8.30-5.00	8.30-5.00	9.30-5.00	8-2 (53.5)	7-2	8.30-5.00	8.30-7.30	8.30-5.00	8.30-5.00	8.30-5.00	8-7 (58)
Laundry	RD	8-4.30	8-4.30	8-4.30	8-4.30	8-8	8-1 (51)	8-1	8-4.30	8-4.30	8-4.30	8-4.30	8-7.30	8-1 (55.5)
Pool	RD	8-4.30	8-4.30	8-4.30	8-4.30	8-4.30	7-1 (48.5)	8-1	8-4.30	8-4.30	8-4.30	8-4.30	8-4.30	7-1 (53.5)
General	8-1	8-4.30	8-4.30	8-4.30	8-4.30	8-4.30	OD (47.5)	8-1	8-4.30	8-4.30	8-4.30	8-4.30	8-4.30	OD (47.5)

KEY: RD = REST DAY   OD = DAY OFF   ( ) = TOTAL WEEKLY HOURS

124

Case Study 3

Summary of Key Points Emerging

— At the hospital studied management and trade unions were facing a number of conflicting pressures which held significant implications for working time organisation. Primarily, as with all NHS establishments, the need to reverse assumptions with regard to the future availability of exchequer resources was apparent. However, at the case study this went hand in hand with a planned expansion of capacity which was going ahead.

— As a result of this fiscal constraint management had for some time been investigating the possibility of increasing the efficiency of labour utilisation, for example, substituting bonus schemes for overtime wherever possible amongst ancillary staffs. Such a move was meeting strong resistance from the portering staff at the time of the study.

— High overtime rates were noted amongst, the portering, kitchen staff and building and engineering workers. As such it appeared strongly sexually differentiated—women working very little overtime; and was linked both to low basic pay and to external labour market shortages in the case of skilled kitchen staff and building and engineering craftsmen.

— Critical *external* labour market shortages were reported for all types of skilled workers. The solutions adopted varied from explicit attempts at improving *external* competitiveness, e.g. in recruitment literature for the senior porters and ancillary craftsmen the availability of contractual overtime was stressed, to implicit attempts to improve the *internal* labour market via the reallocation of non-skilled tasks from Key skilled workers or through the offer of a variety of part-time working forms—particularly important for nurses.

— Working time organisation was largely determined by the structure of the 'patient day' here a mixture of 'custom and practice' heavily underpinned by the 'pecking order' of the medical hierarchy contrived to establish fixed and interlocking patterns of work throughout the day. Additionally, the quality of patient care was held to be sacrosanct.

— Implementation of the 37½ hour basic week for nurses was being actively discussed during the study. At senior management level the 'absorption' strategy favoured involved reducing the overlap time between the morning and afternoon shifts, effectively therefore attempting to increase nursing productivity. This was seen at ward level as a threat to the quality of patient care. The possibility of increasing employment to cover the hours lost was however, equally constrained by the fiscal control exercised through expenditure cutbacks and, for trained nurses, the *external* labour market shortage.

Chapter 7   The Transport Industry: Industry and a Public Service
            Agreement

INDUSTRY STUDY

Road Passenger Transport

The fuller unpublished study is divided into six main sections which are
summarised below, with special emphasis on those features most relevant
to the general discussion on working time in several industries.

Section I looks at *data sources* and finds that the main one is the annual
HMSO publication, *Transport Statistics, Great Britain;* but recent issues of
this contain only one tri-partite table on employment in the industry, and
nothing at all on working time. For statistics on employment, earnings and
hours of work one must resort to the relevant Department of Employment
publications which cover all industries. Other particularly useful sources of
data on the road passenger transport industry are the annual reports of the
Road Transport Industry Training Board (RTITB)—for various employment statistics—and an *ACAS* Report (No. 16), *Industrial Relations in the
Coaching Industry* (1978).

Differences of scope and coverage cause some problems when using the
available statistics; and there are several gaps, notably and unfortunately
on some aspects of working time, such as the shift systems in use and the
extent of regular overtime working; and on the distinction between the bus
and coaching sectors of the industry.

Section II considers those aspects of the *industry's organisation and
structure* which are thought most pertinent to the discussion on working
time.

It is noted firstly that road passenger transport is a declining industry; that,
for example, total users' expenditure on buses and coaches fell from being
equivalent to 1% of GDP in 1967 to being equivalent to 0.85% in 1978:
that the share of buses and coaches in total passenger kilometres travelled
has fallen from 41% in 1954, to 14% in 1970, to 11% in 1978—this decline
must be set against a smaller decline for travel by rail, and an increase in
the share of private road transport from 39% in 1954 (smaller than the
share of buses and coaches), to 76% in 1970, to 81% in 1978 (11 times the
share of buses and coaches).

In spite of this substantial decline in the supply of and demand for public
road passenger transport, the industry's *capital assets* i.e. mainly buses and
coaches, have remained relatively constant at around 73,000 vehicles over

126

the last decade, although there was something of a peak from 1974-76, when numbers rose temporarily above 76,000. However, within this constant total there has been a decline in the number of double-deck buses matched by a rise in the number of single-deck buses (47,024 out of 73,699 buses and coaches were single-deckers at the end of 1978).

This change in the predominant type of vehicle suggests a reasonable renewal rate for the capital stock, and this proves to be the case. There has, in fact, been a continuing and constant acquisition of new vehicles, averaging about 6,000 per year over the last 10 years. As a result, over 60% of public service vehicles registered in 1978 were less than eight years old, and 30% were less than four years old.

The capital renewal of the industry has been facilitated since the late 1960s, it can be suggested, by the 'new bus grant' paid direct from central government and providing 50% of the cost of new vehicles for use on stage services. However, the changing character of the vehicle stock is also associated with the increased use of one-man operated buses, and with the accompanying decline in the number of conductors.

It is seen from data analysing supply of bus and coach services by *type of operator* that the decline of the industry is concentrated in the larger, publicly-owned sector which has existed in its present form since the implementation of the 1968 Transport Act: in contrast the private sector, which consists of about 6,000 mainly very small concerns, has flourished. While private operators accounted for 5.5% of passenger journeys in 1968, compared with, for example, the 28.8% of the National Bus Company (NBC) and the 28.4% of the Passenger Transport Executives (PTEs), by 1978 they accounted for 10.5% of passenger journeys with the percentages of the NBC and PTEs having dropped to 25.0 and 27.5 respectively. However, the private operators also accounted for an increasing proportion of vehicle stock, from 30.0% in 1968 to 38.7% in 1978: these latter percentages related to the proportions of passenger journeys suggest that the increasing role of the private operators may actually result in decreasing capital efficiency in the industry.

The growth of the private operators as a group is shown to be clearly associated with the *growing demand for contract and private hire services,* both types of service where they dominate (84.1% of private hire and 77.0% of contract journeys were accounted for by private operators in 1978). Contract and private hire journeys as a proportion of the total rose from 2.0% in 1959, to 3.8% in 1968, to 8.7% in 1978: and in spite of a declining total, the absolute number of such journeys rose from 393 million in 1968 to 636 million in 1978. In contrast the absolute number of stage service journeys fell from 9,735 million in 1968 to 6,596 million in 1978 and the percentage of the total over the same period fell from 95.1 to 90.3%.

Price movements for the services of the road passenger transport industry can be seen to be both a cause of and a result of declining demand—from the end of 1973 to the end of 1979 the stage service fare index for all operators rose by more than 20 percentage points more than the transport and vehicles element of the General Index of Retail Prices which in turn rose by more than 20 percentage points more than the all-items GIRP. Given that there is a limit, partly centrally and locally determined, to cuts in local stage services, it is apparent that rising fuel and labour costs coupled with falling passenger numbers will be met by higher fares, which further reduces the number of passengers.

It is concluded from the preceding description of certain aspects of the industry: that owing to the structure of the industry and its varied types of service, the 'employment situation' must be diverse: that employment morale and prospects must be affected by the declining status of the industry: and that central and local government financial support has enabled the re-equipment of the industry to take place to the benefit of employees.

Section III considers certain aspects of employment in the industry. It can be seen both from the Department of Employment's statistics and from the figures collected on a slightly different basis by the Department of Transport that *total employment* in road passenger transport fell significantly between 1968 and 1978: on the latter basis the drop was from 253 thousand to 211 thousand. Moreover, the decline was a steady one with only occasional years going against the falling trend, 1975 being the notable recent one.

However, upon further analysis it is discovered that the decline is almost entirely due to the drop in the number of conductors from nearly 70,000 in 1968 to 25,000 at the end of 1978, the other categories of employment having remained remarkably stable over the decade. The steep decline in the number of conductors (and conductresses) must be largely the result of, but possibly also a contributory factor to, the adoption of large single-deck one-man operated buses on many routes, although there is a lack of statistics on this aspect. The decline in demand for local stage services vis-a-vis other types of service, which are less likely to require conductors, must also be relevant.

There is an unusually large and growing proportion of part-time males in the industry (4.7% in 1977), possibly because of the requirements of peak-hour loading on services, and a large but unknown number of casual

128

workers, the result of the seasonal nature of some types of coach services. Both these types of supplementary labour may affect the amount of overtime worked by regular employees at times of heavy demand.

It is observed that the number of employees of each of the public sector *operators* has fallen over the ten years since 1968, while the number of employees of private operators has risen from 28½ thousand to 34½ thousand. The growth of employment in the private sector of the industry is obviously consistent with the increasing proportion of passenger journeys and vehicles accounted for by the sector.

The relationship between employment in the industry and *unemployment* and *vacancies* for the most relevant occupational group is found to be not clear, but it is apparent that labour turnover has been high over recent years, up to 23.7% in 1972-73 according to RTITB data, except in 1975-76 when employment rose and turnover fell to 17.7%. Many of the public sector operators, including in particular the PTEs, have recorded problems of recruitment and turnover in their annual reports.

Section IV is concerned with the *bargaining structure* of the industry, which is severely fragmented, for historical and structural reasons. On the employee side the main dominant union is the TGWU but it has negotiating rights concentrated in the publicly-owned sector but varying from area to area and from operator to operator: the unions' role in the private sector is limited. The employers, on the other hand, have several organisations, some more influential for negotiating purposes than others.

There are two *national* bargaining *organisations*, the National Joint Council for the Road Transport Industry (NJIC), and the National Council for the Omnibus Industry (NCOI), the former being more important for stage service employees. Separate negotiations are held with the London Transport Executive (LTE) for London bus employees.

The national negotiating bodies cover only a proportion of employees but their agreements are copied or noted by other negotiating groups at regional and local level.

Nevertheless it is obvious that the bargaining process is a particularly complex one in road passenger transport and one which must result in considerable variations in wage rates and conditions of employment, even within the public sector, and even for stage carriage drivers within that sector.

Section V deals with *pay and labour costs*, in the light of the fragmented bargaining structure already described.

Considering the basic rates fixed by the three major agreements (LTE, NJIC, NCOI), it is observed that the margin between the rates of drivers and conductors has widened significantly over the last decade, partly as a result of additional payments to one-man-operators but apparent even in the mid-1960s.

The basic rate for LTE drivers and conductors is shown to have been consistently higher than those for NJIC and NCOI employees. However, substantial increases for all three groups were agreed in 1975 and these were reflected in the higher level of employment and lower turnover rate already noted.

Again, with regard to *earnings,* LTE drivers and conductors are found to have been better off than the other two groups, who have in turn been better off than the average for adult manual men but by a relatively small margin: only in 1975 was this margin widened. This observation holds good when looking at industrial data (which includes employees outside the scope of the national negotiating bodies) as well as at figures by collective agreements.

An occupational analysis shows that the average weekly earnings of bus and coach drivers were higher in 1979 at £87.3 than those of train drivers (£86.0) or heavy goods drivers (£84.2), but that these relatively high earnings were achieved by long hours, and that in fact, average hourly earnings at 170.1p were below those of train drivers (193.5p) and even below those of all adult manual men (172.8p).

New Earnings Survey (NES) data shows that the *make-up of pay* is reasonably similar for employees under the NJIC and NCOI agreements, but rather different for LTE employees. For instance, in April, 1979 *overtime* formed a significantly lower proportion of total average earnings for LTE employees (13.5%) than for NJIC employees (24.1%) or NCOI employees (20.6%). The proportion of employees receiving overtime pay was also lower—77.2 for LTE, 86.8% for NJIC and 83.2% for NCOI.

Even if one looks only at those employees who received overtime pay in the survey period in 1979, one finds that such pay formed a lower proportion of total gross average earnings for LTE (16.9%) than for NJIC (26.7%) or NCOI (23.9%) employees.

Again PBR etc. payments formed a lower proportion of total gross average earnings in 1979 for LTE employees (4.2%) than for NJIC (9.3%) or NCOI (7.4%) employees. On the other hand, 100.0 of LTE employees received PBR etc. payments compared with 65.3% of NJIC employees and

44.9% of NCOI employees. So if one looks at only those employees who received such payments one finds a much larger discrepancy in the proportions of total average earnings—4.2% for LTE, 14.3% for NJIC, 16.5% for NCOI.

In contrast, *shift etc. premium* payments form a larger proportion of total average earnings for LTE employees (11.3%) than for NJIC (5.8%) or NCOI (5.14%). But again a much higher proportion of LTE employees receive shift payments (92.1%) compared with NJIC (58.9%) or NCOI (74.4%) employees. The consequence of this is that when one looks at only those employees who received shift payments in the survey period one finds a change in the pattern of the proportion of earnings formed by such payments—only 13.5% for LTE employees, but 22.3% for NCOI employees and a massive 25.3% for NJIC employees.

In spite of the variations in the subtractions from total gross average earnings listed above the proportion of earnings formed by 'all others' pay (mainly basic pay, includes London allowances where applicable) are not greatly dissimilar between the three agreements—in 1978 the percentages were in fact 68.2% of LTE, 65.3% for NJIC and 66.4% for NCOI.

The patterns described above have not changed greatly over the period covered. The main development being the large increase in the weight of shift (unsocial hours) payments for LTE employees between 1974 and 1975, as a result of the 1975 agreement.

Section VI draws together the preceding observations and arguments, before looking at the published data on *working time,* as follows:

In terms of demand for services, the industry has been in decline since the early 1950s. However, investment on a substantial scale has taken place and the capital stock is relatively new—largely because of government (central and local) financial support, to independent as well as the publicly owned operators. Thus technological innovation (mainly through one-man operated buses; and computerised time-tabling) has been facilitated.

Total employment in the industry has fallen substantially over the last 20 years, but this decrease corresponds to the reduction in the number of conductors as one-man operation has been introduced: the numbers of drivers, and of administrative staff, have remained roughly constant. In most years there have been vacancies for drivers and skilled maintenance men; and in some recent years, e.g. 1974-75 severe shortages, which have affected services, have developed. Labour turnover appears to be relatively high.

Earnings for the industry have generally been slightly above the average for

131

adult male manual workers, but only when the differential has been increased, as in 1975, has there been an improvement in the employment situation.

Earnings have probably been lower than they might have been, partly because of the severely fragmented bargaining structure, even in the publicly-owned sector. Obviously, such fragmentation affects agreed working hours, overtime rates and shift premia, as well as basic rates.

It appears that the level of earnings in the industry results from a relatively low basic rate combined with relatively long total working hours. This is particularly true for provincial bus and coach drivers, less true of LTE employees, whose somewhat higher earnings result from higher basic rates and shift premia for shorter total working hours.

Most of the available data on working hours comes from the main agreements and from the NES. Average *normal basic hours* in road passenger transport have declined from 41.0 in 1972 to 40.4 in 1978 and 40.5 in 1979, but have nevertheless been consistently above the average for the whole transport and communications industry, and the average for all industries and services.

Average *overtime* worked has over recent years been generally higher at between 7.5 and 9.7 hours per week for road passenger transport than the average for all manual men which has varied between 5.4 and 6.5 hours per week. Looking at the collective agreements, more overtime hours have generally been worked by NJIC and NCOI employees than by LTE employees: in April 1979 overtime hours for the three groups were 11.9, 10.5 and 4.8 respectively.

The pattern in agreed basic weekly hours as laid down by the collective agreements is summarised as follows:

In 1950 they provided for a 44 hour, 6 day week; in 1966 agreement was reached for a 40 hour, 5 day week and these working hours still prevail. Between 1950 and 1966 there were various combinations of, for instance, 84 hours or 88 hours, 11 day fortnights; 42 hour, 6 day weeks. But the standard 40 hour, 5 shift week has prevailed for a 13 year period from 1966.

Overtime rates, shift premia and holiday entitlements over the past 20 years are described and found to be fairly average among manual workers.

It is now possible to attempt to draw some conclusions on working time with reference to employment and earnings in the road passenger transport

132

industry. A distinction should first be made between working time for LTE road transport employees and those in the provinces, in consequence of which there are differences in earnings. There is also a distinction, although a less clear one, between bus and services and the coaching activities of operators; the conclusions here relate particularly to stage carrier services but are not irrelevant to coaching services, particularly to the coaching services of the public sector operators.

Basic working hours are a standard 40 hours throughout the industry, this is now slightly above average for all manual workers.

However, becasue of the nature of the service provided a substantial proportion of employees work a shift system of one sort or another. The method of remuneration for shift-working is by unsocial hours payment (LTE) or shift allowance (other agreements). A higher basic rate plus substantial unsocial hours payments mean that LTE employees have higher earnings than other employees in the industry for a shorter working week. Nevertheless there have been employment shortages in London, but these appear to have been catered for through service reductions rather than through increased overtime.

Overtime working is considerable for the industry as a whole but more so for non-LTE employees: and outside London it would appear that labour shortages have often resulted in more overtime being worked by existing employees.

Unsocial hours and compulsory overtime can be either an advantage or a disadvantage to recruitment dependent on the compensation offered. For LTE employees unsocial hours working might be said to have been turned to their financial advantage. For other employees this is not obviously the case: for most overtime must be necessary in order to receive reasonable earnings.

The fragmented bargaining situation in the industry must have affected earnings levels: only in 1975 does there appear to have been any concerted action in spite of the fact that the TGWU is the dominant union in all sectors.

Although mainly in the public sector, the industry does not provide secure jobs: the number of conductors has declined substantially; and local bus services have been reduced at the expense of stage service drivers who may find even less secure jobs in the private sector.

Thus public road passenger transport is an example of an industry where working time is relatively long and often irregular, seasonally, from week

133

to week, or from day to day. Shiftwork is necessary but is not on the fixed or rotating systems of manufacturing industry and is compensated for by unsocial hours payments or shift allowances. It is difficult to see how irregular hours could be avoided for a substantial proportion of employees at least.

PUBLIC SERVICES AGREEMENT

CASE STUDY

Case Study 4 Reduced Working Time amongst Post Office Engineers

Introduction

Although not specifically covered by the individual sectors selected for the project, the example of the agreement concluded between the Post Office and the Post Office Engineering Union (POEU) is particularly apposite as an illustration of how working time may be reduced in a public service industry. For this reason we include this brief description of the agreement.

Background to the Agreement

It has traditionally been held by the Post Office Engineering Union (POEU) that the hours of work of its membership should be broadly comparable to those worked in other industries. However, it was clear by the start of the 1970s that this comparison had moved adversely both *externally* (e.g. the NES for 1969 showed that 41.5% of all workers had a basic working week of 38 hours or less) and *internally* since elsewhere in the Post Office clerical, executive and supervisory grades had a working week some 2½ hours less than the average POEU member. Secondly, the productivity increase of the engineers was not in doubt and thirdly, it was clear that technological change would both greatly add to that productivity whilst at the same time creating job displacement pressure.

The claim for a shorter working week was first submitted in 1972 and became bogged down by the Post Office's insistence that any hours reduction would have to be paid for by productivity increases. However, since it was the standard practice in nationalised industries to pass 50% of the benefits of any productivity increase to the consumer, the union would have to agree to a productivity improvement at least twice as much as that which by itself would have compensated for the reduction in hours.

Ultimately the frustration with this ruling together with an increasing awareness amongst the membership of the potential impact of new technology led to unofficial action in a number of POEU branches. An inquiry chaired by Lord McCarthy broke the deadlock by suggesting that an hours reduction should be granted provided it could be shown to have nil cost (in other words, it merely had to pay for itself). Agreement was reached in September 1978 on the broad form in which such a reduction could be arranged to ensure nil cost.

The agreement had three principle objectives:

a)   no loss of cover in services to the public, and where possible an improvement;

b)   no increase in overtime or manpower above planned levels;

c)   no loss of output per man averaged over all POEU grades with the Telecommunications and Postal Businesses each treated separately.

The actual reduction of some 2½ hours per week could be achieved in one of the following ways:

1)   by staff *finishing* half an hour earlier per day, with a complementary number of staff *starting* half an hour later in the morning but finishing at the normal time;

2)   by scheduling 75 hours on either 8 or 9 days excluding weekends in any two week period (the 8 or 9 day fortnight) the working day to fall between 7.15 a.m. and 6.15 p.m., hours scheduled in any full working day to be not less than 7½.

3)   by staff taking one full day off in every 15 days.

The restrictions imposed by the agreement were that no more than 40% of staff were to be allowed to exercise option (2).

The agreement was implemented in December 1978 and the POEU has carried out some limited monitoring of its operation. Out of a sample of 20% of engineering branches carried out at the start of the agreement:

—   only one branch reported that all of its membership had chosen (1)—referred to as the "fall-back" option by the union;

—   apart from this branch, the percentage of members who wished to work 8 or 9 day fortnights or 1 day off in 15 day working varied widely form area to area.

—   seasonal variation in attendance patterns was the most popular form of local agreement. This did not always apply to the whole branch, with some groups maintaining 8 or 9 day fortnights all year round.

—   on average the branches from which questionnaires were received attained 40.1% access to an 8 or 9 day fortnight or 1 in 15 day working

— the one day off in 15 days option was selected by 18% of respondent branches, while about 30% of respondent branches had the whole branch on 8 or 9 day fortnights during 20 weeks of the summer

— the same duty groups were not always accorded the same access to 8 or 9 day fortnights or 1 in 15 day working across different branches due to different management conceptions of the potential benefits to them of the longer day in the 8 or 9 day or 1 in 15 patterns.

INDUSTRY STUDY

Introduction

1.   Industrial Performance in the 1970s

Throughout it is important to distinguish between the "electric" group of industries and the "electronics" group. The "electric" industries after an advance in some sectors in the early 1970s show no overall growth trend. Some of the weakness here directly reflects decline in other industries (thus, electric equipment for vehicles advanced strongly in 1972-73 but has more recently been operating some 25% or more below those peaks). The "electronics" industries have advanced output by almost 40% over the decade (though telecommunications equipment, "telegraph and telephone apparatus" is the official title, has shown marked decline since the mid-1970s). Both sets of industries are markedly cyclical (though the timing of consumer orientated industries may not coincide with that of capital goods manufacturers).

Throughout the decade it is the "electric" industries that have had a consistently large export surplus (the official figures for "principal products" show a surplus of over £500 million p.a. from 1976 to 1978). The "electronics" industries have barely produced an overall balance of imports and exports in depression years, and in years of high consumer spending run large deficits (1973-74 and 1978-9); this reflects the market weakness of consumer electronics. Generally the consumer-orientated industries of both parts of electrical engineering have a weak international trade performance and are subject to high and rising import penetration; the capital goods industries have performed more strongly.

2.   Prospects

This is a period of turbulence and uncertainty. The capital expenditure of the industries concerned rose fairly strongly to 1978 (about 50% higher than in the 1975-6 trough), but has since been falling again. Import penetration rose markedly in some sectors in 1978-9, from already high levels. The upward shift in the sterling exchange rate has contributed to worsening comparative costs. New technology and new products pose difficult questions of the timing and scale of new investment and re-organisation (e.g. in telecommunications).

3. Employment

Employment levels and the occupational balance of the industries have been quite markedly affected, though a near stabilisation of employment overall has emerged after the 1975-6 trough. Displacement of labour has particularly concentrated on female manual labour, and the same category has been most exposed to cyclical variations (with e.g. large scale part-time labour recruitment in 1973-4 and its displacement in 1975-6). A 1979 comparison with 1973 (which may be broadly similar in terms of cyclical timing) shows over 50,000 fewer female manual jobs (a fall of over 20%). Technological changes (reducing manipulative assembly work) and areas of competitive weakness have both played a part in this. Male manual employment includes a high proportion of skilled workers (over 40% of the adult male production workers); there has been a more limited fall in male manual employment (averaging 1% p.a. from 1973 to 1979). Non-manual employment has been very stable overall. Consequently, as the total labour force has fallen—in both electric and electronic industries—labour productivity has risen, most notably in electronics (by nearly 50% in the decade).

4. Working Time

Many of the characteristics of working time are linked to wider patterns and agreements embracing the engineering industries as a whole. The substantial increase in part-time female employment in the early 1970s was rapidly reversed. The basic week of full-time workers has not varied over the decade, and shift working has in the main tended to decrease (it mainly affects manual men). Overtime levels were comparatively high in 1979, and overtime was worked not only by around 60% of male manual workers but by some 30% of non-manual males. These overtime levels co-exist with high absenteeism in some industries in the sector. But there is some cyclicality in overtime levels, and 1979 was a year of fairly high activity (interrupted by major disputes).

Definition of Sector

The electrical engineering industries as a whole (Order IX) have been helpfully analysed by official sources in ways that bring out the significant differences between electronics and electric industries (cf. especially Trade and Industry, 22 September 1978 and 20 April 1979). "Electric" covers: electrical machinery (MLH 361), insulated wires and cables (362); domestic electrical appliances (368) and "other electrical" (369). "Electronic" covers: telegraph and telephone apparatus (363), radio and electrical components (364), broadcast receiving and sound reproducing equipment (365), electronic computers (366), and electronic capital goods (367).

The Electrical Engineering Sector: Aspects of Size and Structure

In 1970 the electrical engineering industries in Britain employed 815,000 workers, one tenth of the total in manufacturing. At the end of the decade their employment had fallen to slightly less than three quarters of a million (a slightly higher share, 10½ % of the manufacturing total); their output accounted for about 7% of the total. The contrast gives some indication of the labour intensity of much of the sector's activity.

Large multi-product firms play an important part in the sector. The giant GEC, the product of earlier mergers of the largest conglomerates, started the decade with over 200,000 employees in the UK (roughly one quarter of the sector's total) but by the later 1970s rationalisation had reduced this by some 50,000. It is heavily export-orientated (in 1977 exports of over £520,000,000 from the UK represented about a third of its UK turnover). Another main enterprise employing just under a tenth of the total British employment in electrical engineering is Lucas, with 79,000 employees in 1970 (scaled down by ten thousand by 1977), and 1977 exports of £140 million representing over a quarter of its UK turnover (heavily concentrated on components for the vehicle and aircraft industry). Both these companies have a wide range of multi-national operations.

The market structure for most of the industry is best described as oligopolistic. An official analysis of product concentration analysed the "5 firm concentration ratios"* of 30 electrical engineering product groups; only 4 of these had concentration ratios of less than 60%, 18 had ratios between 60% and 89%, and only 8 had ratios of 90% or more. In terms of competition it has to be remembered that these ratios relate only to sales based on UK production; imports are a major force in many product groups (a point that is examined subsequently).

The large multi-product firms extend their product range over most of the sector. But for a number of statistical and analytical purposes it is important to distinguish between the electrical and the electronic industries. In both output and employment terms the electronics industries are somewhat larger than the electric industries; by the late 1970s electronics probably accounted for about 56% of the output of the total electrical engineering sector.

* Share of UK manufacturers' sales accounted for by the five largest producers in any particular product group. The figures are for 1975; no substantial change had occurred since 1968 (see Trade and Industry, 20 April 1979).

Within these industries the size structure of establishments is such that a high proportion of employment is concentrated on large establishments. However, this does show some important variations as between major electronics industries:

Table 2.19 Major Electronics Industries: Employment by Establishment Size (percentage of total employees)

Establishment Size (No.)	11–99 employees	100–499 employees	500 + employees
Telephone apparatus etc.	4.8%	15.9%	79.3%
Radio and electronic components	13.3%	34.0%	52.9%
Radio, radar, and electronic capital goods	12.8%	25.2%	62.0%

Source: Census of Production.

It is clear that "telephone apparatus etc." has been far more concentrated in large establishments than the "electronic components" industry, with electronic capital goods occupying an intermediate position. "Components" have been one of the most rapidly growing parts of the electronics sector, whereas "telephone apparatus" has experienced major declines. So it is sensible to assume some shift in employment terms towards the "medium" sized establishment. In some cases the nature of local labour markets may restrain the further growth of the large establishments.

Output, Productivity, Competitiveness

The distinction between electric and electronic industries becomes immediately apparent when their respective patterns of output growth, of productivity, and of international competitiveness are compared. The significant point to make is that the export surplus of the sector as a whole has rested heavily upon the electric industries, and that these have failed to establish any overall growth trend in the 1970s.

Table 2.20 provides the salient data on output, employment and productivity, not only for the whole of electrical engineering, but also for both electric and electronic industries. A number of features are apparent:

i) Cyclicality is strongly marked. The peak of 1974 is clearly identifiable and would have been more strongly marked in output terms but for the extensive disruption to production in the earlier part of that year (due to the coal strike). Employment was built up rapidly to 1974, but this was not matched fully in output terms.

ii) Labour has been extensively displaced in the recession years (1971-2, 1975-6). This was more apparent in electric industries early in the decade, but applied to both major sectors in the mid-1970s.

iii) The output growth shown through the decade (taking equivalent cyclical points) has been almost entirely accounted for by electronics. There output rose almost 40% over the decade as a whole. By contrast electric industries by 1978 had not recovered their 1974 peak and stood only 6% above the 1970 level.

iv) But it is clear also that the dramatic advance in output from 1971 to 1974 (a rise of over 20% in three years, for the whole of electrical engineering) has resumed at a more modest pace since 1975.

v) Over the decade as a whole employment fell by 9%. After the shake out of labour in 1975-6, employment has been virtually on a plateau in both main sectors. We will see later that some part of the employment expansion up to the boom of 1973-4 was based on increased recruitment of part-time labour; this does not appear to have been repeated since then.

vi) Consequently labour productivity has tended to advance faster than the rate of output. This is true of both sectors, though the pace of advance is different (an increase of nearly 50% from 1970 to 1978 for electronics, and under 20% for electric).

In a technologically rapidly advancing sector such as electronics, however, over-emphasis on increases in the volume of output per worker may be somewhat misleading. For some product groups, e.g. in consumer electronics, the wholesale price indices make clear the slower advance in final prices in some sectors of rising productivity. Consequently changes in value added per worker may not match the physical productivity trends.

With this said, it is nevertheless important to note that the output growth in electronics is being met from an employment level that is not expanding (and over the decade has shown some contraction), and that in simple terms labour productivity appears to be rising by 5% p.a. or so. Both the growth rate and the productivity increase are high by the standards of UK industry in recent years.

The balance of international trade provides a further contrast. The slow growing electric sector has a strong net export position (with imports little more than half the volume of exports, in 1975-77). The fast growing electronics sector has tended to run a net export deficit; the trade cycle is important and the net balance of trade has deteriorated in periods of high activity and only improved towards bare balance in the cyclical troughs.

Table 2.20 Production, Employment, Productivity

(1975 = 100)

	ALL ELECTRICAL ENGINEERING			ELECTRIC			ELECTRONIC		
	Production	Employ-ment	Labour productivity	Production	Employ-ment	Labour productivity	Production	Employ-ment	Labour productivity
1970	83.5	106.1	79	96.3	111.5	86	81.8	101.5	81
1971	84.8	104.0	82	95.4	107.8	88	83.3	100.2	83
1972	89.0	101.6	88	94.5	103.6	91	86.9	99.8	87
1973	101.3	103.5	98	103.9	103.0	101	99.0	104.0	95
1974	104.5	108.1	97	104.8	108.2	97	104.1	107.7	97
1975	100.0	100.0	100	100.0	100.0	100	100.0	100.0	100
1976	98.5	95.1	104	97.2	95.3	102	99.6	94.8	105
1977	102.7	97.0	106	99.2	99.2	100	105.8	94.9	111
1978	108.1	(97.4)	(110)	(102.0)	(99.7)	(102)	(113.0)	(95.0)	(119)
1979		(96.6)							

(Number employed in 1975, thousands)

		(768)			(365)			(403)	

Sources: Trade and Industry, Department of Employment Gazette, especially 20 April 1979.

Statistical Notes: The series for electrical engineering output is 1975 based, for 1973 onwards. For earlier years the official practice is merely to link to earlier 1970 based series. The *electric* and *electronic* output series are 1975 based throughout. This leads to some awkwardness in the comparisons of 1970, '71 and '72 output across the three series.

Table 2.21 Electrical Engineering: Exports and Imports of Principal
Products   (£ million: Current prices)

	1971	1973	1975	1977	1st ¾ 1978
Electric					
Exports	359.7	447.0	827.5	1,299.8	1,134.1
Imports	142.0	290.5	420.1	715.3	630.8
Balance	+ 127.7	+ 156.5	+ 407.4	+ 584.5	+ 503.3
Imports as % of exports	39	65	51	55	56
Electronic					
Exports	411.4	598.4	1,034.3	1,739.3	1,348.3
Imports	405.9	887.6	1,033.3	1,908.1	1,492.6
Balance	+ 5.5	− 289.2	+ 1.0	− 68.8	− 144.4
Imports as % of exports	99	148	100	104	111

Source: Trade and Industry, 20 April 1979.

A number of points can be made:

— Neither sector seems able to sustain the import/export ratios of the early 1970s.

— The frenzied consumer durable boom of 1972-73 clearly did great damage in balance of payments terms. This links with the comparative competitive weakness of the electrical and electronic consumer goods industries concerned.

— The two-way trade of the electronics industries is considerably greater than that for electrical industries, so that a deterioration of the electronic balance is of considerable—and increasing—importance for the national economy.

Indeed, more recent data indicates a serious weakening of the overall net export surplus of the electrical engineering industries in the continuing consumer boom of 1979. The net surplus of exports in the first three quarters of 1979 was only £86 million, a deterioration of over £250 million compared to the same period a year earlier.

Within both sectors, capital goods have so far shown relative strength. A very large part of the export surplus of the electrical industries is accounted for by "electrical machinery" (MLH 361); exports in recent years have accounted for nearly half of manufacturers' sales.* "Electronic capital goods" (MLH 367) show a major increase in exports to 1977; but since 1978

* Cf. article on "Import Penetration", British Business, 14 September 1979.

143

the ratio of exports to manufacturers' output (from 44% in 1977 to 34% in 1978-79) has been falling. By contrast, domestic electrical appliances have been an area of weakness with an import surplus (though import penetration has been stable at close to 30%). In electronics, "broadcast receiving and sound reproducing equipment" and "electronic computers" show large and growing import surpluses; in the latter case, although imports occupy most of the home market, production is heavily and increasingly export orientated. Rising levels of two-way trade are characteristic. Over the whole of electrical engineering in 1978-79 imports accounted for over one-third of home demand, but nearly 40% of British manufacturers' output was in its turn exported. But if foreign, especially Japanese, competition in consumer electronics is to be met, it would seem to require the establishment of highly automated plants able to ensure very high product reliability and adequate scale economies.

Fixed investment in the sector did in fact rise strongly to the 3rd quarter of 1978 (rising to about 10% of the manufacturing total), but has since begun to recede.

The Structure of Employment

The sector is a relatively large employer of female labour, particularly in assembly operations. The latest estimates indicate over 270,000 female employees compared with about 465,000 males. The most recent employment census (for June 1977) indicated that just over 20% of the female employees were part-time workers; part-time employment was particularly important in "radio and electronic components" (some 14% of total employment).

Female employment appears significantly more cyclical than that of men, and part-time female employment particularly so. (See Graph 1). Total female employment fell by over 70,000 in the recession from 1974 to 1976 (a fall of over 20%); nearly half of that was accounted for by the fall in part-time female employment (a fall of nearly 40%). By contrast the fall in male employment was one of under 30,000 (some 6%).

In addition to cyclical displacement, female employment falls may particularly reflect technological innovation (and declining market share); this applies especially to telecommunications equipment and television

144

manufacture.* The shift in the employment structure of the industries concerned is revealed when manual and non-manual occupations are also analysed:

Table 2.22   Occupational Analysis of Electrical Engineering Employment
(In thousands)

	Operatives	Admin; Tech; Clerical	Total Employed	Admin. etc. as % of total
October 1973				
Male	282	203	485	41.8%
Female	251	76	327	23.3%
Total	533	279	812	34.4%
October 1979				
Male	264	200	463	43.1%
Female	198	73	271	26.9%
Total	462	273	735	37.1%

Source: Department of Employment Gazette.

The displacement of female manual workers and to a lesser extent male manual workers is combined with a near stable total of non-manual employment. A further official study, which concentrates on male manual workers, indicates the unusual importance of skilled craftsmen among the male manual production workers of the industry; over 45% of the total surveyed were in the skilled categories in 1979. The ratio of skilled had been higher still in 1970 (the structural decline of heavy electrical engineering must play a part in this). Consequently the evidence is of a gradual displacement of manual employment, both skilled and semi-skilled; but within that, female employment with its concentration on manipulative and assembly work has been in most evident decline.

It is true that, as the official study on micro-electronics says, "The major impact of micro-electronics on employment is yet to come". But on the evidence so far it is helping to reduce the number of manual jobs in the production sectors most directly concerned.

* HMSO: Manpower Implications of Micro-Electronic Technology, pages 17-19. "There is the replacement of extensive hard wiring and of discrete components by integrated circuits, resulting in a vastly reduced component count . . . second, the reduction in the number of components has facilitated automatic insertion; something like 60% can now be inserted automatically."

Graph 1   Electrical Engineering: Changes in Female Employment 1971–1977

Source: Census of Employment for Great Britain.

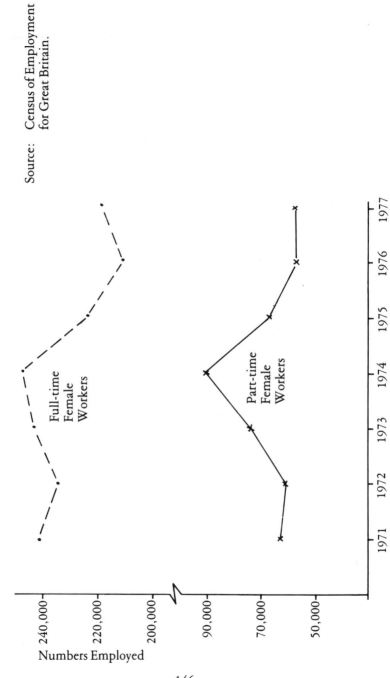

146

Patterns of Working Hours

There are few remarkable features in the overall working time patterns of electrical engineering workers. The following are the salient features (derived from the New Earnings Survey unless otherwise indicated):

Basic Hours

These were recorded in 1979 as follows; they have shown no material change over the decade:

Manual Men	39.6
Non-Manual Men	37.8
Manual Women	39.5
Non-Manual Women	37.2

As the main engineering agreement defines the hours of shift workers as 37½ for double-day or three shift workers "exclusive of half hour break for meals each shift", this is probably recorded as such for shift-workers and helps pull the manual average slightly below 40 hours.

Overtime Working

Overtime hours have generally been close to the manufacturing average. They were cyclically high in the April 1979 survey (probably reflecting attempts to catch up on production schedules after disruption earlier in the year caused by the transport drivers dispute).

Manual Men	average of 6.3 hours overtime
Non-Manual Men	average of 2.4 hours overtime
Manual Women	average of 0.9 hours overtime
Non-Manual Women	average of 0.5 hours overtime

These appear moderately higher than in a year of lower cyclical activity (e.g. in 1975, 4.4 hours average overtime for manual men, and 1.6 hours for non-manual men). Electrical machinery, insulated wires and cables, and electronic capital goods, generally appear as industries within the sector with rather higher levels of overtime working.

The six monthly survey of manual men suggests rather less overtime working among Payment By Results workers (3.6 hours for skilled workers, 2.7 hours for semi-skilled) than among Timeworkers (4.7 hours for skilled, 4.1 hours for semi-skilled) in the June 1979 survey. The difference in overtime almost exactly compensates in earnings terms for the slightly lower hourly earnings of Timeworkers in the case of skilled workers, and largely closes a more substantial hourly earnings gap in the case of semi-skilled workers. Skilled maintenance workers appear to work generally longer overtime than other categories.

Overtime working and overtime earnings are rather more markedly important for non-manual men in the electrical engineering industries than in most other manufacturing industries. The 1979 data on those workers who did work overtime in the survey period brings this out:

Table 2.23   Overtime Workers: Overtime Hours and Pay

	% of total who worked overtime	Overtime hours of these	Overtime pay as % of gross pay
Manual Men	58.3	10.8	22.1
Non-Manual Men	31.3	7.4	18.6
Manual Women	17.6	5.2	14.2
Non-Manual Women	14.4	3.5	10.5

For those who did work overtime, these levels of overtime hours and the proportion of gross pay that the associated earnings produced were close to manufacturing averages. But 31% of non-manual men in electrical engineering worked overtime compared with 23% in manufacturing generally.

Absenteeism
There is some evidence of high levels of absenteeism in parts of the sector. The Sector Working Party (set up by the National Economic Development Committee) for Domestic Electrical Appliances carried out a survey which found that only in two plants was absenteeism below double figures (10%). There was general agreement that absenteeism was a major impediment to production planning for high productivity. The difficulties have been compounded by resort to overtime as a method of coping with casual absenteeism.

Shiftworking
Engineering industries in Britain have not been characterised by high levels of shiftworking; that in electrical engineering is somewhat higher than in mechanical engineering but considerably lower than in manufacturing generally. Thus in the 1979 NES 16.4% of manual men in the industry received shift premia compared with 25.6% in manufacturing as a whole. In addition it should be noted that shift working by manual men has been tending to fall over the decade; 24% received shift premia in 1970, and 18% in 1974. Such industries as electronic components and domestic electrical appliances show significant falls (from around 25% in 1974 to 16% in 1979). The industry with the highest proportion of shiftworking, insulated wires and cables (34% receiving shift premia, in the case of manual men) has also shown a declining trend. The only exception is MLH 369 "other electrical goods" (this includes electric equipment for vehicles,

batteries, and lamps) where shiftworking by manual men has risen from 22% in 1974 to 30%; this certainly reflects capital intensive continuous process work (e.g. in the production of dry batteries).

For other categories of worker, shiftworking is of minor importance (in the 1979 NES premia were paid only to 5.4% of manual women and 4.1% of non-manual men). The only major recorded use of shiftworking for non-manual men is in electronic computer production; this is becoming more capital intensive and the proportion receiving shift premia has risen to 10.5% in 1979.

The shift premia received by manual men actually working shifts averaged £17 in 1979, rather higher than in manufacturing as a whole, but only bringing weekly earnings to a level of about £14 a week above non-shiftworkers.

Outlook for the Sector

Official studies are noticeably unwilling to offer any clear predictions as to the scale of directions of change that may be generated in the sector, and as to the speed with which technologically induced changes may be diffused. Any analysis has to be tentative, since one important dimension that is also difficult to guage is the extent of competitive pressure and the nature of the response to it by UK firms.

The retreat from any confidence in predictive ability is particularly expressed in the highly relevant recent report under Department of Employment auspices on "Manpower Implications of Micro-electronic Technology". On the key conclusion as to employment effects the Report has this to say:

> "The economic factors leading to employment shifts as a result of technological change are complex and inevitably involve both job displacing and compensatory job creating mechanisms. Higher productivity results in reduced unit costs which lead to higher profits and/or lower relative prices. These have direct demand effects on the products initially affected by technological change and indirectly on other sectors. *The overall employment effect is virtually impossible to guage.* However, past empirical work suggests that, in the long run, technological change has been beneficial to both output and employment." (Op. Cit. Page 106. Our emphasis).

It is the kind of statement that can as readily be made before studying a subject as after it.

Within the sector some implications of the new technology and of competitive market pressures are already evident, and have in part already been discussed. It is not only a matter of more automated assembly, and radical changes and reductions in component requirements. Japanese industrial practice has particularly linked this with quality control to ensure extremely high reliability. In some parts of electronics this is already leading to partnership with Japanese enterprise in reorganising UK production (e.g. in consumer electronics). Government policy in the UK (in the name of "industrial strategy") has offered various kinds of selective aid to assist industrial investment. This included an "industry scheme" for electronic components launched in 1977; by March 1979 assistance of £16 million had been offered on project costs of £65 million, with further projects still under consideration. But the electrical engineering sector has only been a relatively small recipient of "selective investment" aid (only 4% of the total assistance given); this hardly suggests a vigorous response so far.

One displacement effect within the sector will be that of electronic components replacing electric ones (e.g. in vehicles). This has, of course, already been a major factor in telecommunication equipment manufacture, but the report already cited emphasises that the major impact in this area has yet to come. "System X" (fully electronic telephone exchanges) starts to be installed from 1981:

> "It has been estimated that, for equivalent capabilities, where the production of electro-mechanical switchgear employed 26 people, first generation semi-electronic equipment employs ten people and System X will employ one person." (Op. Cit. Page 18).

The worst hit establishments will be, in the short run, those still concentrating on electro-mechanical exchange equipment; but the timetable for the full transition to System X stretches through most of the rest of this century. Integrated circuits are similarly displacing older products in transmission equipment and telephone subscriber apparatus.

A further uncertainty is how far or on what scale the telecommunication firms may offset some of such job losses by diversifying into new ranges of equipment associated with the telecommunications network. Such aspirations may be shared by other parts of the electronics industry.

Changes in technology in the industry have already been seen (e.g. by NEDO's "Industrial Review to 1977" earlier in the 1970s) as increasing the proportion of people in the industry required with technical skills, at the same time as reducing the proportion of traditional craftsmen in production processes, and displacing manual labour in face of automation, etc. The "Micro-electronic Technology" report refers to draughtsmen and electronic test technicians as two areas of skill shortage. There are areas of tension as to the demarcation lines, and actual tasks deployment, of professional engineers and technicians. Additional skill requirements may be involved for maintenance craftsmen (e.g. the issue as to whether the common craft rate for a skilled electrician should be breached by an "electronic technician" grade). It is to be expected that design and technology will themselves react to at least some perceived skill shortages. But problems of skill segmentation, and of persistent skill shortages (e.g. of electronics process engineers), are evident; retraining and upgrading within the internal labour market of firms may only be part of the answer.

ELECTRICAL ENGINEERING

CASE STUDIES

Case Study 5

Introduction

The plant investigated in this case study was engaged in the manufacture of capital electronic goods for the aviation industry. The company is part of a major UK based multi-national electronics engineering group. On the site where our study was carried out some 5,000 were employed which included 1,200 engineers of graduate status; 1,200 skilled production workers; 600 semi- and unskilled workers, whilst the remaining 200 were distributed amongst administrative, technical and clerical categories.

The plant is organised into 12 distinct operating divisions all serviced by three central divisions (data processing, personnel services and corporate management and co-ordination). Each operating division is divided into two parts:

The **engineering function** which is responsible for project development, design, and to a large extent the "selling" (which involves the winning of contracts) of the product and is staffed largely by graduate engineers organised into a number of different project groups. A drawing office and a model shop service all the groups.

The **production department** is involved in the actual production of developed models and is operating, normally, some two to five years behind the engineering department. Most production workers, fitters, testers and wiremen are skilled craftsmen.

Since to a considerable extent each one of the "operating divisions" can be treated as a discrete entity, it was decided to concentrate our investigation

151

upon one division, chosen to be more or less typical in terms of size and function. The division chosen was the Instrument Services Division (ISD) which concentrates upon the development and production of air data systems. It should be noted that in most of what follows we report on the engineering function of ISD.

Terms and Conditions of Employment (company wide)

The company is an affiliate of the Engineering Employers' Federation and is thus a signatory to the National Engineering Agreement for manual workers. Most production manual workers on site are members of the AUEW (Engineering Section) or EETPU, whilst AUEW (Technical and Administrative Staffs Section) have bargaining rights for engineers and draughtsmen, and separate representational rights for certain higher management grades. Clerical workers are organised by APEX.

Administrative, Technical and Clerical workers and Engineering staff work a basic week of 37½ hours, with contractual hours from 8.30 a.m. to 5.00 p.m. They have a basic holiday entitlement of 20 days, plus statutory holidays, and service related holidays add up to three further days of holiday.

By comparison, production workers (including monthly paid production superintendents) work the basic 40 hour week, with contractual hours from 7.30 a.m. to 4.30 p.m. All skilled manual workers with more than one year's service, and some with less, have the right to apply for "staff status" (entitling e.g. payments during sickness, and payment on a weekly, rather than an hourly basis). Present holiday entitlements are of four weeks, with service related holidays adding up to another three days.

Since 1975, the establishment has operated a flexi-time system for all employees (except the small number of shift and night workers in the production departments). This may be worked as an alternative to contractual working hours, by agreement with the supervisor of the department concerned. 37½ hour workers have "core times" of 9.00 a.m.-12.00 noon and 1.30 p.m. to 3.30 p.m. with "flexi-times" between 7.30 a.m. and 9.00 a.m. and 3.30 p.m. and 5.30 p.m., whilst 40 hour workers have "core times" of 8.30 a.m. to 12.00 noon and 1.30 p.m. to 3.30 p.m. and "flexi-times" from 7.00 a.m. to 8.30 a.m. and 3.30 p.m. to 5.30 p.m. As a condition of operation of the scheme "clocking" was extended to cover all employees. Employees can choose to take half hour or one hour lunch breaks, and their clock cards are endorsed accordingly. Management reserves certain rights to limit flexibility to deal with sections which need to be covered through the whole working day (i.e. throughout "flexi-time" in addition to "core time"), and may require employees to attend or leave at certain times outside "core times".

The company pays all employees below a certain management level for hours worked in excess of contractual time. Overtime rates are set domestically and for manual workers will normally exceed those set by the National Agreement, in as much as the premium is paid upon personal "hourly rates" rather than on the National Minimum Rate. Premium rates for all workers are time and a third for weekday overtime, time and a half for Saturday working, and double time for Sundays. Production workers are required to work their daily contractual hours, and weekly and monthly staff their weekly contractual hours before overtime is paid. Monthly paid staff must also work a minimum of one hour's overtime on any one day to qualify for payment.

It is a condition of employment for all manual workers that they be prepared to work on such shift systems as are agreed between the company and the trade unions.

Manual workers in the production departments are paid according to various mutually agreed incentive systems. Both group and individual systems are in operation with payment reflecting achievement against "Standard Times".

Instrument Services Division (ISD Engineering Department)

In total ISD employs some 348 persons, of these 187 are to be found in the engineering department. The majority (166) are classified as direct workers, the remainder (21) including some management, cleaners and maintenance workers are classified as indirect.

Before examining the detail of our findings it is worthwhile drawing attention to two factors which interact to condition the individual worker's attitude to his working time. Firstly, there appeared to be a relatively high level of job satisfaction amongst the workers interviewed. This motivation was seen to translate into a willingness either to work overtime or 'a bit harder' in order to meet particular schedules. Secondly, and related to this, in the highly aggressive markets both for defence and civil avionics, the ability to meet tight production schedules is clearly of considerable importance to a company. The workforce appeared very conscious of the market position of the company and indeed saw it as a matter of personal pride to maintain schedules, and thus help preserve the competitiveness of their employer.

The Organisation of Work and Working Time Implications

The engineering department is involved in the high risk activity of winning contracts and the designing and testing of the products which subsequently make up the contract. Accordingly, and given the nature of particularly the defence market, products tend to be either "one-offs" or significantly differentiated from one another. The work-load of the department is also characterised by the differing developmental time scales which an on-going policy of contract seeking must inevitably create.

Each project has its own cycle of growth and decline of activity and as development activity is winding down so production begins—as illustrated in Figure 1.

Figure 1

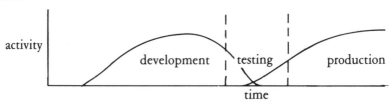

The nature of the business, combined with the life cycle of the project, means that there is the likelihood of a certain "lumpiness" in the activity level of a division. When programming the activity for the coming year a division will be certain of a guaranteed level of activity from jobs already being done, but some of these will be in their growth and some their winding down phases. In addition certain potential activity can be predicted, but it is not necessarily certain that peak levels of activity will be sustained throughout the time period under question as is illustrated in Figure 2.

Figure 2

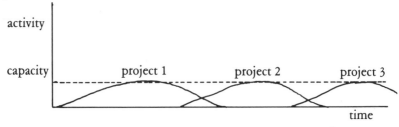

To some extent these fluctuations in the level of activity can be ironed out by the transfer of personnel from one division to another, or more commonly by the transfer of "work packages". In addition, however, a division would seek to fill up periods of excess capacities by "in house work", to develop and research into areas of potential future tendering. This use of "in house work" is illustrated in Figure 3.

154

Figure 3

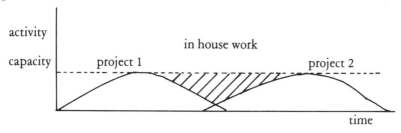

Whilst in extreme cases the excess capacity is so great that it cannot be so filled and so redundancies occur, as was the case in 1972, in the last two years the problem has been very much the opposite one, a situation of a shortage of capacity. Explicitly this has been a function of a shortage of suitably qualified engineers, both of graduate level and of engineers with three or four years experience. This shortage, thought to be a result of both the relatively low professional image of engineering and of the level of salaries offered in comparison to other professions, and also of the quality of engineers from some of the new universities and technical colleges, is anticipated to continue at least into the next few years. The degree of seriousness of the problem is emphasised by the fact that the company has in the past two years been making recruiting trips to Australia, signing up over one hundred graduates on each occasion.

Within this overall position, individual projects in the department become the focus of specific teams of workers. Each project has its own timetable worked out at the contracting stage, and according to which the project team attempts to complete their work. It follows, therefore, that the accuracy of this projected time-table together with the avoidance of unforeseen delays either internal or external to the project team become the crucial determinants over the working time organisation of the project team. Where delays do arise management may consider some rescheduling. The extent to which this is possible depends upon the customer, and the nature of funding of the project. However, the teams do not like to have to reschedule unless absolutely necessary, if for no other reason than that it is a matter of collective and individual job satisfaction to try to complete on time. Thus, when it is acknowledged that either the whole, or particular sub-parts of the project are falling behind, it is the case both that individuals impose a discipline upon themselves to work more than their contractual hours, and that they come under pressure from management to work such overtime. Furthermore, should the time-table be rolled forward, assumptions about a certain level of overtime working are incorporated into the rescheduling.

A check is kept upon levels of overtime worked and limits are set for both individuals and groups, to ensure that overtime working does not become excessive. Excessive overtime is deemed to being worked when substantial numbers in a group are working between 12 and 14 hours overtime per week for about one month (equals two weekends worked, two Saturday mornings and regular evening overtime), and, should this pitch occur, re-scheduling of the project is considered.

Whilst it is theoretically also possible to deal with the pressure points on schedules by drafting in extra engineers from other projects which have temporary surpluses (e.g. that are near the end of their life cycles), in practice this is very difficult. To the extent that the frequent sources of pressure are instances of things-not-working-as-they-were-designed-to-work, this requires the persons involved in the designing to be involved also in the rectification. It was felt that upper management did not always understand the problems involved in bringing in "outsiders" when they suggested this remedy, and in particular the fact that there was in many cases too much of a "learning curve" to make it worthwhile.

It would seem that the company are in the relatively favourable position whereby overtime in the engineering department is seen neither as an intolerable imposition or as the only means of achieving a living wage;* rather it was viewed as an inevitable repercussion of the style and nature of development work. This "professionalism" may also be linked to the significant number of graduate engineers working in the department together with the high overall levels of job satisfaction and loyalty to the company which were apparent amongst the workforce.

The Potential for Shorter Working Time

From the managers we interviewed it was plain that the magnitude of change was seen to be the key factor when considering reducing contractual working time. It was thought possible to cope with an incremental reduction to 35 hours per week either through increased productivity or via more overtime, either course being favoured over the option of employing more workers.

More significant reductions in working time tended to be translated into adverse pressures on the company's competitiveness insofar as it was considered that such change would lengthen the timing of particular projects and hence increase its cost. Again it was clear that increasing

* It was not until the 1970s that overtime payments were in fact negotiated, moreover, one individual interviewed felt that although such payment was nice, without it management could still achieve a significant overtime response from the workforce.

156

employment to counteract any lengthening of project times was effectively ruled out by management. This negative approach, was as we shall show, largely informed by external labour market constraints which the company was currently suffering within the existing patterns of working time organisation. Changing working time and attempting to re-man was seen as exacerbating this difficulty.

Labour Market Constraints

Whilst the company like many of its counterparts complained in general terms of the shortage of skilled engineeering workers on the external labour market, it was clear that particular shortages were creating problems, and that attempts to improve the efficiency of the *internal* labour market were only providing a partial answer. A particularly acute case was found in the drawing office. In the last 18 months vacancies had existed for three senior draughtsmen (the office currently employs 18 staff). The extent of the labour shortage meant that the company had, as part of a scheme generated by the Personnel Department and the unions, begun training draughtsmen at its own training centre, aiming to produce a skilled man after 30 weeks in the centre and two and a half years "on the job". Whilst this was felt to be better than nothing, the chief draughtsman was "not too happy" with the scheme as a way of increasing staff, because he felt that the trainees lacked the "general engineering background" that the traditional four year apprenticeship gives, and that their experience was limited and too specific.

The supply shortage was seen to have several sources, of which two are particularly important. In 1971 when the industry suffered a serious downturn, there had been enforced redundancies, plus others leaving of their own accord. The division had lost 5 out of 26 persons, and these had mainly been the more senior drawing staff. Whilst work levels built up again within two years, the staffing levels never recovered, and it was felt that many people had been entirely lost to the industry.

Furthermore, it was felt that there has been a steady deskilling of the draughtsmen's jobs in recent years, with the design function being taken over by engineering staff. Inasmuch as this has contributed to a decline in job satisfaction it might explain why staff were reluctant to return to the industry, and why they carry on leaving.

The shortage is responded to in several ways. The company makes extensive use of subcontractors—with ISD alone having "employed" 39.5 subcontract draughtsmen in the year to date. It also has to overstress its own capacity, both by using inexperienced draughtsmen beyond their capabilities, which means that supervisors have to spend excessive time explaining matters to them.

Overtime is the other means whereby the company seek to overcome labour supply constraints. Most of the younger staff work 10 hours of overtime per week (three evenings of two hours each and a Saturday morning). Older staff (four) do less—either the evenings, or the Saturday morning, whilst some three or four do little or no overtime at all. (One problem is that the "checkers" fall into this latter category). Supervision of overtime is covered by "section leaders" on an informal rota system. The section leaders do somewhat less overtime than average, between six and eight hours per week.

The branch chairman of the AUEW (TASS) was particularly critical of the effect which the combination of subcontracting and extensive overtime had on both performance and morale in the office.

Management were criticised for being lax, and of seeking to control neither overtime level, nor work-pace during the day. In addition, because many of the section leaders spend a day a week visiting the subcontractors there is both inadequate supervision and a consequent fall in efficiency which lowers the effective input of the given workforce and so exacerbates the problem of shortages.

It is worthwhile noting, indeed it is of considerable importance in the context of future manning levels in the drawing office, that there existed a widespread anticipation that new technology would in the near future solve the shortage of skilled draughtsmen. Computer aided design (CAD) has been making an impression at the company in recent times. It was, for example, pointed out to us that the draughtsmen's job had been progressively de-skilled. The extent of such de-skilling and some indication of the productivity boost which CAD affords the company can be gained if we consider that four years ago, the office was doing some 100 "art works" (printed circuit drawings) per year, it was now, with computer aided systems, doing some 400 per year. With improvements to the technique it was suggested that it would, in one year's time, be possible to cut out all subcontracting of this work. Even more extreme was the example whereby a drawing, which would have taken two weeks if manually made, could be prepared in two hours by means of CAD. In addition, the CAD system would incorporate its own "checking" function, and so could save on this manpower category.

The impact of CAD was felt to be such that in little more than two years there would be no need for any overtime to be worked with present staff levels, whilst, had staffing been at its 1971 level, there would also be the likely need to shed labour. As things stood, however, the advent of CAD meant that management would not have to worry in the next few years about the loss of several of the more senior draughtsmen, particularly the "checkers", through retirement, although in the absence of CAD these retirements would have caused severe problems in finding replacements.

As it stands, CAD can be seen to have both positive and negative potential. In the absence of an agreement linking its introduction with the maintenance of manning levels, CAD could lead to the widespread displacement of drawing office staff—by the erosion of their function through the use of CAD in other departments traditionally reliant upon the drawing office, or by more direct means. On the other hand, CAD could provide the capacity whereby a substantial reduction in working time for existing manning levels was possible.

Workers Preference for Shorter Working Time

Possibly because of the "professional ethic" exhibited by many of the workforce in the engineering department, there was said to be little real grass roots pressure for shorter working time. It was felt that a reduction in the contractual working week would leak 100% into extra overtime. Moreover, the workforce appeared strongly aware of the external labour market constraints which would hamper any skilled remanning consequent on hours reduction. In addition, amongst the workforce no real enthusiasm had yet surfaced for the notion of worksharing. It appeared that if anything lenghtening holiday entitlement was considered to be the most desirable and feasible method to both worker and management, but even here it was pointed out to us that a fairly high degree of satisfaction with the existing holiday entitlement can be found amongst the workforce.

Case Study 5

Summary of Key Points Emerging

— The plant investigated employed a comparatively high proportion of skilled workers, either graduate engineers or 'time-served' craftsmen;

— The particular department studied was engaged in the "high risk" activity of development work and was responsible for winning contracts in the highly competitive aviation electronics (avionics) markets (defence and civil);

— These two factors gave rise within the workforce to both a pride in the work and an acute consciousness of the company's competitive position, this readily translated into a willingness to work overtime in order to maintain the schedules allocated to individual projects;

— A severe skill shortage was noted, which added to the pressure for overtime working. In addition, flexibility in the *internal* labour market was constrained by the esoteric nature of development work which tended to create high "learning curve" barriers around particular projects;

— It was anticipated that the shortage of experienced draughtsmen which had hampered the company would soon be wholly offset by the more widespread use of computer aided design (CAD) techniques.

Case Study 6

Introduction

The company is engaged in the manufacture of electronic components—principally printed circuits. It is a subsidiary of a US based multi-national company and is a member company of the Engineering Employers Federation. The company employs some 500 persons, and the majority of these, the production and clerical workers, are members of the T&GWU (and ACTS). Production jobs are mainly semi-skilled, and some 50% of production staff are female.

The company operates from a main plant in Scotland. It was chosen as an object of research because of an almost unique work time pattern—in essence based upon a four day week. The inception of such an innovatory work time system can be seen to be particularly remarkable when studied in the context of the local culture which has traditionally been dominated by the textile industry (although electronics is now becoming a significant employer) and was until very recently steeped in an almost Victorian set of attitudes towards industrial relations, with a low level of trade union organisation. In the early 1970s the T&G had only some 2,000 members and 20 shop stewards in the district. Now membership is above 5,500 and the number of shop stewards exceeds 160.

To a considerable extent the development of the work time system at the plant was integrally linked to the growth of trade union organisation within the particular plant.

The case study is constructed from interviews with two District Officials of the T&G, one of whom was the principal shop steward at the plant during the period of the formulation and introduction of the radical changes to the

160

work time system. The company itself refused to grant access, or to make any member of management available for comment.

Traditional Work Time Patterns and the Experience of the "Three Day Week"

In the early 1970s the company was expanding and in need of larger premises and moved to a new purpose built factory in the autumn of 1972. At that time the company was very typical of the area. Union membership in the plant was low, limited to some 20% of the workforce, there were no shop stewards, and management prerogative was strong. Wage rates, following those set by the dominant textile industry were low. Working time patterns were typical for the electronics industry—standard day working predominated, although a few departments operated limited "double day" working and there was a very small, female, part-time or "twilight" shift. However, in addition, a high level of overtime was worked by production workers. Overtime was laid on for three or four hours on Monday to Wednesday evenings, on Saturday mornings from 8.00 a.m. to 12.00 midday, and on Sundays from 4.30 p.m. and most male production workers worked a good many of these overtime hours. Indeed, because hourly rates were low they could not afford not to, but again in this respect the company was not atypical—a high overtime culture was general to the area.

The growth of the company, and the consequent growth of the labour force, was, however, having considerable implications for the level and nature of collective organisation and representation. Many of the new employees came from trade union orientated backgrounds, from the pits, and as overspills from the greater Glasgow area. By the end of 1973 trade union density had reached 90% and a shop steward organisation operated. Thus, when the miners strike of the winter 1973/74 led the company to being forced onto the "Three Day Week" in early 1974, the management were prepared to come together with the unions to negotiate how the emergency might be successfully managed.

The unions were prepared to offer, on the basis of it being manned only by volunteers, a 12 hour night shift that, together with a 12 hour dayshift permitted continuous working on Mondays, Tuesdays and Wednesdays of each week. Whilst it was thought that such work time pattern would prove arduous,* in fact, the workforce found the system sufficiently advantageous,

---

* It would seem, at least with respect to male workers, that concern was directed towards the necessity for shift working rather than towards the number of hours worked in any one stint, *since on site time, with weekday overtime, had been 12 hours.* Female workers did not work the night shift; however, they were required to work the 12 hour day stints.

161

particularly with respect to the blocks of free days it created, that they disliked having to go back to five day working once the emergency ceased. However, as well as providing employees with four days off every week, the "three day week" forced both the company and the workforce to accept a "no overtime" situation,* and the benefits of this the T&G regarded as equally significant,** sufficiently so that it asked for the three day week system to be continued beyond the settlement of the miners dispute. Although the company, at the time, refused on the grounds that it was unable to afford it, the union continued to nurture and develop its claim.

Takeover and the Need for Expansion

A takeover of one company by one of its leading customers (the US based MNC) was completed by the end of 1974. It was a very low key affair, involving very little change in substance of management style or conditions of employment, beyond the introduction of a sick pay scheme that was a part of the new parent's general "terms and conditions".

Despite the fact that it was the parent company's policy not to make use of systematic overtime, 1974 and 1975 saw an increase in the incidence and level of overtime working. Whilst there was limited experimentation with shift working—a very small night shift was operated from mid-1974 to mid-1975[†]—traditional shift working systems seemed to prove unsatisfactory to the company, and by mid-1975 even the double day shift had been reduced in numbers from 60 to 30 persons. The T&G as early as mid-1974, suggested two shift operations based upon a four day week, but the company claimed that it could not envisage any new shift arrangements, this not withstanding the fact that orders were increasing and that the factory was working substantially below a theoretical full capacity.[‡] Such was the

* However, under the terms of the Engineering Agreement, four hours of every stint were paid at overtime rates.

** Whilst the workforce might have appreciated it at the time, once the miners strike was settled "within a week it was as if the overtime restrictions had never been there".

[†]It was continued beyond this period in the "drill room" which was operated on a five day semi-continuous basis, using duble day shifts with a complementary (unsupervised) permanent night shift.

[‡]It would seem retrospectively, that the opposition was not so much from the company itself but rather from the parent, who feared that any radical chahges might spill over into their other factories. The Managing Director and the Production Manager in fact saw the potential advantages of four day working and became amongst its staunchest supporters; it was they who ultimately "sold" the system to the parent and without their support, it is thought, the change would not have come about.

T&G's exasperation with the management of working time that in September 1975 they sought to shut down even continuous operations over lunch time.

However, it was recognised that as a preliminary for effective negotiations over working time, or any other matters, an adequate bargaining forum be established. The period end-1974 to mid-1976 was devoted to discussing a comprehensive procedural agreement establishing formal consultative rights and access to the management information system. Once this agreement was concluded the union formally approached the company on the issue of four day working. The case that was presented was very general, the T&G had not worked out any details, and so it was in the period late 1976 and early 1977 that a joint working party systematically examined ideas and possibilities.

The Principles of the Four Day Week System

The changeover to four day working was proposed with the object of achieving four major objectives:

a) a reduction in throughput times
b) a reduction in overtime working
c) an increased capacity reserve
    and
d) sufficient capacity for budgeted sales.

The company required to increase its manufacturing capacity but had run up against the limits of factory size and the length of the *actual* working week. It was possible neither to increase numbers on the standard day shift, since the shift was already fully manned, nor to extend further the working time of the present labour force, since "excessive" overtime was already being worked. In addition, and precisely because these limits had been reached, the company had no reverse capacity to meet exceptional peaks of demand. By going over to shift working the company created the "space" to increase the number of employees, some of whom would have been required—but could not have been accommodated—even if actual hours had remained unchanged, and some of whom were required as a result of the translation of the bulk of overtime hours at present worked into normal hours for additional employees; whilst by going over to four day working they created "space" for any overtime working that might be necessary. At the same time the union succeeded in achieving its twin objectives of a four day work week, in return for which it was prepared to co-operate in extensive shift working, and a virtual elimination of overtime.

In addition, it should be noted that the increase in employment consequent upon the reduction in overtime was greater than a one-to-one translation of overtime hours to normal hours would suggest. Because "equivalent compensation was used as the medium of translation (i.e. because what was required was that projected labour costs remained unchanged), and because normal time hours were cheaper than overtime hours, *each overtime hour eliminated could "buy" more than one additional normal hour.* The joint working party's proposal illustrated this:

Increased Heads by Reduced Overtime

Reducing overtime in production from 20% to 8% (of hours) would increase the year average heads by 16 . . .

Budget year average heads	= 91
Corrected average with Cost Improvement Forecast	= 99
Hours attended per week at 20% overtime	= 4,752
Hours attended per week at 8% overtime*	= 4,277
Savings	= 475
Average Overtime Rates	= 1.65
Overhead labour costs for directs	= 22%
Increase in heads for equivalent compensation	=

$$\frac{475 \times 1.65}{40 \times 1.22} = 16.07**$$

Furthermore there were a series of secondary benefits, consequent upon the change, that the working party recognised. For the company these included:

a) a reduction in cost of services, and utilities—heating, lighting, etc.;
b) easier access to equipment for major maintenance work;
c) a reduction of unproductive time in starting up and closing down, in particular on continuous plating processes, giving better plant utilisation and a better return on assets;
d) an improved recruitment potential***

whilst for employees these included:

a) a reduced cost of travelling to work (20%);
b) a reduction in total travelling time to work.

* It was assumed that a minimal level of overtime working would still be required, although in practice this is less than the 8% planned.

** However, we should note that the introduction of shift working, necessarily consequent upon the change, required that a premium over and above straight time rates be paid to the night shift and this is not taken into account in the calculation here presented.

*** Turnover rates, particularly for the less attractive jobs, are claimed to have fallen significantly, as too has absenteeism.

Against these advantages several possible disadvantages were mooted. It was suggested that 10 hour stints might be over fatiguing; however, when one considers the high levels of overtime previously worked, this could not be considered to be a meaningful objection, at least with respect to the male labour force. With respect to female workers, it probably had more substance, as did the objection that the new daily work times might interfere with domestic or other commitments, although this problem was considerably mitigated by the union successfully pressing for a degree of flexibilisation that permitted women to work less than full-time.* Finally it was suggested that the introduction of a night shift would lead to the loss of the back shift from Monday to Thursday for servicing and repairs, but since the bulk of maintenance work was done at the weekends this criticism did not stand up to real examination, whilst in addition there was still a gap between the end of the day shift and the commencement of the night shift that *could* be utilised if required.

Not mentioned in the joint working party's proposals but raised, in the course of discussions, by one of the domestic unions, the AUEW representing the engineering/maintenance staff, was the objection that the result of the introduction of four day working would not be to decrease actual working time but rather to introduce the opportunity for systematic overtime working, on Fridays, and thus to leave the length of the actual work week unaltered. Pressure from their membership, who saw the tremendous advantages of four day working, was however sufficient to induce the union to participate in the change, whilst in addition the unions collectively sought to ensure that the necessity for any overtime working would have to be fully justified before they sanctioned it. Furthermore, the T&G felt that since the company, as a result of improvements in the basic rate negotiated in the preceding years, was now a relatively high payer, there would *be* less pressure from the workforce for overtime, and in this they were correct. Those persons who felt the potential fall in earnings to be less than tolerable as the price for change, were those who volunteered for the night shift, for which a premium** was paid.

Details of the Four Day System

The contractual week for production workers is 40 hours. The *day shift works*

* NB women also work on the night shift, which is, in fact, now 50% female. For this a special exemption order, from the Factory Inspectorate, was required.

** Now worth 33 ⅓ % on domestic rates.

Monday to Thursday, from 7.00 a.m. to 6.00 p.m. with one hour unpaid lunch break staggered over a two hour period to permit some continuity of production. There is a ten minute teabreak within each half of the working day. The *night shift* works, Sunday to Thursday, 9.15 p.m. to 7.15 a.m. without an unpaid meal break. The two shifts thus overlap for a quarter of an hour to facilitate the changeover between both the workforce and the supervisors, and to allow production to continue uninterrupted over the full two shifts. Despite an actual "on site time" of 10 hours, the *night shift's* 9.15 p.m. start represents a "late start" that was achieved by dropping an equivalent amount of tea break time, whilst the fifteen minute overlap time is counted as overtime. In addition, following an agreement whereby cover is provided over the remaining tea break time, a further fifteen minutes worth of overtime is paid, such that a total of two hours per week of paid overtime is guaranteed to the night shift.

Some overtime is worked on Fridays by day shift dispatch and inspection staff, but this involves only some 10% of the day shift strength. Friday overtime working by other production staff is very rare. Maintenance work which used to be done on Saturday overtime is now largely done on Fridays.

In the *drill shop*, which is operated on a continuous basis, Monday to Saturday, production staff work on a "four day on, four day off" (with Sundays excluded), non-rotating shift system, involving 12 hour stints and an average 36 hour week. Shift changeover times are 7.00 a.m. to 7.00 p.m. and within each shift are two paid 30 minute meal breaks, staggered so that machines are manned 24 hours per day. Shifts working Saturdays have the obligation to provide overtime on the following Sunday, should it be required. The incidence of such overtime working is however very limited.

Four day working also extends to the *clerical staff* in the company. These have a contractual work week of 37½ hours, and work on a flexible rota system, whereby some work Mondays to Thursdays and others Tuesdays to Fridays, to maintain full provision of services through the "normal", five day, working week.

Holiday entitlements for production staff are as per the Engineering Agreement. The bulk of the holiday is taken up by factory closure—one week at Christmas, one week at Easter and two weeks in July/August—but because closures coincide with days when staff would have, in any case, been off—i.e. Fridays for day and night shift workers, "off days" for drill room workers—the union has insisted that, in order to receive the full entitlement *measured in days*, employees be granted additional "floating days" to be taken at discretion. These floating days at present number some nine per cent for two shift workers, and 16 for drill room workers.* Similar arrangements apply for clerical staff who have some 12 floating days of holiday per year.**

Conclusions

The District Office of the T&G had, and still have, a firm bargaining objective embracing the threefold strategy of increasing basic rates of pay, minimising overtime working, and constructing opportunities for a meaningful reduction in working time. At the case study plant the domestic union took this objective seriously. The development of an effective organisation enabled them first to tackle the question of the basic rate, whilst the experience of the three day week showed not only the advantages of a reduced work week and the absence of systematic overtime, but also, it threw up forms of work time organisation that illustrated the possibilities for real reform. There is no doubt that the union was aided by a favourable conjuncture: the virility of the organisation itself might be seen as a function of its relative newness, whilst the circumstances of the company—its need to significantly expand capacity—presented an opportunity without which the impetus for change might well not have borne fruit. However, we should recognise that effective Trade Unionism and constructive collective

---

* In order to ensure continuous operations drill room workers have the obligation to cover all instances of undermanning—holidays, sickness, and other absences, as well as break periods, if necessary by extending the responsibility of one operator from one machine to two, the collective agreement recognising that:
> there will be occasions when both machines demand an operator, which would result in reduced utilisation.

The number of holiday absences in the drill room means that the degree of undermanning can be quite significant. The T&G is pressing for introduction of a "cover" shift, which they see as the embryonic form of a fifth shift, and feel that any further extension of holiday entitlements would make this a practical possibility.

** It was suggested that the apparently very generous holiday entitlements were a source of embarrassment to the company, who had not realised, on agreeing to the four day system, its implications in this respect, and that this was at least one of the reasons why the company itself was not willing to grant research access.

bargaining consists as much as anything else in taking full advantage of those opportunities which do present themselves. *

Furthermore, whilst the management of further reductions in working time was not discussed at length, it was clear that the union at least was prepared to engage further in the exercise of efficiency bargaining over hours of work, recognising that in a situation where operations are already fully manned some further extension of capacity utilisation time would be required to sustain output and competitiveness.

Case Study 6

Summary of Key Points Emerging

— Trade union pressure at the plant had achieved a major change in working time organisation. A standard five day, day working system with high overtime was replaced by a two shift four day week which minimised overtime;

— The pressure for this change was born out of the union's experience at the plant during the three day week of 1974 when two 12 hour shifts were worked as an emergency measure for the three days of operation. In addition management sought to expand their output and found they could not increase their labour utilisation under the existing system where overtime was already running at very high levels;

— Local plant management was a Key factor in persuading the parent company to change to a four day week; it was suggested that the parent company feared that the example would be used to achieve similar working time patterns amongst their other plants;

— The achievement of the union was all the more remarkable since the plant is situated in an area where trade union organisation and militancy has traditionally been suppressed.

* Elsewhere, within the District attempts have been made to introduce the concept of four day working. However, whilst in all the electronics and textile plants, in which the T&G organises, any night shifts which operate are worked on a 4 × 10 hour basis, it is recognised that "the night shift is thought of as a thing apart", to which management are prepared to concede much greater flexibility, and that it is much more difficult to gain acceptance for innovation in dayshift practices.

Case Study 7

The Company and the Product

The company is part of a UK based multi-national, primarily involved in electronic and electrical engineering.

The plant under investigation employs approximately 1,000 (FTE's) manual workers, and is located in the West Midlands.

Much of the electrical engineering (as opposed to the electronics) output of the parent is produced for the vehicle industry, and the case study factory produces solely for this source. Thus demand, and hence activity rates, tend to reflect both the cyclical pattern of that sector's output, and the present depressed state of the UK automobile industry. At the time of investigation the plant was operating at not more than 75% of full capacity, and had had a spell of "short time working" in the preceding weeks.

Settlements of Terms and Conditions of Employment

The parent is a member of the Engineering Employers Federation and as such a signatory to the National Engineering Agreement, the terms of which, with respect to holidays, hours of work, and premia and calculator rates, applied in the case study factory. The workforce is represented by the AUEW (Engineering) and the T&G, the former having some 700 members (craft and semi-skilled), and the latter some 400 (semi-skilled and unskilled). Both unions have a "full-time" senior steward.

The Structure of Employment

The table below shows the numbers employed, in terms of full-time equivalents, on the various shifts in operation at the factory.

Table 2.24

Shift	Skilled (= Craft)	Semi-skilled (= Production, Direct)	Labourers (= Production, Indirect)
6.00 a.m.–2.00 p.m.	109	340	27
2.00 p.m.–10.00 p.m.	73	310	24
Nights	26	59	7

The skilled workers and labourers are virtually all male, as are the night shift semi-skilled. Of the semi-skilled some 65% are female and 35% male, whilst in terms of "heads", some 80% are female.

The size of the two double day shifts is supposed to be equal, the smaller second (2.00 p.m.–10.00 p.m.) shift, particularly for skilled workers, representing an underfilled establishment. The night shift acts as a "top up shift", which can fluctuate in size within a margin of some 20%, as demand requires, but for male semi-skilled workers it also serves as the way into the plant, most new workers seeking to transfer to "double days" as a vacancy arises.

Semi-skilled labour can be trained within one week, and for this there is no local labour market constraint, although the factory does have difficulty in recruiting craftsmen, a difficulty which is exacerbated by the requirement of working shifts.

Work Organisation

Production work is organised in two basic forms within a high volume flow system. In the machine shops the work is largely individually performed, and is flexible to the extent that more or less machines can be manned up. The number of machines for which an operator is responsible is determined after negotiation and regulated by a domestic agreement. In the assembly shops a series of lines are run, with cycle times varying between 7½ and 13 seconds. There is an optional running/manning level for which each line is engineered. Lines must be fully manned, and thus for each 12 operators a "standby" is employed, paid at a higher rate, and able to relieve operators taking a "personal break" (includes tea breaks from the "open vending system"—there are no formal or collective tea breaks).

The Payments System

A piecework system operates which gives an average production worker a weekly wage (including shift premium) of £85 per week. The largest part of the "incentive money", some 90%, is in fact guaranteed and wages tend to fluctuate by not much more than £3 per week. In the assembly shops the bonus paid to the group on group performance, in the machine shops on individual performance. "Waiting Time" is paid at 80% of the factory average.

The Shift System

As illustrated above, the plant operates basically on a double day shift basis, with a top-up night shift that provides the principal means of accommodating to fluctuations in demand.

For male workers the double day system operates in a conventional system, i.e. alternating every week. Female workers, however, do not, except for a very small number, alternate shifts. The early shift of females is then a permanent one, and a full-time one. The second shift of females, on the other hand, is essentially two half-shifts, one operating from 2.00 p.m. to 6.00 p.m. and the other from 6.00 p.m. to 10.00 p.m. The management feel that they are able to offer a wide range of shift patterns to female employees, particularly to those trying to balance their worktime patterns with those of their husbands.

The permanent night shift works a four and a half night week of 4×9 hours (Mondays–Thursdays) and four hours on Friday, this system being introduced to replace a conventional 5×8 hours system some six years ago. The nine hour nights, involving a 9.00 p.m. start (Mondays to Thursdays), and the Friday half shift (6.00 p.m.–12.00 p.m.), necessitate an overlap of shifts, that, at least in the earlier days of the changeover, was a considerable source of inefficiency, since in an already fully manned factory there was little the workers involved could actually do. However, there is now one assembly line which is not run in the afternoons and the night shift operate this during overlap times. (However, according to the senior AUEW steward, this meant a run down of female recruitment, and as such was resented by the female labour force).

There is no "handover" from one shift to the next, each shift change involves a break in production of some 15 minutes, except the changeover of the first and second half-shifts where the break time is of only about five minutes.

Actual weekly "on plant" time for each of the full-time shifts is forty hours, and this includes a daily half hour lunchbreak. This break time is unpaid—i.e. paid time per week is 37½ hours, at 1/40 of the notional weekly rate.

Overtime Working and Flexibility of Production

The incidence of overtime working for production operators is very low because of the role of the night shift, although in exceptionally bouyant market situations Saturday overtime working might be scheduled. However, the factory is very far from being in such a situation at present.

Overtime is, however, worked by the craftsmen, on an informal rota system which brings in some 25% of the craft labour force on Saturday and Sunday mornings for four hours at a time, to carry out necessary maintenance work outside production time. In addition some 5% of the labouring workforce might come in on Saturday mornings.

In addition to the use of the "top-up" night shift as a source of flexibility, there is considerable scope for variation in the work pace using relatively constant numbers employed. Management felt not only that the night shift were adaptable and able to give more effort if short term production demands required it, but also that on the assembly lines a higher rate of output could be achieved if orders, and hence morale, were high, whilst similarly work rates dropped in periods of slack demand.

Finally, short time working does provide a means of reducing capacity, although in fact, its use to date has been very rare, and it is considered a fairly traumatic experience.

Absences—Holidays and Other

Holidays are covered by factory closures, one week in the spring, two in the summer and one at Christmas. These closures are co-ordinated with the closures of the other engineering companies in Birmingham. Certain "Statutory Days" are moved around, by joint agreement, and also in co-ordination with other major local employers.

The plant management anticipates and plans for, in setting establishment levels, a 9-10% absence level. Absence levels fluctuate seasonally, between 8% and 17% and female absence rates are higher than male. Female part-timers have lower absence rates than do their full-time counterparts, whilst male craft workers have lower absence rates than do male semi-skilled workers and labourers.

In cases of above average absence in the assembly shops; operators are transferred from the machine shops, to ensure that the assembly lines remain fully manned.

Shorter Working Time—Employee Preferences

The senior T&G shop steward (female) thought that the female workforce had a strong preference for a reduced working week, above any other form of reduced work-time. Particularly what was sought was the opportunity for earlier finishes within the day. On the other hand according to the senior AUEW steward (male), the male workforce would be more interested in longer holidays, or opportunities for earlier retirement.

The T&G steward felt that there could be some corresponding productivity gains automatically achieved by reduced working time, fatigue would be less, etc., but also thought that any management proposals for changing work methods would have to be looked at very seriously.

172

The AUEW steward felt that under no circumstances would his membership be prepared to trade money, even future earnings rises for shorter working time, nor did he feel that there existed any real pressure to bargain actively about working time.

Shorter Working Time—Management Views

Management were conscious of the costs involved, in a highly competitive and already depressed market, of reductions in working time.

Reduced working time would lower notional full capacity, and in a situation of more bouyant demand they would probably consider looking to an increase in night shift manning levels as a possible means of compensation. On the other hand, in the longer term they would be seeking to examine both the product mix and production technology looking to these as a means of enhancing labour productivity.

It was, however, recognised that in the short term, with the factory operating at well below capacity, any reduction in working time would put no pressure upon ability to maintain output, although it would still be taken into account in appraising future investments.

No real forward planning, concerning means of adaption to various forms of reduced work time, had been done by the plant management. This was seen more as the preserve of the Group Services Division.

Case Study 7

Summary of Key Points Emerging

—   Output at the plant was very much tied in with the fortunes of the major vehicle manufacturers, hence, at the site investigated plant was being operated at not more than 75% capacity;

—   A shortage of skilled craftsmen was noted, which it was suggested was exacerbated by the need to work shifts;

—   A double day shift operated for the majority of the workforce, for men this operated in the normal alternating manner, for women the shift pattern was fixed—the 'morning' i.e. 6.00 a.m.–2.00 p.m. was a full shift whereas the "afternoon" operated in two half shifts, i.e. 2.00 p.m.–6.00 p.m. and 6.00 p.m.–10.00 p.m. this latter arrangement was offered as a means whereby women could better arrange their working time to fit in with their domestic needs;

—   Overtime working was generally low as the pressure for such was "drawn off" and handled by a "top-up" night shift. This was not the case for craftsmen, however, particularly, for maintenance workers who tended to work for two mornings at least one weekend in four;

—   A clear distinction between the men and women employed emerged with regard to the preferred form of working time reduction. Women would opt for an *incremental* shortening, i.e. earlier finishes to the day whereas the men favoured an increase in *blocks* of leisure time, e.g. through extending holiday entitlement;

—   Management identified competitive constraints to the reduction of working time, conscious of the fact that the factory was already operating below capacity in a depressed and highly competitive market.

INDUSTRY STUDY

Introduction

Industrial Performance in the 1970s

The Chemical Industries presented a number of features which were—in combination—unusual in British manufacturing. These industries in aggregate showed strong growth in output, a 40% increase over the decade (more marked in the first part of the decade) but with strongly marked cyclicality too. Capital investment also showed wide fluctuations (with gross spending at constant prices falling from a major peak in 1970 to a rate little more than half that level by 1973 and then climbing to a peak again in 1978). But it was high enough to be remarkable by British manufacturing's standards; at constant prices plant and machinery capital stock in the chemicals industries increased by about 50% in the decade. These industries were also characterised by a substantial net export surplus which, at constant prices, tended to improve at least until 1978; proportionately the net export surplus was most strongly marked for pharmaceuticals.

Prospects

There must, however, be doubt as to whether the characteristics of the chemical industries' performance through to 1978 can be projected forward as a guide to the 1980s. In the face of an adverse shift in comparative costs (made worse by the appreciation of sterling) import volume increased by as much as 18% in the first quarter of 1979 (compared to a earlier) while exports increased by only 3%. Output growth has been slow since 1977 and must now be affected by General industrial recession in 1980-81. Yet very large capital investment was put in in the late 1970s (some £750 million at 1975 prices in the year 1978 alone). So there may be major problems of undercapacity operation, and of depressed capital investment spending, together with sharper reviews of organisation and operations.

Employment

Employment patterns, in this dynamic industrial setting, were surprisingly stable. There were only very slight cyclical fluctuations in total employment around a virtually level trend; this stability extended to most major industrial sectors within chemicals. It applied also to the occupational balance of the labour force during the 1970s, and to the balance of male and female employment. Consequently changes in labour productivity largely

175

mirrored the variations in output level. It raises the question how far such stability of employment might be consciously pursued and might form a general objective around which other aspects of labour utilisation, and policies on working time, might be developed. This stability in employment in the 1970s suggests two aspects in particular: (i) the benefits from scale economies and improving technology incorporated in new investment enabling capacity and output per worker to rise substantially, and (ii) the stability of manning required in capital intensive plant despite cyclical variations in capital utilisation and output.

Working Time

The employment stability was largely matched by stability in patterns of working time. Only the increase in holiday entitlement could be assumed to have reduced slightly the level of annual working time. Apart from some cyclicality there were no significant changes in levels of overtime, which were low for categories other than men manual workers. There was no tendency to displace full-time by part-time workers. The basic week did not change. Shift working overall (largely applying to manual men) showed little change, at just over one-third of manual men receiving shift premia; though there were increases in the proportion concerned in "general chemicals".

Viewed in one way, basic hours, the majority of full-time manual and non-manual workers in chemicals in the 1970s were on a 37 to 37½ hour basic week, (since this basic week applied to non-manual employees, and shift working manual men are on 40 hours *inclusive* of meal breaks). Viewed another way, in terms of *actual* hours, there is a very marked contrast. The majority of non-manual workers worked simply their basic hours (37/37½); the majority of manual men worked approximately 50 hours (nearly 60% typically working an average of 10 hours overtime).

Definition of Sector

For many purposes we make use of the official data concerning the chemical and allied industries as a whole (Order V). However, as the case studies concern both pharmaceuticals (Minimum List Heading 272) and areas within general chemicals we have—where data made this helpful—separately identified these sectors. For some purposes we have grouped together data for general chemicals (including inorganic and organic chemicals), synthetic resins and plastics, dyestuffs, and fertilisers (MLH 271 and 276-278) as the "chemical sector".

The Size Structure of the Industry

In April 1978 there were 1,394 firms operating in 3,226 establishments in the chemical and allied industries, with total UK employment of over

440,000. But such overall figures should not obscure the concentration of a high proportion of capital in the hands of very large firms, and the high proportions of employees working not only in large firms but in large plants ("establishments").

A recent government survey ("How Many and How Big": Trade and Industry, 17 November 1978) of company size by capital employed showed high concentration in the chemical sector. The analysis examined the 1,500 largest industrial and commercial companies registered in Great Britain.* 106 of these were in chemicals, but the three largest of these accounted for over half (54%) of the total capital employed by all these chemical companies. A further 12 companies, the next in size ranking, accounted for a further 28% of the total capital.

An analysis by the chemical industries' Industrial Training Board enables us to identify broadly the proportion of employees in different size categories of firm in the main sectors of chemicals our case studies were located in. Three quarters of employees in the *"chemical sector"* (with total employment of some 220,000) worked in large firms with more than a thousand employees, 19% in "medium" firms with between 200 and 1,000 employees, and only 6% in smaller firms. The figures for *pharmaceuticals* show slightly less concentration; just over 71% of total employment (some 78,000 working in the pharmaceutical sector) was in large firms, 18% in medium, and just over 10% in smaller firms with less than 200 employees.

Employment is characteristically concentrated in relatively large plants in terms of numbers employed (given the high levels of capital per employee such establishments also represent very large units of capital employed). The table that follows shows the proportion of employees in different sizes of "establishment" in 1976 for pharmaceuticals and for "general chemicals" (MLH 271).

Table 2.25 Percentage of Employees by Size of Establishments

Size (number employed)	11-19	20-49	50-99	100-199	200-499	500-999	1,000 +
Pharmaceuticals	8.0	2.4	5.6	5.9	16.3	28.1	40.8
General Chemicals	1.6	4.8	5.7	11.1	20.1	18.8	37.8

Source: Census of Production, 1976.

As can be seen from the table nearly 70% of pharmaceutical employment is

* These 1,500 companies accounted for 85% of the total assets of all British industrial and commercial companies.

177

in establishments employing 500 or more workers. In general chemicals a rather lower percentage (57%) is in the two largest size categories, and nearly one-third (31%) in the medium plant ranges (from 100 to 499 employees).

It is worth noting that there are differences in the *regional* concentration of these sectors of chemicals. The pharmaceutical industry is unusual in having a high proportion (48%) of employees in the South East. The "chemical sector" is heavily concentrated in the North and North West, with over 60% of its employment in regions north of the Midlands.

Ouput and Productivity

The chemical and allied industries in Britain have, at least until the recession of the mid-1970s and slower growth since, been characterised by unusually high average annual rates of output growth.

Thus, over the period 1963 to 1972 (using the 1963 index of production base and weightings) the average annual percentage growth in output was 6%, in contrast to a 3% growth rate for British manufacturing industries as a whole. Within that, the average annual growth rate of the pharmaceutical industries was almost 10%; by 1972 its output was 2.3 times the 1963 base.

Switching to the 1970 index of production base indicates virtually identical rates of growth from 1968 to the peak in 1974. The average annual rate of output advance for the whole range of chemical industries was 6.1%, an even more striking contrast to that of manufacturing industry as a whole, which had slowed to only 2% p.a. The growth rate in pharmaceuticals was again almost 10% p.a.

These output increases occurred with a virtually unchanged level of total employment in chemical and allied industries, though with slight declines in the early 1960s and early 1970s. Thus the rate of advance of output per employee was virtually that of output itself. There was, however, some build up of employment in pharmaceuticals (from just over 60 thousand in 1963 to nearly 80 thousand at the peak in 1974 for employment in Great Britain); allowing for that, productivity was rising by between 7% p.a. and 8% p.a. in pharmaceuticals.

The performance of the 1970s is best viewed by switching to the 1975 index of production base and linking back to earlier series for the early 1970s. What becomes apparent is the slower rate of advance since the 1975 recession. The data available for 1979 (the first three quarters) suggest output and labour productivity only around 10% higher than the preceding

178

peak year of 1974, though some 20% higher than the trough of 1975. It is worth emphasising, however, that this still contrasts sharply with manufacturing output as a whole, which by 1979 had not regained the 1974 level and had only risen 4% above the 1975 trough, (see Table 2.26).

Table 2.26   Chemical and Allied Industries: Output, Employment, in the 1970s (1975 = 100)

	Production	Employment	Labour Productivity
1970	86	103	83
1971	88	101	87
1972	93	99	94
1973	104	99	105
1974	110	101	108
1975	100	100	100
1976	112	98	114
1977	116	100	117
1978	118	100	117
1979 (1st ¾)	120	101	120

Sources: Trade and Industry: British Business; Department of Employment Gazette.

The table serves to demonstrate the minor element of cyclicality apparent in total employment levels (a deviation of at most some 2% from trend), and their overall near stability. Even with the slower advance of output after 1974, the industry increased output by some 40% over the decade, and ended it with a marginally smaller labour force.

Pharmaceuticals were less affected by the 1975 recession. By 1979 their output was some 20% above the 1974 level, but beginning to decline; labour productivity was some 25% above the 1974 level. By British standards these are still high growth rates, but they are less than the 1960s and early 1970s. Over the decade of the 1970s pharmaceutical output rose over 70% and labour productivity by about two-thirds.

Clearly the growth of the chemical industries is in part related to rates of growth—or lack of such growth—in the UK economy's output and final consumption. It has also reflected a strong international competitiveness. Indeed, the net export surplus improved in recent years until 1977 (whether measured at current or at constant prices). More recently, in the words of the Department of Industry:

> "The continuing strength of sterling, high interest rates and rapidly increasing costs are therefore causing considerable anxiety particularly among the sectors most dependent on remaining competitive in international markets". (British Business, 21 December 1979, p.644).

Within chemicals the pharmaceutical sector is strongly export orientated; exports account for nearly 40% of manufacturers' sales and are around two and a half times the level of imports. (Organic chemicals are also heavily export orientated—with exports some 45% of manufacturers' sales—but the net export surplus is relatively small. Two way trade is increasing as a proportion of the UK market and manufacturers' output*).

Investment

Given the capital intensity of the chemical and allied industries and the continuing high levels of gross capital expenditure it is necessary to look briefly at the industry's fixed investment in the 1970s. The most recent peak of such investment spending, in 1978, found the chemical industries accounting for nearly 20% of manufacturing's fixed capital expenditure (though the industry employs only 6% of manufacturing's total labour force).

It is not easy to interpret the strongly marked waves of capital expenditure in the 1970s, since they do not match the four to five year rhythm of the output cycle. Major investment in new plant is likely to look well beyond any current cycle. The most obvious approach is to suggest that bunching of investment spending generated by relatively optimistic growth projections, the high utilisation of existing capacity, and the need to incorporate more modern technology, may be followed by a pause for "digestion", especially if current possibilities for profitable output growth appear limited and surplus capacity emerges. This fits reasonably well the major and rapid fall in chemical industry investment in the early 1970s (in the context of a moderate recession in 1971-72). It may apply at the end of the 1970s. Slow output growth since 1977 has been noted. The fixed capital expenditure cycle which peaked in the second half of 1978, is likely to have fallen some 10% in 1979, and the downward trend is expected to continue.

The Chemical Industries Association anticipate a further fall in real terms of 30% by 1982. In practice the decline in fixed investment may be more drastic; for on the projections of the Association excess capacity by 1982 would have built up to unusually high levels. It is significant that ICI has in 1979 heavily reduced (approximately halved in real terms) its "sanctioned" spending on future investment in the UK (compared with the 1978 level of "sanctions"): this has generally—with a one year time-lag—been broadly indicative of changes in ICI's subsequent actual rates of capital expenditure. The overall figures are as follows:

* See article "Import Penetration", British Business, 14 September 1979.

Table 2.27 Fixed Capital Expenditure: Chemical and Allied Industries

(in 1975 prices)

	£ million	Index (1975 = 100)
1970	786	144
1971	684	125
1972	492	90
1973	389	71
1974	440	81
1975	546	100
1976	583	107
1977	615	113
1978	748	137
1979 (est.)	(675)	(124)

Source: British Business.

The recovery of capital investment spending before the mid-1970s recession and its continued increase in real terms through that recession owed a good deal to the encouragement provided by high levels of government grant aid. As much chemical plant was already located in "development areas" and as grant aid encouraged location in such areas the chemical industries received substantial Regional Development Grants (a total of £380 million between 1972/73 and 1978/79). These industries also benefited considerably from selective aid under the Accelerated Projects Scheme (designed to operate contra-cyclically in the 1975/76 recession) and the subsequent Selective Investment Scheme; for the latter the chemical industries accounted for half the total assistance provided up to end March 1979. (See: Industry Act Annual Report, 1979).

It is, however, not easy to judge the implications for future market competitiveness, for growth in capacity, and for labour productivity and employment levels in the 1980s of the recent relatively high levels of capital expenditure. It should be noted that pharmaceutical investment has been high in the second half of the 1970s, and this may have provided further capacity to sustain the high growth takes noted for that area of chemicals production. There are no official estimates to indicate how much of recent fixed investment was needed to match "retirements" of existing plant. For manufacturing as a whole official estimates indicate over a third of gross capital spending would have been offset against plant "retirements" but the ratio may be less in the growth orientated chemical industries.

Official estimates of national income lump together the capital stock of the chemical and allied industries with oil refineries. In the decade to 1978 the stock of "plant and machinery" was estimated to have increased by 50% (at

181

1975 replacement costs) to £15 billion. Chemical industries' output rose by almost 50% over the same period. But it would be hazardous to guess how much recently installed capacity may provide the base for futher competitive output growth in the early 1980s.

The Structure of Employment

One official series makes it possible to provide not only an overall analysis of male and female, manual and non-manual, employment but also to compare it with the same data for 1973. (Before that the figures were compiled differently). The comparison suggests surprisingly little change in the balance of employment in the chemical and allied trades:

Table 2.28 Occupational Analysis of Employment: Chemical and Allied Industries (In thousands)

	Operatives	Admin; Tech; Clerical	Total Employed	Admin; etc as % of Total
October 1973				
Male	186	114	209	38.0
Female	70	56	126	44.7
Total	225	170	425	39.9
October 1979				
Male	192	118	310	38.1
Female	65	58	123	47.1
Total	257	176	432	40.7

Source: Employment Gazette, Dec. 1979: Great Britain

Very little change in the occupational balance is apparent—in contrast to other manufacturing sectors (e.g. electrical engineering). The largest single group is that of male manual workers, but they constitute less than half of the total labour force (44%). The ratio of non-manual to manual employees is actually the highest of any industrial Order in manufacturing.

The pharmaceuticals sector stands in rather marked contrast to the employment patterns in most other chemical industries. Around 44% of employees are female in the case of pharmaceuticals; female workers account for nearly 40% of process workers and over two-thirds of ancillary workers. This reflects the importance of jobs such as light testing and packaging operations in pharmaceuticals. By contrast the "chemical sector", as earlier defined, is very heavily male orientated with female employment accounting for only 16% of the total. Very few of these are engaged in either direct or indirect manual production tasks.

182

Patterns of Working Hours

Basic Hours. The New Earnings Survey identifies the basic hours of full-time workers. These have shown negligible changes through the decade.

Table 2.29 Chemical and Allied Industries: Basic Hours, 1979

Manual Men	40.0 hours
Non-Manual Men	37.6 hours
Manual Women	39.1 hours
Non-Manual Women	37.0 hours

However, the bargaining agreements make clear that there is an important qualification to be made as to the basic 40 hours of manual workers. For workers *other than* shiftworkers the basic hours are stated *exclusive* of meal times; for shift workers the 40 is *inclusive* of meal times. What this means in reality could be expressed as a 37½ hour week for shiftworkers exclusive of meal times. The distinction is therefore of importance.

Overtime Working. If anything, levels of overtime working are somewhat less than for manufacturing as a whole. Expressed as average overtime hours per week for all workers the 1979 NES showed:

Table 2.30 Chemical and Allied Industries: Overtime hours, 1979

Manual Men	5.9 hours
Non-Manual Men	1.1 hours
Manual Women	0.8 hours
Non-Manual Women	0.3 hours

(For manufacturing overall average overtime hours were 6.2 for manual men and 1.8 for non-manual men).

In consequence, overtime earnings appear as making only limited contribution to the earnings of non-manual workers (only 2.3% for non-manual men, and 1.2% for women) and manual women (2.7%). These are averages. For the small proportions of the total who worked overtime at the time of the survey such earnings would have been more important. For manual men, overtime earnings were distinctly more important, averaging 14.3% of earnings across the chemical industries. A far higher proportion of manual men worked overtime:

Table 2.31   1979 NES: Proportion Working Overtime

(Chemicals & Allied Industries)

	% Working Overtime	Overtime hours of these
Manual Men	58.2	10.0
Non-Manual Men	15.3	6.7
Manual Women	16.7	(4.8) estimated
Non-manual Women	7.1	(4.0) estimated

Shiftworking will be analysed in a subsequent section, but it intrudes into the analysis of overtime working, because of the somewhat lower average level of overtime hours worked by shiftworkers (this is mainly due to a lower proportion, 50%, of shiftworkers working overtime). This, again, is mainly associated with continuous three shift working (average of just over 4 hours' overtime, according to a separate Department of Employment survey); other male manual workers average nearly 7 hours' overtime.

This general pattern of overtime is entrenched in the industry and shows some variation over the years only as a response to cyclical levels of activity (e.g. manual men's average overtime hours fell from 5.4 in 1974 to 4.1 in the 1975 recession). The second quarter of 1979, during which the NES was taken, was a period of high output in the industry (following supply dislocations earlier in the year).

Regional data is interesting since it suggests some tendency for higher levels of overtime to compensate for lower levels of hourly earnings (excluding overtime premia). In 1979 inter-regional differences in the hourly earnings of "general" workers were as much as 20%; they had been much wider in 1970 (when earnings in the highest earnings region were nearly 50% higher than in the lowest, for time-workers). In 1970 in the lowest earnings region (East Midlands) average overtime worked was nearly 10 hours, in the highest (Scotland) it was just over 4 hours. For craftsmen in 1979, with the same regions representing the lowest and highest earnings (an earnings difference of over 20%) the respective levels of overtime hours were almost identical (9.4 and 4.3 respectively). Most other regions were scattered between these two points. So much might the overtime variation be seen as compensating for differences in hourly earnings, that in 1979 *weekly earnings* of craftsmen in Scotland and East Midlands differed by less than 4%, and the weekly earnings of craftsmen in four other regions fell within the same weekly earnings band (over £100 but under £105). (Source: Employment Gazette, November 1979).*

* The survey of occupational earnings etc. in chemicals covers chemical manufacture within MLH 271-273 and 276-278.

On this interpretation overtime levels are inversely related to underlying levels of hourly earnings. But particular regions appear to have a distinctive overtime culture. Thus Wales, one of the higher earnings regions in chemicals would be expected to have *relatively* low levels of overtime; in fact it has *unusually* low levels of overtime (3 hours a week or less). On the other hand the South Western Region appears in recent surveys as a region that combines high hourly earnings with high levels of overtime working.

Shiftworking. A weakness of the New Earnings Survey data on shiftworking is that it identifies workers receiving shift premia, but this may not coincide with all types of shiftwork. For instance in pharmeceuticals no manual women are recorded as receiving shift premia; there are, however, "twilight" shifts of part-timers. However, we can broadly trust the main finding, namely that shiftworking is primarily a male manual phenomenon. Only 6.3% of non-manual men in the chemical industries received shift premia in the latest survey, less than 2% of non-manual women, and only 4.6% of manual women. In all these cases the value of shift premia accounted for less than one per cent of average earnings for these categories as a whole.

The NES identifies 35% of manual men in chemical and allied industries receiving shift premia in the 1979 survey; the figure was higher (41%) in general chemicals and lower (22.6%) in pharmaceuticals. The proportion receiving shift premia was almost as high overall (34%) in 1970, but appears to have risen (also from 34%) in "general chemicals" over the decade. A separate survey covering "general" workers engaged in chemical production shows a much higher proportion of workers in the category of shiftworkers, slightly over two-thirds, working on one type of shift system or another. If the sampling frame is correct there were about 72,000 manual men in the category of "general" production workers in the chemical industries surveyed in 1979. The breakdown as between day workers and workers on different shift systems was as follows:

Table 2.32 Chemical Industries "General" Production Workers: Shiftwork

Type of shift	Percentages of the total	
	1970	1979
On: Day work	36	32
Continuous 3 shift	49	47
Non-continuous 3 shift	7	11
2 shift	6	8
Others, including night	2	2

Source: Employment Gazette, June surveys.

The importance of continuous 3 shift working emerges clearly, though it is the other shift systems that have shown proportional increases during the 1970s. It is worth noting that overtime working is at higher levels on the shift systems other than 3 shift continuous, where it averages less than 5 hours a week. There appears to have been some increase in the total number of "general" production workers working shifts during the 1970s; from the survey data an increase from under 40,000 to around 50,000 in the industries covered by the survey.*

From the New Earnings Survey we can identify broadly the average value of shift premia to those manual men in chemical industries who worked shifts. In the 1979 survey these shift premia averaged just over £15 in the survey week (the same as the manufacturing industry overall figure for shift premia). This is largely reflected in the higher weekly earnings of shift working manual men in chemicals, £108.80, compared with those of manual men who did not work shifts, which can be estimated to be £94.30—a difference of £14.50 in favour of the shiftworker.

CHEMICAL INDUSTRIES
CASE STUDIES
Case Study 8

Introduction

The company researched for this case study is jointly owned by two multi-national companies, one UK-based, one US-based. It operates on a single site and employs some 500 persons, 386 of whom are "industrial staff", the remainder being administrative, managerial and clerical staff. As the accompanying detail suggests, access to both management and union representatives on site was readily forthcoming.

The company produces "Carbon Black"—used in the manufacture of motor tyres to harden the rubber—via an oil "cracking" process. It is one of three such producing companies (and plants) in the UK, although until very recently there were five indigenous producing plants. The company's output of "Carbon Black" in 1978 was nearly 62,000 tonnes (31% of UK output), of which nearly 16,000 tonnes (26%) was exported.

As well as producing "Carbon Black" the company has, on the same site, a brickworks. This relatively recent addition to activities was made to take advantage of the surplus of power generated by the company's own electricity plant that serves the "Carbon Black" production process. Some 80 of the company's "industrial staff" are here employed, but in this study we are concerned only with the "Carbon Black" activities.

The raw input for "Carbon Black" manufacture, semi-refined oil, arrives by

* Minimum List Headings (MLH) 271-273 and 276-278.

sea, which explains the plant's location on the estuary of the river, and is taken into the factory by pipeline. The final product, a fine black powder loaded in drums, is transported out by road.

Terms and Conditions of Employment

"Industrial staff" in the company are represented by the Transport and General Workers' Union (process and semi-skilled workers) while the various craft unions represent the skilled workforce. There is a post entry "closed shop", and a "check off" system operates.

The company is a member of the Chemical Industries Association, and as such is a signatory to the "Heavy Chemicals" National Agreement.

The company has, since 1968, developed considerable experience of productivity bargaining, indeed this study is very much concerned with the first of these bargains, and with innovatory practices, the latest being (July 1979) to introduce a "threshold" (indexation) clause into the current domestic wage settlment. It is generally agreed that terms and conditions of employment are very competitive, in local terms, and this explains a relatively low rate of labour turnover (8% for manual workers), and a waiting list of potential new employees. One of the particularly favourable aspects of employment conditions was felt to be work-time patterns and durations.

However, it should also be added that the work itself is extremely dirty. The "cracking" process generates a fine black dust which gets everywhere in the production areas. Operatives are required to wear special overalls, which must be removed outside the production areas, and have to bath thoroughly at the end of the shift. Both "dressing up time" (10 minutes) and "bathing time" (30 minutes) are outside "normal time" and are not paid for by the company.

Work-Time Patterns and Durations

The production of Carbon Black is necessarily a continuous process, continuous for 24 hours per day, 7 days per week, 365 days per year. The company is located in an industrial complex composed primarily of other oil and chemical products plants, thus is one of several where continuous operations occur, and as such is in an area where there is a "shift working culture". In this study we are principally concerned with the work time patterns of the continuous process workers (at present some 125 of the "industrial staff").

i) Work Time Patterns Pre-1968

Prior to the 1968 productivity deal work time patterns were like those found in many continuous process plants. Under the 48 hour week, shifts were arranged on a seven week cycle, using three and a half teams, and for any one individual were as below:

	Sun	Mon	Tue	Wed	Thur	Fri	Sat
Week 1	R/D	2-10	2-10	2-10	2-10	2-10	2-10
Week 2	2-10	R/D	10-6	10-6	10-6	10-6	10-6
Week 3	10-6	10-6	R/D	6-2	6-2	6-2	6-2
Week 4	6-2	6-2	6-2	R/D	2-10	2-10	2-10
Week 5	2-10	2-10	2-10	2-10	R/D	10-6	10-6
Week 6	10-6	10-6	10-6	10-6	10-6	R/D	6-2
Week 7	6-2	6-2	6-2	6-2	6-2	6-2	R/D

Shift times: Morning shift   6.00 a.m.– 2.00 p.m.
             Afternoon shift   2.00 p.m.–10.00 p.m.
             Night shift   10.00 p.m.– 6.00 a.m.
             R/D = Rest Day

When the working week was reduced to 44 hours a new shift pattern was introduced having a four week cycle, and using four teams (i.e. an additional half team was recruited). The shift pattern is illustrated below:

	Sun	Mon	Tue	Wed	Thur	Fri	Sat
Week 1	R/D	R/D	2-10	2-10	2-10	2-10	2-10
Week 2	2-10	2-10	R/D	R/D	6-2	6-2	6-2
Week 3	6-2	6-2	6-2	6-2	Spiv	R/D	10-6
Week 4	10-6	10-6	10-6	10-6	10-6	10-6	R/D

In order to produce the 44 hours outcome it was necessary to have 22 8-hour shifts worked in any four week period. This explains what was termed the "Spiv Day", on which the workers came in on a day shift (8.00 a.m.–5.00 p.m.) and worked on odd cleaning jobs (i.e. "spiving" the plant up). When the working week was reduced to 42 hours the "Spiv Day", generally admitted as not very productively used, was replaced by an additional rest day.

On the reduction of the working week to 40 hours a further minor modification was introduced. To produce a 40 hours average only 20 days had to be worked in any four week period. The basic shift pattern remained unchanged—i.e. two days "off", seven days "on", two days "off", seven days "on", two days "off", seven days "on", and then one day "off"—but one of the morning shifts was also taken off, as a "lieu" day. To fill in the "gaps" thus created a special 6.00 a.m.–2.00 p.m. shift, of five persons was recruited.

188

ii) The 1968 Productivity Deal

It first must be stressed that the ideas generated, and the changes in work organisation made, in the 1968 productivity deal were *entirely* local in origin. Neither the company or the local unions made use of any national facilities (i.e. of the CIA's or the national unions' resources). The agreement applies to all "industrial staff" but we shall see first its implications for continuous process workers.

The changes made in 1968 were an attempt to break out of a "high absenteeism, high overtime syndrome", i.e. one in which the rate of individual, unplanned absences was high and there was a consequent need to make use of overtime to cover these absences, which in practice meant the necessity for operators to work "doublers" (or double shifts). The productivity deal stated as one of its principal objects the intention:

To share the benefits of increased productivity with employees by

a) eliminating overtime and achieving an average 40 hour week as far as possible;

b) providing each employee with a stable wage not dependent upon overtime earnings and with greater financial security.

The introduction to the agreement subsequently continued:

The Company and the Trade Unions, agree that overtime is undesirable and should only be performed when essential and should not be used as a regular means of maintaining an acceptable level of earnings; but that it is essential that extended hours within the terms of this Agreement must be worked to satisfy essential production needs.

To discourage resorting to overtime, it was no longer to be payable, but to be taken as *Time off in Lieu* (TOIL) *on an hour-for-hour basis*. It was also, however, agreed:

. . . that an employee may be required to work incidental overtime in order to complete a job on the following basis.

Short periods of overtime, the need for which arrives during the course of the day, amounting to not more than 30 minutes in any day and totalling not more than one hour in any pay week, shall be treated as incidental overtime and shall not rank for time off in lieu . . .

This arrangement applies equally to shift workers delayed through the late arrival of a relief.

In order to maintain wages average overtime earnings were consolidated and an annual salary was calculated. This salary is paid monthly, in arrears, in 13 instalments.

Operators would continue to provide "overtime" cover for the *first day* of sickness and other absences* (although not holiday absences and planned absences) if another shift worker were not available, albeit that this meant the working of a second shift (double shifts were to be preferred to "call in" another worker both because they minimised the inconvenience of calling in and were cheaper—i.e. did not require "calling in payments" to be made). However all hours so worked became an entitlement to time off.

In order to provide for opportunities for this time off to be taken without disrupting manning levels on the continuous production process, shift patterns were re-arranged onto a five week cycle. The system, as instituted, now required five teams to man it, and we shall discuss later the manner whereby this fifth team was "created". The shift pattern looked as follows:

	Sun	Mon	Tue	Wed	Thur	Fri	Sat
Week 1	R/D	2-10	2-10	2-10	2-10	2-10	2-10
Week 2	2-10	R/D	R/D	6-2	6-2	6-2	6-2
Week 3	6-2	6-2	6-2	R/D	R/D	10-6	10-6
Week 4	10-6	10-6	10-6	10-6	10-6	R/D	R/D
Week 5	R	R	R	R	R	R	R

R/D = Rest Day   R = Relief Shift

Under this system the fifth week was the occasion when operators took time off for overtime worked (on a day "suitable to the management, after consultation with the employee, whose wishes will be met whenever practical") and also took their "lieu days" (i.e. those necessary to produce the 40 hour week). It was from the Relief Shift that cover for the second day of unplanned absences, and for all planned absences was taken, and the operator would work on the appropriate shift. If an operator was not required for cover then he would work (Monday to Friday) on days, doing cleaning and other odd jobs.

There were however problems associated with this system. Firstly, it was never certain how many people would be available on the relief shift after TOIL entitlements had been dealt with. Secondly, the jobs done by those on "days" were not considered very useful, and supervision created difficulties. The first modification to the system was one whereby operators actually on the shift provided *all* the cover for the shifts, and the fifth week was used for TOIL or for day working. The second modification was more important, for

* The agreement states:

A double shift will be worked or another suitable relief will be provided if a shift worker does not arrive within the following periods from his starting time: Morning shift 2 hours; Afternoon shift 1 hour and Night shift 30 minutes.

It both dealt with the unproductiveness of day working, by abolishing it, and introduced the concept of "annual hours".

The Annual Hours Contract

The final modification to the shift system left the five week cycle with five teams unchanged. However all unplanned absences and short term sickness* plus one week per person of winter time holiday were to be covered by "overtime" either by the half or the full shift, worked by those actually working shifts. The fifth week was now to be time off. In other words every fifth week would be a free week, and since it is buttressed on each side by rest days thrown up by the normal shift cycle—two days preceeding it and one day succeeding it—the actual break is of eleven days. Summer time holidays of three weeks are rostered into the system such that during the holiday period a system of four team working is reverted to. Because the fifth team is on holiday there is no rest week every fifth week.

It should be noted that the system has been altered from a slow to a fast rotating one. This is because, if relief cover has to be provided, a fast rotating system eliminates the burden of covering one particular operator's absence from falling entirely upon another particular operator, rather it will necessarily fall on several persons.

The concept of annual hours is important to this system since it provides the obligation for the provision of "overtime" cover. The annual hours contract is calculated in terms of the number of hours *owed* to the company, by an employee, working a notional forty hours per week, and entitled to four weeks vacation, and 8 days of statutory holidays per year. These parameters are set by the National Agreement, and the company's domestic agreement left them unchanged. What it did do, however, was to radically alter how these hours were distributed through the working year.

Each employee owes the company 1,856 hours per year (= 52 weeks × 40 hours—4 weeks × 40 hours—8 days × 8 hours). The company requires continuous cover throughout the year, or 8,760 hours of cover (= 365 days × 24 hours) and has five teams available to provide that cover. Thus each team is required, all things being equal, for 1,725 hours (= 8,760 ÷ 5), but any individual is, in fact, contracted to do 104 hours more than this. The agreement rounds this down to 100 hours, and the company is entitled to "claw back" these 100 hours in the form of "overtime cover". This is where the obligation to cover for sickness, absence, and winter holidays comes from.

* Sickness of less than one month.

191

In practice any one individual will only tend to work some 50 of these "overtime" hours. For this there are two reasons. Firstly management monitors very carefully each person's "overtime" record, and when "overtime" appears to be "too high" (>50 hours) will ensure that subsequent cover will be provided by another operator from another work group, or in the case of larger work groups from the same work group, who can perform his functions, or, if there has turned out to be a case of longer term sickness, put in a replacement operator to eliminate the need for cover. Secondly, absence rates tend to be low in any case. Work groups are small (the maximum size is 10, most are five—i.e. one person per team) and there is a high degree of solidarity which ensures that people are aware of the inconvenience to another that an unnecessary absence will cause. In addition the fact that one week in five is free means that there is little need for casual absence—free time is always fairly imminently available. The company claim as a consequence of the original agreement, and the new patterns of working time that it threw up, a substantial saving on overtime payments that would otherwise have been paid, and argue that this was the result of a considerable fall in the rate of absenteeism.

In 1977 as part of a "self financing productivity deal" in which process operators agreed to carry out certain quality control exercises, payment is now made for any "overtime" worked.   This payment comprises the "premium element" only.

Both management and unions agree that the present work time system, based upon the annual hours contract, represents the perfection of five-team, no-overtime working. However they also recognise that it was probably very necessary to move through all the various steps on the way to the creation of that system, believing that the learning process involved was a vital one.

The Creation of the Fifth Team

The Creation of the fifth team, an organisational requirement for the new worktime pattern, was an essential element of the productivity bargain. The introduction to the agreement stated:

> The Trade Unions jointly undertake that . . . agreed flexibilities will be maintained and the company undertakes to take such measures as may be necessary to achieve the aim of a true 40 hour week as far as possible.

The flexibilities that the unions agreed to were very significant. The unions agreed to impose no restrictions on "the employment of any operator in any other operating capacity *when necessary*" or on "training or the use of trainees on operating jobs''. More importantly they agreed to participate in *a major "demanning exercise''*. In the words of the agreement:

> To enable the (fifth team) to be formed without a significant increase in the number of operators and to improve efficiency the manning of the plants will be reorganised on a team basis. The grade of Charge Hand will be abolished with five promoted to Assistant Foreman and 3 re-deployed to Panel Control Operator. Shift Drivers will be re-deployed.

What, in fact, the unions were agreeing to was a 25% demanning of each of the existing four shifts, thus enabling five teams to be created out of the manpower of four. This was considered to be perfectly possible for the process jobs, since they contained only a small element of manual work, and mainly involved watching dials and monitoring. In other words there was considerable scope for job enlargement.

Work Time Patterns of "Non Continuous" Staff

Most other "industrial staff" including maintenance craftsmen, packers, and labourers work days (8.00 a.m. to 4.30 p.m.). "Bulk loaders" (those loading the final product onto road transporters) work a system of three weeks on days followed by two weeks on "double days" which enables an extended time for loading. (The 1968 Agreement introduced this shift working as a replacement for overtime working).

The principle of TOIL applies to overtime worked by non-process workers, and the non-process areas were also subject to the agreements to enhance the flexibility of utilisation of labour. These included the phasing out of the use of craftsmen's mates and the introduction of a grade of "maintenance assistants", and the consent of the unions to the use of craftsmen across more than one skilled area. Workers in the loading areas committed themselves to an increased daily output rate.

Day workers are liable to work up to 10 weekends per year, as required. For maintenance workers some of this time is rostered. All weekend working is eligible for TOIL. Actual overtime in the day working area tends to be low (it was averaging 3.5 hours per week for all day workers at the time of the study) and management claimed that, since the foremen were committed to getting work done in normal time, this had a salutory effect upon the workforce.

Day workers, subsequent to the 1977 deal, do have the choice of taking overtime as TOIL, or of receiving payment for it. Individual preferences tend to be a function of age/financial responsibilities.

The premium payment for overtime was reintroduced, in part, to expand the amount of overtime worked in the maintenance department. The company wished both to re-equip, and to do a backlog of maintenance that had been put off during the mid-1970s downturn. To do this it was necessary to extend the maintenance input, and this had to be done via overtime rather than recruitment a) because the company is physically unable to increase its labour force—it has no space, b) because there was need for much of the work to be done outside normal hours, and c) because it was felt that, even if additional labour could have been recruited, there was not enough sustained work to justify recruitment.

Shorter Working Time

Both management and unions thought that any reduction in the basic working week would flow over, 100%, into overtime. Both were agreed that the present work time pattern gave employees as much leisure as they could handle, or wanted, and thus that preferences would be for actual hours and work patterns to stay unchanged, with earnings being the medium of adjustment. Whilst, theoretically the slack in the system would mean that an additional week's holiday could be accommodated, because, on average, each shift worker still owes the company 50 hours per year, it is possible that employees would be reluctant to "give up" any of those hours without being paid for them (albeit that they were, in fact, the company's to claim).

Significant reductions in actual annual work time would be sufficient to make the introduction of a sixth team necessary. However, whilst it was felt *technically* possible to repeat the demanning exercise of 1968 again in order to create a sixth team, it was doubted whether it would be *politically* possible, on the grounds that there were "no longer the carrots there" to induce the unions to participate in the exercise (because people do not want any more free time).

There was an extreme consciousness of the physical constraints of the site which would militate against any possibility of increasing the size of the labour force in response to shorter working time. The recent closure of two UK "Carbon Black" plants, and hence a severe shortage of manufacturing capacity in the country, had recently put considerable pressure upon the company. They had sought to increase both their packing and cleaning staff and had already run up against the problem of the physical size of the plant, and the difficulty of getting any more persons onto it.

194

Case Study 8

Summary of Key Points Emerging

- The plant investigated displayed a steady evolution of its shift system as it adapted to reduction in basic contractual hours, i.e. from 48 to 44 to 40;

- As an attempt to break out of the "high absenteeism—high overtime" syndrome which had characterised its working time patterns it embarked upon a productivity deal to eliminate overtime and provide financial stability and security via the basic wage;

- Overtime was compensated only by time off in lieu (TOIL);

- In order to provide the necessary flexibility a fifth shift was created: this was conditional upon the trade unions agreeing significant increases in the flexibility and deployment of labour whilst also agreeing that the manpower for the fifth shift be drawn from a 25% demanning of the existing four shifts;

- The development of the working time system at the plant also introduced the notion of contractual hours being negotiated on an *annual* basis;

- The evolution of the shift system and the organisation of working time appears to have been wholly carried through at local level, and has been characterised by a degree of willingness on both sides to attempt to develp innovatory solutions to standard manpower problems. The learning curve thus generated also seems to have been appreciated by both sides.

Case Study 9

This case study comprises the tablet factory of a major UK based pharmaceutical company. The site investigated is situated in the Midlands. At the Tablet Factory the company *makes* tablets essentially in four operations—mixing the constituents, granulating the mixture, pressing out, and finally, as necessary, coating the tablets—and also *packs* the finished product. Since the product range is wide, production is by the *batch*. Production runs for any particular product will vary in length, but each change of product requires a complete cleaning of the production areas and equipment.

In the interests of brevity it should be noted that after some preliminary comments this case study concentrates on working time organisation in the packing department of the plant. The other three departments were studied, but the reports remain unpublished.

Settlement of Terms and Conditions of Employment

Hourly paid workers in the factory are represented by USDAW, which, together with the T&GWU is party to a Company wide closed shop agreement for all production and warehouse workers. The company is a member of the Chemical Industries Association, and is a signatory of the "Drug and Fine Chemicals" National Agreement, which for the company determined overtime premia, "call in" payments, hours of work and holiday entitlements and arrangements. Separate company and National agreements cover engineering/maintenance workers, who are represented by the appropriate craft unions.

Collective bargaining, covering such areas as rates of pay, shift premiums, and conditions of working, including the terms and the operation of the Job Evaluation Scheme regulating the grading of workers, is conducted at Company level, there is no local (site or plant) bargaining. The terms of the Company Agreement grant considerable scope for managerial prerogative with respect to work organisation and work methods, in as much as:

> "The unions recognise the management's right to plan or organise and manage the operations of each factory and warehouse in order to achieve and maintain maximum efficiency of operation".

Present Working Time Patterns (plant wide)

The basic work week, for full-timers, is of forty hours, Monday to Friday. The annual holiday entitlement is of four weeks, and in additon employees receive eight statutory days of holiday. There is no annual factory closure period, bar the three days off at Christmas. Annual holidays can be taken as desired, save that line management has the right to operate a "first come first served" system to ensure that holiday absence within any particular period does not rise above levels detrimental to planned production.

Both shift working and day working are to be found in the factory. Tablet *production operations* are performed on a two shift, "double day", basis, with the first shift commencing at 6.00 a.m. and finishing at 2.00 p.m., and the second shift commencing at 1.30 p.m. and finishing at 9.30 p.m. Each shift includes a half hour's paid meal break, and shifts alternate on a weekly basis. The half hour overlap, a relatively recent modification, was introduced as the result of a local initiative—for which there is scope in the company agreement—to produce a more socially desirable finishing time for the second shift, whilst, at the same time, providing considerable benefits to management and the production process. Shift premiums are paid at a flat rate—the same for both shifts, and are worth some 21% of time rate to a normal—Grade F—production worker.*

Packing operations are performed on a day shift basis, with a standard day starting at 8.00 a.m. and finishing at 5.00 p.m., and including a one hour's unpaid lunch break. In addition a part-time, "twilight", shift works form 5.00 p.m. to 9.00 p.m.

Whilst the factory itself is part of a complex on which fairly extensive incidences of shift working, including seven day continuous shift working, are to be found, and this complex itself is in an area where other major employees also operate shift working, so that a "shift working culture" can be said to prevail, tablet production is considered, at least by the workforce, to be a double day operation and management feel that it is not possible to change this. Furthermore, the operation of two shift working in one area—production, and single shift working in another—packing, is reinforced by a sexual division of the labour force. Production is considered to be a "male job" (although, not quite all production employees are male) and men are more prepared/less constrained to work shifts, whereas packing is considered to be a "female job" (and indeed all the packing staff are female), and, as such is felt unsuitable, for both social and legal reasons, for shift operation. The assumption is that cultural norms are, and will remain, rigid, and that in consequence dependent work organisation norms are also rigid.

PACKING OPERATIONS

Establishment, Functions and Shift Pattern

Packing is performed exclusively by females, and the present day shift complement is 110. This total is, and has been, fairly stable. In addition, working days, are 19 "morning part-timers" working from 8.00 a.m. to 1.00 p.m., and 14 "afternoon part-timers" working 2.00 p.m. to 5.00 p.m., all of whom are long servers—the company does not recruit day part-timers—these are drawn from either full-timers who have sought to reduce their hours, or are evening part-timers who have sought transfer to day working. The day shift is complemented by the part-time evening shift which serves to absorb peak loadings of work. The present part-time shift complement is 44 but it was emphasised that, as a function of its

* The range is from 24% to 19% across all grades of worker covered by the agreement.

197

"back-up" role, numbers varied considerably over time, and as required. Totals as high as 90 and as low as 25 were both fairly recent, and turnover rates are sufficiently high to give management all the flexibility they require over manning levels. Over the past twelve months the shift had been run down from over 80 strong, and the factory was still not replacing leavers, in order to reduce numbers yet further.

Ancillary functions to the packing process—the servicing of the packing lines, the setting up of equipment—are carried out by male workers. One of these works days, but the rest, twelve plus two supervisors, are divided into two shifts and work the standard "double day" shifts. This provides ancillary cover over the whole of the packing day, as well as time at the beginning of the day to prepare and supply the packing counters. In addition the supervisor of the second shift has overall supervisory responsibility for the part-time evening shift.

In addition there are eight engineers/maintenance workers attached to the department. Four of these work days and the other four are divided into two shifts to provide cover during the full "double day".

Organisation of Work

Some 20 counters are available for packing, with different counters having different speeds of operation and suitability for different products. Present product mix consequently means that some counters are used more than others, some being used continuously, others hardly at all. Counter running speeds are fairly flexible, in that between certain limits there is a one-to-one relationship between manning levels, on a counter, and hence line speeds, and counter output. However, beyond a certain level diminishing returns set in, although it is possible to mitigate this temporarily by adding additional equipment to the counter. Those lines which are in more or less continuous operation, the fastest lines, processing the major share of output, are already manned up to their limits and it is not possible to increase output by increasing manning and hence line speeds. It is, in consequence, on these lines that the evening shift is employed, supplementing capacity by extending counter running time.

Effective Working Time

Within paid hours day shift packers have a 10 minute break, in the middle of the morning work period. On the evening shift there is a five minute, informal, break.

The paid breaks of the male ancillary workers are staggered over a period of some two and a half hours and in addition these workers are able to take informal breaks, as the work load itself determines. The overlap of the two shifts was felt to have had no impact upon effective working time—given that the function of the ancillary workers is to service the packing lines very little work needs to be done after the counters cease running, and certainly very little used to be done after 9.30 p.m. when the 10.00 p.m. finish was standard. On the other hand the overlap has lead to substantial benefits in solving problems of communication between shifts and in this sense time has probably been saved.

Use of Overtime

Overtime, for the packing staff, is only very infrequently worked. When it is laid on, to meet peaks of production, the normal form is to work two additional hours in the evening, Monday to Thursday. The response rate is never more than 50% and sometimes as low as 10%. Overtime is never laid on for more than one week at a time, and rarely for more than four weeks in a year. Very rarely the evening shift is extended by one hour, and very occasionally volunteers are drawn from both shifts to work on a Saturday morning, from 8.00 a.m.–12.00 mid-day.

Throughout most of the year weekend overtime working can be offered to/is required from the ancillary workers. A rota system, in which most participate, brings in four men for four hours on Saturday mornings, doing work on cleaning and setting up of equipment. Such overtime accounts for 95% of overtime worked by the ancillary workers, the rest, involving early starts or late finishes, is required to deal with highly specific and immediate tasks.

The engineering/maintenance staff work occasional Saturday mornings and this is the extent of their overtime working. This very limited overtime, is, however, a recent phenomenon. Until some six months ago all the engineers were day workers, and evening cover was provided by overtime. The introduction of shift working was designed to eliminate this need for overtime, but the change over was resisted by the workers involved—who earned more with overtime than they would by simply being in receipt of a shift premium, and was only made possible by allowing the day shift to run down through natural wastage, and by recruiting new workers to make up the shifts.

Absences

Absence rates vary significantly across the different categories of worker, the principle source of difference being the incidence of short term (less than three days) absence. Part-time women have the best record of attendance with very little absence, whilst full-time women have the highest absence levels. Male workers' patterns fall between the two.

Since the absence level of full-time females is fairly constant a "plus element" is built into manning levels to cover for it. The "plus element" is further increased to take account of holiday entitlements, although, in addition, a certain peaking of holidays, within a fairly narrow, three to four week, period, is anticipated, and built into production schedules. Holidays of part-timers tend to occur at the same time, and as such are similarly anticipated, whilst the generally low level of absence does not necessitate any "plus manning". Should there be an exceptional shortfall on a particular day it is usually possible to make it up by borrowing staff from another factory on site.

Absences, including holiday absences, amongst the ancillary staff tend to be covered from within the work group, "by asking people to work a bit harder". Long term absences are covered by borrowing from elsewhere, within the factory or the site.

Possibilities for Flexi-time

There are two principle constraints on the operation of a flexi-time system for packing operations.* Firstly, the nature of the packing process means that full attendance is necessary for effective operation of the packing lines. Secondly, the fact that 90% of the female workforce travels to and from work on contract hire buses means that starting times have to be common, since the majority of women would be unable to supply alternative transport.

However, for the ancillary workers, who supply their own transport in any case, it is possible, on an informal basis, for individuals to swap shifts, whilst in addition a system whereby, with agreement, a person's opposite number on the other shift covered by his own early arrival, for an early finish, was also considered to be a practical possibility.

The Potential for Shorter Working Time

Given that the work time durations of ancillary workers are dependent upon those of the packers, investigation concentrated upon the effects of shorter working time for the packing staff.

* NB. Considerable use of flexi-time is made on site amongst clerical and administrative grades, but management have proved reluctant to extend the practice to productive grades.

Management felt that there existed little potential for savings of time within the normal working day as a source of compensation for reductions of basic working time, since time was felt to be efficiently used already. On the other hand, operations were for the first time being subjected to work-study, which might suggest more efficient line layouts and reveal potential manpower savings or increases in productive capacity. Notwithstanding this, the principle source of increased productivity was felt to be via investment in new and faster equipment.

A reduction in the length of the basic work week, e.g. a 35 hour week taking the form of five seven-hour days, would suggest two possible forms evening shift. This was because the latter shift's starting time cannot be and those which are not, are not appropriate to the present product mix, a shorter working week would all things being equal, reduce productive capacity. One way to restore this capacity would be to move over to two shift operations, with smaller sized shifts. However, such a radical change may, in fact, be unnecessary. Already planned and soon to be installed new equipment will reduce the required running time of these lines for any given level of output, and will of itself be sufficient to compensate for the effects of a reduced work week.

Moreover, a change to 2 shift working in the packing department would run up against the seemingly fixed perception of the workforce already referred to, that packing is strictly a day shift occupation. Whilst management might seek to break this cultural "norm" perhaps by employing more male workers (i.e. more sympathetic to shift working), a second "norm" would then act as a constraint, i.e. that packing is a "female job". Despite the fact that packing jobs are not the lowest grade in the factory and that some males might be better off financially in the packing department, to date no males have ever applied for jobs in what is seen as a strictly female province.

The planned installation of new equipment providing increases in production capacity illustrates the vulnerability of the part-time evening shift. Indeed, it was this anticipated increase in spare capacity which had led to the running down of the twilight shift observed at the time of our investigations. Managment on site felt that it would not be removed entirely, i.e. a much reduced manning level may be maintained "just in case" the new equipment did not produce the expected increases. However, it was made clear to us that the twilight shift would have a much better chance of surviving, notwithstanding the new equipment, if it were operated in conjunction with a shortened basic week for the day workers. Even so, such a reduction in the basic week to say 35 hours per week would have to be concentrated at the start of the day in order to fit in with the evening shift. This was because the latter shift's starting time cannot be brought forward without disrupting arrangements for child-minding that are essential, particularly for those whose ability to leave home is dependent upon the fact that their husbands have already arrived home from work.

Working Time Preferences (plant wide)

Shiftworking is considered to be generally acceptable to the extent that it does not interfere with the traditional weekend. Consequently there would be resistance to the introduction of continuous operation, whilst in addition there is aversion to any extension of the limited instances of night working.

Within the present contractual work week rearrangements were favoured which reduced Friday finishing times, both for day workers and for those on the second shift of the double day, and thus extended the weekend break. There are examples on some company sites of arrangements whereby day workers have reduced their lunchbreaks to permit an early finish on Friday, although it was recognised that where *large* numbers of workers were serviced by a central canteen a compressed lunchbreak would be organisationally impossible.

Whilst workers were looking for reduced work-time the chief shop steward suggested that there was uncertainty as to the form in which it was desired. As such he felt that a "framework agreement", granting a reduction in annual hours of work but allowing the form of the reduction to be dictated by the nature of the operations involved*—e.g. for some a reduced working week, for some an increase in the holiday entitlement, would be a practical proposition, and that, were the company able to make out a good case for the need to differentiate between different groups of workers, the arrangements would be acceptable to the workforce.

Constraints on the Management of Change

It was felt that the management of change was the responsibility of the company, and that the unions would look to the company and individual plant managers to present to them their formulae for its successful management, but saw their role as to assess the credibility of these formulae and to advise their members accordingly.

Given the nature of the industrial relations environment it was thought that maximum co-operation would be given in the management of

* NB. This was the formula anticipated by the Company Industrial Relations Manager, and to the extent that any reduction in working time was accepted, according to him, favoured by the CIA.

change, and it was felt that increased productivity would be the principle source of compensation. Whether this would mean an explicit productivity deal around the working time reduction, or a productivity deal linked to a simultaneous or consequent wage increase, was uncertain, but as a consequence it was felt that the employment effects of shorter working time would be very limited. This was seen to be not only a function of management's desire to seek a least cost solution, but also it was suggested because of the workforce's apparent lack of sympathy for the unemployed.

Were an increase in the holiday entitlement to be granted it was felt that the unions would insist that at least some of it be available to be taken over the summer months, although a closure between Christmas and the New Year absorbing three additional days would be acceptable. The company has never operated a summer holiday closure, arguing that the nature of the business, the need to continuously supply the retail trade, does not allow for it, and as such an increased holiday entitlement would affect the volume of labour available in the summer months. At present this greater than average level of absence is covered in two ways—by those remaining on the jobs working a bit harder (not necessarily overtime), and by taking temporary labour (e.g. students), usually onto the lowest grades and temporarily upgrading permanent staff, sometimes straight onto production jobs. The role of both of these methods might be increased, suggesting that where there is demand for additional labour it would only be for temporary labour.

Flexi-Time and Alternative Hours System

Flexi-time systems have been operated in the company for some five years. Most of the schemes are of the standard form involving two "core times" within the day, a flexible lunch time, and flexible start and finish times. Some schemes permit the carrying over of hours within the week, others require that the full day be worked each day. The vast majority of the schemes cover only administrative, clerical and scientific staff.

There are, however, two instances of flexi-time for production workers. One of these involves a small number of male ancillary workers operating on a double day shift system and servicing a day and twilight shift packing line (similar to the situation found in the tablet factory). The first shift can come in between 6.00 and 6.15 a.m. and leave eight hours later, the second shift can start between 1.30 and 2.00 p.m., again finishing eight hours later. The nature of the work done means that only during the time when the packing line is running is it necessary to have the full complement of ancillary staff, and that at other times manning can be varied. In the other instance of flexi-time for production workers again the nature of the work done means that it is not necessary to have the full workforce there at the same time. The scheme operates for day workers engaged in "specials manufacturing" which involves more or less individual working on the manufacture of small batches, and is an example of a standard two "core" times flexi-day system.

Where working involves collective operations, and flexi-time is consequently not appropriate, the scope for variation is more limited. However, there are three examples within the company of "alternative hours" systems. Two of these involve double day shift workers and offer alternative hours for the second shift, a fifteen minute early start for four days of the week and one hour early finish on Fridays, the third involves day shift workers, and offers the opportunity to take either a 45 minute lunch break five days per week or a 30 minute break and a one hour 15 minute early finish on Fridays.

However, it is worthwhile noting that union interest in flexi-time systems for production workers had been greatest at the time of their first introduction into the company, but that, once the practical difficulties of their implementation had been appreciated, interest, and any concern for parity of treatment, seemingly had diminished.

Case Study 9

Summary of Key Points Emerging

— Collective bargaining is carried out at company level. The company agreement provides considerable management autonomy in the organisation of working time;

— Clearly defined *temporal* and *sexual* norms were identified with respect to working time organisation, i.e. the packing operation was seen as a *day work female* job whereas production was seen as a *shift work male* province. These cultural rigidities apparently conditioned the responses of both management and trade union to the notion of reduced working time;

— A part-time all female "twilight" shift which operated at the end of the basic day shift in the packing department displayed both the immediate flexibility which management can achieve and the vulnerability of this particular shift form—manning had fluctuated between 90 and 25 in the recent past;

— New equipment soon to be introduced at the plant was thought to promise sufficient increase in labour productivity to both absorb potential reductions in basic working time, whilst drastically reducing the requirements for the "twilight" shift;

— No clear preferences for the form which reduced working time might take were identified, other than a general desire for early finishing on

Fridays—thus maximising the weekend break. The leading shop stewards were in favour of a "framework agreement" which would provide the flexibility for local negotiations to agree the form of any reduction within an annual hours guideline;

— The existence of significant *internal* labour market flexibility was denoted by a facility which the company used to "borrow" workers from within the plant to provide extra cover for particular operations.

Case Study 10

Introduction

The company researched in this case study is wholly owned by a US multi-national. It operates a number of sites in the UK and is amongst the five biggest chemical companies in the UK. The works studied was situated in the Midlands and was principally engaged in the production of phosphorus and phosphor compounds. It employed some 780 persons on site comprising 150 non-manual and 630 manual employees.

Considerable access and co-operation was provided to the researcher by both management and unions on site. *

Settlements of Terms and Conditions of Employment
(Manual Workers)

The company is a member of the Chemical Industries Association, and as such is a signatory to the relevant national agreements. These agreements determine basic hours of work, basic holiday entitlements, and overtime premia percentages.

Wage rates (until 1979), shift premia, and most other terms and conditions of employment are settled at site level and embodied in local agreements. At the site the signatory unions are the AUEW (Engineering Section) and the EETPU (Electrical Section) covering craft workers, and the GMWU covering process and all other manual workers. The parties have a long tradition of productivity bargaining.

In 1979 company level negotiations concluded with agreement on a Wage Rationalisation programme designed to introduce uniform rates of pay

* We use the words "works" and "site" to indicate a particular establishment, the word "plant" in the Chemical Industry referring to a particular piece of equipment, within a works, producing a particular product. Thus at the site there are some 20 plants, each producing a particular compound.

across all sites. Company level rates already exist for supervisory staff, and the existence of a multiplicity of rates for manual workers—a function of the fact that the company in part grew by merger and acquisition—had produced the unsatisfactory state of affairs of a multiplicity of differentials between supervisors and the supervised. The Wage Rationalisation deal was designed to put an end to these anomalies, and necessitated the raising of rates at all sites to the level obtaining at the highest paying site. At the case study site this required an average increase of 15% on basic rates. The settlement was to be phased over four years but the agreement made provision for individual sites to pay sooner provided the increase could be funded by productivity, and at the case study site management and unions decided to take advantage of this, with the full 15% paid at once in return for a major productivity deal—the Works Wages and Conditions Rationalisation Agreement.

Current Working Time Organisation

The Shift System

The works at present employs under 300 process workers of whom rather over 200 are shift workers. Most of the producing plants on site are run on a continuous basis, although some of the smaller ones are run on days only and one is run on a five day semi-continuous basis.* Continuously operated plants are covered by four shifts, but some plants, or groups of plants, have one or more day workers attached to them to cover certain ancillary functions (e.g. packing), and on one plant output is supplemented during week days by the use of day operators.

The standard four team shift system uses twelve hour shifts, a day shift running from 6.00 a.m. to 6.00 p.m. and a night shift from 6.00 p.m. to 6.00 a.m. Operators work on a "four shifts on, four shifts off" basis and the system has a cycle of 16 weeks.

The Twelve Hour Continuous Shift System (Four teams, A, B, C and D)

Shift	M		T	W	T	F	S	S	M	T	W	T	F	S	S	etc.
Day	A		A	A	A	C	C	C	C	B	B	B	B	D	D	
Night	B		B	B	B	D	D	D	D	A	A	A	A	C	C	etc.
Rest	C		C	C	C	A	A	A	A	C	C	C	C	A	A	
	D		D	D	D	B	B	B	B	D	D	D	D	B	B	

* Certain of the smaller plants can be taken off continuous operation if demand for the product falls.

206

The twelve hour shift system was introduced in the early 1970s at the workforce's request and replaced an eight hour slow rotating system.*

Those workers interviewed were very enthusiastic about the system, arguing that shift start and finish times were much more attractive in that they followed more closely normal day working patterns, and that the system gave time off in significant amounts and at less anti-social times (e.g. there are six full weekends off in 16 as opposed to one in four with the eight hour system).**

Management too recognised advantages, notably that there were now only two as opposed to three disruptive shift changeovers per day. However, it was also felt that the rota did cause some problems for supervision. Shift supervision is by a leading hand on each plant, with the foremen all working days, and it is consequently possible that a foreman has to wait up to fifteen days before an operator he wishes to see is back again on days.

Within the twelve hour shift are 50 minutes worth of paid break time. Operators are allowed a 30 minute mealbreak between 1.00 p.m. (a.m.) and 2.00 p.m. (a.m.), to be taken in two shifts to allow production to be continued uninterrupted, with the half of the shift still present covering for those away, and two ten minute teabreaks, one to be taken between 8.00 a.m. (p.m.) and 9.00 a.m. (p.m.) and the other between 3.00 p.m. (a.m.) and 4.00 p.m. (a.m.), again staggered to permit continuous cover.

Shift changeovers take place on the job with the oncoming operator changed ready for work. Shift workers are required to remain at work until the relieving operator arrives, or for a maximum of two hours, until alternative arrangements are made by the management—e.g. an alternative operator is "called in" to work one of his rest days, and extra time so worked is paid as overtime. It is also possible for operators to enter into transactions with their opposite numbers in other teams to cover for a late start or an early finish, or an entire shift, although any additional working is not counted as overtime.

* e.g. seven morning shifts, two shifts off, seven afternoon shifts, two shifts off, seven night shifts, three shifts off.
** We should note, of course, how committed shift workers tend to be to "their" system and to defend it as the best. Those interviewed made reference to rapid rotating eight hour systems, which they had never worked, and suggested that these would be particularly unacceptable "because you would never know where you are with them". However, those who work this system will argue that if one must work shifts, then, because it does not involve prolonged spells on any one shift, it is the best way.

Present Patterns of Overtime

The four team continuous shift system produces a rota giving a 42 hour working week (= 168 hours ÷ 4) over the four week cycle. The basic work week as defined in the national agreeemtn is 40 hours but shift workers are contracted by the site agreement to a normal basic week of 42 hours (Weekly Staff Agt., Clause 11), and thus are "conditioned" to an average of two hours' overtime per week,* paid at time and a half on the works basic rate. On the other hand, whilst holiday pay is calculated on the basis of a 42 hour week—the four week holiday for shift men is considered to consist of 21 standard shifts** (Contract of Employment App. I), the latest works productivity deal eliminates these two hours as "guaranteed overtime" such that "guaranteed hours" for continuous shift workers are now 40 per week.

However, a significant amount of overtime, over and above the two hours "conditioned" by the shift system is worked and the average hours of those actually attending are some 50 per week. This overtime involves workers coming in on what would normally be their "rest days", and it is worked for four principle reasons, discussed in order of significance below.

1)   To meet normal cover requirements. Each plant is operated all through the year except for the period of the annual two week closure, thus, each plant requires an annual 8,424 hours of cover (= 365 days × 24 hours—14 days × 24 hours). Using "four teams" this requires each team/employee to provide 2,106 hours cover per year (= 8,424—4). However, each employee is contracted (in terms of the National Agreement) to a 40 hour work week and to four weeks*** and eight "statutory days" of holiday per year, in other words is contracted only to provide 1,856 hours of cover per year (= 52 weeks × 40 hours—4 weeks × 40 hours—8 days × 8 hours). The difference between contracted and demanded hours, an average of 250 hours per employee/team per year, some 13% over and above contracted hours, is made up by overtime working and

* This practice is specific to the works rather than the company. At certain other sites within the company the work's agreement schedules employees one rota day "off" every four weeks, such that only 20 shifts (producing an average 40 hour contractual week) are worked within each cycle. The system of 12 hour shifts operated at the works makes such a proposition organisationally much more difficult, since it relies upon eight hour shifts.

** A "Standard Shift" is defined as of eight hours duration.

*** The site agreement grants workers with 25 or more years service an additional 5 days holiday.

208

produces an average working week of just over 45 hours. The existence of this overtime reflects the fact that, in order for any one shift worker to take that part of his holiday entitlement not accounted for by the period of plant closure,* it requires another shift worker to provide, by working a full shift on one of his "rest days", a complementary amount of overtime cover, to ensure that the plant remains fully manned.**

2) To cover unplanned absences. As well as holiday absences short term sickness and other casual absence has to be covered by rest day overtime working. On average some 10% of the work force are absent for all unanticipated reasons and thus the average work week of those at work is approximately 50 hours.

3) To cope with new plant coming "on stream". The works has been the recipient of considerable investment designed both to update and to increase capacity. The operation of this equipment requires additional training, and such training is scheduled, as a day activity, on "rest days". In addition Health and Safety training, and other company initiated education/training programmes, involving shift workers are rostered to take place on "rest days".

4) To meet peaks in demand. In some production processes there is a direct relationship between plant output and plant manning levels. Whilst this form of relationship primarily involves ancillary operations (e.g. packing), which are more normally performed by day rather than shift workers, there are *limited* instances of overtime serving, in continuous shift operations, its "traditional" function of providing a means whereby fluctuations in demand can be accommodated to.

Overtime is not, however, the only means by which absences, of any form, are covered. A domestic agreement provides that cover might be supplied from within the work group—i.e. via undermanning, at times when the plant is less busy. Such cover can only be used on a short term basis (up to

* An employee is allowed to take this holiday in single days or in blocks of up to a week's duration as he wishes, by arrangement with the relevant head of department, subject to the proviso that not more than 20% of any one section normally be away at any one time (Contract of Employment, App. I).

** The implication of this is that the more recent increases in the annual holiday entitlement have not in fact led to a reduction in annual working time but rather to an increase in the number of hours paid at overtime rates.

two days) and the remainder of the work group share between themselves two-thirds of the basic hourly rate applicable to the absent operator.

Most recently, and as a result of attempts to tighten up on efficiency of labour utilisation as a means of funding the recent Wage Rationalisation deal, management has been looking at overtime working and asking themselves, on each occasion, whether it is really necessary to cover the particular absence by calling in an operator, or whether the absence can be covered from within the group. The incidence of overtime working has fallen, such that average weekly hours of work are now approximately 46.

We can look at the savings to the company involved by comparing the movement in earnings of a hypothetical grade 6 operator, using new wage rates.

OPTION A 10 hrs O/T old rates			OPTION B 6 hrs O/T new rates
Basic rate for 40 hours	71.77	82.34	Basic rate for 40 hours
Shift pay for 40 hours	23.75	26.13	Shift pay for 40 hours
10 hours O/T @ 1½	26.90	18.35	6 hours O/T @ 1½
Shift supp. for 10 hours O/T	1.90	1.14	Shift supp. for 6 hours O/T
		2.28	Working conditions payment
		.34	Work conditions supp. for 6 hours O/T
Gross earnings	124.32	130.76	Gross earnings

The example above illustrates that whilst basic rates increased by some 15% gross earnings only rose by some 5% (excluding the bonus for providing cover from within the group).

There is some union resistance to the increased use of intra-group cover for absences, the domestic unions feeling that management now relies too much on undermanning, and that the strain on the work groups involved is sometimes too great. Furthermore, they argue that management only became conscious of the need to limit overtime working once the premia paid became "too high", and that in the early 1970s, when the effective premia were time and one-sixth, and time and one-fifth on Sundays, management were far more willing to schedule overtime than at present, when the premia are time and a half and double time.

The Potential for Reducing Working Time

Generally speaking overtime working at the site falls into 2 broad categories that which is foreseeable, i.e. arising from the "continuation" of the shift systems; and that providing cover for holidays, sickness and absence (all relatively stable at the site) and that which is *non-foreseeable*, i.e. coping with sudden peaks in demand.

It could be argued that the high level of overtime worked, and the fact that by far the largest part of it falls into the category of being foreseeable, would suggest that there is scope for the translation of overtime hours into additional jobs, jobs that would provide an element of "plus manning" that would cover not just normal sickness and casual absence, but also holiday absences, and some form of "rota day" absences necessary to produce a true 1,856 hour year, 40 hour week. The magnitude of this plus manning element would, in fact, have to be significant. Assuming a no sickness/casual absence situation it would require the workforce to be increased by rather over 13%, whilst 10% on top of this would be necessary to cover unplanned absences, meaning that the total increase would be of the order of 25%.

In the following table we provide a hypothetical comparison of the cost to the company of operating on current manning with 10 hours per week of overtime with the cost of "plus manning" by 25%. It can be seen that the effective costs are very similar. However, the translation of overtime hours into additional manning is not, in fact, as simple as it might appear. Whilst 25% plus manning suggests the use of one additional operator for every four presently used, there certain *organisational* difficulties associated with implementing this approach. Primarily these are a function of the relatively small size of the work groups involved, for the total complement, *per shift*, on any one plant equals or exceeds four only on seven of the twenty plants on site, and only on a maximum of five do the number of persons (including leading hands) of the same grade and performing interchangeable functions equal or exceed that number.

It would appear, at this stage, that there is little, in terms of cost, to choose between the two options, that overtime and additional employment are close substitutes for one another. In other words despite the fact that the *apparent* marginal cost of overtime—time and a half on basic rates—is greater than the *apparent* marginal cost of employing additional labour—overhead labour costs = ⅓ basic rates—the *effective* marginal costs are similar, at 21% and 24% respectively.

Thus, in some of the small teams to increase manning by one would incur more than the present overtime cost. Moreover, a higher degree of mobility

211

Table 2.33   The Cost of Overtime Compared with The Cost of "Plus Manning"

NB. Throughout this example we have used the current works pay and allowances for a grade 6 operator.

	Option A 10 Hrs. (25%) O/T worked	Option B No. O/T, 25% "Plus Manning"
Basic pay for 40 hour week	82.34	82.34
10 hours O/T @ 1½	30.88	
Shift pay for 40 hours	26.13	26.13
Shift supp. for 10 hours O/T	1.90	
Working conditions pay for 40 hours	2.28	2.28
Working conditions pay for 10 hours O/T	.57	
Total wage costs per man	144.10	110.75
O'head lab. costs @ 30% gross wage costs*	43.23	33.23
Total lab. costs per man	187.33	143.98
Option B × $\dfrac{125}{100}$		179.98
Index of total lab. costs (Option A = 100)	100.00	96.00

* This figure is used by Central Office Personnel Department in calculating total labour costs.

between tasks and grades than is currently achieved would be needed. This, however, might well form the substance of an efficiency bargain.

However, the incentive not to disturb the status quo is not simply a function of the organisational difficulties associated with change. Two factors would appear to be relevant here. The domestic unions and employees interviewed suggested (and management accepted) that in the past a significant amount of overtime working was necessary to produce an acceptable level of earnings, implying that historically there was pressure to build regular overtime working into the system. Whilst both sides agree that over the years basic rates have been raised to a level that makes overtime earnings now no longer "necessary", overtime working appears to have become "institutionalised", and in as much that 10 hours overtime adds some 30% to gross weekly earnings it is difficult to refuse.* This aspect could be compounded by the effects of the second relevant factor the nature of the shift system, which makes it appear, as employees admitted, that the normal work week is only of three and a half days duration and thus that to work an additional shift during the week does not unduly encroach upon leisure time.

The Possibility of a Fifth Shift

We should note that many of the organisational problems disappear if we think not in terms of *"horizontal"* but rather of *"vertical"* plus manning. 25% horizontal plus manning which we described above, consists of increasing the manning levels on any one team by 25%. 25% vertical plus manning consists, rather, of increasing the number of teams by 25%. Obviously this second alternative means that the problem of overmanning does not arise, and it does not, *in itself,* call for any greater flexibility of working than exists at present. Employing the concept of "annual hours" we can see that whilst cover demanded remains at 8,424 hours, using five teams this requires each team to work 1,685 hours. Assuming an absence rate of 10% 168.5 of the required hours will not be provided and will necessitate, as now, "overtime" cover. However, since each employee is contracted for 1,856 hours, or 171 hours more than required hours (= 1,856—1,685), each employee "owes" to the company sufficient hours to cover all anticipated "overtime" needs. The difference, between the two forms of plus manning is illustrated in the table below.

Methods of using the fifth team vary, one way being to use the fifth week of the cycle as a relief week and to draw on the team currently on relief to cover any absences (planned and unplanned) on the other four teams, another way being to use the fifth week as a completely free week and to provide absence cover, as at present, out of the four teams at work.

The attitudes of the workforce who admit that overtime working is not financially necessary are important here. Those employees with whom the question of overtime working was discussed went further in that they suggested that they felt "trapped" by overtime—it was there, and if they did not work it somebody else would. Similarly, and precisely for this reason, not one of them was prepared to not work overtime, although if there were an externally imposed ban on overtime working this would be acceptable, indeed it was argued that this was what was needed. In one

---

* There did not appear to be any significant pressure from the workforce to reduce overtime working. By comparison, the factory manager was concerned about the level of overtime and appeared willing to consider ways of reducing it.

Table 2.34 The Impact of Different Types of Plus Manning

Present situation		25% horiz. plus manning			25% vert. plus manning		
Team size	Comprising of 4 teams	Team size	Comprising of 4 teams	Actual plus manning	Team size	Comprising of 5 teams	Actual plus manning
2	8	3	12	50%	2	10	25%
3	12	4	16	33%	3	15	25%
4	16	5	20	25%	4	20	25%
5	20	7	28	40%	5	25	25%
6	24	8	32	33%	6	30	25%
7	28	9	36	29%	7	35	25%
8	32	10	40	25%	8	40	25%

sense to introduce 25% plus manning, horizontal or vertical, does precisely this, for it means that the Company can cover all the hours it requires without calling for overtime, except in a limited number of unanticipated cases.

Thus it might be possible to argue that five team operations provide the medium for giving effect to a not explicitly stated, or necessarily even recognised, coalescence of interest between management, who want to reduce overtime but not do know how to, and the workforce, who do not particularly need overtime but will not give it up as long as it is there to be had.

On the other hand whether the workforce would in fact be prepared to accept a considerable drop in gross earnings—albeit a smaller drop in net earnings—is a crucial question, for whilst overtime earnings are not "necessary", consumption patterns are built around this additional source of income and the change is bound to be disruptive.

Those instances of overtime elimination in continuous shift working concerns that we do know of have involved the consolidation of overtime earnings into an annual salary, i.e. no fall in gross earnings, and the 25% increase in manning has been achieved by a 25% demanning of all jobs, for which, given the changes conditional upon it, the incentive was there.

Management at the site felt that the creation of a fifth shift was dependent upon the ability to demand jobs. They pointed out that the long history of productivity bargaining at the plant had steadily increased labour productivity and removed slack manning of jobs. For example, the bulk of the productivity increases negotiated in the most recent (Wage Rationalisation) deal were of this sort, involving commitments to operate additional, new plant, and to increase output rates on existing plant—rather than towards shedding labour, but the Personnel Manager thought that this in itself ensured that labour utilisation was about as effective as it could be, and that the scope for demanning was very small, maybe 5% across all process operations—approximately the amount achieved in the latest productivity deal.* On the other hand the Factory Manager considered that if possibilities for inter plant and inter functional mobility were fully explored the scope for demanning might be considerably greater, sufficient to produce perhaps half of a fifth shift. The most recent productivity deal did in fact provide instances of such increased mobility that did allow for demanning, instances both of full mobility across a small group of plants, and of increased functional interchangeability on a single plant, and the manpower saving effected in these particular, but limited number of, instances was quite significant.

* In practice this demanning has meant that vacancies created by natural wastage have not been filled.

215

A general proposition made by management was that the nature of process jobs, the fact that a lot of the work is instrument watching and thus that further activity is only intermittently required, meant that process workers only actually worked for about seven out of the twelve hours of the shift,* which suggests in itself that, were sufficient incentive offered, there is considerable scope for "job enlargement". It was to this that the Factory Manager was also referring when pointing to the potential scope for a demanning exercise.

Labour Market Constraints

If the fifth shift is to be less than entirely internally generated then there would have to be labour available on the local labour market. Management claimed that recruitment on such a scale would present them with serious problems, and that whilst there were plenty of persons registered at the local labour offices these were not of the quality demanded (indeed the local labour office was rarely, if ever, used to recruit process workers). It was argued that the nature of the work had changed, operations had become far more sophisticated and demanded a far higher calibre of recruit than thirty years ago. Whether this proposition is valid it is difficult to assess, but it does suggest that there is at least a perceived *supply* constraint upon shorter working time having an employment effect.

Reduction of Contractual Working Time

We have already shown that to produce a true 40 hour week—48 week year with eight statutory days of holidays would require a significant increase in employment, or a similar enhancement of productivity such that a fifth team could be operated. However, it was also part of our brief to examine the potential effects of a reduction in contractual as well as actual working time.

Management's response to the introduction of a shorter working week was that it would require more overtime to be paid, and indeed this also was the implied response with respect to increased holiday settlements. Members of the workforce also suggested this as a likely reaction, and one to which they would not be adverse—e.g. "the 35 hour week would mean five more hours of overtime". In management's view a 100% overtime leakage would be cheaper than recruiting an additional shift, whilst in any case labour supply problems would make the adoption of the latter difficult to say the least.

* NB. This was one of the principal reasons why management consented to introduce the twelve hour shift system.

On the face of it, the argument concerning relative costs seems not to hold. Again comparing the situation of a hypothetical grade 6 operator working either 46 hours per week as at present but now doing 11 hours overtime, with the same working 38 hours per week—i.e. with three hours of overtime, on a five team system,* we see that the net effect upon labour costs is the same—i.e. in both cases labour costs increased by some 17%.

Table 2.35 Comparative Labour Costs

	Option A 4 teams 35 hours + 11 hours overtime	Option B 5 teams 35 hours + 3 hours overtime
Basic pay for basic week	82.34	82.34
Shift pay for basic week	26.13	26.13
Work conditions pay for basic week	2.28	2.28
Total pay per person for basic week	110.75	110.75
O/T @ 1½	38.82	10.59
Shift supplement for O/T	2.24	.66
Work conditions pay for O/T	.72	.20
Total O/T pay per person	41.96	11.45
Total wage cost per person	152.71	122.20
Overheads lab. cost @ 30% gross wage costs	45.81	36.66
Total lab. cost per person	198.52	158.86
Option B × $\dfrac{125}{100}$		198.58
Index of total lab. cost (lab. costs for 40 hour week = 1.3 × £130.76 = £169.99 = 100)	117.00	117.00

* We again use the "annual hours" method of calculating notional average weekly hours.
  Required work time per team = 1,685 hours (= 8,424—5) = 3% more than contracted work time of 1,624 hours (= 48 weeks × 35 hours—8 days × 7 hours) = 36.3 hours per week. Assume 10% absence, for which additional overtime is required, so that actual average weekly hours = 40 = 5 hours overtime. Assume, however, that, as at present some 40% of these notional overtime hours are, in fact, covered by undermanning so that actual overtime = 3 hours and average actual weekly work time = 38 hours.

Adopting Option A would increase gross earnings per person by 17% whereas with Option B, because the amount of overtime required is less, both relatively and absolutely, than at present, earnings would fall by nearly 7%. Option B requires paying for more operators but because these operators are paid less hours the actual cost of the two options is very much the same.

If, into the bargain, we could assume that 50% of the fifth shift—the most optimistic assessment—could be internally generated then labour costs would rise by only just over 8%.* It is perhaps important to note that this kind of productivity effect is only likely to be achieved via the formation of a fifth shift, when the specific incentive is there, and that is unlikely to be realised in the absence of such a strategy.

If we were to assume that the effect of the reduction in work time consequent upon the introduction of a 35 hour basic week and five shift operations was to diminish the incidence of sickness and other short term casual absences, as a result of it providing substantially more free time (e.g. 6 days off) then the overtime requirement would also fall and this would cheapen the fifth shift option.

Maintenance Workers—Negotiated Overtime Reduction

There are some 200 maintenance workers on site, of whom 130 are craftsmen, 40 are craftsmen's labourers (maintenance assistants) and 30 are apprentices. The maintenance workforce is responsible for all routine maintenance and installation work, and for repair work including emergency repairs.

All the maintenance workers work days except that there is one maintenance fitter and labourer attached to each shift. Emergencies beyond the competence of the shift fitter require additional maintenance workers to be "called in" on overtime and a "duty rota" determines obligations in this respect,** whilst provision is also made for temporary shift working to cope with longer but immediately necessary jobs—e.g. emergencies and new installations.

* Assuming the labour costs to be some 15% of total costs (average for the Chemical Industry) the net effect on total costs would be just over 1%.
** Night time "call ins" for all employees grant entitlement to paid time off in lieu as well as overtime and call in payments, e.g. an employee arriving home up to midnight will not be expected to commence work until 9.00 a.m.
An employee arriving home after midnight will not be expected to commence work until 1.15 p.m. An employee who has worked two or more hours after midnight will not be expected to commence work until 7.45 a.m. on the following day.

Until recently the level of overtime working was relatively high. The average weekly hours of maintenance workers were just over 46, and much of this was contributed to ,by weekend working for routine maintenance and installation, and to provide additional emergency cover. Again a "duty rota" operated for this weekend working.

However, much of the weekend overtime working has been eliminated as part of the Wage Rationalisation deal for maintenance workers. In order to fund the increase in basic rates, management and domestic unions sought to reduce man hours required and concentrated upon reducing overtime. A new "shift system" using four "teams" was introduced, whereby every fourth week an employee is required to work Monday to Friday, Saturday and Sunday mornings, and, by arrangement with supervisors, two out of three days Tuesday to Thursday. For this week of 40 hours, 46 hours are paid.

This new system, together with a commitment (which so far seems to hold reasonably well) by both sides not to use overtime except when absolutely necessary, has led to the length of the average work week now being little over 40 hours.

Case Study 10

Summary of Key Points Emerging

— The company had in the early 1970s changed its shift system from a more traditional eight hour three shift to a 12 hour two shift system for its process workers;

— Although the working day was longer the workforce preferred the starting and finishing times and the more significant—both quantitatively and qualitatively—amounts of leisure time which the two shift system yielded them;

— Management found two changeovers as opposed to three less disruptive, although they did appear to incur slightly more supervision difficulties since the foremen all worked days;

— Fairly extensive overtime working—around 10 hours per week—was common, but latterly management had reduced this to six hours on average. It was suggested that management had been forced into this as a result of "high" overtime premia. Our calculations showed, with the new productivity agreement operating in conjunction with the reduced overtime, that basic rates increased by 15% but gross earnings (including overtime) only increased by 5%;

— It is possible to demonstrate the scope for and cost of reducing overtime still further whilst increasing manning at the plant. This can be achieved by (a) increasing manning horizontally on each team. For a typical operative team we calculate that to remove overtime but increase manning levels pro rata would not add to the overall labour cost to the firm, although it woud reduce gross earnings per operative. The constraints to this exercise are related to the small size of many operative teams and the lack of interchangeability of many operative tasks. The alternative method (b) of increasing manning involves a *vertical* increase in effect the creation of a fifth shift. Again, we estimated that for a typical operative team such a change—dependent upon some demanning of the existing shifts, hence the *internal* generation of the fifth shift—would not add to the total labour cost to the firm although again it would reduce individual earnings as a result of the reduction of overtime pay. The *vertical* route offers the advantage of not requiring any greater flexibility of working than exists at present and would yield extra leisure time to the individual operative.

INDUSTRY STUDY

The Structure of the British Motor Industry

The motor industry is usually defined as comprising Minimum List Headings 380, 381.1 and 381.2 (1968 SIC), that is wheeled tractor manufacturing, motor vehicle manufacturing and trailers and caravans. Indeed, under the earlier 1958 Standard Industrial Classification all were grouped under the same heading and many firms are engaged in activities in more than one of these areas. Ford and BL, for example, both produce agricultural tractors.

However, it is desirable to make a distinction between these sectors, for as Table 2.36 shows, tractors, trailers and caravans are peripheral to the motor industry in terms of both production units, output and employment. In 1968 (analogous figures are unavailable later but the situation remains similar) wheeled tractor manufacturing accounted for about 6-7% of total motor industry output, trailers and caravans a mere 2½%, with employment percentages of the same order.

This study, therefore, concentrates upon MLH 381.1 motor vehicle manufacturing, which encompasses over 90% of the total industry and is primarily concerned with the production of cars, commercial (goods and public service) vehicles, their parts and accessories. Although it is sometimes necessary to rely upon data for the whole of MLH 381, or occasionally even under definitions of the industry, the predominance of motor vehicles means this is not a serious problem.

The British motor vehicle industry is characterised by a large number of small enterprises manufacturing a multitude of different components for assembly in the plants of the few volume producers. These are dominated by the ''big four'' car and CV manufacturers: BL (formerly British Leyland, effectively state owned), Talbot/Dodge (formerly Chrysler but recently taken over by Peugeot-Citreon), Ford UK and Vauxhall (wholly owned subsidiaries of the American multi-nationals Ford and General Motors).

Their factories are often extremely large, Ford's four main car body and assembly plants each employing around 5,000 manual workers, with a total of over 24,000 operatives at the Dagenham site and 12,500 at Halewood. By contrast, commercial vehicle plants tend to be somewhat smaller, especially those of the lesser manufacturers, such as Seddon-Atkinson,

Table 2.36 Employment and Output in the (United Kingdom)[1] Motor Industry in 1968

Minimum List Heading (1968 SIC)	Sub-divisions of the Industry	Enterprises	Establishments	Total Employment	Gross output £'000	Percentage of sales taken by largest five enterprises
380.0	Wheeled Tractor Manufacturing	20	28	26,083	181,966	94.6
381.0	Complete Vehicles and Chassis with engines					
	Cars	11	43	168,216	1,306,229	99.2
	Commercial Vehicles	30	46	43,233	259,974	91.2
381.1	Parts and accessories for Cars and C.V.s					
	Motor bodies	87	124	50,723	176,286	
	Engines and parts thereof	33	49	20,436	72,111	97.0
	Other parts and accessories	224	395	137,883	570,317	63.2
381.2	Trailers, Caravans and parts thereof	63	88	11,271	68,408	44.2
380-1	Totals of establishments employing 25 or more persons[2]	488	850	469,023	2,683,500	89.9
	The Motor Industry	1,629	2,075	483,500	2,765,793	n.a.

Source: 1968 Census of Production, Chapters 81, 82, Tables 1 and 4.

Notes: [1] All lines except the last refer to establishments employing 25 or more persons. The last line provides totals for all establishments in the motor industry.
[2] The sum of figures for the sub-divisions does not equal the total for the industry's larger establishments because enterprises made returns for more than one sub-division and the 'remainder' of MLH 381, (77 establishments employing 11,000 people with a gross output of £48m) have been excluded from this table.

222

ERF and Fodens. Indeed, while the "big four" account for over 99% of new car production in Britain—the remainder made up by specialist producers like Lotus and Rolls Royce—their share of CV production is slightly lower at 97% and throughout Europe the CV sector is significantly less oligopolistic than the car industry.

The volume producers are supported by two thousand or more component manufacturers. Some of these such as Lucas and GKN are sizeable companies with several factories, indeed, the five largest firms supply half the market and the ten largest nearly two-thirds. However, the vast majority are small, many making only one or two products and totally dependent upon the health of one or more of the "big four" for their survival.

Thus, in 1977 (the latest year for which figures exist), over 93% of the 1,750 enterprises classified directly to MLH 381.1 employed less than 100 people, 55% of them 10 persons or less; yet this group constituted only 5.4% of the industry's total employment of 474,500. At the other end of the scale, however, a mere six enterprises (or seven establishments with over 7,500 workers) employed more than 55% of all persons engaged in motor vehicles manufacturing; while three companies with over 10,000 employees accounted for exactly half the total workforce. In terms of gross output, the enterprises with less than 100 employees produced some 7% of goods and services, but the firms with more than 7,500 workers produced 63% and the three with over 10,000 at least 57% of the industry's total production. *

With partial exception of Ford (to whom we shall return later) British motor vehicle manufacturing is a highly interdependent, horizontally integrated industry. The large assemblers ultimately rely upon raw material suppliers and the plethora of independent component companies, whose (often unique) products are vital to the production process. At BL's Cowley plant, for example, 800 firms supply more than 7,000 different parts and over the industry as a whole around 60% of the production costs of a car are accounted for by bought-out components; the percentage for CV's is even higher. ** This situation is in marked contrast to Europe and the United States where vertical integration is the norm and its origins lie in the history of British industrial organisation. The motor industry grew out of the small engineering firms of the West Midlands at the turn of the last century and the two sectors have always been closely related; not only in terms of location, production and personnel, but also (perhaps inevitably) with regard to such factors as payment systems, trade union organisation and collective bargaining arrangements.

* Census of Production, 1977.
** Central Policy Review Staff "The Future of the British Car Industry" (1975) p.5; House of Commons Expenditure Committee 14th Report, "The Motor Vehicle Industry" (HC 1974-75,617) p.19. Hereafter CPRS and HC respectively.

A prominent feature of the British motor vehicle industry is therefore its locational concentration. Beginning in the Midlands, it developed in the South-East between the wars with the American firms opening plants at Dagenham and Luton. Then in the 1960s there was a further expansion into Merseyside in response to government regional policy (buttressing the heavy CV makers already located in Lancashire) and three new integrated car plants were built at Halewood, Ellesmere Port and Speke, owned by Ford, Vauxhall and BL (then Triumph) respectively. Meanwhile Chrysler opened a new complex at Linwood, Scotland, and component manufacture developed in South Wales.

While there has been a relative decline, then, in the two traditional car making centres, the motor industry remains concentrated along the main South East/North West industrial axis of Britain. Throughout the 1970s around one-third of total employment in MLH 381.1 was centred upon the West Midlands, with a further 30% in the South East (including Bedfordshire and Oxfordshire) and about 15% in the North West.*

Moreover, if allowance were made for the component firms classified under other headings, particularly electrical engineering, the preponderance of the Midlands would be even more pronounced.

A recent attempt at quantifying the total employment dependent upon motor vehicle manufacturing concluded that it amounted to around 5% of the national workforce. While in the West Midlands the "first round" dependence alone is as high as 16%, with the economic base of towns as large as Coventry and Oxford in large measure dependent upon the continued presence of the major producers. The knock-on effect of any plant closures by the "big four" would therefore be immense, even for the large component manufacturers.**

The Production Process

While initially a considerable advantage to British motor manufacturing, a strong independent component sector is something of an anomaly, perhaps even a liability, in the context of current trends towards high volume production of common component models by vertically integrated multinational corporations. The explanation for this is grounded in the nature of the production process.

There are a large number of discrete operations involved in automobile production. At each step in the process different types of machinery and

* Census of Production.
* * HC pp.15-16, see the comments of the Chairman of GKN, ibid. p.28.

equipment are required and while a growing number of operations are almost fully automatic, many others will still require considerable amounts of labour. Similarly at each stage there is a minimum efficient size below which unit costs begin to rise. Thus efficient production requires not only the realisation of scale economies but also careful scheduling and balancing of each activity to ensure a smooth and uninterrupted flow of materials and components through each operation.

Despite the almost infinite number of parts and multitude of different jobs, the production process can be divided into four basic groups of operations:

i) **Panel Production.** Body panels are produced by stamping sheet metal in a press shop where typically there may be 15-20 lines, each producing 12-20 parts a minute. While automatic presses are extremely expensive they last for many years and investment is largely concentrated upon the dies which must be changed with each new model. A set of high volume dies costs tens of millions of pounds and as their potential life is far longer than that of a single car model, manufacturers try to write off their tooling costs quickly by employing the same basic panels on several different models. The press shop is therefore highly capital intensive, its operations forming only about 10% of the total labour hours required to manufacture a finished car.

ii) **Body Assembly and Painting.** Car bodies are then constructed by welding various panels together into sub-assemblies that finally form a rigid body, which in turn is cleaned and painted in a separate paint shop. The number and precision of welds and the quality of paint finish demanded means that in some large companies these operations are already becoming the province of robots. In the past however body assembly was labour intensive, accounting for 30% of a manufacturers' workforce. Painting, although requiring less than 10% of total labour, is highly skilled.

iii) **Powertrain Production.** The production of engines, transmissions and axles employs about a quarter of a car assembler's workforce and a substantial proportion of total investment. Rough castings and forgings (which may be bought-in) are machined on sophisticated automatic lines, allowing hundreds of separate operations in rapid succession. Since tooling and development costs for a new engine can amount to £150 million (1975 prices) and for a new gearbox half of that, successive models ranges are designed around common powertrain units. This extends their lives beyond the 7 to 8 years normally accorded a volume car. As with body assembly, production targets must be met otherwise the final assembly lines will be undersupplied and buffer stocks, which tie up capital, will have to be maintained.

iv) **Trim, Final Assembly and Rectifications.** As the painted body moves along the trim lines, thousands of parts and purchased components are installed. This is a long and complex process involving a number of separate sub-assembly operations at some of the 70-80 different "stations" along the line. Powertrain units are then installed on the final assembly line, tyres, etc., added and the car driven off the line for quality checks and rectification. As nearly every piece of the car is assembled by hand, trim and final assembly lines are highly labour intensive, accounting for at least 20% of the workforce. Here more than anywhere else in a vehicle plant, teamwork, consistency and continuity are essential to achieve planned output levels.*

It is evident from this description of the production process that two elements are essential for efficient and profitable automobile manufacture. On the capital side very high levels of investment and large model runs are necessary to achieve the economies of scale vital in order to avoid serious competitive disadvantage.** On the labour side continuity and flexibility of production are demanded to ensure maximum use of expensive facilities and the ability to vary the product mix in order to supply a capricious and volatile market. The overriding concern of the industry's managers is therefore the level of capacity utilisation, the major determinant of profitability.

The Performance of the Motor Vehicle Industry

While always inherent in the production process, size only became vital to automobile manufacture with the resurgence of demand conditions in the 1960s. It was apparent that medium size producers could no longer compete in the volume car market and the decade witnessed a series of mergers and takeovers culminating, for example, in the creation of the British Leyland Motor Corporation in 1968. This was accompanied by the increased participation and eventual control of Chrysler in the Rootes Group and, in sum, the division of the assembly industry between the "big four" manufacturers. However, the rapid growth in costs during the 1970s and greatly increased competition in the context of a world market soon made it clear that concentration of ownership is not in itself sufficient.

* CPRS pp.11-17 for all this section.

** The minimum efficient size for each operation (measured in identical units per plant per year) was estimated by the CPRS to range from 100,000 for engine block castings, to half a million for powertrain operations, with 250,000 for final assembly.

Table 2.37 Motor Vehicles in the UK, 1968-1979: Production, New Registrations, Exports and Imports

Year	UK domestic production	New registrations	Output as % of new registrations	Thousands Exports	Imports
Cars					
1968	1,816	1,104	164	677	102
1969	1,717	965	178	772	102
1970	1,641	1,077	152	690	158
1971	1,742	1,286	135	721	281
1972	1,921	1,638	117	627	450
1973	1,747	1,661	105	599	505
1974	1,534	1,269	121	565	375
1975	1,268	1,194	106	516	449
1976	1,333	1,286	104	496	534
1977	1,328	1,324	100	475	698
1978	1,223	1,592	77	466	801
1979	1,070	1,716	62	362*	890*
Commercial Vehicles					
1968	409	244	168	142	3.9
1969	466	257	181	181	5.5
1970	458	257	178	172	10.3
1971	456	257	177	195	18.6
1972	408	n.a.		140	34.9
1973	417	300	139	163	36.9
1974	403	237	170	161	39.6
1975	381	220	173	180	25.6
1976	372	209	178	188	27.4
1977	386	225	172	192	36.9
1978	385	256	150	142	46.6
1979	408	306	133	125*	56.5*

Source: SMMT, 'The British Motor Industry' (Various Editions)
SMMT, 'Monthly Statistical Review' December 1979

Note: * Figures for 10 months only

During the 1960s governments of all shades pursued 'stop-go' economic policies designed primarily to reduce the balance of payments deficit. Purchase tax and credit restrictions were used to dampen consumer spending and encourage manufacturers to export. However, the overvaluation of sterling before 1967 restricted both the number and profit margin of foreign sales. Profits were low among all the assemblers with Chrysler and to a lesser extent Vauxhall regularly reporting losses. British car manufacturers therefore lacked the money to finance capital expenditure and although the industry had planned to invest £980 million in the period 1964-70 only £450 million was actually spent. New models stayed on the drawing board, the replacement of aged plant and machinery was again postponed and the industry entered the 1970s ill-prepared for the challenge facing it.

In Europe and Japan, meanwhile, governments had been stimulating their home markets and, free from restrictions, continental manufacturers enjoyed unprecedented expansion. By the end of the 1960s they were already making inroads into the British market as they built up dealer networks (from BL and Ford cast-offs) in anticipation of the UK joining the EEC. In 1972 the Heath government slashed credit controls in a "dash for growth", but at the same time the GATT Kennedy Round halved the import duty on cars to 11%, while the transitional arrangements for EEC entry reduced the tariff on European models still further to 44%. Conservative British designs, the producers' inability to satisfy demand, and the ready availability and fresh image of foreign cars meant that the explosion in consumer spending resulted in a flood of imported cars. By the time of the 1974 oil crisis foreign manufacturers had taken a firm hold upon the UK market, with a share rapidly approaching 30%. In the post oil-crisis era they have consolidated and expanded their position, capitalising on the domestic manufacturers' ageing and inadequate range of small cars, as buyers switched to smaller, fuel-saving models.

British motor industry volume is therefore determined not only by the size of the UK market for new vehicles, but also by the share taken by imports and the penetration of UK manufacturers into export markets. Table 2.37 shows that trends in all those areas, not just imports, have been adverse and that as a result the car sector is declining both relatively and absolutely.

While the motor industry is clearly subject to the extremes of the business cycle, there is no mistaking the downward trend in domestic car output: the 1976-77 revival fell more than half a million short of the 1972 peak of 1.9 million and the 1979 production level of barely one million (when registrations set a new record at 1.7 million) was lower than at any time since 1961. The tenfold increase in imports to nearly one million in the decade to 1979 would have been less significant, if car exports had been

228

maintained, yet they are now running at only just over half the 1969 peak of 772,000 while output as a proportion of new registrations has fallen steadily from 168% in 1969 to a current low of 62%.

By contrast, the commercial vehicle sector has shown more resilience and, while it too has suffered from production losses and import penetration, exports have been generally upheld and CV's have escaped the precipitous decline of the car industry. However, as the CV market is worth only around one-quarter of the car market, this has not preserved the balance of trade. Britain became a net importer of cars in 1976 and the ratio by value of exports to imports, which stood at 6:1 for cars and 20:1 for CV's in 1968, had fallen to only 1.1:1 for the whole of MLH 381 by 1978.

When discussing the performance of motor vehicle manufacturing it is therefore important to make the distinction between car and CV manufacture; nevertheless the recurrent crisis facing the car industry during the 1970s overshadows all else and has called into question the survival of some major manufacturers. A number of reasons have been adduced to explain this decline and together they amount to a vicious downward spiral.

The over-capacity facing the industry since the early 1970s due to the high level of import penetration has had a disastrous effect upon the capacity utilisation of British manufacturers and therefore on their profitability (the UK industry needs 72% utilisation merely to break even). Profits have consequently been inadequate to finance the investment necessary to introduce new models at the same rate as the competition. Model lines have become dated, the competitive position worsened and the market share fallen. This in turn has led to lower volumes, higher costs per unit and a further deterioration in profits, investment and ultimately market share.

The insecurity which this promotes among employees has exacerbated the industry's chronically bad industrial relations, deriving from a tradition of mutual distrust and entrenched positions. Dispute levels have remained high, productivity low, with the result that lost production and poor quality here worsened the competitive position still further. Companies have sought to reduce their fixed overheads (even to the extent of closing major plants) and serious disputes have arisen over manning levels and work practices.

Developments among Car Manufacturers

This is essentially the same downward spiral in which the British motor cycle industry was caught and indeed other sectors of British manufacturing industry. To a greater or lesser extent it applies to all the "big four" motor manufacturers, none of whose car production has yet recovered to the heights of 1971-72. However, there are significant differences in the performance of these companies, which stem less from the operational factors outlined above than from structural causes, notably size and integration.

i) **BL** epitomises the problems facing the British motor industry. As the most traditional of British manufacturers it was also the most vulnerable to imports, its market share dropping 9% in 1971-2. Over the decade as a whole it halved to less than 20% and exports have fallen as models have become increasingly dated and the company has suffered from serious production failures due, in part, to dire labour relations.* In 1975 BL came under the ownership and guidance of the NEB following the publication of the Ryder Report, which revealed several management deficiencies including the failure to integrate production facilities (with 55 plants, 9 bodies and 12 engine types) and a catastrophic lack of investment (half the machinery was over 15 years old) as too great a proportion of profits was distributed to shareholders.

However Ryder's projections for future sales and profitability proved wildly optimistic, the £1,000 million investment plan scarcely sufficient, and BL is now in a severe crisis with thousands of unsold cars and doubts as to whether it can survive until new models appear early in the 1980s. The management response has been a policy of retrenchment and brinkmanship, and BL is now the smallest and weakest full-range motor vehicle manufacturer in the world . . . pitifully short of skilled technical and engineering resources.** Official analyses in the 1970s concluded that BL was sufficiently large to reap its own economies of scale, but it is now clear that the only viable future for the company lies in full partnership with another producer, rather than mere assembly under licence, which is the essence of the current arrangement with Honda.

ii) **Vauxhall and Talbot/Chrysler** have experienced similar difficulties, but in their case within the context of multi-national corporations. As the smallest of the major British manufacturers they carried horizontal integration to extremes and in the mid-seventies 85% of the material cost of Vauxhall cars and over 70% of Chrysler cars was accounted for by bought-in components.*** However, the external economies scale of component manufacturers have been an adequate

---

* For all production and sales figures in this section, See Table 2.38.
** Eurofinance Report on BL, p.6.
*** HC, Table 6.

Table 2.38 The Performance of UK Motor Car Manufacturers Production and New Registrations (1969-1979)

	UK Production		UK New Registrations		
Year	Total	Allocation for Export	Group imports	Total	Market share %

BL/British Leyland

Year	Total	Allocation for Export	Group imports	Total	Market share %
1969	830.9	408.5	—	388.5	40.3
1970	788.7	368.4	—	410.5	38.1
1971	886.7	385.8	—	516.3	40.2
1972	916.2	347.3	—	542.4	33.1
1973	875.8	348.0	—	529.6	31.9
1974	738.5	322.5	—	415.4	32.7
1975	605.1	256.7	—	368.7	30.9
1976	687.9	320.8	—	352.7	27.4
1977	651.1	293.3	2.6	322.1	24.3
1978	611.6	247.9	15.7	373.8	23.5
1979	503.8	—	—	337.0	19.6

Ford

Year	Total	Allocation for Export	Group imports	Total	Market share %
1969	531.6	247.9	—	264.0	27.4
1970	448.4	185.7	—	285.7	26.5
1971	366.6	127.1	—	230.9	18.7
1972	546.7	126.6	—	402.0	24.6
1973	453.4	112.0	1	376.2	22.6
1974	383.7	93.2	—	288.4	22.7
1975	329.6	89.2	—	259.1	21.7
1976	383.2	108.2	28.9	324.7	25.3
1977	406.6	132.4	86.8	340.3	25.7
1978	324.4	102.4	138.4	392.4	24.7
1979	398.7	—	227.1*	485.6	28.3

Talbot/Chrysler (including sales of Simca Cars)

Year	Total	Allocation for Export	Group imports	Total	Market share %
1969	173.9	91.5	3.7	97.1	10.1
1970	217.0	99.7	7.9	120.5	11.2
1971	281.5	143.3	24.2	159.4	12.4
1972	263.9	98.6	32.9	186.7	11.4
1973	265.4	111.9	28.8	190.4	11.4
1974	261.8	144.0	23.4	137.6	10.8
1975	226.6	161.0	16.9	95.5	8.0
1976	144.6	103.8	10.7	82.9	6.5
1977	169.5	127.7	15.1	79.7	6.0
1978	196.5	132.0	18.1	112.6	7.1
1979	103.0	—	—	119.4	7.0

Vauxhall, i.e. General Motors (including Sales of Opel Cars)

Year	Total	Allocation for Export	Group imports	Total	Market share %
1969	171.7	72.9	1.5	114.2	11.8
1970	178.1	65.7	2.6	110.2	10.2
1971	199.1	55.2	8.7	146.9	11.5
1972	184.0	37.2	15.2	162.4	9.9
1973	138.4	26.3	15.8	148.7	8.9
1974	136.9	28.6	8.7	101.0	7.9
1975	98.6	21.3	11.1	98.7	8.3
1976	109.1	29.2	45.6	130.4	10.1
1977	93.2	16.8	56.6	137.3	10.4
1978	84.0	9.4	59.7	154.1	9.7
1979	58.8	—	44.5*	140.9	8.2

Table 2.38 *continued*

Year	All UK Manufacturers new registrations of UK assembled cars		All Imports UK new registrations	
	Number	Market share %	Number[2]	Market share %
1969	865	89.6	101	10.4
1970	923	85.7	154	14.3
1971	1,038	80.7	248	19.3
1972	1,253	76.5	385	23.5
1973	1,206	72.6	456	27.4
1974	915	72.1	354	27.9
1975	797	66.8	397	33.2
1976	798	62.1	488	37.9
1977	723	54.6	601	45.4
1978	807	50.6	785	49.3
1979	750	43.7	966	56.3

Source: SMMT, 'The Motor Industry of Great Britain' (various editions)
SMMT, 'Monthly Statistical Review' December, 1979 and earlier editions

Notes: [1] It is known that Ford was importing units from continental plants as early as 1973. However as the figures are wholesale, not retail and some may have been re-exported they are not directly comparable. Between 1973 and 1975 Ford's wholesale of imported units varied between 16,000 and 25,000. Chrysler and General Motors did not begin producing European models (as opposed to European makes) before 1975-76.
[2] The figure given here for imports is somewhat lower than that in Table 2, due to a slightly different accounting base.
* Figures are for 11 months only.

232

compensation for their small size. The market share of both companies (including group imports), has fallen from around 12% at the beginning of the 1970s to current levels of 7-8% with the drop in UK production even more pronounced—from a 1971 peak of 281,000 for Chrysler and 199,000 for Vauxhall to 103,000 and 59,000 respectively in 1979. The difference is accounted for less by the relative level of group imports (although these have risen since General Motors introduced European models—as opposed to makes—after 1976) than by the virtual cessation of Vauxhall car exports from the UK.

The experience of Chrysler and Vauxhall illustrates the problems of dealing with multi-national companies on a merely national basis. Largely because of their size and structure the British subsidiaries of these companies have experienced a poor rate of return on capital and been unable to finance a new investment from retained profits. They have therefore had to obtain funds from the parent companies (or as a last resort from government, as Chrysler demonstrated), however their poor performance compared to their European brothers, particularly with regard to labour productivity, has meant that new models have generally gone to the continent not Britain. The multi-nationals have been transferring R&D and machine tooling capacity abroad, UK assembly facilities have been constrained and the British plants have increasingly become component supply centres (where the labour input is less than in assembly) rather than car-making concerns. A reflection of their European geographical and market positions: peripheral rather than central.

iii) These tendencies have received their furthest development with **Ford UK**. Ford have not escaped from the misnamed 'British disease' (a complex of factors inherent in deindustrialisation) and actual UK car outputs is now some 150,000 lower than early 1970s levels. Production schedules at major plants are rarely met, labour relations are strained and, until 1978, investment per head in real terms was falling annually. Nevertheless Ford are the only major UK car producers to have maintained (and lately increased) their market share and profitability.

This has been achieved principally by the vertical integration of all Ford's European operations into a single production system based on the multi-sourcing of complementary components. Faced with growing competition and a reduction in profit margins Ford were ahead of GM in adopting a total European approach to product development and the allocation of production between countries in order to achieve maximum economies of scale. As early as 1975 they had only four basic body shells and engine ranges and in the succeeding years over £450 million was invested in developing the Fiesta models. In consequence only three of Ford's five basic models sold in Britain are now assembled here, group imports to the UK have rocketed since 1976 from 30,000 to over 220,000 per year, and the company's British facilities are increasingly devoted to component and KD production.

From Ford's point of view the strategy has been extremely successful. For example, the major strike in 1971 cost the company at least 45,000 new car sales nearly 8% of its market share, yet due to the availability of group imports the two month strike in 1978 resulted in a loss of only 1% in market share and in boom conditions new registrations of Ford cars rose by over 50,000. Historical cost profits, which doubled to over £240 million in 1977 only fell to £217 million in 1978; in real terms the value of sales jumped 50% between 1975 (the same levels as 1970) and 1977-78, total payroll employees increased by 8,000 to 74,000 while productivity (sales per employee) rose by over 55%.*

Three important points emerge from this analysis of trends among car manufacturers. First, that notwithstanding the manifold problems of the British motor industry, both market and production conditions favour the 'global federals', Ford and GM and to a lesser extent the 'zonal federals' like PSA. They are firmly against the 'national direct exporters' such as BL, whose lack of foreign production facilities hinders access to export markets and whose limited capacity impairs competitiveness in the high-volume, low cost component production already dominant among successful manufacturers.

Second, that the multi-sourcing and complementation of componenets practised by Ford and GM raises the issue of the accountability of multi-national companies, both to employees and to governments. Paradoxically, of the British based manufacturers only BL is able to export world-wide without any restriction of parent company policy or model design.** Moreover multi-national corporate policy and transfer pricing is now in the control of private bodies such as Ford Europe, over whom no government has legislative power.

Third, and most germane to the present study, there are three groups among the British manufacturers, divided according to ownership, size, structure and production: Ford, Talbot and Vauxhall, and BL. However, in terms of market leadership (both in products and in products processes, wages and work organisation) they effectively divide into only two—Ford

* Ford Annual Report and Accounts.
** HC, para. 268.

and the rest. In the case of employment and working time issues this is reflected in a distinction between demand-led and demand-constrained companies.

In these conditions, it becomes particularly difficult to discuss likely future trends of employment and productivity in a meaningful way, not least in relation to the "car" industry. Weaknesses on the supply side, major fluctuations in the domestic demand for cars (with exaggeratedly high rates of increase in 1972, and in 1978 and 1979), major shifts in the exchange rate and consequently in international competitiveness (a major fall in the sterling exchange rate in 1976; substantial increases in 1978 and 1979), have all affected the outturn. It remains significant that even so, one major manufacturer, Ford UK, has shown substantially improved profitability since the recession of the mid-1970s; the competitive pressures on the other manufacturers and assemblers has been the more intense.

Employment, Productivity and Industrial Disputes

It has been a constant theme of the analysis that capacity utilisation is fundamental to motor vehicle manufacturing, for it is here that labour enters into the equation and that the demands of capital and labour conflict. Excluding bought-in components, labour costs amount to about half the cost of building a car and in Britain this means they comprise roughly 20% of the total production cost of a car. A company's labour costs are composed of two elements: the wages cost per hour and the number of man hours it takes to build a car, i.e. productivity. While the former is simply a function of employment and wage levels and is to a large degree within company control, the latter is dependent upon shopfloor practice, where workers' attitudes and trade union reactions hold greater sway. The cost of the bad labour relations endemic in the motor industry—in lost production, low levels of utilisation and productivity, and poor quality—must therefore be immense. Industrial disputes are variously estimated to account for between half and two-thirds of the industry's lost production.

However, both productivity and industrial relations vary greatly between companies, plants different stages of the production process and hence different groups of workers. For Ford, for example, the CPRS found (significantly) that the gap between the labour input required in Britain and on the continent for powertrain and component manufacture was only that observed in vehicle assembly. Productivity varies according to many non-labour factors such as product-mix, reliance on bought-in components, plant layout and equipment; stoppages in strategic production areas can rapidly halt a whole plant, while others merely hinder production in particular sections and have only marginal or long-term effects. In short, unless facilities and manning are identical, labour productivity can only be measured and compared upon a financial basis. This ensures that the following brief analysis of employment, productivity and industrial disputes can be no more than a rough guide to an extremely complex and multi-form situation, one which may occasionally defy meaningful generalisation.

Table 2.39   Indexes of Output, Employment and Productivity for Motor Vehicle Manufacturing (MLH 381) and all Manufacturing Industries, 1960-1979   1970 = 100. 1968 SIC

| | Motor Vehicle Manufacturing | | | All manufacturing |
Year	Output	Employment	Productivity	Productivity
1960	71.6	84.8	84.4	74.2
1961	64.5	80.6	80.0	73.2
1962	68.5	83.2	82.3	74.0
1963	79.8	87.2	91.5	77.9
1964	89.1	92.9	95.9	83.8
1965	89.7	95.7	93.7	85.3
1966	88.5	96.0	92.2	86.9
1967	83.8	90.3	92.8	90.0
1968	93.5	91.1	102.6	97.0
1969	99.1	96.2	103.0	99.3
1970	100.0	100.0	100.0	100.0
1971	100.5	99.2	101.3	102.8
1972	102.2	96.4	106.0	109.0
1973	104.6	100.4	104.2	117.4
1974	95.5	97.8	97.6	115.5
1975	87.8	89.9	97.7	113.4
1976	89.4	88.2	101.4	118.9
1977	94.2	91.3	103.2	119.8
1978	91.0	95.2*	95.6*	121.7*
1979	87.2	92.9*	93.9*	123.7*

* 1978-79 figures are provisional.

Source: 'Department of Employment Gazette' 'Monthly Digest of Statistics' (various editions). 'Economic Trends' November 1973.

Note: Output figures are taken from the 'Index of Production'. 'Productivity is therefore a crude volume measure of the value of output per person.

i) Employment and Productivity

The changes in the volume of output, of employment and of productivity since 1960 are outlined in Table 2.39. The following points are noteworthy:

a) Though there is a clear cyclical variation in employment there is surprisingly little change in the level of total employment over the last four trade cycles; cyclical peaks (in 1966, 1970, 1973 and 1978) are all within a range of about 5% of each other (over 480,000 under 510,000). A more serious problem of manning and employment is evident at the end of the 1970s, with BL in particular emphasising the need for a major reduction in employment and associated plant closures and re-organisation.

b) Output of the sector peaks in 1973 (31% higher than a decade earlier); since then performance has been unusually weak, and only one year (1977) has even come within 10% of the 1973 level.

c) The crude indicator of productivity derived from the output and employment series shows only subdued improvements in the decade to the output peak in 1973. Over the same decade productivity in the UK manufacturing as a whole rose considerably faster (approximately by one half). In more recent years, labour productivity in the motor industry has remained below the 1972/73 levels (again by contrast with the rest of manufacturing industry) and has now declined to the same level as fifteen years ago.

ii) Industrial Disputes

A full analysis of stoppages of work due to industrial disputes in the motor industry is given in Table 2.40. This shows that the number of disputes fluctuates widely from year to year, but that only once in the past decade has the total number of working days lost in the motor vehicle industry (MLH 381) fallen below one million, an increasing proportion of them at the establishments where the disputes occurred. Moreover, it must be remembered that the official statistics understate the level of disputes since they exclude all stoppages entailing the loss of less than 100 working days where they involved fewer than ten workers or lasted less than one day. Some indication of the comparative severity of industrial disputes in the motor industry and elsewhere can be obtained from the figures for "incidence rates". These demonstrated that in terms of working days lost per 1,000 employees, motor vehicle manufacturing is considerably (anything between two and twenty times) more prone to dislocation than the average of all industries and services.

Table 2.40 Stoppages of Work due to Industrial Disputes in the Motor Vehicle Industry,[1] 1969-1979

Year	Number of stoppages beginning in period	Stoppages in Progress		Working days lost at establishments not involved in the dispute	Total working days lost in the motor vehicle industry	Working days lost per 1,000 employees[2]	
		Number of workers involved	Aggregate working days lost			Motor vehicle industry	All industries and services
1969	276	276,000	1,636,000	860,000	2,496,000	3,100	300
1970	336	271,400	1,105,000	523,000	1,628,000	2,150	475
1971	241	340,300	3,100,000	95,000	3,195,000	6,150	600
1972	217	247,300	1,355,000	115,000	1,470,000	2,750	1,100
1973	297	442,600	2,082,000	330,000	2,412,000	4,100	325
1974	223	296,600	1,755,000	201,000	1,956,000	3,534	647
1975	150	164,000	829,000	203,000	1,032,000	1,814	265
1976	191	206,000	785,000	178,000	963,000	1,751	146
1977	212	283,800	2,605,000	315,000	2,920,000	5,455	448
1978	194	234,300	3,495,000	320,000	3,185,000	7,214	414
1979 *	152	199,500	1,555,000	n.a.		3,307	1,302

Source: Department of Employment Gazette, annual survey; incidence rates, August 1974, page 710, January 1979, page 33.

* Provisional. The 1979 figures for the motor vehicle industry are an underestimate as the effects of the national engineering dispute have not yet been distributed among associated industries.

[1] 1969 = 1958 SIC; 1970 to date = 1968 SIC.

[2] The incidence rates refer only to the working days lost at the establishments where the disputes occurred. The official statistics understate the number of stoppages of work since they exclude: a) stoppages involving, fewer than 10 workers or lasting less than one day, except where the total days lost exceed 100, and b) any dispute not connected with terms and conditions of employment. Fortunately the motor vehicle industry is the only one for which the DE provides estimates of time lost at one establishment resulting from a stoppage at another.

238

Further examination of the causes of disruption suggests that wage rates and earnings levels have regularly accounted for between 40% and 50% of the larger stoppages, and 60% to 80% of working days lost. However, manning levels, working time and conditions, disciplinary measures and trade union matters are all significant causes of industrial strife in motor manufacturing and it is clear that there are many complex, deep-rooted and often interdependent problems affecting the industry's labour relations.*

— "A lack of confidence in the prospects for the industry and employment within it.

— A long history of disagreement has led to a serious lack of trust and faith between the two sides in the industry:

— Poor communications between management and labour

— Introduction of measured day work (MDW) at BL and Chrysler has caused new problems

— Decentralised wage bargaining (now forcibly centralised at BL)

— Fragmented union structure."**

Other commentators may have utilised different categories, but all the evidence points to the chronic state of labour relations at shopfloor level throughout the motor industry.

Collective Bargaining, Occupations, Pay Systems

As the analysis of industrial disputes suggested, the motor industry provides major contrasts in collective bargaining, and connected contrasts in pay systems. Broadly, the UK subsidiaries of United States companies developed company wide bargaining and pay structures, with emphasis on time rates of wages for production workers as well as other grades. The plants of United Kingdom firms developed far closer to engineering industry practice, with localised bargaining and pay rates, and extensive use of group payment by results systems. BL is most recently attempting the difficult task of shifting across to company wide pay structures, having in the earlier 1970s largely replaced plant level payment by results systems by "measured day work" (arguably with detrimental effects on labour productivity).

A substantial part of the industry, and notably BL plants, are parties to the engineering industry agreement—which sets minimum pay rates and

* Department of Employment Gazette. Annual Survey.
** CPRS, p.101-3 for the detailed exposition.

establishes hours and other conditions of work—and are thus affected by the recent agreement (and were affected by the industrial action that preceded it) with its provision for the 39 hour week late in 1981.

With a high proportion of workers employed in large plants, unionisation of manual workers in such plants is virtually complete, reinforced by "closed shop" arrangements. Membership of particular trade unions reflects skills and historical patterns of union organisation in specific plants. The T&GWU has emerged as the trade union with the largest membership in the industry, with the amalgamation of the Vehicle Builders in the T&GWU in the early 1970s being an important influence.

Returns from motor industry firms to the Industrial Training Board give the following approximate occupational proportions:

Managerial and supervisory	7%
Scientists, technicians	5%
Admin., professional, clerical	12%
Craftsmen	14%
"Operators"	33%
Other employees	29%

Tension persists over the occupational differentials of skilled workers. The differential in hourly earnings between skilled and semi-skilled workers has, according to NEDO studies* become unusually small (only an estimated 3% in 1979 for timeworkers). Such differentials have been diminishing since the late 1960s in other engineering industries as well. Perhaps the special feature in motors was the extensive change over in the early 1970s from payment by results (especially for semi-skilled production workers) to measured pay work; the high earnings of PBR workers were transformed into high time rates under measured day work.

Some estimates of the decline in PBR in the motor industry is given by Table 2.41. It is noticeable that incentive schemes have been preserved most among skilled craftsmen such as fitters, turners and sheet metal workers; perhaps in order to maintain high earnings levels. However, the lowest proportion of PBR workers is found amongst toolroom and maintenance men, so these differences may reflect the varying proportions of each group employed with the major manufacturers and component producers respectively. There may be also be a slight cyclical trend on the incidence of PBR working.

* NEDO: 'Engineeering Craftsmen: Shortages and Related Problems' (1977).

Table 2.41 Payment-by-Results Workers in the Motor Industry

Classes of Workers (MLH 380-382)	Percentage of Payment-by-Results Workers									
	1979	1978	1977	1976	1975	1974	1973	1972	1971	1970
Fitters (skilled—other than toolroom and maintenance	38	46	42	56	54	57	51	57	57	56
Turners and machinemen (other than toolroom and maintenance)										
a) rated at or above fitters' rate	52	63	55	70	60	66	66	76	82	84
b) rated below fitters' rate	65	62	47	70	67	67	64	84	93	92
Toolroom fitters and turners	7	14	13	14	6	13	11	10	10	11
Maintenance men (skilled)										
Skilled maintenance fitters	8	12	12	13	6	10	11	12	14	12
Skilled maintenance electricians	7	11	10	10	4	8	8	9	11	12
Other skilled maintenance classes	5	6	6	6	—	4	4	6	8	12
Patternmakers	20	22	22	18	—	14	13	14	13	13
Sheet metal workers (skilled)	43	50	46	52	68	72	71	74	73	74
All other adult skilled grades	39	39	34	41	41	47	45	42	47	48
All other adult semi-skilled grades	16	21	19	22	21	24	27	32	38	40
Labourers	20	24	23	19	14	19	17	16	20	25
Male manual workers MLH 380	61.0	44.8	38.1	24.7	35.6	—	47.1	n.a.	n.a.	49.5
MLH 381	34.0	42.6	29.2	33.7	30.9	30.5	39.1	n.a.	n.a.	34.7

The NES is a sample survey of all employees, however the DE June Survey sample omits transport workers, storemen, warehousemen, canteen workers and the like. But while the NES includes, at most, one per cent of employees, the June Survey "numbers are equivalent to about four-fifths of all adult male workers in the occupations concerned in all establishments".

Source: Department of Employment Gazette, June Survey
    New Earnings Survey
   — = not given (sample too small)

Pay and Patterns of Working Time

The 1979 New Earnings Survey provides a useful outline of the make-up of earnings and the main characteristics of working time for broad categories of workers in the industry in April of that year. This material relates to those workers who worked a full week (so it does not indicate the effects of industrial disputes), and relates to a period of high demand for motor industry output. It is useful to contrast 1979 with a year of declining demand (1974) in the middle of the decade, and with the opening of the decade (1970, which saw some minor decline in activity).

The data for *male manual workers* bring out clearly the major shift in the pattern of pay since 1970, but there are other points that are worth noting:

Table 2.42   Make-up of Pay: Manual Men, Motor Manufacturing

Year	Av. weekly earnings £	Percentage of earnings from			Earnings as % of manuf. Av.*
		overtime	PBR	Shift Premium	
1970	33.1	11%	24%	6%	116
1974	49.7	9%	10%	5%	110
1979	103.5	13%	7%	6%	106

* Comparison with earnings of all manual men in manufacturing.
Source: NES: 1974, 1979.

The major reduction in the importance of payment by results (PBR) systems, as a result of changing to measured day work, is evident. A cyclical swing in overtime use provides the best explanation for contrasting percentages of overtime pay. Even so, it is interesting to note that average overtime hours in 1979 were 5.8 to produce total average weekly hours of 45.6 and this was slightly less than in manufacturing generally (6.2 hours overtime: 46 hours worked). Shift premia have been a stable element (with some decline in a period of low activity such as 1974); the main form of shift work in the industry is night work alternating with days.

But in addition it is important to notice the decline in the level of earnings as compared with those in manufacturing generally. Despite the survey week in 1979 relating to a period of high demand and some increase in overtime working in motors, earnings were only 6% higher than in manufacturing generally, whereas in 1970 they had been 16% higher.

There are rather different trends apparent in the make-up of pay of *non-manual men* in motor manufacturing.

242

Table 2.43 Make-up of Pay: Non-Manual Men, Motor Manufacturing

Year	Av. weekly earnings £	Percentage of earnings from			Earnings as % of manuf. Av.*
		overtime	PBR	Shift Premia	
1970	38.4	7%	2%	1%	105
1974	59.5	4%	1%	1%	109
1979	124.8	10%	1½%	1%	106

* Comparison with earnings of all Non-Manual Men in manufacturing.
Source: NES: 1970, 1974, 1979.

The swing in the proportion of earnings accounted for by overtime are more pronounced than for manual men, and it is apparent that overtime work has built up to comparatively high levels. This is unusual for non-manual men in industry. Thus in the 1979 survey week, non-manual men in motors worked on average 4.6 hours overtime to make a total of 42.7 hours worked; by contrast in manufacturing only 1.8 hour overtime were worked on average to make a total of 39.6 hours actually worked.

This factor has to be borne in mind when looking at the comparative earnings of non-manual men in motor manufacturing (compared with manufacturing as a whole). At first sight a fairly stable relative position appears to be indicated. But by 1979 hourly earnings had fallen below those of manufacturing generally. Thus it would seem that both manual and non-manual men in motors have experienced a decline in their relative earnings position, but for non-manuals this is masked by considerably increased overtime working.

The data available for *women* workers (some of it is incomplete for earlier years) shows only limited overtime worked (1.3 hours average for manual women, 0.7 for non-manual in 1979). However, the earnings data for manual women (under 5% of the total labour force in motors) is of some interest; in 1979 the average weekly earnings were £72.4. This was 25% higher than the manufacturing average for manual women full-time workers. 11% of the total earnings in motors were accounted for by payment by results payments; this is less than in 1974 when PBR accounted for 18% of total pay. So the "myth" of the comparatively high paid motor industry worker apparently can only be said to apply to the small proportion of its workers who are women manual workers.

It should be borne in mind when interpreting the connection between hours of work and patterns of working time (e.g. shifts) on the one hand and average earnings on the other that varying proportions of those "average" workers work shift systems, or work overtime in the survey week.

243

Thus, in the case of manual men some 60% worked overtime in the 1978 survey week. (In the cyclical downturn in 1974 only 50% worked overtime during the survey week). Nearly 31% received shift premia in the 1978 survey week considerably higher in the course of the cyclical activity to the industry (it was lower in 1975 and higher in 1977). Detailed studies of shift working in the industry, indicate that a considerably higher proportion of male manual workers are working within one or other sequence of a shift system than might be assumed from the NES information on shift premia in the survey week.

As for non-manual men, some 43% received overtime pay in the 1978 survey week. The proportion had been considerably less (30% in 1974) in the downturn of the mid-1970s, and will almost certainly be higher than 43% in the 1979 survey week, when the further details are published. But only 5½% received shift premia according to the 1978 survey; the contrast with manual workers' experience here is extreme.

Clearly, the UK motor manufacturing industry faces major problems of organisation and competition. It has not only experienced instability and turbulence in external market factors affecting its performance, but labour relations and dispute levels also present many unresolved problems. Serious issues of the displacement of plants and workers are currently arising, and the relatively stable level of employment provided by the industry over the last decade and more may now be under greater threat. It is within this context that changes in the patterns of working time have to be reviewed.

Definitions

1968 Standard Industrial Classification

MLH 380   Manufacturing and assembling three- and four-wheeled and half-tracked tractors. Manufacturing parts and accessories (other than rough or semi-finished castings and forgings) when made wholly or primarily of metal and not specified elsewhere. Industrial tractors are classified in Heading 337, road tractors in Heading 381 and electrical accessories and equipment in Heading 369.

MLH 381.1 Manufacturing and assembling passenger cars, commercial goods vehicles, road tractors solely for tractor-trailer combinations, buses, battery-electric vehicles, and three-wheeled vehicles. Manufacturing engines, bodies chassis, chassis frames, seats and safety belts for motor vehicles, cabs for commercial vehicles and motor body shells. Manufacturing all other parts and accessories (other than rough or semi-finished castings and forgings) when made wholly or primarily of metal and not specified elsewhere. Establishments specialising in reconditioning engines and gearboxes are included.

Powered invalid carriages and industrial trucks are classified in Headings 382 and 337 respectively; electrical accessories and equipment in Heading 369; parts and accessories made wholly or primarily of asbestos, glass, rubber or plastics in Headings 429, 463 and 496 respectively.

MLH 381.2 Motor drawn trackers, caravans and freight containers.

MOTOR VEHICLE MANUFACTURING

CASE STUDIES

Case Study 11

Introduction

The case study was made up of two separate on-site investigations (referred to here as Plant A and Plant B) into the working time organisation of this US owned multi-national company. It should be noted that with the limited exception of Plant B management co-operation in this study was not forthcoming. The researchers were, therefore, forced to rely to a large extent on published company data to elicit basic economic performance indicators. Fortunately, through the good offices of the T&GWU and the local shop stewards interviewed, some internal company data on manpower was accessible.

This lack of access inevitably means that the likely management reactions to shorter working time options cannot be adequately commented on or evaluated by the study. Moreover, detailed attempts to cost out such options must await a more enlightened management response. Insofar as a demand for a reduction in the basic hours of work has featured in the last two annual wage claims submitted to this company by their signatory unions, the "territory" to be studied is not new to management. It would also appear from the company's reply to these claims that some rudimentary costings of the unions' claims for a reduced basic working week have been carried out. That management refused to co-operate with our research is perhaps an indication of their sensitivity to the concept of reduced working time as a realistic subject for bargaining. Be that as it may, and observers of corporate styles of information disclosure may simply recognise this as a typical response of a US owned MNC, it is not altogether unreasonable to conclude that the company is unlikely to give up its rigid control over the length of the working week (and the high levels of overtime which it appears to prefer) without considerable persuasion from the trade unions it recognises.

Economic Context

As previously mentioned, the responses of individual parties to the case studies have to be seen against the economic context and market environment which the enterprise finds itself operating within. A brief review of the performance of the company in this study provides, perhaps, some insight into the management's refusal to co-operate with the research and sheds a good deal of light on the company's more immediate arguments against bargained reductions in working time.

On superficial indicators it would appear that the company has fared markedly better than its UK based competitors, experiencing peaks in sales in 1972 and 1977 and increasing its UK market share steadily over the last decade. Whilst the company have not completely escaped the effects of the recession, it is clear that they have a solid presence in the commercial and export markets, and that any adverse effects have been less marked than those suffered by their main competitors, hence the company's market share has increased. Of greater significance, insofar as potential reductions in working time and possible increases in employment opportunity are concerned, are the increasing imports of cars made elsewhere in the European operations of the company for sale on the UK market. The fact that sales in 1977 equalled the 1972 previous peak, but that in 1977 home production fell some 30 points below that of 1972 indicates either a production shortfall or a major change in the product mix of the final output of the UK operation. Either way, some 90,000 cars were imported in 1977 whilst in the following year, disrupted by a major strike, over 150,000 units were imported to maintain the market share. The ability to bolster home output in this way is an impressive display of multi-national strength, but along with the continuing high external value of sterling does not look promising for future investment by the company in the UK.

Like other factors employment levels are subject to cyclical trends, however, whilst white collar employment at the company has been progressively declining since 1973 (the introduction of electronic data systems meant the loss of over two thousand salaried jobs by 1976, a trend that was barely arrested by the conditions of 1977), the hourly paid staff by comparison have increased by more than ten per cent. The June 1979 figure of 58,500 was nearly seven thousand higher than three and a half years ago, and manual employment must now be at its highest ever level at the company.

With these historically high manning levels it would seem most unlikely that the company would view reductions in working time as anything other than a means to raise labour productivity, either by more effective work organisation or through increased capital intensity. In any event it would appear that the optimum consequences for the trade unions involved would be a maintenance of the workforce at existing levels with any reductions in actual hours being bargained against whatever "slack" that can be identified within the current system of labour deployment.

The Regulation of Terms and Conditions of Employment

Terms and conditions of employment for both manual and non-manual employees at Plant A and B are subject to annual negotiations through the respective national joint negotiating committees. The T&GWU has the major membership share at the company and tends to lead both negotiations. The AUEW (Eng.) also has sizeable membership but the majority of engineering craft unions are represented on the NJNC.

Prior to our case studies, we were led to believe that the control of terms and conditions was highly centralised and could only be changed through the NJNC. The evidence gained from Plant B however showed that some scope for local autonomy in terms of changes in working time organisation does exist. This is an important point since the degree to which stewards and convenors at local level feel constrained from impinging upon the NJNC's bargaining province clearly represents a negative influence over the possibility of "breakthrough" initiatives at individual plants. Whilst the changes in working time negotiated at Plant B might indeed be considered as a "breakthrough", it is equally illustrative of the centralising power of the NJNC that this example has not been used to force similar agreements at other plants in the company's UK operation.

PLANT A—PRESENT WORKING TIME ORGANISATION

At the site all aspects of production are carried out, ranging from foundry work, to body pressing to pre-assembly, to final trim and assembly, and including upholstery work and the manufacture of certain components. Each of the plants on site, consequently, has its own peculiar pattern of work organisation, related both to the nature of the technological process of production, and to the nature of the particular unit produced and its relationship to the final production process.

The basic company-wide grading and shift systems operate at the plant. Hence manual male workers are distributed across five grades: A-E (grade A being unskilled labourers, B, C and D semi-skilled production and grade E for skilled craftsmen—apprentices have a separate grade) and may operate on any one of five individual shift systems;* female manual workers

---

* Five day continuous, seven days continuous, alternating, permanent days, permanent nights.

247

are distributed across grades A, B and C and are almost totally deployed on permanent day shift. Aggregate employment data for the company shows that the majority of manual males are in grades B and C (around 80% of male manuals) and that the majority are employed on alternating shifts (65%) with five day continuous being the next most utilised shift system (20%). There is little reason to suppose that the specific distribution of labour at Plant A would deviate significantly from this overall company pattern.

Shift Systems

"Seven day continuous" shift working is limited, mainly, to workers in "service occupations", those tending to the boilers and heating, security staff, etc. "Five day semi-continuous" shift systems operate for certain of the pre-production process such as the press shop and machine shop. In the latter type of shop it can be introduced to replace two shift working, as a means of accommodating sustained (i.e. anticipated to last some 18 months at least) increases in demand, as an alternative to using overtime to increase capacity.

The majority of assembly workers, including the line and final assembly workers, work on a two shift "alternate day and night" system, as do the majority of maintenance workers.

Rotations are fixed section by section. The alternate day and night shift rotates fortnightly, the three shift systems anything between weekly and monthly. However, where an individual worker is not part of an integrated production team he is able to make his own arrangements for rotation.

Within the two shift systems possibilities exist in certain sections for the use of permanent day and permanent night teams. Whilst this system is not applicable to final assembly operations, it can be found in sections concerned with certain pre-assembly processes—e.g. in the KD plant, and in sections where a relatively large number of women are employed—e.g. in the plant where seating and upholstery work is done.

Shift working is seldom popular, and when the company had originally introduced the alternating system in the early 1960s hundreds of previously day shift workers had left the company in response to the demand for them to work nights. Now, however, the stewards recognise that shift working is widely accepted as a necessary evil by the workforce in order to boost earnings.

Overtime Working

The company's Overtime Agreement specifies overtime working as serving to enable the company to meet peaks and troughs of demand without

248

recourse to layoffs.* However, demand for the product is both high and stable, indeed demand cannot be met, and thus overtime does not fluctuate significantly on a week by week basis. Overtime thus serves largely "institutional" purposes, although, of course, it also serves an important purpose in extending capital utilisation time and thus lowering unit costs—particularly to the extent where additional manning, or the introduction of additional shifts, is neither practical nor acceptable to the workforce.

Differing overtime arrangements can be distinguished on a section by section basis.

Line workers (on the two shift system) work one hour's overtime at the end of each shift—making the actual working day one of nine hours. This arrangement is sanctioned by formal agreement, and whilst the additional hour is not compulsory almost everybody will work it. Saturday morning overtime is not however normally worked by line workers because it is found that not enough want to work at the weekends and thus it is not viable—in terms of the company being able to efficiently man up the line. It might however be used after a sustained strike to rebuild up stocks, and in these circumstances the workforce normally has a sufficiently financial interest to ensure high attendance levels. Non-assembly or pre-production workers and machine shop workers—will tend to do the one hour's overtime at the end of the shift and also a five hour half-shift on Saturday or Sunday (depending on which shift they are working).

Skilled workers will work similar patterns to other pre-production workers except that they might do up to an hour and a half overtime at the end of each weekday shift.

Maintenance workers who are working the two shift system will put in extensive overtime after the normal shift time, and also do a considerable amount of weekend working. For this category of worker it is of course necessary that a certain amount of his work be done at times outside the working hours of others.

It was felt however that the principal function of high levels of maintenance overtime was to attract and retain labour, via its ability to enhance wages.

This is particularly the case for skilled workers, tool room workers especially, who would not stay with the company if the overtime was not

* By comparison, in certain of the company's continental plants where much less overtime is worked, layoffs are for this reason used to a far greater extent.

249

available. The company in seeking to recruit skilled workers, advertises the availability of overtime with its subsequent effects upon earnings levels. Consequently, it can also be seen that overtime earnings serve to maintain earnings differentials between skilled and line workers—given the longer average overtime worked by the former.

Whilst the stewards tend to think that the amount of overtime worked is excessive most of the workforce are willing, because of the money, to work the overtime demanded, e.g. 70% of those who are offered it work the Sunday morning half shift. Whilst nearly all work the one hour's overtime at the beginning and end of the shift.

This raises the problem of what would be a sufficiently high basic wage to make overtime working unnecessary, and what would be the implications of introducing such a rate.

Given the pressure from the shop floor for overtime, whatever their own views, the stewards do not interfere by, for example, seeking to initiate a reduction in the level of overtime. Rather they concern themselves more with its allocation, on making sure that there is "fair play" if limited overtime is shared out.

Absenteeism

The notion that absenteeism was the result of the long hours worked was rejected. Rather, where high absenteeism was a problem it was seen as a function of high marginal rates of taxation such that, it was suggested, if a person had the opportunity to work compensating Saturday half shift (worth about £23 gross) his net of tax earnings would be only £2 less if he took off a day in the week. Thus the fact that compensating overtime opportunities exist facilitates absenteeism, but overtime is not the cause.

The Potential for Shorter Working Time

It should be noted that historically reductions in the basic week at the plant have been both gradual, i.e. from 44 to 42½ in 1955; to 41¼ in 1959 and finally to 40 in 1961, and accompanied by high overtime leakage which has maintained actual weekly hours. This, for example, was explicitly recognised in the agreement struck in 1955 which stated:

> "In consideration of an assurance given by the Trade Unions that, because the Company's facilities are inadequate to meet current demand on the production capacity, there will be no reduction in the present minimum level of actual working hours, the Company agrees . . . to reduce the standard working week from 44 hours to 42½ hours without loss of pay"

whilst later agreements were in a similar vein. Reductions in actual hours tended to come subsequently and were the product of drops in final demand which caused the company of its own accord to reduce its demand for overtime, although it was workplace organisation, producing pressure for agreements which constrained the scheduling of overtime to within particular limits,* which prevented the company subsequently, as demand recovered, reverting to former overtime levels.

The historical experience, then, does not suggest any exclusive and immediate linkage between reductions in basic hours and increases in employment, although it is possible that the overtime restrictions detailed in the footnote may have led to some increased manning as demand recovered.

In the recent past (the last two years) the company have rejected the union side claim for a 35 hour week; it was argued that they would not be able to recoup the lost output implied, since the possibilities for any compensatory speed up and remanning were critically impaired by the extent to which they considered the company's facilities were already overmanned.

Whilst the unions were critical of the descriptions of the state of affairs as one of "overmanning", since this suggests an under-utilisation of labour —they did agree that manning was very high on the production lines, as a result of their already high speed, and that further speed up would be impossible simply because there was no physical space on the lines to put in more people.

Only in the engine plant was there considered to be the physical space necessary to realistically increase line manning—indeed such a practice was carried out in this section (in addition to increased overtime) in order to meet temporary peaks in demand.

The lack of physical space on the majority of assembly lines, together with the apparent tightness of the work-studied schedules which govern them, was clearly identified as a constraint by stewards at the plant against remanning subsequent to any reduction in the basic weekly hours of work. Moreover, the increased cost of creating additional space for assembly lines to accommodate reduced hours and higher manning was seen as a powerful company argument. In these circumstances increases in overtime begins to be seen as a "rational" solution by both management and workforce.

This is not to suggest that there are no possibilities for reducing working time at the plant. Where work is *operator* as opposed to *machine* paced,

---

* For instance, now, overtime can only be scheduled for one hour at the end of the shift plus five hours on Saturday and Sunday mornings.

i.e. in some sub-assembly areas—there was indeed evidence of workers creating their own working time "space" by operating at a pace faster than the standard times set for them which enabled unofficial breaks to be taken. In addition, experience at the plant showed that changeovers from two to three shift operation with downward adjustments in manning per shift (but overall achieving an increase in manning) were possible in sub-assembly and pre-assembly areas. However, a similar adjustment of final assembly areas apparently remains critically constrained.

A further constraint can be found in the dependency of the working time patterns of indirect workers on direct workers. For example, a considerable amount of maintenance is carried out after the completion of the direct workers' normal shift time. Increasing shift utilisation would effectively squeeze the time available for maintenance jobs to be carried out. Such a balancing of tasks is not impossible to achieve, but it remains an easier organisational option for management (even though it means the tolerance of significant amount of non-effective working time for maintenance workers) to operate on a two shift basis and merely have to balance maintenance time with high overtime working of direct workers.

Briefly then, our study at the plant showed that reductions of working time were possible particularly where work was operator paced (of course, this is not surprising and the practice of "job and finish" has a long pedigree throughout the motor industry) and that changeovers to three shift working could be achieved with increases in manning. The constraints however, which seemed to be exerting a fairly powerful influence on the shop stewards were to be found in the existing very high manning levels on the assembly line, the limited physical space on the lines, and the feeling that since the company had all the operations timed to the last second there was very little room for manoeuvre. Against this backdrop overtime was seen as being a supportable solution.

This does not however suggest that the workforce did not want a reduction in the basic working week. The women in particular favoured a 35 hour week.

Extending Holidays

One of the alleged drawbacks of the shorter working week is that it does not create time off in useful sized blocks. The utility of an extra half an hour of leisure time at the end of the day is probably not very great, and may explain the willingness of workers to put in odd hours overtime at the end of the day, which would facilitate the "overtime leakage" reaction to a shortening of the basic week. To this extent it appeared that increasing holiday entitlement, either across the board via an increase in the basic entitlement, or through improvements to the 'extra days for service' scheme which the company operated would prove a more popular way of reducing annual working time. In this context the notion of a staggered paid personal holiday scheme (a system recently negotiated in the US vehicle industry) which would operate throughout the year as an *addition* to the normal holiday entitlement, clearly suggests that more novel and more effectively job creational approaches could be tried—the idea was in fact raised by the union side in the most recent wage negotiations.

Paid Personal Holidays (PPH)

In essence a PPH system runs as follows:*

In the first year of its operation all auto workers with at least one year's seniority received five personal holidays, the number rising to seven in the second. These PPH's must be taken as days off and they are scheduled by a computer, to be evenly distributed across the working week and between shifts. At present the PPH's are planned to fall only between October 1 and May 31, so as not to aggravate manpower shortages that occur in the summer because of regular vacations, and in the period October 1978 to May 1979 (180 work days), one free day falls every 28 days. On any day, for example, 2.8% of the labour force is off work on PPH, although the company has found it necessary to hire a slightly lower percentage to serve as replacements.

The advantages of the system from the point of view of our analysis are three-fold. Firstly, it has the advantage of leaving present capital utilisation time unchanged; it does not upset what is apparently quite a finely balanced production process, in which work-time durations are a crucial part of that balance. Secondly, whilst it involves admittedly highly complex planning** it makes use of—albeit that it qualitatively expands—a system already in operation in the industry, that of a "plus level" of manning. Already each production area is overmanned by a certain percentage to cover for sickness and other absences—the precise percentage we found varies from plant to plant, and from work area to work area, and is a function of both the geographical area, and hence, local culture, in which the plant is situated, and of the nature of the work involved—and the

---

* The model used here is derived from that negotiated in the US Automobile industry by the UAW in 1978.
** Chrysler and General Motors set up new offices to manage their PPH operations.

introduction of a PPH type scheme would merely increase the level of this "plus manning".* Thirdly, it would appear to produce more nearly a "one to one relationship" between the reduction of working hours and the creation of jobs, as it would not be open to either overtime or productivity leakages. Finally, because it would not require any complementary investment along with the additional jobs, it would be less costly than other alternatives, and the only costs, above overheads of administration, would be labour costs. However, were the system applied to give as many hours off within the working year as would a reduction of five hours in the basic week it would render each worker 30 PPH's within the year, which if these were evenly distributed through the year would have (a maximum of) a 3.3% employment effect.

An additional benefit would be that by taking a person out of work for a whole day the costs of travel to work, and of being at work—e.g. meals, would be avoided. Given the relatively long travelling time found at Plant A it is estimated that the saving here is not inconsiderable.

Finally, the scheme does come within the experience of the workforce—it has been an element in the company's wage claim, and an accepted tradition of work-time management in the UK—we can cite the use of "rota days", one per month, in continuous process industries to produce a 40 hour week from a system which in itself generates a 42 hour week, and even the granting of an additional "rota day" in Electricity Generation to cope with the 38 hour week that exists there.

PLANT B—PRESENT WORKING TIME ORGANISATION

Plant B employs some 2,000 persons. It is involved primarily in the manufacture of machined components and supplies these to company plants throughout the country. In itself this makes the plant unusual in that it concentrates only upon pre-production and is not involved in any final assembly. This factor explains some of the work patterns to be found on site. However, it is important to contrast the changes in working time organisation which have been negotiated at Plant B compared to the more rigid managerially imposed and sustained patterns detailed in the review of working time organisation at Plant A.

It should be noted that as for Plant A the company wide grading structure applied at Plant B, as did the variety, although as will be seen not the same utilisation, of shift types.

* It should be noted that at our case study the service holidays granted to workers with long service—three days for those with 10 years service, five days for those with 25 years—are already covered in this way.

254

The Change from Two Shift to Three Shift Working

The company commenced production on the site in 1966. Originally the company imported traditional (as operated at its other plants) work patterns, and principally this entailed operating a two shift (alternate day and night) system.

However, the plant is in an area of coal mining and steel production in which two shift working was an alien tradition. Local culture favoured five day 3 shift operations, and these were fairly rapidly introduced so that now some 73% of the hourly paid workforce—i.e. all the machine shop workers—are on such a system.

The changeover brought with it some changes in the organisation of work. Whilst the two shift system had involved a "heavy" manning of equipment (2 × 12), the introduction of a third shift had been conditional upon agreement to "man down" equipment (to 3 × 9 system).* However, it also involved an expansion in output, which was in accordance with company plans for the plant and a consequent increase in the labour force in the order of 12½%.

Most of the rest of the workers (some 20% of the hourly paid staff) remained on a two shift system, these people being principally engaged on sub-assembly work.

It should be noted that the whilst three shift working is appropriate to the local culture, it is also appropriate to the sort of production operations carried out at the plant. In motor manufacturing as a whole, much pre-production work is organised on a three shift basis, whilst two shift systems are applied to (final) assembly work. Thus, the type of operation performed made adaption to the local culture less problematic.

The Changes in the Three Shift System

The three shift system as introduced operated upon a traditional 6.00 a.m. to 2.00 p.m., 2.00 p.m. to 10.00 p.m., 10.00 p.m. to 6.00 a.m. pattern. Workers were "on plant" for 40 hours but each shift included a half hour's paid meal break.

However, the employees were concerned about the five night week, worked by those on the third shift, which was potentially disruptive to the

---

* i.e. on two shifts for a given number of machines 12 men were used, on three shifts for the same number of machines nine men were used.

255

enjoyment of the weekend. Arriving home after a 6.00 a.m. finish effectively rules out much of Saturday as a day of leisure.

In 1977, after some three or four months of negotiation, a substantial rearrangement of the system was agreed. The first (or morning) shift now works Monday to Thursday from 6.00 a.m. to 2.00 p.m., and on Friday from 6.00 a.m. to 11.30 a.m. The second (or afternnon) shift works Monday to Thursday 2.00 p.m. to 10.00 p.m. and on Friday from 11.30 a.m. to 5.00 p.m. The third (or night) shift works Monday to Thursday 10.00 p.m. to 6.00 a.m. and Friday from 5.00 p.m. to 10.30 p.m.

This system means that those on the second shift are now able to have Friday nights off whilst those on the third shift do not finish at an unreasonable time on Friday night, and do not therefore have their Saturday leisure time eroded by the need to rest, although the high level of weekend overtime worked suggests that it is the free Friday night that is most valued.

"On plant" time is now 37½ hours per week (previously 40) but "effective working time" has not been reduced. Under the original three shift system 58 minutes of each day were paid but not worked—this non-working time consisting of the half hour meal break plus 28 minutes "personal allowance" (including tea break time); under the new system meal breaks were reduced to 20 minutes, and personal allowance time was reduced by 20 minutes to 8 minutes. Thus whilst under the old system four hours 50 minutes of time "on plant" was spent not working, now only two hours 20 minutes is so "lost". The loss of break time during working hours is felt to be compensated for by the reduction in time spent "on plant".

At the same time as the Friday night shift was abolished for three shift workers a similar change was made to the work patterns of two shift workers. The original system was a night shift operating from 10.00 p.m. to 6.30 p.m. but with an addition on each end of one hour's overtime (no longer obligatory, as a condition of employment, but still worked) such that actual hours were 9.00 p.m. to 7.30 a.m.—for five shifts per week. This pattern was maintained for Monday to Thursday operations but on Fridays the night shift now comes in at 4.00 p.m. taking over straight away from the day shift, and works until 9.30 p.m.

Positive Effects of the Changes

In the opinion of the convenors the change in work patterns has had a beneficial effect upon the rate of absenteeism. Under the old system the Friday second shift had been characterised by early leaving whilst the third shift had suffered from people not turning up at all. The rearrangement of shift patterns in such a way that end of week and weekend leisure time was less encroached upon, lessened the need to resort to early leaving/absence and indeed people now looked forward to Fridays.

Management agreed that the change to four and a half day working for shift workers was probably "socially desirable". They recognised that the change had brought about a decline in early leaving, although they felt that "under the old system management was at fault in allowing people to go early", and that now early leaving was easier to control. On the other hand management contested the union's claim that there had been any change in absolute absence levels since the 1977 change.

If anything else the changes that took place in patterns of work time do indicate a considerably greater degree of plant autonomy than one would, at first impression, think would be the case within the company's highly centralised management structure. For example, during the 1977 (12.10.77) Joint Negotiating Committee negotiations over the 1977 wage claim the company refused to consider any proposals for the introduction company wide of a nine night fortnight to ameliorate conditions for shift workers, fearing that it would mean a "de facto" shorter working week. Experience at Plant B however, shows that some reform is possible without their being any disruption of output.

Patterns of Overtime

In common with other plants elsewhere in the company's UK operation at Plant B overtime levels are above average. This reflects the company policy of undermanning and making use of overtime to meet peak production requirements.*

Whilst the three shift system precludes overtime at the beginning and end of the shift, overtime can be worked at the weekends in 4 6-hour half shifts. According to the level of demand management operate half shifts on Saturday morning, Sunday morning and Sunday afternoon. Overtime is not obligatory (although it used to be) but the convenors think that some 90% of workers will normally work the additional half shift if it is available. Management, commenting on what they perceived as a positive demand for weekend working, suggested that if weekend work were not offered to enough persons then the workforce would refuse to comply with the request for weekend working. The company wages structure, which

* Evidence of this practice can be gained from the New Earnings Survey. Disaggregating for this particular company shows manual workers' overtime hours increasing from an average of 6.2 hours per week in April 1978 to 9.0 hours per week in April 1979.

257

produces high rewards but only at the cost of high overtime clearly contributes to this pressure for overtime.

As was said above, two-shift workers normally work an additional hour's overtime at the beginning of the night shift and a further hour at the end of the shift—perhaps because the additional social disruption is only marginal. In addition the two-shift workers have opportunities for weekend overtime, again by the half shift.

Whilst the convenors felt that overtime working at the plant was excessive, they, like their counterparts in Plant A, recognised that because of the workforce they found themselves seemingly "locked in" to an overtime system. Not surprisingly, they did not feel able to "unlock" the system by any local initiatives. Rather, they were seen to favour unilateral action from the union nationally or even a directive from the TUC. Optimism was expressed that either form of pressure would be successful on the grounds that "people down here are constitutionalists".*

The Potential for Shorter Working Time

Their achievement of a 37½ hour "on plant" week for the majority of shift workers led the stewards to believe that the desire for a further reduction to 35 hours was blunted to some extent. Nevertheless, the possibility of further reductions had clearly exercised their minds since they had quite definite views as to how it may be achieved. For three shift workers the short (5¼ hours) Friday shift could be extended to operate on Thursdays as well—the short shift being extremely popular amongst those affected. For two shift workers the cessation of Friday night working was mooted. Clearly, both of these possibilities would have to operate against the virtual exclusion of overtime if they were to achieve a real reduction.

Whether or not preliminary and presumably informal exchanges had taken place with management is not known, but the stewards were of the view that management might well attempt to accommodate the 35 hour working week by restoring non-working time (either meal breaks or personal relief time) such that actual "on plant" hours remained the same but actual working time was reduced. This would obviously have the advantage as far as management were concerned of minimising disruption since the present shift patterns and changeover periods could be maintained. Moreover, with staggered meal breaks involving temporary covering by individual work groups, potential output and productivity leakages could be effectively prevented. It is quite possible that the stewards felt

---

* Recent industrial problems in this particular region have shown the singular accuracy of this comment.

that this was a probable management strategy because non-working time had been used as part of the bargaining counter to achieve the short shift agreement. It does however raise the question as to whether the individual worker would accept the distinction between reduced actual working hours and reducing actual "on plant" hours.*

For their part, the stewards felt that there was little chance of the company absorbing a further reduction in actual working hours through increased productivity. This was seen as only possible through a "speed up" and such things were strictly regulated by the "Works Standards Agreement", and were in any case hotly (and by implication would continue to be) contested by the stewards. It was not thought, however, that a one for one employment effect was necessary to maintain output. It was felt that with some additional manpower coupled with a reorganisation and remixing of manning that some of the machine "slack" could be taken up. Thus, at the end of the day, the stewards did appear to be implying that some marginal increases in labour productivity were both achievable and bargainable.

Increased Holidays

Present holiday arrangements at the company are more generous than the norm for production workers. The summer holiday shutdown is of three weeks duration and the Christmas shutdown lasts for two weeks. In addition workers with more than 10 years service receive an additional three days' "service holiday".

The convenors thought that minor increases in holiday time, were not a positive way of achieving shorter working time and that indeed as a strategy could be diversionary, and hence were not particularly impressed with the concept of the Paid Personal Holiday system (PPH) suggested in their recent wage claim.

Additional holidays were thought to be worthwhile only if these came in significant blocks of additional free time. Whilst the convenors themselves favoured a shorter working week, they felt that their membership might prefer an equivalent reduction in annual worktime in the form of increased holidays (one hour off the work week being equivalent to one week's additional holiday).

* It is significant that in a recent agreement concluded by Volkswagen production workers and line workers will, from September 1979, be able to take within each working hour, a rest break of six minutes, and from September 1981, of eight minutes. In other words whilst being at work, or in the factory, for 40 hours, production workers at Volkswagen will in effect only be working for approximately 35 hours. (Le Monde 30.3.79).

A possible form that an increased holiday entitlement might take, and that was thought to be desirable, would be a provision that each worker received one week off following each twelve weeks of work. Staggering each person's entitlement would not require any additional closedown of the whole plant, and could have an employment effect.

Case Study 11
Summary of Key Points Emerging

At Plant A:

— The fact that collective bargaining is conducted at company rather than plant level appeared to exert some restraining influence over possible local initiatives on reduced working-time on site;

— Overtime levels for all manual grades were very high. This did not appear to be related to low basic rates. Although the stewards disapproved of the level of overtime working they could see no pressure from the shop floor for its removal;

— In part this acceptance was built upon their recognition that the company faced severe physical space problems which effectively constrained increased manning on the lines. In this context, faced with a high level of demand for the product overtime was seen as a "rational" solution;

— By implication management invoked a competitiveness argument against expanding physical space via extra capital investment—the argument appeared to be largely accepted by the stewards;

— The company's traditional resistance to productivity bargaining together with their emphasis on a tightly work studied system of measured day working again appeared to exert a restraining influence over local initiatives on working-time organisation;

— Some change, e.g. from two to three shift working had been effected at the plant;

— Scope for individual reductions in *effective working* time, where the job was operator paced was indicated;

— A fairly clear cut difference in the preferences of men and women with regard to the form of working time reductions was identified. The women tended to favour an *incremental* shortening of the working day whilst the men seemed more inclined to favour increased *blocks* of leisure in the form of days off;

— A shortage of skilled craftsmen was noted. This was both *externally,* underpinned and *internally* sustained. The crude solution of high overtime availability for skilled workers was an attempt to improve *external* competitiveness whilst providing some *internal* counterbalance to the erosion of differentials between semi- and skilled workers.

At Plant B:

— Local initiative was apparently less constrained by the centralised company bargaining structure;

— Two significant changes had been negotiated at the plant. Firstly, the two shift system employed at the commencement of the plant's operation was changed to a three shift system with reduced individual shift manning, but increased aggregate manning in the order of 12½%. Secondly, in 1977 it was agreed that hours worked by all three shifts be reduced by 2½ hours. *Effective* working time however has been maintained since this reduction was offset by the workforce giving up 2½ hours worth of paid break time spread across the working week;

— As at Plant A high overtime was worked by all manual grades and there was no significant workforce pressure against this;

— Also similar to Plant A the shortages of skilled craftsmen were noted;

— Preference for reduced working time was expressed in terms of increasing usefully sized blocks of leisure.

Case Study 12

Introduction

Our investigations for this case study embraced two plants, referred to here as A and B of this UK owned MNC. By comparison with case study 11 local management co-operation was forthcoming and in consequence some detail can be provided and evaluated which can be supplemented by that gained from our interviews with trade union representatives at both plants.

The Regulation of Terms and Conditions of Employment

The company is a member of the Engineering Employers Federation, and basic hours of work and holiday entitlements are determined by the National Engineering Agreements. These also determine the premia and calculator rates paid for, e.g. overtime and shift working. At the time of the interviews, either the recent engineering dispute had not commenced or was in its very early stages, and thus the now agreed 39 hour working

261

week (with effect from November 1981) was not a major object of investigation. Our interviewees were, therefore, discussing hypothetical rather than real possibilities.

The Economic Context

When the case study fieldwork was carried out, and as subsequently revealed in greater detail, the company has undergone (and is still experiencing) a crisis in its trading position with regard to its volume car output. A major fall away in market share has been followed by substantial losses being announced. As a result the company is embarking on a drastic reduction in manpower and a substantial closure programme. Knowledge of this adverse trading performance plus the fact that "overmanning" as a major contributory factor has become conventional wisdom amongst management and workforce alike crucially influenced the responses to our investigation.

By comparison with the plants covered in case study 11, the plant in this case study did not suffer high, persistent levels of overtime (the present case study did, however, as will be seen, have its own particular constraints which tended to complicate work time organisation). This was clearly related to market factors—the plants investigated were operating well below optimum capacity, but it was also a function of a managerial philosophy which actively discouraged overtime which helped to explain the absence of an overtime ethos amongst the workforce. The singular exception, and this is where case study 12 closely resembles case study 11, was to be found amongst skilled workers where the same combination of external shortage and internal differential erosion brought forward the same response, i.e. longer hours—via overtime—for this particular group.

PLANT A

Plant A is composed of a series of different shops that together build the bodies of five of the company's basic models of passenger car. The plant provides the finished bodies for an assembly plant to which it is connected by moving tracks, and here the cars are painted, trimmed and have the powertrain added. Certain cars, however, leave the plant in a painted and trimmed condition and are transported by road to plants elsewhere for powertrain addition.

Shift Systems

Certain conditions are standard to the whole plant. These include factory hours and the shift systems. Nearly all operations are performed on a two shift basis with a permanent day and a permanent night shift. Factory hours for the day shift are from 7.15 a.m. until 4.15 p.m. Monday to Friday with a one hour unpaid break for lunch. For the night shift hours are from 8.00 p.m. until 7.00 a.m. Monday to Thursday again with a one hour un-paid break—i.e. 4 × 10 hours, common to much of the engineering industry.* Night working is paid at a premium of time and one-third.

Overtime Working

Despite the management argument that "the most efficient way of making a car is without overtime, because then you can be more certain that everybody is there", and although the company in general exhibits relatively low overtime working, we found that it did exist and was more prevalent in Plant A—the body plant, than Plant B—the assembly plant. This was largely because overtime in the former was necessary to compensate for breakdowns and other disruptions which were more frequent occurrences than in the assembly plant.

Day shift overtime tended to be worked as two hours on the end of the shift on Mondays to Thursdays. Saturday morning overtime was not popular but was occasionally worked (quite frequently in fact for particular groups, e.g. toolmakers). Overtime on the night shift tended to be worked as either a half or whole shift on Friday night. Whilst the frequency of overtime working varied between groups of workers there was some suggestion that the change from payment by results (PBR) to a measured day work (MDW) system of payment effected by the company in recent years had raised the overall incidence of overtime working. Under the old system the practice of "job and finish" clearly operated against overtime since the whole purpose of the practice was to finish in advance of the allocated time and hence reduce the individual's "on plant" time. In addition, with the introduction of the MDW some of the operations which under PBW would have been allowed to have been performed *during* shift time, for example some cleaning jobs, now have to be carried out outside the normal shift hours.

Overtime levels are much higher for skilled pre-production workers than for semi-skilled production workers. High overtime is worked by tool-makers and patternmakers and this is necessary since this category of worker is in short supply. The overtime enhancement to earnings is also necessary to maintain competitiveness in the labour market. But it should be remembered that super-normal overtime is very often required simply to

* Previous reductions in hours of work, at least for the day shift have concentrated on moving forward finishing times, leaving starting times unchanged.

263

complete the work; consequently, for toolmakers and patternmakers there is an "open house" on overtime, with regular Saturday morning working and with the permanent night shift coming in on Sundays during the day.

Potential for Reducing Working Time

The potential for reducing working time and any assessment of possible employment effects has to be seen against the major manpower changes already announced by the company. The pressure for these changes is not merely a reflection of the deteriorating market position of the company, in fact, it stems far more directly from the degeneration of the manning levels which followed on from the company's move away from PBR to MDW.

Under the old system where individual effort and reward were clearly related the collective strength of work groups focused on keeping manning levels to a minimum in order to maximise individual earnings—in effect a self policing system which ensured "tight" manning. Under the new system where the scope for increasing individual earnings has been removed (in an effort to restore managerial control over labour costs and labour utilisation) the collective strength of the shop floor has focused in the opposite direction (apparently with considerable success) to 'bid-up' the number of individuals required to do a particular job. Hence, in management terms manning levels have become 'slack' whilst for the individual worker the job has become (seemingly) less demanding.

Recently, there have been clear indications that the workforce accepted (albeit that the adverse position of the company has been heavily dramatised by both management and the media) the need for a radical restructuring of manpower. The company's initial plan to reduce the labourforce by 15% in 1979 (already 9% below its 1978 level) was rapidly followed during the recent (current at the time of writing) wage negotiations with the argument that any increase was dependent upon a 20% increase in productivity which would require a further reduction in labour in the order of 10%.

The company makes no secret of the fact that acceptance of the incentive scheme will involve fundamental changes in working methods, the implementation of which will significantly diminish the traditional power of the shop stewards to control manning levels and the pace of the job, allow time and motion studies to be used to explore possibilities for increased efficiency, and permit much greater mobility of employees within any plant.

Principally, the productivity plan will affect semi-skilled production workers and, should the company be successful in implementing it, the scheme should throw up sufficient surplus labour to more than compensate for any reductions in labour supply consequent upon reduced working hours.* This is particularly true with respect to the marginal reductions envisaged so far, and suggests that if reduced working time is to have any employment effect at all it will be an employment saving rather than an employment creating one.

Moreover, the extent to which even a neutral employment effect can be salvaged, will depend crucially upon the strength of the shop steward system at plant level. The limiting factors here must be the successes which the management have had so far in forcing through their restructuring plan, and the consequent weakening of the workforce's collective ability to enforce the spirit of existing manning agreements.

Manning levels associated with particular track speeds are the subject of union/management agreements. If track speed is increased and returns, as a result, to a level at which it operated at some previous period, then the manning level associated with that previous period has to be respected. The unions see these agreements as important safeguards against "speed ups". However, if management claimed that in a situation where the need to increase line speed was the result of an agreement to reduce working hours, they would not consider themselves bound by any previous agreements with respect to manning levels. In other words, management would seek to use the opportunity to redesign tasks and intensify the labour of the workforce, and would accordingly attempt to keep the increase in manning associated with the new and faster line speeds to a minimum.**

PLANT B

The plant is adjoining Plant A and is linked by a number of tracks which take completed "white" (i.e. unpainted), and sometimes painted, body shells, from the latter plant to the assembly plant where they are painted,

---

* NB. It is the semi-skilled production workers who do little overtime and whose actual worktime is closely determined by contractual worktime. This is less the case for craft workers.

** It should be noted that the October 1979 National Engineering Agreement which grants a 39 hour week from November 1981 also emphasises that management should extract productivity concessions in return for changes in the length of the working week. The unions have agreed to a clause specifying:

"maximum co-operation at domestic level so that improvement in productivity will ensure that no increases in manufacturing costs arise as a result of the shorter working week".

which would provide management with a basis for seeking to impose the kind of changes described.

265

trimmed, and have the completed powertrain attached. Completed cars are then tested any rectifications made, and finally taken for storage and delivery to distributors.

Whilst the two plants can, in technical terms, be treated as two parts of an inter-related whole they are separate in terms of historical development, and in consequence in working practices and cultures. This is inspite of the fact that they draw from the same local labour market. Moreover, until recently, indeed at the time of the investigation, the payments structures too were different, although not radically so. Furthermore, whilst Plant A is principally T&G organised, Plant B is an AUEW stronghold, the majority of semi-skilled, as well as skilled, workers belonging to this union, although representation rights are shared with the T&G.

Shift Working

Production is organised essentially in the same fashion as in Plant A, i.e. it involves "line type" operations, worked on a two shift, day and night basis. However, shift working came somewhat later (the early 1960s) to the assembly plant than to the body plant (where a small permanent night shift that could be increased in size for "top up" purposes had already existed for many years) and as a result of its being a wholesale changeover took the form not of two permanent shifts, but of an alternating "two weeks about" system. As a "sweetener" to shift working the night shifts took the form of four and a half night weeks (10 hours Monday-Thursday, four hours Friday) which subsequently became four night weeks with the introduction of the 40 hour week.

Whilst the majority of production workers on shift operations are in fact working the alternate pattern, there are opportunities for permanent day and permanent night working.

These systems are organised by work groups themselves, and arrangements affect only the discreet groups. However, whilst an individual is obliged to conform to the practices of the groups to which he is attached, he cannot, as a consequence, be obliged to work a system "inferior" to (i.e. giving more night working than) the fortnight about system, which must prevail in cases of dispute. He can however be obliged to work more days (i.e. on permanent days) since this is considered a superior situation.

In addition to two shift operations some lines are operated on days only. This tends to be the case for lines assembling models for which demand is low, whilst a fall off in demand might itself lead to a changeover from two shift to single shift operations. Frequently, this latter will involve an increase in output on the single shift (i.e. it need not necessarily involve output being reduced by 50%) and this is effected by increasing line speed and manning levels, thus serving to absorb some of the labour being displaced from the second shift (the rest being distributed elsewhere in the factory). Given the deteriorating market performance of the company there were several instances of this kind of changeover occurring at the time of the investigation.

Finally, in certain of the indirect "service" areas—e.g. boiler rooms three shift, or even continuous systems operate, but these affect only a very limited number of persons.

Overtime Working

Systematic overtime is not (for most of the same reasons as in the body plant) used in the majority of production areas, although it might be used to cope with occasional peaks in demand. Day shift workers work overtime when required for one or two hours after the Tuesday or Wednesday shift (pay day is Thursday), whilst night shift workers will work half (or whole) shifts on Friday night. It was suggested that the day shift gets more opportunities for overtime than does the night shift.

We did find instances of overtime being used for "catch up" purposes particularly in the rectification block. The input to this area is a function of the daily output of the assembly lines, and given that by this stage the product cannot be easily stockpiled it is necessary to move through each day's input, by means of overtime if necessary. Whilst at present rectification does not appear to operate with a higher level of overtime than do the assembly lines it should be noted that at present only one of the two lines is operating on two shifts, and thus daily output is no more than three quarters of any theoretical maximum. Once, however, maximum production is again achieved the physical constraints of the rectification area could make overtime a necessity.

We did find examples of considerably higher levels of overtime working amongst certain of the indirect workforce. The obvious example is that of maintenance workers who must necessarily do a substantial part of their work outside normal production time. However, in all plants we visited we found that the normal work time patterns and durations of maintenance workers were the same as for direct workers—i.e. they worked the same shifts, so that they necessarily were required to work extensive overtime. At the assembly plant a general pattern of hours for mechanical maintenance workers is set down in a local agreement that provides for 51 hours of maintenance time for each shift, giving twenty four hour maintenance cover during the Monday to Thursday week by boosting both the day and night shifts with overtime, and also providing for Friday night working (seven hours) for the night shift and Saturday morning working (six hours) for the day shift. Whilst no individual is obliged to, or indeed does, work the complete 51 hours. there is an obligation to provide for cover, within the patterns described. This cover is provided by the use of rota systems which do seem to permit a fairly high degree of personal flexibility—e.g. there exists the opportunity to come to swapping arrangements, and in addition participation appears to be voluntary, so that each worker is able to achieve the patterns and durations suited to his own preferences. On average 12 out of 56 pairs of maintenance workers within any normal week will offer themselves, and since six pairs are required, overtime (two and a quarter hours) is worked every other day when on the day shift. Similar arrangements permit the night shift to come in early (three quarters of an hour) to restart the production process. Additional rotas, involving only one pair at any one time, provide for a 24 hour seven day a week "safety cover".

Friday night or Saturday morning overtime necessary to provide for more major work attracts about 50% attendance as does a Sunday morning shift manned out of both shifts. On the weekend effort levels are thought to be relatively low, work being stretched to fit the full shift time—but the state of affairs is accepted by management. Again it was frequently suggested, as at all the plants, that the offer of extensive overtime was necessary to provide sufficiently attractive earnings to skilled workers, whilst some of the workers themselves seemed to find, e.g. Sunday morning working as providing an opportunity to "get away from under the wife's feet".

Labourers involved in cleaning up operations at the end of the shift must also necessarily work overtime,* and again we found built in overtime patterns, incorporating provisions for early starts and late finishes and weekend working. Lower basic rates of pay produce pressure for overtime in order to achieve parity of earnings; the levels of overtime involved mean that earnings could be higher than "on the line". Again we found indications that not all the overtime hours are effectively worked—i.e. effort levels are low.

Where some form of continuous cover is required five day semi-continuous shift systems are most frequently used and these are supplemented by the use of overtime to provide some element of skeleton manning at the weekends. At the assembly plant we found an example of a conditioned Sunday night/Monday morning shift (i.e. the obligation to do at least one

* It was suggested that since the introduction of Measured Day Working the incidence and duration of that overtime had increased. This is because under the Payments By Results system there had been considerable opportunities for "job and finish", allowing production workers to leave before time and allowing the cleaners to move in.

extra shift every three weeks) for boiler attendants (necessary to prepare the paint ovens for the week's production) operating in addition to the rotas for providing the full seven day safety cover. Work conditions were felt to be poor, compared to line conditions, and hence there was a high labour turnover, and it was alleged that given a grading system which failed to recognise the skills and responsibilities involved, the unsocial hours element in the job and the inability—because of cover needs—to take breaks away from the work position, the conditioned overtime provided the only means of producing an acceptable earnings level.

Reduced Working Time

Previous reductions of basic hours of work (44-42-40 hours) have at the plant been matched by similar sized reductions in actual hours of work, and the shop stewards interviewed were insistent that this would happen again were reduction in hours to be achieved in the future. On the other hand, if we examine the historical experience we should remember that, at the plant at the time, work was organised on a Payment By Results basis, and one of the results of this system was the existence of substantial "job and finish" working. This "job and finish" was real "job and finish"— *on completion of output quotas people actually went home.* As a consequence there was a lot of "slack" in the organisation of production and this slack was taken up, in part, by the reduction of hours of work. This sort of slack, now that a Measured Day Working system operates, is no longer there.

On the other hand a considerable degree of another sort of slack is to be found, a slack that is a function of the plant operating well below capacity. On one particular model assembly line current hourly output per line was 21 cars. Given a 35 hour week, seven hour day, an extra 21 cars would have to be produced within normal time giving an hourly output of 24 cars. Yet, the same lines have in the past been producing the same model at a rate of 26 per hour, with a higher manning level.* Whether, in fact, the higher hourly output rates necessary to prevent a loss of output would be produced by remanning the line, or by "speed ups", is open to question, and would depend very much upon the context in which the reduction in working time were to be bargained.

Finally, another aspect of existing excess capacity is the fact that, not only are lines running below their maximum speeds and manning levels,

* On the other hand whilst the assembly line itself might be capable of producing a higher hourly output it is not certain that post assembly areas would be able to cope. Physical space constraints limit the ability of the rectification block to absorb more than a given hourly output without resorting to the need for overtime working.

but also that the possibilities for shift working are not used to the fullest, since on many lines it is now possible to supplement total output rates simply by re-introducing an additional shift.

Taken together these facts suggest that at company 2, the organisational, if *not the economic,* scope for adjusting to reduced working time by increasing manning, is considerably greater than at company 1, particularly Plant A.

Clearly the poor market position of the company must be the most important short-run determinant affecting the judgement of both management and unions at Plants A and B with regard to the priority given to reducing working time. Thus it is far more likely that the two sides will focus their attention both nationally and locally on getting the manning levels right. In other words the union strategy will presumably attempt to reduce and slow down the labour force retrenchment which management is currently pressing for.

Against this sort of background it may be some time before the cost effectiveness of reduced working time is perceived by management, it may equally, however, prove one of the few potent arguments left to the trade unions in their efforts to preserve some semblance of both the manning levels and the effort/reward relationship which they have built up.

Cast Study 12

Summary of Key Points Emerging

At both Plants A and B:

— The adverse market position of the company tended to dominate and constrain both management and trade union responses to the question of working time reductions—simple manpower restructuring in absolute terms was seen as the immediate priority;

— The change from a predominantly piecework conditioned payment system to measured day work has shifted the focus of the shop floor organisation away from a "self policing" tightly manned organisation of work which *maximised* individual earnings and *minimised* (through 'job and finish') individual on site time towards the active bidding up of manpower requirements in order to *maximise* employment density and improve the individual effort required to complete a particular job;

— *Externally* marked and *internally* sustained skill shortages were noted, as was the crude response of high overtime availability for skilled workers;

270

— Overtime was relatively low, except for skilled and maintenance workers; in the latter case overtime was necessary since basic working patterns of maintenance workers were coterminous with production workers and much maintenance work could only be carried out *after* the shift had finished. However, management were against overtime working, and the workforce in general did not display any significant enthusiasm for overtime working;

— The plants were operating at levels some way below optimum capacity utilisation as a result of the company's market position hence, it was felt that significant 'slack' existed which could be utilised to absorb any reductions in working time without consequent remanning. Indeed it was suggested that management would ignore existing manning agreements to speed up the lines hence minimising the need to re-man in the event of a reduction in basic hours.

SOME LESSONS

Throughout our case studies the objective has been followed of presenting the data and our interpretation of it in a form which can be readily identified by collective bargainers. We have focussed on what has happened, what currently happens and what might happen with respect to the organisation of working time at the level of the individual case study. In the course of this we have identified various critical factors which either singularly or, more commonly, in combination continue to create either a *constrained* or *unconstrained* setting against which potential working time reductions have to be set and evaluated.

Our intention in these concluding comments is not to extract from this a simple checklist of factors to be worked through in the course of any negotiation on working time, but rather to group the factors under 5 broad headings which seem to us to offer at least the beginning of an analytical framework designed specifically for the use of bargainers as opposed to their being confined to the more esoteric corners of academic debate.

The broad headings which seem most useful are as follows:

— Labour market constraints;

— Social and economic determinants of working time patterns;

— Costs and competitiveness;

— Bargaining structures;

— Worker preferences.

It is clear that these are by no means the only headings that could be utilised and it should be noted that they are not arranged in any particular order—e.g. we do *not* suggest that labour market constraints are, for example, more important in informing the bargaining priorities than are worker preferences on working time (the reverse, in fact, is more likely to be the case). What we are suggesting is that it is likely that an interplay of these factor groupings has conditioned the evolution of working time patterns at any particular place of work and that a crucial part of maintaining that evolution (or even changing it dramatically) must involve the bargainers in a fairly detailed appraisal as to where these factors may provide either fruitful avenues for development or solid obstacles in the way of progress. Only if this analysis is both actuated and subsequently drawn upon in the agreement of alterations to working time systems can the process of change be said to be either "managed" or jointly determined.

272

Labour Market Constraints

Frequent mention is made throughout our case studies of labour market constraints which are said to exist *internally* or *externally*, either representing a potential difficulty in terms of being able to increase manning levels subsequent to any reductions in working time.

It is important, then, to distinguish here *internal* from *external* labour markets. By *internal* we mean that pool of labour already directly employed by the company on site. *External*, therefore, describes the generality of the potential supply of labour which might be attracted to a particular company were it either expanding its labour requirements or replacing parts of its existing workforce. Most companies seem to operate with a reasonable notion of the geographical boundaries of their external labour market. It is important to note that such boundaries are not fixed; employers in extreme cases may be forced well outside traditional geographic areas, as for example one of our case studies showed—the shortage of skilled engineers of graduate status had forced the particular company to extend its recruitment activities as far as Australia. By and large, however, the geographic boundaries are determined by transport availability and the pressure of labour demand amongst a company's competitors within what can be considered a reasonable commuting distance (labour market theorists will hopefully forgive these sweeping generalisations). It follows that improvements in a company's relative terms and conditions of employment, e.g. through a reduction in basic hours of work, should, all things being equal, improve the attractiveness of that company to the *external* labour market and consolidate and improve, for example, by reducing absenteeism, the *internal* labour market. Such beneficial effects depend, however, on a high degree of mobility and the existence of the "right kind of labour at the right time".* Evidence from the majority of our case studies suggested that this latter requirement was particularly absent from certain types of skilled worker. Hence, reducing working time where this may be dependent upon the ability to increase manning fairly rapidly bumps against external labour market constraints.

The obvious example which stood out in our case studies was that of the skilled engineering worker. Difficulties here were encountered and foreseen on the *external* and *internal* labour markets. *Externally*, the labour markets seemingly irrespective of geographic location were regarded as being actively short of mobile, skilled workers. *Internally*, the erosion of earnings differentials which has taken place in many manufacturing establishments between skilled and semi-skilled groups of workers

---

* We might also add, somewhat cynically, but not in view of the low basic rates paid to skilled engineering workers, "at the right price".

273

combined with the traditional demarcation "defence" operated by the former groups has served to seriously constrain the internal mobility of labour.

The crude solution which tended to be adopted by companies finding themselves in this position was to offer significant opportunities for overtime working to skilled workers.* It was claimed that this at least maintained some degree of competitiveness on the *external* labour market, whilst at the same time providing a stabilising influence on the *internal* market. At best such an approach can only provide temporary relief. However, the more obvious long term remedy of increasing the rates paid to skilled workers can by no means be considered a straightforward option. For it has to be appreciated a) that any widening of the skilled/semi-skilled differential is likely to be strongly contested by unions representing the latter groups; b) that an increase in skilled wage rates may be followed by the company's counterparts in the *external* labour market hence no comparative advantage would exist to release more mobile skilled workers and c) that the increased wages cost implied may be more than the company is prepared to bear. Whilst bargainers facing up to skill shortages must obviously examine the extent to which wage differentials could be successfully altered to ease the situation, it has also to be recognised that some skill shortages may not be wage induced. It appeared, for example, from our NHS study that the shortage of trained nurses was in a sense a real one, i.e. it was not the case that trained nurses were choosing to work elsewhere in the local labour market in order to gain higher earnings.** In these circumstances (and they may be more common than is frequently assumed) the bargainer is forced to consider what other inducements might help solve the problem. At our NHS case study it was recognised that a supply of trained nurses could be tapped by allowing a variety of part-time hours patterns to be worked, thus, trained nurses who had left the profession in order to look after their families, could be "filtered" back in to the service by allowing them to adjust their working hours to fit in with their domestic needs. This plainly yielded beneficial results both to the employee and the employer.

Again, where the shortage may not be wage induced, the provision of training facilities both *internal* to the establishment and those that may be *externally* situated, e.g. skill centres, technical colleges, and polytechnics must inform the bargaining process. The point to be made here is that

* It should be noted here that for some skilled workers, e.g. maintenance workers overtime very often resulted from the organisation of working time whereby much of the work could only be carried out at the end of shift times and during the weekend.

** It was not, for example, suggested to us that trained nurses were being "poached" by private sector health care establishments even though it is reputed that earnings are higher in such establishments.

reductions in working time cannot be seen in isolation from the other influences which help determine the supply of skilled labour. It may be that in bargaining for reduced hours a trade union side may also find themselves arguing for a parallel boost in training provision in order to combat the labour market constraints operating on their claim. (In view of the generally low level of training provided by the majority of British industry such a pressure may have long awaited benefits.)*

Our case studies showed that scope can normally be found to improve the efficiency of the *internal* labour market and hence minimise skill shortage effects. All three of the main methods which we identified require careful evaluation since without proper safeguards they can produce adverse effects in the long term. Firstly, as Case Study 5 showed the introduction of new technology was confidently expected to solve the shortage of skilled draughtsmen that they had been experiencing. The difficulties here do not require much elaboration, suffice it to say that "solving" the shortage may also result in a general de-skilling of the workforce concerned and possibly significant displacement of individual jobs. Hence the need to safeguard this particular route with some form of technology agreement is clearly of prime importance.

Secondly, and particularly appropriate to maintenance workers, is the possibility of re-organising the working time of skilled workers to maximise their effectiveness and reduce non-working time, i.e. concentrating their normal, as opposed to their overtime hours, on the parts of the day when the demand for their services is at its greatest. Related to this, the third method involving internal efficiency improvement could be seen to have operated in the NHS case study, where non-skilled tasks previously undertaken by nurses were re-allocated to non-nursing staff. There are clear limits to this strategy—for example the nursing officer at our case study argued that this "paring down" process had gone as far as it could go, i.e. the 37½ hour week was not going to be absorbed via further changes to nurses' duties—but as a means of relieving pressure on scarce skills (whilst at the same time possibly raising and enlarging the job of the recipient). The strategy clearly merits the attention of bargainers.

Whilst it is hoped that these comments may represent helpful "markers" for bargainers we should note, that no such labour market constraints

---

* We should note in passing here the historical constraints which operate on improving the supply of skilled workers, e.g. from skill centres. The fear of "dilutees" can still be identified as a potent barrier to entry of anything other than a "time served man". An unfortunate consequence of this, is the classic "baby" and "bathwater" exercise about to be undertaken by the MSC in closing some 30 odd skill centres and skill centre annexes.

either *internal* or *external* appeared to operate at any of our case studies for semi- and unskilled workers.

Social and Economic Determinants of Working Time

In general historical terms it is reasonable to suggest that economic factors have played the most significant role in determining the broad patterns of working time which can be found in the manufacturing sector of our economy. For example, some processes require 24 hour operation for purely technical reasons, whereas in others a continuous operation is required either to achieve low unit costs—crucial in highly competitive industries—or to amortise high levels of capital investment. Changing demand conditions for the products of the company can also give rise to significant changes in working time organisation (see for example Case Studies 12 and 6) as can major changes in the technology employed.

In the service sector of the economy, by comparison, social factors have tended to play a bigger role. The NHS, for example, is a 24 hour 'continuous process' industry not for the reasons outlined above but rather to meet the requirements of a society which falls ill or has accidents at any time of the day, all the year round.

Our case studies identified the interplay of social and economic forces and the working time systems which resulted; equally they showed how the injection of a demand for a change in working time (not necessarily a reduction) could potentially upset this "balance".

The crucial point to be grasped here is that whereas in the past the *supply* of labour and the social factors which condition such a flow have largely reacted and adapted to the *demand* for labour conditioned by the sort of economic/technical factors already cited, the demand by organised labour for reduced working time represents a major break and a reversal of the direction of the forces which are normally influencing the capital/labour mix at any one enterprise. As such it is important that bargainers have a thorough grasp of the particular social and economic factors which have determined working time patterns at the enterprise in question.

As stated the process typically can be thought of as a set of requirements flowing from economic and technical factors; these are reacted to and modified by the availability of labour and the social factors which act upon it. The stability of any resulting organisation of working time then depends significantly on the *rigidity* of both the economic/technical factors which condition the demand for labour and more often than not, the predictability of the social factors which condition the supply.

It was apparent from our case studies that very few working time systems were stable since in almost every case we could identify changes in the factors contributing to the demand for labour, e.g. falling or expanding markets, the introduction of new technology and so on, all of which tipped the balance and required an adjustment in the supply, e.g. a reduction in labour supply, or perhaps greater overtime or a re-arrangement of shift patterns. It was equally the case that our research showed that the management of this dynamic adjustment varied considerably and was influenced significantly by social factors. For example, the rigid cultural norms identified in Case Study 9, provided a very real constraint to the introduction of 2 or 3 shift working in a particular department.

On the other hand the "professionalisation" we noted amongst the workforce at Case Study 5 provided management with considerable flexibility insofar as intensifying effort was concerned.

Case Studies 8 and 5 provide examples where the joint management of working time change can be discerned. It is notable that in both cases comparatively innovatory systems have evolved which seem to be designed far more explicitly than is common to account for the economic/technical needs of the company and the social/economic needs of the workforce. Moreover, it should be noted that in both instances the minimisation of overtime was one of the main objectives.

It is obviously dangerous to generalise from such limited evidence; however, it does appear that the issue of overtime can very often mask for both parties far more fundamental changes which threaten the labour/capital mix. Whilst overtime can, and clearly does, provide a temporary "escape valve" for pressure that has built up within a working time system in no way can it remove the causes which have led to the pressure in the first place. Thus, whilst we suggest that overtime is a straightforward obstacle to the achievement of reduced working time (and generally acknowledged to be so) we would also suggest that it is far more diversionary within the bargaining process than seems to be acknowledged, in that it leads the bargainer away from a more thorough analysis of the underlying problems in managing the change of working time systems, towards an over concentration on just one solution to the *symptoms* of the malaise. As we shall see in the following section, this 'side tracking' of the bargaining process has not been helped either by the falling real cost of overtime, or the understandable acceptance of overtime by sections of the workforce seeking ways of maintaining their real earnings in the face of low basic rates, restrictive incomes policies and rampant inflation.

Costs and Competition

It is a reasonable assumption that the majority of employers will seek to manage their working time organisation in order to *minimise* its costs and *maximise* its return. It follows, then, that any 'agent' seeking to change the working time patterns of a particular enterprise must be able to convince management that the present system is either not *minimising* costs or not *maximising* returns and that the change mooted will improve one side or the other of this simple equation.

In most instances our case studies showed that where management were hostile to the suggestion of reducing working time it was related to their perception of the adverse effects on their unit costs that such a change would make either linked to a) loss of output or b) increased overtime or c) increased manning. These were rapidly translated into loss of competitive edge and hence indicated a change to be resisted.

Where management were sympathetic to reduced working time it was normally as a result of such a change translating, e.g. through more effective use of labour (reducing absenteeism and overtime) or through an extension of shift working, into an advantage insofar as *maximising* the returns from the working time system was concerned.

Our case studies provide some guidance to bargainers tackling the adverse cost argument. For example, the changes in the working time organisation described in Case Studies 8 and 6 were achieved without adding significantly to costs—in both instances changes in actual working time were balanced by improvements to effective working time (via the creation of a fifth shift at Case Study 8 and via the changeover from predominantly day working to two shift working at Case Study 6) and in both cases overtime was reduced substantially. It is crucial that bargainers facing up to a management defence based on the cost increase perceived should explore and organise the offsetting benefits which can accrue either through increased flexibility of labour deployment (as instanced in Case Studies 8 and 6) or through the minimisation of negative supply effects such as high absenteeism and high labour turnover.

The type of calculation which we provide at Case Study 10 (which could well provide the starting point for an efficiency bargainer) in fact shows the negligible difference in labour costs to the employer where high overtime has been the norm between continuing with such a system and increasing manning levels (either with the existing shift system or via the creation of a fifth shift) to provide the requisite effective hours of work. The proximity of these final costs is all the more remarkable when we consider that the relative 'cost' of an hour's overtime has been falling in recent years.

Across a whole range of industries it can be shown that effective overtime rates have fallen whilst overhead labour costs have risen, and indeed that overhead costs on the way up have probably passed overtime rates on the way down, making the substitution of overtime for persons increasingly attractive. At least a part of the fall in effective overtime can be attributed to successive incomes policies granting pay increases as supplements that were not consolidated into the basic rates used in calculating overtime premia. In many of our case studies the devaluation of the effective overtime rate appears as a function of the fact that a supplement of considerable magnitude, the shift premia, is not consolidated into the overtime calculator rate.

As a general proposition we would suggest that whatever else their function overtime premia now fail in terms of their original justification, that of making the method of increasing the labour input by extending the actual hours of current employees rather than by recruiting additional employees punitively expensive to the employer. Taking a long term perspective we would attribute this effect more to movements in overhead labour costs—the increasing significance of the employer's National Insurance contribution, the spread of paid holidays and pension schemes and of other social benefits and facilities provided, including the introduction of redundancy payments schemes, and the increasing importance of training, On the other side "wage drift", the difference between actual hourly rates and basic rates prescribed in National Agreements and used as calculator rates, has without doubt also played a part.

Clearly, the extent to which any addition to unit costs can be minimised by the *form* which a negotiated reduction in hours takes must become an important variable in the individual bargaining process. However, it is equally important *strategically* to consider the competitive position of the company or enterprise. Whilst in most instances we consider the management argument, that any individual action on their part would endanger the competitive position vis-a-vis their market, to be over-stressed, there is little doubt that some companies as a result of their competitive strength are in a far more favourable position to undertake working time reductions (in this sense the "lead" companies in a particular sector could be considered to be at least potential "change agents") than others.

That this is the case may be seen, for example, if we compare Case Studies 11 and 12. The somewhat obvious point to be made here is that both in terms of its "demonstration effect" on the rest of the industry and its medium to long term viability, a 'key' efficiency bargain with a strong competitor, e.g. the company in Case Study 11 is of much greater significance than the achievement of working time reduction with a company, e.g. Case Study 12 who are facing severe market share losses. In this sense the unilateral agreement reached in both the engineering and retailing sectors on marginal reductions in working time by 1981 and 1982 respectively are a disappointment and indicate that both the time scale and size of the reductions agreed have, perhaps, been critically constrained by the fact that the negotiations were unilateral and that the needs and abilities of the weakest and strongest employers in the respective sectors were weighed. The resulting agreements can both be fairly described as very cautious. Moreover, neither are likely to have the impact of the agreements reached either with the Post Office Engineering grades or with nursing staff in the NHS.

Bargaining Structures

In most instances our case studies suggested that trade unions locally were the most obvious agent of change, and that the bargaining process formed the "agency" whereby changes in working time organisation were agreed. There were, however, exceptions to this, for example, whilst union pressure may have led to the setting up of an inquiry, it was the inquiry itself which laid down the requirement that the NHS should implement a 37½ hour week for nurses by 1981. Moreover, the negotiation of specific objectives can set up a powerful reaction within management which if recognised and used, as for example by the local unions in Case Studies 8 and 6, can draw management into the bargaining process on more or less equal terms and with equal commitment to a workable solution.

Picking up on the point made at the end of the last section, the actual bargaining structures are critical here. It is surely significant that the most positive joint initiatives recorded by our case studies took place against the backcloth of relatively autonomous local bargaining frameworks, unconstrained by "national" or "sectoral" considerations.* Moreover, as can be seen, "national" pressure has tended to produce only slight incremental movements in working time, e.g. in engineering and retailing. Alternatively, national trade union pressure may have finally led to the 37½ hour week for nurses in the NHS but it has also created an as yet uncharted "sea" of local bargaining as management and unions at hospital level begin to thrash out the operational reality of reduced working time for nurses. In this context, the "learning curves" which are discernible in both Case Studies 8 and 6 represent a far more robust approach to providing workable solutions.

The gap identified between "national" and "local" bargaining structures, in terms of what has been achieved so far as working time reductions are concerned, is perhaps unsurprising given the pluralistic nature of the British system of industrial relations. It does, however, sharply raise the question as to the usefulness of bargaining at the national level for these particular ends. After all, many of our bargaining structures are national in coverage and are

* The constraint in this sense for example in Case Study 6 was primarily the "knock on" effect within the parent company's span of operation.

unlikely to be otherwise. Are workers in industries covered by such bargaining arrangements going to be limited to only modest incremental changes in working time? It may be argued that what happens in the NHS over the next year or so will provide a critical pointer in this respect and that the agreement between the Post Office and their staffs indicates some grounds for cautious optimism that significant changes can be achieved through a nationally struck bargain. Even so, and the latter example amply illustrates it, the scope for local bargaining about the particular form in which reduced working time may be implemented must remain as being considerable.

A reasonable compromise, as suggested in Case Study 9 and apparently one which underpins the agreement with the Post Office engineering staffs, is for the "national" agreement to lay down a broad framework within which local bargaining can recognise and adjust for local preferences and needs. Whilst such a relationship would seem to make obvious sense it should also be noted that an extensive process of consultation between the two levels of bargaining form a crucial pre-condition to the agreement. This is what distinguishes the outcome of the Post Office deliberations from those concerning nursing hours in the NHS. Whereas industrial action by Post Office engineers forced its own particular form of "consultation" between local and national union levels the same cannot be said of unions representing nurses in the NHS. Thus, where the Post Office agreement was based upon options known to be broadly acceptable locally in advance of the agreement, in the NHS the process of discovering locally acceptable options was begun after the Whitley Council for nurses sanctioned the McCarthy recommendation for a shorter working week.

Worker Preferences

Although providing the concluding part of this review of the key factors emerging from the case studies, worker preferences regarding both the desirability of and form in which reduced working time may be negotiated are by no means the least important factor. Indeed, a strong case can be made for such preferences to represent the starting point of any efficiency bargain which concerns the re-organisation of working time.

The main distinction identified in the preferred form of reduced working time lay between men and women. The former overwhelmingly favoured reductions which would yield useful blocks of time—typically a whole day or series of extra days off. The latter, probably influenced by domestic considerations tended to favour earlier finishing times. The women's need to confine the working day was also emphasised by their resistance to overtime working, very few instances of which were uncovered in our case studies. By comparison overtime and weekend working were fairly common practices amongst men workers in the case studies.

Leaving aside for a moment the possible causes of this distinction, the implications for bargainers are significant. For example, in the context of a predominantly female workforce the demand for a 35 or a 30 hour week would probably win support, whereas additional holidays, whilst supportable, may be seen to be less of a priority. By comparison, in a male dominated workforce negotiating longer holidays, particularly if workers experience the "locked-in-to-overtime" syndrome may prove the most effective bargaining strategy to reduce annual working time.

Plainly, then, the sexual make up of the workforce is an important characteristic in the pre-planning of shorter working time bargaining, but one that has, perhaps, not received the detailed attention which our case studies suggest that it should have had.

Whether or not these marked differences in preferences are likely to move towards a more easily managed concensus must remain open to doubt at least in the short to medium term. Both sets of preferences appear to be firmly rooted in the cultural conditioning which has given rise to fixed attitudes to work, working time and the balance between work and leisure. In the short run marginal changes to working time patterns are unlikely to alter greatly these fixed perceptions. As we argue in the following chapter individuals are maintained in a culturally hidebound state by our rigid definitions of "full-time" and "part-time" work. Indeed, the fact that work is typically measured in "weeks" is yet another example of the short term focusing which characterises our thinking on working time organisation. (In this sense the concept of "annual hours" reported in our Case Studies 8 and 10 should be seen as a welcome breakthrough).

The persistence of relatively high levels of overtime working appears to be critical with regard to male/female preferences. Whilst this poses short run obstacles to bargained reductions in working time, it also raises questions over employment security which, because they are largely medium to long term, have a tendency to be overlooked. For example, the characteristic patterns of female hours of work provide ample flexibility of working time up to a 40 hour limit, whereupon further ' marginal' extensions are strongly resisted (indeed, the growth of female employment particularly part-time probably reflects to a significant extent the value of this recognisable flexibility). By comparison, the 'marginal' flexibility of male hours of work in the manufacturing sector tends to be located beyond the basic 40 hours. Whilst this may be tolerable to an employer where the relative cost of overtime has declined (as we suggested earlier), it will probably not remain the case if the relative cost of overtime begins to rise.

Here then would appear to be the real dilemma for trade union bargainers facing 'institutional' overtime practices. For whilst overtime persists it militates against employment creation and against changes in working time. Moreover, the maintenance of overtime is likely to depend increasingly upon its relatively low cost to the employer. This, in itself, is a direct challenge to the traditional trade union approach which seeks to make overtime 'expensive'—implicit in this strategy lies a cost pressure which should make the individual employer more efficient in his/her utilisation of labour. However, raising the relative cost of overtime (which must surely feature in coming wage negotiations) may also accelerate the substitution either of *capital* for labour (as the marginal efficiency of male labour declines) or of female for male labour since the marginal cost of female labour is still lower than that of the male.

In this sense the real force of the locked-in-to-overtime syndrome can be appreciated. Not only does the individual worker feel trapped into the system* but the system itself has set up its defence in terms of the control it exerts on both employer and employee preferences.

Working Time in Services and Manufacturing: Diverging Possibilities?

Since we have grouped our data into these two broad categories, it is relevant to review what points of similarity or departure arise. Plainly, if significant differences are discernible this must be of major interest to collective bargainers since it may give rise to the need for totally differing bargaining strategies.

To begin with a caveat. The distinctive features which have emerged at case study level, that we have loosely grouped into either "sponsoring" or "limiting" factors, may simply exist and be entirely peculiar to that particular enterprise. In the absence of a good many more case studies and information from other industries within the manufacturing and service sector, it is precarious to offer anything more than the most tentative of generalisations. This being said, one or two more general features are worthy of further comment insofar as they would appear to distinguish the possibilities for achieving major advances in reduced working time between the two broad sectors.

It seems to us, for example, that the state and nature of the labour market, together with the bargaining power which this apportions to management and trade unions, is significantly different in two of the three service industries we examined. In the case of retail distribution, which is probably typical of the broader miscellaneous services sector, the major retail

* This is not always caused, as our case studies showed, by low basic wages, but where it is then overtime is not merely tolerated but actively defended and worked for.

283

companies draw upon a virtually limitless female labour market, increasingly segmented by part-time working and increasingly de-skilled. These developments inevitably place the unions concerned in a weaker bargaining position insofar as winning further reductions in the basic hours of full-time workers is a major objective. Management domination over any negotiated change in working time is further reinforced by the structure of bargaining residing as it does either at national or company level. As already stated this allows strong competitors to "shelter" behind the more critical cost portion of their weaker counterparts where they are grouped together in national agreements. Company level bargaining particularly where it isolates a strong competitor may prove a more fruitful form of union pressure, but even here the ready recourse to part-time workers remains a powerful disincentive to "rock the boat" too far or too fast.

The situation in the NHS exhibits some similarities insofar as the labour market for unskilled ancillary workers is relatively unconstrained by supply problems. Equally, management have recourse to a growing part-time component amongst their female workers. The distinction between the NHS and retailing lies in the fact that the former does experience serious skill shortages in certain occupational groups—which so far have proved incapable of solution through de-skilling. Whilst this has given rise to a variety of short-time working patterns being offered to induce trained nursing staff back into the profession it appears to have developed more or less spontaneously without a high degree of joint control. The extent to which NHS managers could utilise more part-time nursing staff to blunt the job creational effect of the 37½ hour basic week is probably not as great as a similar option in retailing; it remains, however, a possibility which unions in the service will need to keep a close check on.

As in retailing, the unions in the NHS appear to be in a relatively weak bargaining position with regard to major reductions in working time. This has less to do with the labour market (although it does have an influence) but rather more to do with the exchequer control over NHS finance. In a sense neither management nor unions dominate the bargaining process, they merely exercise a protracted 'brokerage' over what the treasury sees fit to allow in their budgetary allocation. Movement towards shorter hours is further constrained in the male dominated parts of the manual occupations by low basic pay giving rise to high levels of institutionalised overtime. Attempts to reduce these overtime levels via locally negotiated bonus agreements seem to have had only limited success, but seem likely to be stepped up as the regime of financial stringency proceeds. The point to be made here is that a bonus scheme may lead to a fall in actual hours worked, but is unlikely to affect basic hours and will move strongly against any job creational effects that might be expected to accrue from the curtailment of overtime.

In the case of the Post Office Engineers the shortage of skilled workers, added to the rising demand enjoyed by the telecommunications section of the Post Office, has plainly tended to equalise the bargaining positions of management and the union. The agreement on reduced working time appears to have been additionally facilitated by the practice of efficiency bargaining which has developed between the two sides since the early 1970s. There are, however, significant differences between the POEU case and those of retailing and the NHS. In a sense the POEU example provides a "bridge" between the service sector and the manufacturing sector, since both in labour market and in the inherent threat from new technology it more closely resembles the three manufacturing industries studied.

The obvious points of departure between the manufacturing and service sectors stem as much from the labour market as from the obvious differences in the style and nature of the work. Our case studies showed a high degree of congruence in that all exhibited marked labour market shortages for skilled workers; all had faced severe disruption in their markets as a result of the recession; shiftworking was common and all faced an impending increase in high technology capital equipment. The manpower implications and working time organisation were, however, handled differently. The key determinant here, as already noted, appeared to be the location of the bargaining power centre. Where plant level bargaining took place the response from both management and union side was comparatively unconstrained and significantly more innovatory.

The manufacturing case studies were stongly distinguished from those in the service sector, particularly retailing and the NHS, by the absence of part-time working and the predominance of male workers. To this extent the bargaining position of the unions was constrained more by the nature of the firm's competitive position and the need to defend job rights against increasing capital intensity. To this extent bargained changes to shift systems, for example the creation of a fifth shift, offered a practical response which both reduced actual hours and provided some consolidation of employment levels.

The defence of overtime by management in the sector, as a means of partially offsetting skill shortages and maintaining flexibility, and by unions (locally if not nationally) as a means of boosting earnings during times of high inflation, does, however, appear to be a precarious strategy when seen against the probable changed labour market conditions of the 1980s.

In this sense, a concerted union offensive in the immediate future on these negative working practices, which new technology will rapidly show to be anachronistic, may prove far less painful (and costly in control terms) than the longer term prospects of forced adjustment to much lower absolute levels of employment.

Chapter 12   Why Change?

The earlier analysis of the 1970s, and (with a few notable exceptions) much of the atmosphere of the plant and company level studies, reveals a world in which the main styles of working time are barely questioned, or only marginally changed. Indeed, in many cases the continuity of at least full-time patterns of working-time—length of basic week, propensity to overtime work, the nature of and extent of shift systems—appear as one of the few fixed elements in a fairly rapidly changing and sometimes markedly unstable economic environment. It is clear that even when working time has been an element in the collective bargaining process— and for much of the 1970s even this was inhibited by incomes policies—it has hardly been given strategic weight. The main exception to that, in the late 1960s in particular, were a number of "productivity bargaining" agreements that reduced or eliminated overtime work as part of a major re-organisation of labour utilisation and the structure of earnings.

And yet it appears less and less likely that the perpetuation of "traditional" patterns of working time, combined with the passive acceptance of some of the new trends identifiable in the 1970s (not least the rise in part-time employment), can meet the new social and economic needs of the 1980s. Indeed, it is surprising that these traditional levels of working hours, and annual working time, could have co-existed with growing levels of persistent unemployment in the last decade without earlier meeting social challenge. Perhaps the high unemployment of the mid-1970s was seen for a while as largely cyclical, rather than the opening of a new phase in national economic development and management.

But it is important, at this stage, to pass in review the critical issues which, in combination, make urgent an exploration of both new patterns of working time and (for many full-time workers) reductions in total working time. For in one industry, or one plant, not all these issues will necessarily be apparent at once, and it is natural that response may be piece-meal and limited if analysis is itself fragmentary.

The Context of Employment and Unemployment

Earlier post-war assumptions were that production, labour productivity and real incomes could be envisaged as rising fairly steadily. The largely unresolved crises of the 1970s have displaced such expectations, not only in Britain, by those of hesitant growth (and in many sectors zero growth or outright decline) within a rhythm of more strongly marked trade cycles. In Britain in particular the associated rise in unemployment of recent years has occurred despite a very marked check to the earlier trends of rising productivity. Consequently, a return to higher rates of productivity improvement may imply more displacement of labour, and cannot be assumed to go hand in hand with the generation of more employment.

From a number of directions the rise in real incomes has faltered. This was in the mid-1970s most directly associated with worsening terms of trade in face of the oil price increases; later, for Britain but not for other European countries, this was largely reversed. The slowing of real income growth has been connected also with failures in competitiveness and deterioration in productivity in some industrial sectors. The tension over income expectations has hardly been resolved in the later 1970s by supporting personal disposable income through direct tax cuts while curbing the "social wage" through curtailment of public services. Higher inflation has been one evident sign of greater difficulty in managing the processes of the distribution of income in face of competing claims.

In Britain unemployment has reached higher and higher levels in each of the trade cycles of the 1960s and 1970s. No-one doubts that it is going to reach unprecedented post-war levels in the recession of 1980-81. Even the latest government assumptions (in the White Paper on public expenditure) assume a rise in the average adult unemployed total to 1.8 million in the fiscal year 1981-82. It is equally clear, as a result of governmental analysis, that the unemployment of young workers will rise more than in proportion to the general rise in unemployment. This may well mean two-thirds of a million unemployed under the age of 25 by 1981-82 *as well as* higher unemployment of "school-leavers", that is of those entering the labour market for the first time.

Nor can it be assumed that such levels of unemployment will recede subsequently through strongly renewed growth. Both governmental and other forecasters expect only very slow overall growth rates to resume, and these will rest heavily on increased output of North Sea oil (which has an unusually small employment effect).

We consequently find *existing* patterns of working time alongside a rapidly growing army of unemployed workers. Within the total of the unemployed are, and will be, disproportionate numbers of young workers. In British experience also, a high proportion of the unemployed are male manual workers, and this contrasts directly with the extended work week (some 60% of adult manual men working an average of some 10 hours overtime) of those in employment.

It is important to emphasise the *recognised* dimensions of unemployment that are foreseeable in the first half of the 1980s in Britain, built as these are on assumptions that working time patterns will substantially continue.

But in addition the 1980s will see increasing effects from new technology. The official view on this is that:

"over the next five to ten years the effects of micro-electronic technology in reducing industry's demands for labour are unlikely to be any more dramatic than those of many previous examples of technological improvement". (DE Report, "Manpower Implications of Micro-Electronic Technology", p.14).

But the nature of the new technology will mean that it will particularly tend to reduce much routine, repetitive work. On the one hand this may involve the reduction of burdensome work; on the other hand the freeing of human resources from such work may accentuate at least medium run problems of structural unemployment. The problems of discontinuity appear formidable. Since the pace of change is largely the result of dynamic competition (seeking cost-reductions in production processes; seeking new applications and products) by multi-national companies, the rate of diffusion of new technology can barely be thought of as within social control.

This adds, therefore, further elements of risk and uncertainty to any discussion of employment and unemployment in the 1980s. It does not alter the need to recognise the new and persistently higher levels of unemployment that stem from present markets, public policies, and the existing pattern of working time.

The defence of existing working time practices, and especially the extended annual working hours required of many workers, in face of large scale unemployment has largely taken the form of emphasising costs and real income demands as constraints. The constraints, and the light our studies throw on them and on how they may be overcome, form the main part of a later section of this report. But even at this stage what needs to be emphasised is that *the costs and the real income effects of perpetuating current patterns of working time are worsening*. Unemployment is a cost that falls on business costs and on personal disposable income alike. New working time patterns may offer businesses benefits from a wider re-ordering of resource use, potentially improving both capital and labour utilisation. And increased access for the full-time workers to leisure time, especially at times or in amounts that are particularly valued, represents a notable gain in real welfare. Meanwhile the moral challenge represented by the co-existence of mass unemployment and the old stereotypes of working time remains.

Part-Time Work

In the previous section what was examined was the displacement of workers into unemployment, together with the special problem of the new entrant to the labour market. But there are also serious problems arising from the displacement of full-time work by part-time work.

Earlier in this report we have discussed the surprising scale of the expansion of part-time work in the economy of the 1970s. In some cases what has been apparent, and this applies in terms of rapidly changing *proportions* of female employment, has been large scale displacement of full-time work by part-time work. Thus in retail distribution between 1971 and 1977 virtually all the change can be thought of in terms of such displacement (full-time female employment fell over 70,000 to 560,000; part-time employment rose nearly 140,000 to 674,000). But much the same *proportional* change was true in "miscellaneous services"; between 1971 and 1977 (combining both male and female employment) part-time employment rose 50%, while full-time employment rose only 6%. On a calculation based on "full-time equivalents", had the proportion of part-timers in the labour force in "miscellaneous services" remained the same in 1977 as in 1971 there would have been *100,000 more full-time jobs by 1977* than in fact there were.

To a considerable extent the advantage to the employer in increasing part-time employment may reflect the disadvantages experienced by workers concerned. Our study has shown that in manufacturing in particular it was part-time female workers that were shed in the recession years on a disproportionate scale—having been recruited on a disproportionate scale in the boom (see electrical engineering).

Apart from job insecurity, the part-time worker is likely to be disadvantaged as against the full-time worker so far as access to pension schemes is concerned (and therefore the build-up over a period of years of some future income entitlements). Other elements of benefit, such as paid holidays, may also be affected. There is some likelihood that lower rates of hourly pay may be involved (though many bargained agreements appear to prevent this); for one thing, the access that the employer has to part-time labour in a local labour market may enable him to meet his labour requirements at a lower rate of hourly earnings than if he had to attract solely, or largely, full-time workers—even if no formal inequality is involved. As to pay rates, the Employment Appeals Tribunal has in particular cases decided that working substantially fewer hours than a full-time employee might constitute a material difference that justifies a different (i.e. lower) rate of pay than for full-time work.* In a number of ways, part-time workers (depending on the hours worked) may fall below the levels of weekly hours that bring some degree of protection under labour legislation.

This differentiation in the standing of part-time and full-time workers may be reinforced in practice by greater difficulties in recruitment and

* Kearns v Trust House Forte Catering Ltd. and Handley v H. Mono Ltd.

retention in trade union membership; even for members, trade union bargaining priorities may not materially change the position of part-time work.

Yet all the trends of activity rates of married women (especially for the age groups 35 and upwards), and these are the main source of the supply of part-time labour in the economy, indicate increasing participation in the labour force. The rise in the estimated numbers of married females in the labour force from 1971 to 1977 (just over one million) is not surprisingly close to the rise of 860,000 over the same years in female part-time employment. Official estimates projecting such rising activity rates forward suggest another one million married women in the labour force by the late 1980s. It hardly looks either economically practical or socially acceptable to take a negative view of the employment needs of these would-be workers.

Besides, the health service studies have served to emphasise the important point of the reservoir of skills that may be available—e.g. nursing skills—in the local labour market, but largely accessible to employers only if considerable flexibility in offering or accepting varied levels of working hours is shown. Since the community has in the past invested considerable resources in the training and development of workers and of such skills, it is important to be able to tap these skills to maintain or improve levels of hospital service provisions without further major increases in costs (including additional training and accommodation costs).

If the community may benefit from the flexibility that could accompany recruitment of workers offering different levels of labour time, we have to re-evaluate the "traditional" categories of both full-time and part-time work. The danger of the recent drift into significantly higher proportions of part-time work is that they may indicate not only some socially useful and acceptable substitution effects, but also the attraction (to employers) of lower labour costs and fewer job rights in the traditional handling of part-time employment. For the trade unions these subjects represent serious issues of policy, of priorities, and of control (or lack of it) of the conditions of work and workers. In these circumstances the passive acceptance of present trends and attributes of part-time work is no longer possible.

"Traditional" Manual and Non-Manual Working Time

In Britain, perhaps more than in some continental countries, it is not possible to discuss the organisation of working time without paying the greatest attention to the differentiation between manual and non-manual patterns. For many manual workers in Britain current arguments about reducing working time are *both* related to concerns such as maintenance of employment opportunities *and* represent a response to part of the structure of differentiation between manual and non-manual working conditions.

These extend into other associated aspects of the management of working time as well as the "basic week", but that is a central issue.

The differentiation in the "basic week" of manual and non-manual workers has been discussed at length in the first part of this report. However historically explicable such differences may be, they do not stand up well to the presentation of any rational case for their continuance. The shorter week of non-manual workers does not compensate for other disadvantages; on the contrary, it is generally part of a further differentiation of working conditions and income security largely in favour of the non-manual employee. (The possibility that treatment of overtime is in part an exception to this is considered subsequently.)

In consequence, as we have already shown, British employers are very far removed from being able to explain or defend the "necessity" of maintaining a 40 hour week. It would be more than a little difficult when 77% of non-manual men in 1979 and 79% of non-manual women were on a shorter "basic week" than 40 hours. Moreover, one of the big groups of non-manual workers hitherto on a 40 hour "basic" week, nursing staffs, are now in the process of transition to a 37½ hour week.

This element of manual/non-manual differentiation was also clearly a factor in the pressure of the Post Office Engineering Union for shorter hours in 1978. In practice, post office telecommunications needed to develop close working links between "manual" engineering workers and "non-manual" technicians, and in such circumstances a differentiation in basic working hours appeared to them anomalous.

But given the separation of manual and non-manual bargaining processes that is true of most industries, this matter of the differentiation in working time patterns is a matter of great complexity and sensitivity. Reduction of such differentiation, or assimilation to a common set of conditions, raises many problems of institutional practice and power. This may explain some of the survival of "traditional" working time distinctions without however providing a justification for them.

The present pattern of "basic weekly" hours is, therefore, essentially irrational and unsustainable in Britain. It may be that a 35 hour week is the only round figure that might emerge *if* some future stabilisation were to be sought. It offers some measurable improvement to many non-manual workers, and it offers—if uncertainly—some prospect that a closing of manual and non-manual differentials would in this sense be widely accepted. That, it should be noted, implies a conscious move away from "traditional" working time practices. The more that "traditionalism" is defended the more likely it would be that a degree of "leap-frogging" on hours reductions might open up in an unplanned and unco-ordinated way.

The problems of the present traditional differentiation in working time are compounded in many other ways. Differentiation in annual holiday provision has been discussed in the first part of this Report. Non-manual work has in recent years also developed more flexibility in "flexi-time" variations in starting and stopping times for the individuals, as well as in the degree and nature of direct supervision over working time. There are in many industries differences still in the factors that lead to loss of pay, including absence due to sickness, with much more security of income traditionally arising for non-manual workers. Changed processes, changed proportions of manual and non-manual labour, new technology, new skill mixtures, new requirements for direct team-work involving manual and non-manual work, all these must continue to raise fresh areas of challenge to the traditional occupational differentiation.

In all this, one critical area is the use of overtime. As a major aspect of British "traditionalism" in working time it requires separate treatment. But in some categories of "staff" status work, at least small amounts of overtime may be worked without being recorded and paid; for some higher grades hours may not be formally recorded. The persistence and import- ance of the overtime of manual men is exerting a pull upon the working time of many non-manual men (supervisors are an obvious example). In some case study areas some upward drift of overtime hours of non-manual men seemed apparent (e.g. in the motor industry). Here too the tradi- tional occupational patterns of working time may be setting up sets of "invidious comparisons" that pull working time in undesirable directions. *

Overtime

Overtime is undoubtedly the most criticised aspect of the "traditional" working time pattern in Britain. We have earlier referred to the major NBPI Report of 1970 which dealt extensively with overtime in its study of "Hours of Work, Overtime, and Shiftworking". Probably the most effective critical study, still almost entirely relevant, was prepared for the Royal Commission on Trade Unions and Employers' Associations in 1968; this was "Overtime Working in Britain" by E. G. Whybrew. Our own industry studies have shown the persistence of relatively high levels of overtime on the part of manual men in the 1970s, despite major recessions and in some sectors a more general decline in the rate of output growth. The case studies have frequently indicated the extent to which enterprises appeared locked-in to particular levels of overtime work, or were prepared to assume that shorter basic hours would "leak" into overtime.

* Not least if managerial and supervisory workers develop a direct vested interest in arranging or tolerating manual overtime working.

Some traditional defenders of the levels of male manual overtime have argued in terms of the operational necessity generated by, e.g. emergency work, and work that cannot be performed during normal working hours (including maintenance). There may also be a reluctance on both sides to recruit and then discharge labour to meet seasonal or cyclical swings in demand. However, these factors would have meant that overtime would have more clearly marked cyclicality and seasonality than it actually does, if they were more than a small part of the explanation.

A more important set of arguments relate to the recruitment and retention of workers in particular labour markets. For instance, an enterprise operating nationally (such as many public utilities) with national wage rates may have difficulty in retaining and recruiting in "high wage" areas unless take-home pay is enhanced by overtime working. This may not mean a failure to maintain efficient work standards, since the enterprise is likely to hold "manning" below its formally promulgated "establishment". Moreover, on such an approach to "manpower planning" if there is a run-down of activity it may be handled relatively painlessly by temporarily curtailing overtime, thereby checking recruitment and weakening retention, until the adjustment has been made; this may also avoid direct redundancy and its associated costs.

There is a further factor of importance in some service trades, as well as in production industries. Levels of demand for products, or pressure for extended hours of customer service, may be met from an addition of overtime to "normal" hours *without* embarking on shift working systems. This may appear to avoid the difficulties of negotiating—where it does not exist—provision for shift or staggered hours of working, and in cost terms the effective overtime premia may not appear even as costly as shift premia.

But such rationalisation of the existence of overtime on such a large scale does not meet the counter-argument that there are formidable reasons for seeking to reduce overtime working. Most surveys have shown that a high proportion of establishments work regular and effectively permanent overtime. The apparent heavy dependence on overtime applies not only to employing firms but to employed workers, in the sense that many workers working substantially regular overtime are dependent on its maintenance for a significant proportion of total take-home pay.

This in many cases may lead over protracted periods of time to built-in habits of operation and sets of expectations and demands that may even push overtime to yet higher levels. Moreover, the widespread connection between low hourly earnings and relatively high levels of overtime working may reinforce each other across a number of industries. Such a circular reaction of lower pay (relatively) and longer hours of work may be perpetuated *without* either side seeking more efficient solutions to the "target" earnings that are implied, or to the output needs of enterprise.

There may be an important concealed economic cost to the enterprise (and to the national economy) from the regular operation of permanently high levels of overtime. Such a mode of operation may reduce the ability of the enterprise to respond adequately to market opportunities presented by increased demand for the product. In one of our case studies the level of output required by high demand could not be met from persistently high overtime; a radical re-organisation of working time was required and this did not succeed in overcoming the constraint on output.

There is, however, little evidence to support the extreme view enunciated by the Whybrew research paper to the Royal Commission that:

> "Far from making possible essential additional output, much of British overtime now seems to arise out of a desire to waste time at work in order to obtain a living wage". (Op. Cit. p.2)

Indeed, such a view was clearly not seen as credible by the subsequent NBPI Report which instead had this to say:

> "It is not common for overtime to be foisted on managements which know that they cannot use it by workers in the pursuit of overtime earnings. That is not to say that it never happens. Instances can be cited . . . On the whole however, these are exceptional and occur in situations where many other difficulties beset the efficient use of manpower". (NBPI "Hours" p.32).

The instances the NBPI cited included an establishment with a high rate of absenteeism in normal hours and high rates of overtime. In one of our case studies we identified a similar pattern for one group of workers. Broadly we would agree with the NBPI view. But this may still mean that pressures from both sides go to establishing a prevailing level of overtime working, out of "custom and practice", and that this may not be conducive to high productivity.*

Certainly, the sources we have been quoting were able to identify a number of case studies not only in which "high overtime and inefficient use of manpower and resources (were) . . . found side by side in British

---

* One of the NBPI survey questions found that employers of nearly two-fifths of the overtime workers covered believed that workers' productivity was affected by a desire on their part to safeguard overtime opportunities (only "occasionally" for 35% of the workers, but "frequently" for a further 7%).

industry'' (NBPI, p.37) but also in which major reductions in overtime hours had been put through without loss of output, particularly within a "productivity bargaining'' framework. The "status'' agreements in the electricity supply industry in the 1960s provided an example of corporation (in this case an industry) level bargaining leading to the reduction of overtime from high to very low levels. Not only did some of these "productivity'' deals of the late 1960s bring together a consideration of the many factors bearing on low productivity and long hours so that new patterns of labour utilisation could be achieved, but some of them sought to prevent the re-emergence of regular overtime by providing for temporary overtime in the future to be compensated for by time off in lieu. Yet this constructive re-organisation of working time did not spread. Our own case studies, where they involved major changes in working time practices, indicated once again the genuine scope for raising hourly productivity in the context of reduced hours of work. It need hardly be emphasised that a) in a context of large scale unemployment there are severe constraints on the willingness to bargain for enhanced labour productivity and improved labour utilisation if this would directly reduce employment; consequently the association of such efficiency bargaining with the reduction of hours (and maintenance of employment) becomes a key requirement; and b) that in a context in which reductions in "basic hours'' are beginning to be negotiated for, the connection of this with a renewed attempt to re-organise working time—and to challenge existing modes of regular overtime working—becomes of the greatest importance.

Once again, therefore, the "traditional'' working time patterns of British industries and services need to be challenged if both sides are to unlock constructive approaches to pay, employment levels and efficiency. The syndrome of low hourly pay, persistent overtime working for manual men, and scope for raising hourly productivity is particularly one that once again needs challenging. This is necessarily so if a reduction of "basic'' working time is to come through as a reduction (indeed, potentially, a greater reduction) in actual working time, but together with greater efficiency in operation.

"Absenteeism"

High levels of absenteeism are one of the indicators of stress and tension in the existing pattern of working time. Some elements of this have appeared in our case studies' areas. One major motor manufacturer has argued the severity of its absenteeism problem and the adverse effect on production planning in its collective bargaining, and sought to remedy this by attendance bonuses. Yet, at the same time the company has a style of management of working time that involves high levels of persistent overtime. The co-existence of high overtime patterns and absenteeism has been commented on earlier, in general and in other contexts.

To some extent this may hinge on the unpopularity of particular shifts (such as the last shift worked before the weekend). In other cases the problem may particularly affect married women workers (e.g. the need to provide care and supervision of children in school holidays). These kinds of social pressures and the urgency of individual needs may not fit neatly into the "traditional" working time, and the definition of full-time work and of actual working hours may be rigid and unresponsive. In one of our case studies a local response was to foreshorten a five day shift cycle to finish earlier on Friday; this was possible even within the rigidity of a "costless' solution by maintaining effective working time but marginally shortening breaks. The point that can be emphasised is that there may be inefficiencies and high costs (especially of foregone production schedules, or of covering for absence through overtime working) associated with unplanned absence from work. These problems may be accentuated if sick pay schemes are to some extent used by workers who have gone absent.

The "traditional" working time pattern has not learnt to cope with the needs that prompt many workers to work *less* than the "basic week" for some of the time. The costs of this are apparent in failures to meet production schedules, recourse to attendance bonuses, and development of a combined build-up of absence and overtime. The traditional system is geared to offer or require the basic week or more (persistent or periodic overtime). There might be important efficiency gains, welfare gains to existing workers, and increased employment opportunities if new patterns of working time were explored.

"Unsocial" Working Time

The history of shiftwork and "compensation" for it was given a fresh impetus in Britain by a provision written into the Pay Code of the 1973 incomes policy. This was essentially designed to offer a major increase to coal miners (whose shift premia were very low) but not a general advance. In practice, however, the definition of unsocial hours for which compensatory shift work premia could be paid was such that other bargaining groups were able to lay claim to premia. These other groups included shopworkers whose full-time work week required them to work on Saturdays.

The point is instructive; it serves to remind us that the tendency has been for more recognition to be given to particular patterns of working time (very early starting, late finishing, weekend working within the "basic week", as well as shift systems themselves) as involving loss of social opportunities to the workers involved. The two main types of work that are caught up in such requirements are capital intensive industries (seeking to operate with high utilisation) and personal and consumer service industries (public transport, health services, and, potentially to an increasing extent, retailing). But the pattern of compensation has, overwhelmingly, been thought of as a directly increased labour cost in the form of premium payments.

Both the scale and the cost of this "unsocial" working time has tended to increase in the post war period, industrial shiftwork more rapidly expanding in the 1960s than in the 1970s.

But the "compensation" for shiftworking has concentrated on pay premia. The only significant extent to which there has been any working time concession is that for continuous shiftworkers meal breaks are taken within the eight hour shift. So little have shiftworkers been seen as having some priority claim in terms of reduced working time that there is clear evidence—which has already been referred to—that continuous working with four crews implies an effective working week obviously in excess of 40 hours. Without re-organisation of such shiftwork we have a situation in which shiftworkers so far from being compensated for "unsocial" working time by some reduction in working time are actually *adding* overtime hours to their basic shiftwork hours. Manual men receiving shift premia averaged 6.2 hours overtime in the NES 1979 survey period so far as manufacturing was concerned (the figure is as high as non-shiftworkers); outside manufacturing the average overtime hours of men receiving premia for shiftwork were 8.8 hours a week (higher than for other workers). Particularly in transport and in some manufacturing industries the overtime hours of shiftworkers are disconcertingly high (for instance nine hours a week in "coal and petroleum products", which mainly embraces oil refineries).* These patterns are persistent, and if anything show a slight upward drift since 1974 (when the data were first published).

It is with these cumulative weaknesses, social tensions and inefficiencies that "traditional" working time in Britain is confronted by the enormous social and moral challenge of growing unemployment, not least of the young, alongside those in work.

In the course of the 1970s, in round terms, full-time employment fell by a million (to 17¾ million in Great Britain), while part-time employment rose by over a million (to 4.4 million in Great Britain) and registered unemployment rose by three-quarters of a million (to over 1¼ million in Great Britain). It is time to unlock the constraints of the "traditional" approach.

* Some of the worst examples of relatively low hourly pay, shiftworking and excessive overtime occur in the food and drink industries. Thus, in the whole group of food industries shiftworking manual men secure gross pay £7 a week less than the manufacturing average for shiftworking manual men, but average 10.4 hours overtime (4.2 hours more than the average) to achieve that result. (1979 NES data, Table 85).

Chapter 13   How to Change?

Overcoming the Constraints

In a number of the case studies there is a sense of the parties involved in industrial relations at plant level feeling "locked-in" to their existing situation. For one thing there are in practice likely to be important elements of inter-connection between the factors that make up the effort-reward bargain. Thus, basic rates, job specification, effective working time and "custom and practice", earnings objectives, differentials (in both pay rates and earnings terms), and hours ("basic" and actual) are all inter-linked to form the familiar outturn. Besides, the enterprise has normally developed some adjustment to its external labour market, and may feel there is limited room for manoeuvre. For instance, some differential change might enhance its ability to recruit particular categories of workers, but this might set off a whole chain of consequences in its internal labour market.

In addition, the wider climate within which such opinions are formed has often been hostile to experiment. The larger firms may be influenced by the consistent opposition expressed by the CBI to bargaining for shorter weekly hours. Successive governments have denied any place to reductions in working time in the framework and norms of repeated exercises in incomes policy, and have outside such periods attempted to lead an anti-inflationary emphasis in public sector pay bargaining. There was only a brief and highly restricted exception to that in 1978 when the then government contemplated reductions in hours if they led to no net increase in unit costs above the pay guidelines. * This guarded invitation to efficiency bargaining over hours was important in opening the way to a settlement of the issue of shorter working time for post office engineers.

What Time Horizon?

It is important, therefore, to offer some comments on the ways in which constraints of different kinds, that are seen as preventing constructive steps to reducing working time, may be overcome. These are, it must be said, connected with the question of the time-horizon of change as compared

---

* See, "Winning the Battle against Inflation", Cmnd. 7293, Para. 23, "The Government can accept a reduction in hours as part of a normal pay settlement on condition that it is demonstrated that the settlement as a whole does not lead to any increase in unit costs above what would have resulted from a straight guideline settlement on pay".

with present patterns of institutional operation. Thus, the dominant collective bargaining time-horizon (largely reinforced by incomes policy) has been one year; in the first half of the 1960s it was by contrast increasingly seen as two or three years as "long term agreements" (including reductions in hours) were developed. Manpower planning needs a medium term time-horizon if it is to be deployed efficiently, but in recent years (and notably in regimes of successive expenditure cuts) this has tended to give way to shorter run expedients. Various employment support schemes on the part of the government have in practice been short run, and built up only to be run down again or terminated abruptly. One necessary requirement in many industries would be a readiness to plan for inter-connected changes in hours, job content, training, etc., over a medium term period, and to roll forward the time horizon so as to maintain an emphasis on forward planning.

Internal Labour Markets

It is mainly in a framework of "efficiency bargaining" that the overcoming of internal constraints can be envisaged. This is discussed in more detail in a subsequent section. But a number of case studies have indicated in different ways how adaptation can be made to particular kinds of, e.g. skill shortage, and how this may reduce costs of particular levels of employment and "output". The experience of the health service is significant, as both the industry study and the hospital level case study demonstrated. We saw "the central feature of hospital manpower policy" as releasing "trained medical care staff from extraneous tasks, allowing them to concentrate upon their central clinical and curative functions". This has involved a degree of substitution of less skilled medical nursing staff to carry out relevant functions, increased use of technical support staff, and the transfer of more "housekeeping" duties to ancillary staff (thereby relieving nursing staff for other functions).

This kind of *active* manpower policy *internal* to the enterprise would be of great importance where major reductions and changes in working time were being attempted, so as to reduce the requirements that might otherwise arise for increased employment of relatively scarce skills.

There is some contrast here between the situation of the service trades we examined and that of some of the industries. It is clear from the retailing studies as well as from the health service that management has for much of the time been able—with or without active bargaining and joint agreement on the part of trade unions—to alter the balance of the labour force and allocation of tasks in ways that reduced the costs of expansion. In these cases, a continuation of such flexible deployment of labour (preferably within the scope of procedural and substantive agreements with the trade unions concerned) can be envisaged as working hours are reduced, or the shift utilisation of plant revised. One could assume that change could proceed by a series of "marginal" changes if need be (such as the transition in multiple shops to a basic week marginally below 40 hours, already negotiated).

In other cases a bolder re-organisation of working time, shift utilisation, labour utilisation, might need to be attempted in order to make it seem worthwhile to both managements and unionised workers to make the considerable effort involved in "unlocking" existing internal arrangements. Such planning and bargaining for change would, in an important sense, have to combine major changes in routine—such as were explored in some of our case studies—with longer term changes in recruitment and training policies, and in the occupational balance of work allocation.

External Labour Markets

We have noted already that at the time of our case studies there were some examples of constraint felt as a result of the "shortage" of particular kinds of skilled workers. Such apparent barriers to change require closer scrutiny:

— The problem may (as to some extent in 1979) have been cyclical; initiatives timed at points of high cyclical activity are likely to be impeded by labour mis-match at least in some regional markets and for some occupational categories;

— The pressure might be eased if it were possible to use the kinds of internal labour market initiatives described in the previous section;

— Then "shortages" may relate to the levels of pay, and the nature of working conditions and "quality of working life" on offer. There may be difficulties in altering the package of "differentials" to attract or retain particular groups of workers (in isolation these might be resisted by other groups). The employer may be reluctant to face the cost implications of raising his bids for the labour he is seeking on a particular local labour market (either as a "monopsonistic" response, or because there are direct or indirect linkages to national pay and hours structures for his enterprises).

— Longer term development policy issues may be relevant. There has been a fairly widely marked tendency for the average (employment) size of the plants of multi-plant companies to fall in recent years.* This may relate to changing perceptions as to scale economies in the plant production process on the one hand, and potential diseconomies to further growth for plants that are large relative to their local labour markets on the other. Barriers in one labour market may be overcome by re-allocation of plant work-loads and development in less constrained labour markets (with or without new plants being opened).

* On this, see S. J. Prais, "The Evolution of Giant Firms in Britain", Chapters 3 and 4.

300

The barriers, then, are relative rather than absolute. They may be less likely to be major constraints overall in the generally depressed labour market conditions of the early 1980s. By contrast, the years in which earlier reductions of basic weekly hours were concentrated were characterised by more nearly full employment in most of the country's labour markets, and they preceded also the more active labour market management policies associated in the 1970s with the Manpower Services Commission, and preceded also the extensive experience of "productivity bargaining" that many trade unions and managements acquired in the later 1960s. *

But it is clear that one necessary condition for the reduction of labour market constraints on reductions in working time is that the Manpower Services Commission should maintain and indeed increase its positive manpower policies. These programmes have been enlarged in the 1970s and in 1978-79 involved the spending by MSC of over £300 million on its Training Services Division function (including £90 million contribution towards the work of Industrial Training Boards). This was apart from further large scale spending on its special programmes (mainly aimed at young workers). It should be emphasised that:

— The net cost of additional training programmes is relatively low over a period of time if they contribute to the attainment of rising levels

* Most of the fall in "basic hours" from 44 to 42 was concentrated in the years 1959 to 1961; the reduction from 42 to 40 was mainly bunched in 1964-66. In each period the official index of normal hours for manual workers fell by 3.7%. At the time the fall in "actual" hours was less pronounced in 1959-61 (1.9%) but continued into 1962. A rising level of economic activity in 1959-60 gave way to recession in 1962. In the circumstances it is interesting that hours actually worked fell as much as they did. In 1964-65 labour market conditions were similar to those of 1960, but 1966 saw a minor recession and a marked reduction in actual hours worked. This timing of "normal" hours reductions despite appearing cyclically unsuitable did not cause any noticeable problems of accelerated inflation. In 1959-61 employment income per unit of output rose just over 7%; this was less than in the equivalent years (1954-56) of the previous trade cycle when no reduction in normal hours occurred. In 1964-66 wages and salaries per unit of output rose by 9½% across the economy; this compares favourably with the 15% rise in such costs in the equivalent years of the following trade cycle when no hours reductions occurred. Although many other factors are involved, it is worth noting that in the recessions following each of these previous reductions of normal hours the unemployment peak remained below 600,000. By contrast the unemployment peaks in the trade cycles of the 1970s during which no significant reductions in normal hours occurred were very much higher.

301

of employment (and therefore tax receipts to the Exchequer) and help prevent constraints on such employment and output growth.

— The emphasis on a medium run programme, related to the labour force training needs associated with phased programmes to reduce the working time of workers in different industries, may in practice help maintain and increase levels of industrial training provision. Otherwise there is a danger that training provision may be the casualty of a deep and prolonged recession. This was true of the recession in the early 1970s, and in the mid-1970s and beyond much MSC initiative and expenditure had to be directed at contra-cyclical support for industrial training. The present danger is in addition that MSC itself will be expected to curb its training support in the name of short run "savings" in public expenditure.

In practice, external labour market constraints may prevent the actual hours of *some* key workers from falling in line with more general reductions of working time. But this looks like a short run effect, capable of being minimised by initiatives in the internal and external labour market of establishments, and with limited exceptions (e.g. possibly new ranges of skill needed in electronic technology) such constraints are less serious in the heavily underemployed labour markets of the early 1980s.

It is indeed possible to reverse the argument. The most likely out-turn in the early 1980s will be heavy falls in employment in a wide range of manufacturing industries. Unless this can be offset to a marked extent, and especially for skilled workers, by more retention of such workers within the context of reduced working time (including recession-induced work sharing) there might be a major and more or less permanent loss of skilled manpower in manufacturing. Skill shortages might subsequently re-appear in any recovery in manufacturing output at even lower levels of manufacturing employment (and higher levels of unemployment) than before. *Not* acting to reduce working time is no guarantee of the removal of later constraints on output growth due to labour force imbalance and skill shortage.

Are Costs and Competition Constraints?

There are a number of general considerations that are worth identifying before moving on to some of the particularly interesting lessons that emerge from the case studies.

One is the uncertainty as to what the *net* costs to an enterprise would be from reductions in working time. In the subsequent section we go on to examine in analytical terms the main opportunities presented by "efficiency bargaining" over working time, and the offsetting benefits that can be identified as accruing to plants and firms. These opportunities could well mean, as was apparent in a case study involving this type of approach, that no major net costs of the process could be identified and that *opportunities* especially of more efficient capital utilisation and production planning might be opened up.

Net costs might appear to be higher where the enterprise, as in retailing (through greater flexibility in opening hours of shops and of deployment of full- and part-time staff) or the hospitals (through revision of job functions internally), is already securing over a period of time a stream of benefits from improving labour efficiency. To this there are two answers; one is that a relevant way for labour to share in the continuing deployment of more efficient combinations of capital, plant, labour, and labour time, is for there to be periodic reductions in normal and actual hours without loss of pay. The other is that for certain categories of workers (particularly married women) a shorter work week would be an attractive force, helping both recruitment and retention of staff, with resulting benefits to the enterprise.

A further distinction that needs to be made is that between private costs (and benefits) and public or social costs (and benefits). Insofar as employment is sustained at a higher level through reductions in working time there are likely to be important benefits to net public expenditure. The Department of Employment calculated the net effect on public expenditure from a reduction in normal hours to 35, using various assumptions as to the employment and productivity effects generated. In 1977-78 prices the outcome ranged between a £650 million and a £950 million net fall in public expenditure (arising from reduced unemployment outlays, and some increases in revenue from taxes on employment income, etc.)* It is a wider policy question how such benefits in public expenditure terms might be signalled to bargainers, and how far private estimates of costs and benefits might be modified (for instance by reducing national insurance payments by the employer on incremental employment). But at least in the case of *public services* it is worth recognising that the *net* cost of changes in the direction of shorter working hours would be—in terms of the public expenditure process generally—less than the apparent cost to the service in question.

It is sometimes argued that what is being asked for involves ''sharing the misery'', that is that reduced working time will deprive workers of some element of real income. One of the functions of productivity bargaining is obviously by helping to raise real hourly productivity (and/or capital productivity) to provide a basis for real hourly earnings also to rise. As to the possible loss of real weekly hourly income from the typical full-time worker working fewer actual hours, this would depend on:

* Department of Employment Gazette, April 1978, p.402.

—   The balance of hours reduction, and gains in hourly efficiency and pay;

—   The valuation of increased access to leisure, that is the real welfare gain of shorter working time.
(There would also be gains in at least a proportion of families' total incomes as a result of any employment increase arising from the work sharing effects of shorter working time).

But is there a major residual problem of "competitiveness"? In general terms it is difficult to quantify what this might involve, although the standard criticism is that "reduced competitiveness" might appear or reduce employment. One possible point of departure is to accept the Department of Employment estimate (as the CBI appears to have done) that on a range of assumptions about loss of output, rise in output per man-hour, overtime hours, and employment increase:

> "A reduction of normal weekly hours to 35 . . . if weekly earnings were maintained . . . could increase labour costs by between 6% and 8%." (Gazette, April 1978 p.401).

To put that in perspective we might recognise that an overall reduction of weekly "basic" hours on that scale would take some time; even on assumptions of an accelerated process one might think of three years, or possibly of the time period of a trade cycle (five years). Over the five years to September 1979 unit wage and salary costs in British manufacturing industries doubled (a rise of 101%); over the three years to September 1979 they rose 42%. Thus, it hardly seems that the labour cost increases that might be associated with the process of a major downward shift in working time would bulk large against the recent pace (which has since accelerated) of overall increases in unit labour costs. *

But in competitive terms, internationally, what would be significant would be whether one country alone, or European trading partners more gener-ally, embarked on a major exercise in bargaining reduced working time. The issue is seen by the trade unions as one involving pressure by bargainers to reduce working time on a European scale, and the Commis-sion of the EEC appears likely to share that attitude. In Britain's case a rising exchange rate and a high internal rate of inflation have between them led to a serious deterioration in comparative costs, and therefore in the competitiveness of manufacturing industry. This deterioration since

* Indeed, it could be argued that were a substantial process of hours reduction to be an element in the medium term it might—insofar as it was was seen as a real income/welfare gain—moderate the general pace or pressure of demands for pay increases.

1978 is already many times what would have been involved even on the worst possible assumptions about the costs of reducing working time, even if that had taken place unilaterally. The problem of comparative costs is real, but phased changes in working time have not been a factor so far, and appear as a minor element in the evolution of potential comparative cost changes in the 1980s.

Internally, competition looks less of a constraint. One obvious reason for this is that movements towards shorter working time may either come from guidelines or agreements in industry or sector-wide bargaining (e.g. engineering), provincial newspapers, or may stem from the bargaining of what might be termed "strong competitors". The latter can be instanced from the experience of retail trade; it has above all been the multiple firms that have developed increasingly efficient organisation of their establishments, flexible use of labour, and resulting high labour productivity. It is these firms, through their joint collective bargaining machinery, that have started to reduce the basic week in retailing below 40 hours. They do not risk their competitive postition in doing so. The likely response is that their competitors will come under pressure to follow suit. Meanwhile, they benefit in labour market recruitment and retention by offering an effort/reward package that is marginally more attractive than that offered by firms that lag behind in reducing working time. There are no signs here of competitive constraints.

Bargaining for Change

Running through the argument of the preceding sections has been the assumption that the reduction of working time can take place in ways, including an active deployment of "efficiency" bargaining, that will raise labour efficiency per hour, possibly offer scope for increased utilisation of plant capacity, and therefore offset some of the "cost" of reduced working time. On such assumptions there would be an admixture of benefits to labour from improvement in real hourly earnings, increased access to leisure, and an increase in overall employment. This latter might appear to the employer as part of the "cost" of reducing working hours, but he may offset some of that by improved labour and capital utilisation, and by reduction in overtime working and costs (if that can constitute part of the bargained "package").

In practice, it is necessary, to think of three levels of response by organised labour to the bargaining process that is required.

One of these is at *the level of the movement as a whole,* the TUC. This is likely to take a number of forms such as:

— The exchange of best practice;

— International co-ordination of bargaining for shorter working time as a priority;

— Discussion with trade unions at sectoral or industry level about the pace and content of change;

— Pressure on agencies such as the Manpower Services Commission to develop further the positive manpower policies that would be needed (improving and extending skill training, etc.). At this level of response it would be important to bring out openly into discussion the need to re-examine the scale and incidence of overtime working and to discuss ways of preventing falls in basic hours "leaking" into overtime working instead of helping to generate additional jobs.

The second level of response is that of major federated bargaining units, Joint Industrial Councils, etc. It is unlikely in practice that the question of a strategy on hours reductions, and other changes in the practice of working time and its management, can be—or should be—separated from other developments that will be occurring in the medium term, including the more widespread adoption of new technology.

At this level—broadly JIC level—it would be particularly helpful to establish guidelines that would *enable* broadly equivalent processes of "efficiency" bargaining to proceed in the specific circumstances of part-icular firms and plants. It is not possible to prescribe such guidelines, but it is possible to indicate what they might embrace:

— Some limit might be set as to the rise in unit costs that could be allowed for in reducing working time.

— Alternatively some target could be set for plant level bargaining as to what proportion of the cost of a given reduction in working time should be offset by improved working efficiency.

— Guidelines could be given as to the monitoring and joint control of overtime and for avoiding any increase in overtime working beyond its previous levels (or with special emphasis on reducing overtime where excessive levels are prevalent).

— There could be special attention to the interests of shiftworkers. This might include more emphasis on reduction of actual hours and remanning of shifts.

These initiatives would need to be supplemented by work both within EDCs and ITBs to improve medium run manpower planning and relevant changes in training priorities.

The third level of response would be that of handling the re-direction of "efficiency" bargaining towards reduction of working time, primarily at plant or multi-plant company level. The case studies have helped to illuminate what some of the bargaining opportunities might be. We are here making two assumptions:

i) That the bargaining objective of the trade union side is a reduction of working time without loss of pay for the "normal" week;

ii) that the bargainers are concerned to ensure that the costs of reduced working time without loss of pay are offset—to some extent—by the generation of compensatory benefits to the business.

The main bargaining approaches that appear of the greatest relevance are as follows:

1) Reducing the "normal" working week in conjunction with a planned and controlled reduction in overtime.

This bargaining approach can be thought of as seeking to achieve a fall in *actual* hours of work greater than the fall in "normal" hours. Cost savings from reducing overtime could help finance a reduction in normal hours without loss of pay. In practice there may be a significant *indirect* cost savings as well as the ones directly recorded (for instance if overtime is excessive it may impair performance through fatigue).

In addition, the Department of Employment and the TUC have both been emphasising the potential scope for increased employment as a result of planned reductions in overtime; consequently there are substantial public or social benefits insofar as such an approach leads to re-manning and an increase in numbers employed. These may only indirectly and in part feed back as benefits to the enterprise, but this does not make them less real. A rational economy would support such bargaining by offering financial assistance to firms that were prepared to increase their total employment in this way, e.g. by helping to finance an accelerated recruitment programme, or financing the training and preparation of labour for any phased re-manning as actual hours as well as normal hours fell, or by direct subsidy to the increased employment generated. Even if substantial aid were to be offered by the state it would still be likely to represent a net reduction in cost to the public finances.

2) Offsetting the cost of shorter working time by improved capital utilisation through extended hours of operation.

In this case we are exploring the benefits to the enterprise if *reductions* of working time for *individual* workers are linked with *longer* hours of commercial use of the capital stock. In some industries, such as distribution, employers have already been seeking such an extension of operating hours by such devices as staggering working hours and deploying more part-time labour—but in the main *without* linking this with a planned reduction in working hours.

Within this particular approach there may be even more flexibility than is apparent. For instance, workers may work fewer days but for a longer shift time (this is a feature of the Post Office agreement on a voluntary basis); they may work a shorter shift time, but shift utilisation of plant may be extended (on a full-time or a part-time basis).

This approach could have widespread application in service trades, e.g. extended opening hours in distribution, banking and insurance, and other leisure and finance industries. A recent BIFU agreement, for the Brent Cross branch of Barclays, is of significance. Under the agreement the branch opens from 9.30 a.m. to 8.00 p.m. Monday to Friday, and 9.00 a.m. to 6.00 p.m. on Saturday. The agreement provides not only for high shift premia but also for reduced hours; in the week in which staff work a Saturday the working week has been reduced to by two hours to 33, and it is also reduced to 33 in the week following the working of a Saturday.

In industry, and in commerce, an approach on these lines would be especially advantageous where the market opportunities available to firms could be more fully met by such increased utilisation of existing capital. In such cases there could be increased employment opportunities both full- and part-time. The increase in unit labour costs could be offset by substantial savings in unit capital costs associated with higher rates of capital utilisation and increased volume of output or turnover per unit of capital. Besides, working capital requirements per unit of output (or in services, transactions) might be reduced. Costing the direct and indirect benefits involved would mean looking at many elements of business costs, in some cases at investment appraisals, and would probably require examination of marketing studies as well.

3) Offsetting the cost of shorter working time by increased capital utilisation during shift times.

There are a variety of ways in which a reduction of hours of work could be linked to a reduction in the "down time" of equipment, machinery, and associated production processes *during* the shift time. This might arise from revisions of maintenance systems, or working practice, or increased managerial efficiency. It could arise from re-phasing work to avoid bottlenecks; an interesting example is provided by the Post Office agreement with the POEU. In this agreement the reduction of the length of the working day is handled by half the staff starting at the normal time (and finishing half an hour early) and half starting half an hour later (finishing at the normal time). This will reduce bottlenecks caused by peaking of administration, scheduling and reporting, and vehicle movement from depots at the beginning and end of the working day.

Flexibility may be increased even more by *combining* economies from increased capital utilisation during the normal shift, in the context of a shorter working day, with economies from lengthening the shift and the working day but reducing the number of days worked (four day week; eight or nine day fortnights). The Post Office agreement uses all these elements to reduce ''ineffective time'' from a variety of directions. For instance, for ''external'' construction work at a distance the longer day may reduce the ratio of the shift spent in travelling to and from the job, whereas for other work the economy of ''staggered'' but shorter hours—described above— may be significant).

4) Offsetting the cost of shorter working time by improvements in labour utilisation during shift times.

This approach involves re-examining working practices that may be currently geared to the present length of the shift time and to existing patterns of working time. For instance, work breaks and relief times, start-up times and arrangement for flexibility and overlapping when shifts change, might be relevant. In some industries, of course, recorded and paid working hours are *less* than the time that workers actually require to spend on the employers' premises, i.e. the time required for preparation (changing, putting on special protective clothing and gear, getting to the work station once inside the works) and for cleaning up at the end of a shift may not be fully compensated or treated as part of working hours. This has appeared as a potential issue in mining, the motor industry, and else-where. So it cannot be assumed that bargaining can avoid such issues once a close study of actual working hours and labour utilisation takes place— some negotiations about labour utilisation may therefore tend to *raise* costs, if ''unpaid'' hours are more adequately recognised and compensated for.

However, as with a considerable amount of ''efficiency bargaining'' in recent years, further study of labour utilisation in the context of working hours may indicate scope for cost savings. The important point to make here is that costing such savings may be quite complicated. If the same output can—through re-organisation of the use of labour—be achieved in a shorter working time, the cost savings are not limited to ''direct labour''. There would be likely to be important savings in overhead costs per unit of labour, including possibly savings in indirect labour costs. Consequently, a serious approach to reducing the net cost of shorter working time must involve major questions as to the disclosure of (and, indeed, reliability of) data on costings. To take a simplified example, supposing a work team agreed to maintain fully previous levels of shift output within a shorter shift time for no loss of pay. This is not the simple exercise in "costless" reduction in working time it might seem. The employer may have secured significant cost savings *per unit of output* in heating, etc., possibly in power requirements, almost certainly in staff costs. He may be able to reduce maintenance costs. And these cost savings might be even more significant if he were, in connection with this, able to maintain—let alone extend—his shift utilisation of plant.

5) **Linking reduced working time with planned improvements in attendance (and reductions in labour turnover).**

In many establishments there are severe cost diseconomies and major losses of planned output due to relatively high rates of unscheduled absenteeism. In some cases, employers have grasped that they confront a major cost problem, but have not seen the possible connection with hours of work—and a possible constructive solution via a conscious link with reduced working time. There is a recent example in the much-publicised 1978 Ford pay dispute. In the "Company Reply", Ford has this to say:

> "Casual absentees cost us 2.1 million man hours in 1977. That means that approximately 1,200 employees were absent without permission every day. These were absences that could not be planned for and which will have had a more serious effect upon production than even their numbers suggest because of all the re-arrangements that have had to be made to re-adjust production plans to the labour available."

> "Our absenteeism on Mondays and Fridays is about 2% higher than on other days and trends in absenteeism are on the increase."

However, Ford in its "Reply" avoided any suggestion that absenteeism might be connected with its practice of long actual hours of work, or any thought of linking reduction of absenteeism with reduction of working hours—which it totally resisted. Perhaps this was the more surprising since the trade union case had not only emphasised that both absenteeism and labour turnover (wastage rates) were increasing, but had specifically connected this with possible efficiency gains from shorter hours. The trade union case had also revealed that nearly one third of Ford's manual employees were working over 50 hours a week (compared with less than one fifth for the industry generally). This would not be the first example of a company whose persistent use of extensive overtime was associated with high and rising levels of absenteeism, with its associated costs.

Whether absenteeism is a seasonal phenomenon, or connected with particular weekly shifts, the costs associated with it may build up from many directions, including loss of capacity utilisation, unbalanced work

310

teams, and attempts to maintain total output by further overtime working. In such conditions it may be attractive to connect reductions in working time with co-operation in improving attendance and in time-keeping. A constructive approach that has been used in the USA in that of building up an entitlement of paid rest days ("Paid personal holidays") which cannot be cashed in but can only be taken up as rest days. In some cases the particular shifts (e.g. Monday and Friday shifts) that have been focal points for absenteeism might be shortened in direct connection with improved attendance.

Bargainers may also find it useful to examine the scale and characteristics of labour wastage. In some cases this may be a direct reflection of an unattractive combination of pay and patterns of working time (e.g. the full forty hour week may put undue pressure on many married women workers). Given the costs of labour turnover, of recruitment, training, and loss of "learning curve" benefits, reductions in working time may be of significance in reducing the costs of such factors by curbing labour wastage. Thus, up to now, the unattractiveness of particular shift patterns of "unsocial" hours has been "compensated" for by premium payments, whereas compensation through shortening the working week or through additional paid rest days may offer for many workers a constructive new approach and one that will lower turnover rates.

6)   Re-allocation of work tasks.

One way of either 'expanding' or 'improving' the efficiency of the *internal* labour market is via the re-allocation of work tasks across existing work groups. Where either external labour market shortages or changing demand or work organisation conditions continue to create pressure on specific work groups, i.e. those whose expansion through extra recruitment is constrained, the re-organisation and re-allocation of tasks carried out by this critical occupational grouping may prove an effective (albeit subject to clear limits) remedy. In the last few years such a practice has been exercised, for example, within the NHS to pare down the activities normally undertaken by trained nurses (now in critically short supply) and the consequent re-allocation of many non-nursing activities to ancillary staff. In essence this acts both to de-pressurise the skilled worker whilst making a more optimal use of his/her skills.

The extent to which such an approach could improve many of the skill shortage problems identified by our case studies may depend crucially upon willingness to examine critically and openly traditionally demarcated working boundaries, a process rendered less easy (but equally, no less important), by the inherent threat to such boundaries posed by the

311

impending implementation on a mass scale of micro-processor based technology.

7) Re-organisation of shift manning.

Where shift systems operate alongside high levels of overtime, and, in all probability high levels of absenteeism; the costs incurred by the firm and the negative social costs borne by the individual worker may be more rationally accounted for by the creation of an additional shift to draw off the pressure from the existing shift system. Our case studies include a successful example whereby in exchange for increased flexibility of manpower utilisation and the internal generation of manpower via "saving" on the existing four shifts, a fifth shift was created which yielded stabilised earnings, virtually no overtime and significant increases in useful blocks of leisure time for the workforce involved.

Such an outcome depends upon the commitment and integrity of the parties to actually 'bargain' labour efficiency in a way that accepts what may be quite radical changes in established working practices.

8) "Job and Finish" and the shorter "normal" week.

This could be considered a sub-set of the theme (heading 4 above) that emphasised "improvments in labour utilisation". The case for setting it out as an aspect on its own is that in some industries "custom and practice", if not fully regularised arrangements, has over many years established some scope for "job and finish". This may point to a working solution to some of the problems discussed (in 5 above) of absenteeism, particularly for certain shifts where the problem is most acute—such as the last working shift of the week. In any case, the experience of such "job and finish" is likely to be worth analysis, and may lend itself to wider application in the phasing of reduced working time. As was emphasised in the earlier discussion, the cost savings that may be associated with this kind of approach, particularly if it is regularised and becomes a basis for revised production planning (e.g. more opportunities for planned maintenance during the week), would include elements of overhead costs.

9) Older workers: phased reductions in working time.

In this case, too, it could be argued that the approach could be considered mainly as a sub-set of heading 5 above (with its emphasis on absenteeism, etc.). But the issues involved are more complex and require specific concern with an additional range of factors.

In a crude way the labour government, in the late 1970s, through its "job release" scheme for workers aged 64, had begun to explore the employment creating aspect of shortening working time for older workers. But it has sought to use merely the technique of subsidy (weekly grant) to encourage early retirement. At least this illustrates the point, that there are significant benefits accruing to public finance from the employment creating aspects of reduction in working time, and that it is rational to recognise this and to "signal", e.g. through appropriate grants/subsidies—that the social benefits may be greater than the "private" benefits (to companies or individuals).

Earnings and other data indicate that older workers tend to work a shorter *actual* working week than younger adult workers. This is true of those who work a full week (that is, less overtime is worked than by other adult age groups—this is mainly of importance for male manual workers). But, in addition, health may affect attendance.

There are three reasons why attempts to plan for phased reductions in working time for older workers may be especially attractive for collective bargainers. Firstly, the "costs" of such an approach—for instance of holidays, or additional rest days—may be offset by important gains. Such measures may both aid retention of skilled and experienced personnel, and may help sustain the health and well-being of older workers. Secondly, with the major development of industrial pension schemes at company level that has taken place, there may be additional flexibility in approaching questions of retirement (age of retirement and level of pension entitlement, and "phased in" retirement—e.g. half-time work in a period preceding complete retirement). Thirdly, since past governments have already accepted through, e.g. the "job release" scheme the positive social benefits of the employment-creating aspects of reduced working time for older workers there may be scope for increased flexibility in the government approach to early retirement in the future. This might help to alter the sums of "costs" and "benefits" as perceived by companies and by the older workers themselves.

Efficiency Bargaining: Some General Considerations

This brief analysis of the scope for "efficiency" bargaining in connection with reducing working time does lead to some important generalisations.

i) A "leisure" trade-off instead of an "earnings" trade-off in efficiency bargaining may open up fresh opportunities for reviewing capital and labour use, and the scale of output (whether goods or services). The Post Office agreement would appear to be a case in point.

ii) In Britain we are fortunate in having a great deal of experience of company and plant level bargaining which can help relate particular patterns of reduced working time to particular needs/opportunities

313

of the business enterprise. This hardly suggests that the "net" costs of reduced working time are prohibitively high; it offers a relevant dimension for constructive collective bargaining.

iii) Under current conditions of large scale unemployment in most regions of Britain there are important expenditure cost savings to the government from employment maintenance and additional job creation. This means it would be irrational of the government if it adopted a negative attitude to either short term "work sharing" proposals or "efficiency" bargaining on the lines indicated. This applies in the handling of the employers' response to bargaining on working time in the public services, and it could justify various types of fiscal support for employment creation through such bargaining in the private sector.

iv) Efficiency bargaining on the lines suggested raises many questions as to the need for access to a wider range of cost information. Joint examination of patterns of working time, actual and proposed, cannot yield the full advantages of a consciously rational measurement of costs and benefits without a much more sustained study of operating and capital costs, and market (product and labour market) opportunities. The full exploration of such options, and their connection with changing technology, must require collective bargaining to face forward and examine jointly what is in effect the choices as to an efficient development path for the enterprise.

v) It is the centrality of the question of reduction of working time that opens up these constructive possibilities for bargaining. Without that element there would be the seriously divisive prospect of efficiency bargaining requiring as its counterpart the reduction of job opportunities either in the internal labour market, or in the firm's demands on the external labour market, or both. In a context of mass unemployment that is clearly repugnant.

New Working Time Policies

One undertone in the discussion so far has been that we are discussing more than a set of mechanical demands for less working time. It is not simply the same recognisable system of the management of working time but with fewer annual units built into it, nor just a demand for social justice and the removal of artificial and illogical distinctions between the terms and conditions of employment of manual and non-manual workers. The new technology will be reshaping many work processes. Arguments for constructive "forward looking" bargaining are likely to link with the persistence of the claim that organised workers should, through whatever mechanisms of "industrial democracy", be directly involved in the determination of their own industrial future. Out of, and partly because of, the structural crisis of employment within our present categories these new pressures for change and a more constructive shaping of the future of work are steadily gathering force. It is not only the present levels of working time, but also the categories themselves that will be brought under closer scrutiny in the next stage of bargaining over hours.

A simple way of approaching these wider issues of the future of working time is to consider why the crude complaint that what is really being advocated is "work sharing", "sharing the misery", still has any pejorative force. After all, why not share work? The trade unions have all along been arguing about the distribution of output, or the fruits of that output viewed as purchasing power. A sense of social justice has been built up and may command wider social significance than would the mere rhetoric of sectional interests and their claims. To take up the note that the last section ended on, organised labour is now confronted with the need—moral as well as economic—to find in new and more difficult economic conditions the means of ensuring paid work for all. It cannot for much longer remain within institutional practice and priorities that offer earnings for some but unemployment for many others. We are talking about a new dimension of the claim for distributive justice that organised labour must assert. Why then the awkwardness about accepting the taunt of "work sharing"? The answer perhaps lies in the sense it conveys of enforcing a reduction of working time on unwilling workers, of an enforced equality of working time contribution. But does the emphasis on reducing working time actually lead in that direction? Even if it did, one would have to balance the coercion of unemployment—of *that* version of enforced idleness—against the apparent coercion of requiring some workers to work less than they wish—a rather different dimension of enforced idleness. But the sense of a levelling process proceeds from the "traditional" rigidity of our conception of full-time working hours. Do we need to re-think our categories?

If we seek an analogy, it could lie in the critical discussion in Europe directed against the enforced work rhythms of the assembly line. That is one symbol of work as involving a dictated, an imposed, rhythm; of the search for a framework of more freely determined choices in the handling by individuals and work groups of the required work process. May not working time be another? May not the inflexibility of the management of working time represent another enforced work rhythm?

Redefining Full-Time Work
In bargaining for less working time can we bargain for the reshaping of working time to match more closely the changing needs of individuals for different combinations of work, study, leisure, and voluntary service?

We have earlier noted that both young and old workers tend to take up overtime working less than the 30-49 age range of men. The resistance of full-time women workers in many cases to overtime work signals a major element of resistance to long working hours. There is some indication, too, from our case studies, that while women workers may prefer shorter hours within the five day week, manual men may find a longer daily shift acceptable *if* this means a four day week, or in another case a nine day fortnight.

There is, then, a problem of the compatibility of differing preferences for the length of the working day, and the shape of the working week or year.

One way of reviewing the possibilities that open up is to reflect that under "traditional" work weeks, the pattern of expected working hours is more tolerant of *extension* of working hours than of their *reduction*. Thus, while the basic hours are 40, the actual work week for manual men is likely to centre around 45 hours or more.

There would seem to be a number of ways of building a more flexible framework of full-time work around a lower level of "basic" weekly hours:

— There could be more recognition of the need for alternative forms of compensation for shift workers with their "unsocial" hours. This could involve priority in the reduction of the length of the basic week, limitation of overtime by re-manning shift teams and shift cycles, and a shift of "compensation" for shift work towards increased access to paid rest days.

— More generally, time off in lieu could be used as recompense for temporary overtime working.

— Workers could have more opportunity of offering a range of weekly hours (say, 30 to 35) while retaining the status, the job rights and working conditions and benefits, of full-time workers.

— Workers who meet agreed standards of attendance and work performance could build up entitlement to planned rest days with pay.

In all these ways planned manning to ensure the achievement of production schedules and the efficient use of capital can go along with reshaping of working time to meet a wider range of individual preferences and needs. If nothing else, the handling of full-time work might reverse the existing pattern; it could be more resistant to the extension of actual working time through persistent overtime, and more ready to accommodate a range of somewhat shorter hours planned and agreed in advance.

316

Redefining Part-Time Work

At the same time, there are a number of reasons to re-think the nature and character of part-time work.'

There is no obvious necessity, in terms of the needs of enterprise for workers at a set retirement age to make as complete, abrupt and arbitrary an exit from full-time work to retirement as they do. The growing power, and potential flexibility of superannuation funds could allow a more flexible transition. This could include for workers nearing retirement access to planned blocks of leisure, sabbaticals, designed to help the adjustment to full retirement; or it could involve a period of half-time work.

Similarly, for many young workers a combination of part-time work or work experience, access to vocational training and further education, and help with constructive use of blocks of leisure time, may be socially and individually preferable to immediate entry into full-time work for some and unemployment for many others. Here, it is already accepted that public funds are deployed flexibly to assist in the varied needs of adaptation to the world of work. The shortened working time of young people under such admixtures of work and training does not have to involve inferior or casual status.

The redefinition of full-time work in a more flexible way would enable more women workers to undertake such work. But there is obvious scope for trade unions to bargain about the rights of part-time workers, their access to training, and the possibilities of exercising options to move between full-time and part-time work with an enterprise, and vice-versa.

In a similar way, bargaining—and government encouragement—might enable workers to reduce their paid work for periods of time in order to undertake voluntary social service, and representative (not merely trade union representative) commitments, without losing job security and without undue loss of income. One way in which this may naturally develop would be through negotiation of paid educational leave, and the connection of this training and education, for social service and voluntary activity.

In all of these ways bargaining over working time could move on from the immediate priorities of reducing the levels of working time, both normal and actual, to creating more flexible (but jointly determined) patterns of working time that *enable* the individual to express personal and social preferences and commitments without undermining the efficient planning and conduct of production and service of activities, and without weakening joint control of working time by trade unions and employers.